DOUBLE INSURANCE AND CONTRIBUTION

CONTEMPORARY COMMERCIAL LAW

Causation in Insurance Contract Law
Meixian Song

Insurance Law in China
Edited by Johanna Hjalmarsson and Dingjing Huang

Maritime Law in China
Emerging Issues and Future Developments
Edited by Johanna Hjalmarsson and Jenny Jingbo Zhang

Illegality in Marine Insurance Law
Feng Wang

Insurance Law Implications of Delay in Maritime Transport
Ayşegül Buğra

Online Arbitration
Faye Fangfei Wang

Double Insurance and Contribution
Nisha Mohamed

For more information about this series, please visit: www.routledge.com/
Contemporary-Commercial-Law/book-series/CCL

DOUBLE INSURANCE AND CONTRIBUTION

NISHA MOHAMED

informa law
from Routledge

First published 2019
by Informa Law from Routledge
2 Park Square, Milton Park, Abingdon, Oxon OX14 4RN

and by Informa Law from Routledge
711 Third Avenue, New York, NY 10017

Informa Law from Routledge is an imprint of the Taylor & Francis Group, an informa business

© 2018 Nisha Mohamed

The right of Nisha Mohamed to be identified as author of this work has been asserted by her in accordance with sections 77 and 78 of the Copyright, Designs and Patents Act 1988.

All rights reserved. No part of this book may be reprinted or reproduced or utilised in any form or by any electronic, mechanical, or other means, now known or hereafter invented, including photocopying and recording, or in any information storage or retrieval system, without permission in writing from the publishers.

Whilst every effort has been made to ensure that the information contained in this book is correct, neither the author nor Informa Law can accept any responsibility for any errors or omissions or for any consequences arising therefrom.

Trademark notice: Product or corporate names may be trademarks or registered trademarks, and are used only for identification and explanation without intent to infringe.

British Library Cataloguing-in-Publication Data
A catalogue record for this book is available from the British Library

Library of Congress Cataloging-in-Publication Data
Names: Mohamed, Nisha, author.
Title: Double insurance and contribution / by Nisha Mohamed.
Description: Abingdon, Oxon ; New York, NY : Informa Law from Routledge, 2018. |
  Series: Contemporary commercial law library
Identifiers: LCCN 2018009930 | ISBN 9781138944732 (hbk) |
  ISBN 9781315671710 (ebk)
Subjects: LCSH: Insurance policies—English–speaking countries.
Classification: LCC K1241 .M64 2018 | DDC 346/.086—dc23
LC record available at https://lccn.loc.gov/2018009930

ISBN: 978-1-138-94473-2 (hbk)
ISBN: 978-1-315-67171-0 (ebk)

Typeset in Times New Roman
by Apex CoVantage, LLC

This book is dedicated to my parents, to Cassim Ahamed Mohamed (LLB (London)), to Abdul Meerakal Kadhija Beevi, Advocate (BA, LLB) who made it all possible, and to my sister, Dr Shaheeda Mohamed.

CONTENTS

Acknowledgments   xvii
Foreword   xix
Preface   xxi
Table of Cases   xxiii
Table of Legislation   xxxiii

	Part A	1
CHAPTER 1	AN OVERVIEW: DOUBLE INSURANCE	3
CHAPTER 2	GENERAL PRINCIPLES	9
CHAPTER 3	EFFECT OF DOUBLE INSURANCE ON CLAIMS	29
CHAPTER 4	LEGISLATIVE REFORM OF DOUBLE INSURANCE	51
	Part B	115
CHAPTER 5	THE MEANING OF CONTRIBUTION	117
CHAPTER 6	WHEN THE RIGHT OF CONTRIBUTION ARISES	131
CHAPTER 7	THE RIGHTS OF AN INSURER TO SEEK CONTRIBUTION AND ENFORCEMENT	147
CHAPTER 8	ASBESTOS LITIGATION FROM AN INSURANCE PERSPECTIVE	169
CHAPTER 9	CONTRIBUTION UNDER COMMON LAW AND ITS EQUITABLE POSITION	207

CHAPTER 10　CONCLUSION 221

Index 225

DETAILED CONTENTS

Acknowledgments	xvii
Foreword	xix
Preface	xxi
Table of Cases	xxiii
Table of Legislation	xxxiii

	Part A	1
CHAPTER 1	**AN OVERVIEW: DOUBLE INSURANCE**	3
1.1	Background: the theory of double insurance	3
	1.1.1 Problems with double insurance	3
	1.1.2 Insurance premiums	3
	1.1.3 Development of the insurance industry	4
	1.1.4 Regulation of the insurance industry	4
	1.1.5 Attempt to define double insurance	5
	1.1.6 Requirements of double insurance	5
	1.1.7 Type of clauses	6
	1.1.8 Uncertainty	6
	1.1.9 Contribution	6
1.2	Different approaches: possible solution	6
	1.2.1 Australian legislation	6
	1.2.2 Should the Australian position be followed?	7
CHAPTER 2	**GENERAL PRINCIPLES**	9
2.1	The history of double insurance	9
	2.1.1 The Chamber of Assurance	9
	2.1.2 The Marine Insurance Act 1906	9
2.2	The concept of double insurance	13
2.3	Cases on double insurance: is there double insurance?	14
	2.3.1 *North British Insurance v London, Liverpool & Globe Insurance*	14
	2.3.2 *Mathie v The Argonaut Marine Insurance Co Ltd*	14
	2.3.3 *Union Marine Insurance Co Ltd v Martin*	15

	2.3.4	*Godin v London Assurance Co*	16
	2.3.5	*Union Marine Insurance Co Ltd v Martin*	16
	2.3.6	*Rathbone Brothers plc v Novae Corporate Underwriting Ltd*	17
	2.3.7	Conclusion	18
2.4	Recovery from insurers		18
	2.4.1	An assured's right of recovery	18
	2.4.2	Conclusion	20
2.5	Interpretation of policy wording in double insurance clauses		20
	2.5.1	Contractual and legislative exclusions	20
	2.5.2	Interpreting clauses: Singapore High Court	21
2.6	Contribution as a general concept		22
2.7	Premiums		25
	2.7.1	Return of premiums when the insurer refuses to pay	25
	2.7.2	Legislative framework of the return of premium	25
	2.7.3	Position of premiums prior to legislation	26

CHAPTER 3	EFFECT OF DOUBLE INSURANCE ON CLAIMS		29
3.1	The rights of an assured		29
	3.1.1	Restriction by insurers of assureds' rights	29
3.2	Effect of "other insurance" clauses		29
3.3	Combination of clauses in policies		30
3.4	Complexities of double insurance illustrated		30
3.5	Policy considerations		32
3.6	A comparison: the Australian position		32
3.7	Types of clauses		32
3.8	Uncertainty of such clauses		33
3.9	Concurrent "escape" clauses		33
	3.9.1	Absolute escape clauses	33
	3.9.2	All policies containing absolute clauses	35
	3.9.3	Self-cancelling clauses ineffective	36
3.10	Has the *Weddell* principle been followed in other jurisdictions?		39
3.11	Escape clause against excess clause		41
3.12	Concurrent "excess" clauses		43
3.13	Rateable proportion clauses		44
3.14	Clauses in combination: excess or escape clauses against rateable proportion clauses		46
	3.14.1	*National Farmers Union Mutual Insurance Society Ltd v HSBC Insurance (UK) Ltd*	46
	3.14.2	The principles and approach adopted in *NFU*	47

CHAPTER 4	LEGISLATIVE REFORM OF DOUBLE INSURANCE	51
4.1	"Other insurance" clauses – Australian legislation barring double insurance exclusion clauses	51

4.2	Australian Law Reform Commission, Report on Insurance Contracts, Report No 20 (1982)		51
	4.2.1 Terms of reference		51
	4.2.2 The guiding principles		52
	4.2.3 Major recommendations		52
4.3	Australian Law Reform Commission: the draft legislation		53
	4.3.1 Existing problems		53
	4.3.2 The draft legislation		53
4.4	Combination of limiting or exclusion clauses		53
4.5	Cover note		54
4.6	"Other insurance" provisions: Insurance Contracts Act 1984 s45		54
	4.6.1 The application of s45		54
	4.6.2 Time "other insurance" entered into		54
	4.6.3 Severance		55
4.7	Severance		56
4.8	Meaning of "the assured" – any difference from "any assured" or "an assured"?		56
4.9	Meaning of "entered into": does it include non-party assured?		57
	4.9.1 *Zurich Australian Insurance Ltd v Metals & Minerals Insurance Pte Ltd*		57
	4.9.2 *Vero Insurance Ltd v QBE Insurance (Australia) Ltd*		58
4.10	The term "other insurance"		59
	4.10.1 What is considered to "enter into"?		59
	4.10.2 Extension of *Nicholas v Wesfarmers Currangh Pty Ltd* to beneficial third parties		61
	4.10.3 The proper approach of the courts		62
4.11	An easier way out? No double insurance		62
4.12	The exceptions under s45		63
	4.12.1 Exception 1: not being a contract of insurance required to be effected by or under a law, including the law of a state or territory		63
	4.12.2 Exception 2: s45(2) Subsection (1) does not apply where some or all of the loss is not covered by a contract of insurance that is specified in the first-mentioned contract		64
4.13	The meaning of "specifically" under s45(2)		65
	4.13.1 *HIH Casualty and General Insurance Co v Pluim Construction Pty Ltd*		65
	4.13.2 Conclusion		67
4.14	Requirement for an assured to notify the insurer: validity of s45(1)		68
	4.14.1 Notification clause		68
	4.14.2 *Steadfast Insurance Co Ltd v F&B Trading Co Pty*		68
	4.14.3 *Home Insurance Co of New York v Gavel*		70

		4.14.4	Should a more stringent approach be adopted?	72
		4.14.5	Policy terminates before loss	72
	4.15	The Canadian position		72
	4.16	The correct approach		72
	4.17	Proposed legislative provision		73
	4.18	Effects of s76 Insurance Contracts Act 1984		74
	4.19	Section 45 and its impact on excess clauses, exclusion clauses and rateable proportion clauses and when the clauses work in combination		75
		4.19.1	Recommendations of the ALRC	75
	4.20	True excess liability in a policy		76
		4.20.1	Limits on recommendations	76
		4.20.2	Exemptions: true excess clause	77
	4.21	Discussion		85
	4.22	Severance of void parts in clauses		86
		4.22.1	The Explanatory Memorandum (Insurance Contracts Bill 1984)	86
		4.22.2	Should the void clause be severed?	87
		4.22.3	Is there sufficient protection for the insurer?	88
	4.23	Specified in the policy?		88
		4.23.1	Parties specifying terms in contracts	88
		4.23.2	Possible definition of "specified"	89
		4.23.3	The Appeal: Court of Appeal	91
		4.23.4	The Appeal: High Court of Australia	94
	4.24	Review of the Insurance Contracts Act 1984		100
	4.25	Analysis of the cases		102
		4.25.1	Was the courts' analysis correct?	102
		4.25.2	True excess clause	102
		4.25.3	Are the tests adopted by the courts confusing?	102
		4.25.4	Parent and subsidiary companies: top and drop policies	103
		4.25.5	How to overcome the practical problem?	103
	4.26	The effect of the "other insurance" clause – the American position		104
		4.26.1	The circular reasoning	104
		4.26.2	Main approaches to resolve the problem	106
		4.26.3	Presence of a combination of the clauses	106
		4.26.4	Should the American approach be adopted?	107
	4.27	The Canadian position on double insurance		107
		4.27.1	The Canadian solution to avoid the circular approach	107
		4.27.2	The Canadian approach to "other insurance" clauses	108
		4.27.3	Ascertaining intention	109
		4.27.4	Conclusion	109
	4.28	Possible solutions to the clauses		110

4.28.1	Suggested solutions	110
4.28.2	Should rights of parties be considered?	110
4.28.3	Other UK legislative protection: are these sufficient?	110
4.28.4	Other Australian legislative provisions	111
4.28.5	The test of fairness	112
4.28.6	Trade Practices Amendment (Australian Consumer Law) Act 2010	114

Part B — 115

CHAPTER 5 THE MEANING OF CONTRIBUTION — 117

5.1	History of contribution?	117
	5.1.1 Common law contribution	117
	5.1.2 Equitable contribution	119
5.2	When does contribution arise in double insurance?	126
5.3	Balancing the interest of the insurer and the assured	128
5.4	Contribution: common law or statutory?	129
5.5	Limitation period for contribution claims	130

CHAPTER 6 WHEN THE RIGHT OF CONTRIBUTION ARISES — 131

A	The UK position	131
6.1	Factors required for contribution in double insurance	131
6.2	Same subject matter common to both policies and each policy must cover the same interest in the same subject matter	131
6.3	Each policy must cover the same risk	134
B	The Australian position	142
6.4	The policies must be in force and valid	144

CHAPTER 7 THE RIGHTS OF AN INSURER TO SEEK CONTRIBUTION AND ENFORCEMENT — 147

7.1	Contribution: principles of equity	147
7.2	Entitlement to contribution	147
7.3	Policy providing method of apportionment	148
7.4	Methods of calculating insurer's liability for insurance	148
	7.4.1 Maximum potential policy	148
	7.4.2 Independent actual liability	151
	7.4.3 Common liability test	154
7.5	Where policy does not cover a specific loss but a wide range of events	154
7.6	Where there is property insurance	155
7.7	Where there is marine insurance	156
7.8	Criticisms and possible solutions	157
	7.8.1 The Australian Law Reform Commission	157
	7.8.2 The draft Insurance Contracts Bill 1982	158

7.9	Volunteers and the right of recovery		159
	7.9.1	Should *Legal & General v Drake Insurance* be followed?	160
	7.9.2	Where both policies contain rateable proportion clauses	161
	7.9.3	Other jurisdictions?	162
	7.9.4	Event after loss and insurer denies liability	163
7.10	Whether incidental overlaps allow for contribution?		164
	7.10.1	Mortgagor and mortgagee	164
	7.10.2	Landlord and tenant	165
	7.10.3	Vendor and purchaser	166
	7.10.4	Primary and excess cover	167

CHAPTER 8 ASBESTOS LITIGATION FROM AN INSURANCE PERSPECTIVE — 169

8.1	Development of mesothelioma: application to double insurance		169
8.2	Development of mesothelioma cases: the law		169
8.3	The impact of mesothelioma litigation		170
	8.3.1	The decision in *Fairchild v Glenhaven Funeral Services Ltd:* Court of Appeal and House of Lords	170
	8.3.2	*Bolton Metropolitan BC v Municipal Mutual Insurance Ltd*	178
	8.3.3	*Barker v Corus:* revisiting *Fairchild*	180
	8.3.4	*Durham v BAI (Run Off) Ltd* – a review of the cases	183
	8.3.5	*Zurich Insurance plc UK Branch v International Energy Group Ltd*	193
	8.3.6	*Cape Distribution v Cape Intermediate Holdings plc*	197
8.4	Reasoning of mesothelioma cases: what is the possible solution and does it apply to double insurance?		198
	8.4.1	Approach of the courts	198
	8.4.2	The extension of the general rule of causation: double insurance cases	199
	8.4.3	Compensating mesothelioma victims	199
	8.4.4	Does the *Fairchild, Bolton* and *Durham* line of cases provide a solution?	199
	8.4.5	*Investors Compensation Scheme Ltd v West Bromwich Building Society*	200
	8.4.6	Further criticism	200
	8.4.7	The implications of the Employers' Liability (Compulsory Insurance) Act 1969	201
	8.4.8	Is there sufficient protection under the law of tort?	202
	8.4.9	Does the type of liability insurance matter?	202
	8.4.10	Implications for insurers?	203
8.5	Should liability be divided proportionately?		203
	8.5.1	*Fairchild v Glenhaven Funeral Services Ltd*	203
	8.5.2	*Barker v Corus (UK) Ltd*	204

	8.5.3	*Phillips v Syndicate 992 Gunner*	204
	8.5.4	Conclusion	204
8.6	Can these principles be extended to double insurance?		205

CHAPTER 9   CONTRIBUTION UNDER COMMON LAW AND ITS EQUITABLE POSITION   207

9.1	Contribution under common law and equity	207
9.2	Joint liability and contribution: its implication for insurance	207
	9.2.1 Does the same damage mean the same tort?	208
	9.2.2 Same damage: joint tortfeasors and several tortfeasors	208
	9.2.3 Where there is a release of one tortfeasor	209
	9.2.4 Possibility of double recovery	209
9.3	Contribution or reimbursement: restitutionary in nature	209
9.4	Distinction between common law and equity	209
9.5	Co-sureties	210
9.6	Law Commission: Law Reform (Married Woman and Tortfeasors) Act 1935	211
9.7	Implementation of the Civil Liability (Contribution) Act 1978	211
9.8	Application to double insurance	212
	9.8.1 Interpretation of ss1(1) and 6(1) Civil Liability (Contribution) Act 1978	212
	9.8.2 Does the Civil Liability (Contribution) Act 1978 apply to claims between indemnity insurers?	213
9.9	Subrogation and indemnity	217
	9.9.1 The difference between contribution and subrogation	218
	9.9.2 *Austin v Zurich Insurance*	218
	9.9.3 *Caledonia North Sea Ltd v London Bridge Engineering*	219

CHAPTER 10   CONCLUSION   221

Index   225

ACKNOWLEDGMENTS

I would like to thank the following people who have helped me through this journey:

(1) Dr Gerard McCoy QC, SC, SBS (my Head of Chambers) who is a brilliant advocate, an invaluable source of knowledge, ideas, encouragement, and support, and who has made a remarkable contribution to the law.
(2) Professor Robert Merkin QC (my PhD supervisor) who is an expert in his field, and who provided invaluable guidance during the writing of this book, and my doctorate.
(3) Mr Alexander Hickey QC (my pupil master) who was always happy to discuss, and challenge, my ideas.
(4) Professor Philip Joseph (at the University of Canterbury) who gave me invaluable assistance and very helpful feedback on how to develop the ideas in the book.
(5) Mr Mike Arthur (Barrister at law) who has always showed confidence in my ability and work.
(6) Mr. James Thomson (my pupil master) for his kind support, constant encouragement and guidance.
(7) Ms Katy, Kwok So Sum (郭素心) (my personal secretary) who is an excellent secretary, and who has helped, and supported me throughout my career.

A special debt of gratitude is acknowledged to Mr Kim J McCoy, Mr Timothy Harry, Dr P.Y. Lo, Mr Allan Wyeth, Mr Douglas Clark, Mr Daniel Hui and Ms Katy H Chung, who have offered collegial guidance, expertise and encouragement.

I would also like to thank with gratitude, the support and encouragement of Ms Carolyn McCombe, Mr Christopher Moger QC, Mrs Prue Moger, Mr Jeremy Nicholson, Mrs Elizabeth Nicholson, Mr Patrick Maddams, Ms Kate Livesey, Ms Juliet Forrest, Mr John Forrest, Mr Grey Pynt, Mr Declan McDaid and Ms Serap Topkaya Ipek.

FOREWORD

This excellent book provides a comprehensive review of the history and development of the law of insurance and the approach of the courts in determining issues that arise in the double insurance and contribution context. It delves into a challenging area of law and highlights the issues faced by the courts and the legislature in balancing the principles of equity, justice and fairness between the interest of victims, the insured and insurers.

The author has conducted a multi-jurisdictional study of the courts in England, USA, Canada, Australia, South Africa, China, Singapore and India. From this, she has made clear legislative and principled recommendations about how to deal with the problems which arise in double insurance which this jurisdiction might find it prudent to heed. The way the cases have developed around the world highlights that the practical problems with double insurance are shared with our common law neighbours, which makes the breadth of this study all the more important.

I expect practitioners will find the book's detailed discussion of approaches to the interpretation of different policy wording in double insurance policies particularly useful. The issue of how to deal with conflicting clauses in different insurance contracts, which purport to cancel each other out, is one which continues to challenge the courts. There is an inherent unfairness in providing no cover to an insured who has paid premiums to multiple insurers but there is the opposing challenge of respecting the rights of parties freely to enter into contractual agreements and to decide on contractual terms.

It is appropriate that the author chose to include both double insurance and contribution in the same book. This work will be of real assistance to insurers for whom the issue of contribution causes uncertainty where double insurance is established. This is due to the wide discretion granted to the courts when deciding between the different methods of calculation so as to ensure a fair and just result. The book's thorough analysis of the case law, and clear presentation of the relevant calculations in numerical form, provides a key tool for parties trying to understand the different approaches. It breaks it down such that even the least numerate lawyer can cope.

There is a very useful chapter on asbestos litigation from an insurance perspective. I imagine there is a law finalist somewhere searching a university library for a chapter that analyses the decisions in this complex area with the level of clarity and detail to be found in this book. The court's response to the mesothelioma problem has been to adapt the general rules of causation. This issue is further complicated by questions around double insurance and contribution. Complex questions can arise in practice: for example, is an insurer entitled to present each outwards reinsurance claim to any single triggered reinsurance contract of its choice; second, if so, how are the resultant rights of recoupment and contribution, arising from the Supreme Court decision in *IEG v. Zurich Insurance plc UK Branch* [2016] AC 509 to be calculated? Sadly, I expect this chapter to become more important as mesothelioma affects more people.

Although there remain a number of unresolved questions, this book goes some way to providing clarity to a particularly complex area of the law. I congratulate Nisha Mohamed on providing a valuable tool for those engaging with double insurance and contribution in regulatory matters, litigation and arbitration. Although this is a book about insurance, I expect it to assist parties, practitioners and members of the judiciary in a wide range of commercial contexts where ultimately it is the insurer who foots the bill.

Elizabeth Gloster
The Right Honourable Lady Justice Gloster DBE
Vice-President of the Court of Appeal of England and Wales
(Civil Division)
Royal Courts of Justice
Strand, London
April 2018

PREFACE

This book aims to provide an authoritative guide to double insurance, its practice and recent developments.

Double insurance is an issue which frequently arises in practice. An assured is usually unaware of the existence of double insurance or takes out numerous policies in the hopes of better protection when a claim is made. This can have major consequences for an assured, as it carries the risk of an insurer relying on policy wording to limit or completely exclude liability.

This book delves into the problems which arise in double insurance, and the court's attempt to provide a solution to the uncertainty created by double insurance.

The book begins with a fascinating look at the history and development of the law of double insurance. It outlines how the law relating to double insurance has developed, and the factors that the courts may take into account when deciding such cases. It attempts to provide a common law solution where no legislative provision exists. It covers contemporary instances of double insurance by focusing on:

- the relevant clauses (such as rateable proportion, excess, escape and other insurance clauses);
- the difficulty of the courts in providing clear principles in cases of double insurance;
- attempts to limit or exclude liability by the insurer;
- how the clauses work in practice;
- court decisions in various jurisdictions;
- the Australian position under s45 of the Insurance Contracts Act 1984; and
- whether the Australian position can be adopted in the United Kingdom.

This text combines practical experience with academic rigour and will be of significant interest to lawyers, academics and insurance industry professionals alike.

TABLE OF CASES

Accident Compensation Commission v Baltica General Insurance Co Ltd
 [1993] 1 VR 467 147
Akai Pty Ltd v People's Insurance Co Ltd (1996) 188 CLR 418 95
Albion Insurance Co Ltd v Government Insurance Office (1969) 121
 CLR 342, [1969] HCA 55 .... 9, 11, 79, 117, 127, 128, 134,
 140–143, 147, 214
Alexandros T, Re the [2013] UKSC 70, [2014] 1 All ER 590 208
Allianz Australia Insurance Ltd v Territory Insurance Office (2008) 23
 NTLR 186 .... 127, 142
Allianz Australia Workers Compensation (NSW) Ltd v
 NRMA Insurance Ltd [2007] ACTSC 40 166
American Surety Co of New York v Wrightson (1910) 16 Com Cas 37,
 (1910) 103 LT 663, (1911) 27 TLR 91 .... 24, 120, 128, 133, 135, 136, 143, 147
AMP Workers Compensation Services (NSW) Ltd v QBE
 Insurance Ltd (2001) 53 NSWLR 35 133
Andrews v Patriotic Assurance Co (No 2) (1886) 18 LR Ir 355 .... 166, 167
Antrobus v Davidson (1817) 3 Mer 569 126
Association Ltd v General Accident Assurance Corporation Ltd (1892) 19 R 977 140
Astra Zeneca Insurance Co v XL Insurance (Bermuda) Ltd [2013]
 EWCA Civ 1660, [2014] 2 All ER (Comm) 55 18
Austin v Zurich General Accident & Liability Insurance Co Ltd [1945]
 KB 250 .... 20, 43, 44, 48, 49, 51, 129, 132, 218
Australasian Medical Insurance Ltd v CGU Insurance Ltd [2010] QCA 189 62
Australian Agricultural Co v Saunders (1875) LR 10 CP 668 .... 73, 74, 135, 143, 144
Australian Eagle Insurance Co Ltd v Mutual Acceptance (Insurance)
 Pty Ltd [1983] 3 NSWLR 59 .... 11, 80, 147
Australian Iron & Steel Ptd Ltd v Government Insurance Office of
 New South Wales (1990) 20 NSWLR 633 133
Austress-PSC Pty Ltd and Carlingford Australia General Insurance Ltd
 v Zurich Australian Insurance Ltd (unreported 1 May 1992) 54, 65, 66, 81, 97

Bank View Mill v Nelson Corp [1942] 2 All ER 477 208
Bankers & Traders Insurance Co Ltd v National Insurance Co Ltd [1985]
 1 WLR 734 .... 33, 41
Bankers Insurance Co v South [2003] EWHC 380 (QB), [2004] Lloyd's Rep IR 1 111
Banque Keyser Ullman SA v Skandia (UK) Insurance Co Ltd [1990] 1 QB 665 52

TABLE OF CASES

Barclays Bank Ltd v TOSG Trust Fund Ltd [1984] 1 All ER 628.................................. 120
Barker v Corus [2006] UKHL 20, [2006]
   2 AC 572....................................169, 170, 180–183, 188, 191, 192, 195, 203, 204, 208
Baulderstone Hornibrook Engineering Pty Ltd
   v Gordian Runoff Ltd (2008) 15 ANZ Insurance Cases 61–780............................ 134
Bechervaise v Lewis (1871–72) 7 CP 372.. 126
Berkeley v Berkeley [1946] AC 555.. 97
Birkley v Presgrave (1801) 1 East 220 at 227, 229, 102 ER 86.................................... 120
BMA Special Opportunity Hub Fund Ltd v African
   Minerals Finance Ltd [2013] EWCA Civ 416... 200
Boag v Economic Insurance Co Ltd [1954] 2 Lloyd's Rep 581...................... 24, 133, 164
Body Corporate 74246 v QBE Insurance (International) Ltd [2015] NZHC 1360.......... 18
Body Corporation 398983 v Zurich Australian Insurance Ltd [2013] NZHC 1109......... 20
Bogart v Twin City Fire Insurance Co 473 F 2d 619... 13
Bolton Metropolitan Borough Council v Municipal Mutual Insurance
   [2006] EWCA Civ 50, [2006] 1 WLR 1492.............. 163, 169, 178, 179, 190, 194, 198
Bonner v Tottenham and Edmonton Permanent Investment Building Society
   [1899] 1 QB 16.. 117, 209
Borg Warner (Aust) Ltd v Switzerland General Insurance Co Ltd (1989) 16 NSWLR
   421, (1989) 5 ANZ Insurance Cases 60–905.. 134, 143, 147
Bousfield v Barnes (1815) 4 Camp 228... 10, 13, 19
Bovis v Commercial Union Assurances [2001] 1 Lloyd's Rep 416................................... 5
Bovis Construction Ltd v Commercial Union Assurance Co plc
   [2001] Lloyd's Rep IP 321, [2001] 1 Lloyd's Rep 416............................ 128, 129, 213
Bovis Construction Ltd v Government Insurance Office of
   New South Wales (1967) 121 CLR 342 134
Bovis Lend Lease Ltd v Saillard Fuller & Partners [2001] 77 Con LR134 213
Bowditch v Green 3 Met 360... 123
Boy v State Insurance General Manager [1980] 1 NZLR 87 11
Boys v State Insurance Australia Ltd (t/as NRMA Insurance) (2008) 15
   ANZ Insurance Cases 61–761 133
Boys v State Insurance General Manager [1980] 1 NZLR 78 (SC).......... 9, 147, 164, 165
Breaux v American Family Mutual 553 F 3d 447 (6 Cir 2009)....................................... 13
Brisbane City Council v Attorney General for Queensland [1979] AC 411.................. 209
Brook v Bool [1928] 2 KB 578.. 207
Brook's Wharf and Bull Wharf Ltd v Goodman Bros [1937] 1 KB 534....................... 210
Brown v Cork [1985] BCLC 363, CA 122
Bruce v Jones (1863) 1 H & C 769.. 10, 13, 14, 19

C E Heath Underwriting & Insurance (Aust) Pty Ltd v Edwards Dunlop
   & Co Ltd (1992–1993) 176 CLR 535 56
Caladonia North Sea Ltd v British Telecommunications plc and
   Others [2002] Lloyd's Rep IR 261 .... 23, 130, 141
Caledonia North Sea Ltd v London Bridge Engineering [2000]
   1 Lloyd's Rep IP 249 .... 129, 214, 219
Calf & Sun Insurance Office [1920] 2 KB 366... 80
Canadian Imperial Bank of Commerce v Vopni [1978] 4 WWR 76 123
Cape Distribution v Cape Intermediate Holdings plc [2016] Lloyd's Rep IR 499........ 197
Castellain v Preston (1883) 11 QBD 380.. 138

TABLE OF CASES

CE Health Casualty & General Insurance Ltd v Grey (1993) 32 NSWLR 25 84
CE Heath Underwriting & Insurance (Aust) Pty Ltd v
    State Government Insurance Commission (SA) (1983) 34 SASR 1 135
Chartbrook Ltd v Persimmon Homes Ltd [2009] UKHL 38, [2009] 3 WLR 267 20
China Insurance Co (Singapore) Pte Ltd v
    Liberty Insurance Pte Ltd (formerly known as Liberty Citystate
    Insurance Pte Ltd) [2005] 2 SLR 509 .... 22, 131
Chui Man Kwan v Bank of China Group Insurance Co Ltd
    (DCMP 211/2008, unreported) 33, 34
Clarke v Fidelity Fire Insurance Co of New York [1925] OJ No144 165
Clements v Langley (1833) 5 B & Ad 372 118
Coburn v Wheelock 34 N Y 440 (1868) 123
Collyear v CGU [2008] NSWCA 92 13
Commercial & General Insurance Co Ltd v
    Government Insurance Office (NSW) (1973) 129 CLR 374 .... 142, 147
Commercial Union Assurance Co Ltd v Hayden [1977] 1 QB 804, [1977] 1
    Lloyd's Rep 1 .... 126, 128, 149, 151, 152, 153, 155, 157
Commercial Union Assurance Co New Zealand Ltd v Murphy [1989] 1
    NZLR 687 .... 42, 43, 145
Commercial Union Assurance Co of Australia Ltd v
    Commissioner of Insurance [1980] VR 443 135
Compare Newland v Nominal Defendant [1983] 1 Qd R 514 143
Coope v Twynam (1823) Turn & R 426 .... 118, 121
Co-operative Bulk Handling Ltd v State Government Insurance Commission
    (1990) 3 WAR 145 9
Co-operative Retail Services Ltd v Taylor Young Partnership Ltd [2002]
    UKHL 17, [2002] 1 WLR 1419 215
Cowell v Edwards (1800) 2 Bos & P 268 122
Craythorne v Swinburne (1807) 14 Ves 160 .... 118, 122, 124, 125, 126
Cruse v Paine (1868) Law Rep 6 Eq 641, 4 Ch 441 126
Cutter v Emery 37 N H 567 (1859) 123

Darrell v Tibbits (1880) 5 QBD 560 140
Davies v Humphreys (1840) 6 M & W 153 .... 126, 130
Davis v Gildart (1777) 2 Park's Marine Inscc 8th Ed, p 424 20
Davjoyda Estates Pty Ltd v National Insurance Co of New Zealand Ltd
    (1965) 69 SR (NSW) 381 .... 74, 134, 166
Deaves v CLM Fire and General Insurance Co Ltd (1979) 23 ALR 539,
    [1979] HCA 12 .... 54, 73
Deker v Pope (1757) Selw NP (1812 edn), Vol 1, 71–2 207
Denton's Estate, Re, Licences Insurance Corporation and
    Guarantee Fund Ltd v Denton [1904] 2 Ch 178 125
Dering v Lord Winchelsea (1787) 1 Cox Eq Cas 318, 2 Bos & P 270 ... 118, 119, 120, 126
Dickenson v Jardine (1868) LR 3 CP 639 219
Direct Line Insurance plc v Fox [2009] EWHC 386 (QB),
    [2010] Lloyd's Rep IR 324 (QB) 111
Dominion of Canada General Insurance Co v
    Wawanesa Mutual Insurance (1985) 64 BCLR 122 (SC) 108
Downs v Chappell [1997] 1 WLR 426 216

TABLE OF CASES

Dragages et Travaux Publics (HK) Ltd v RJ Wallace [2004] 1 HKC 478 57
Drake Insurance plc v Provident Insurance plc [2004] Lloyd's IR 277 24
Drayton v Martin (1996) 67 FCR 1, (1996) 137 ALR 145 .... 149, 151, 152, 155, 218
Dubai Aluminium Co Ltd v Salaam [2001] QB 113 213
Dunn v Slee (1816)1 J B Moo 2 118
Durham v BAI (Run Off) Ltd [2008] EWHC 2692 (QB), [2009] 2 All ER 26;
   on appeal [2010] EWCA Civ 1096, [2011] 1 All ER 605; on further
   appeal [2012] UKSC 14; [2012] 1 WLR 867 .... 169, 183–194, 198, 203, 204, 205

Eagle Star Insurance Co Ltd v Provincial Insurance plc [1993] 2 Lloyd's Law Report
   143; on appeal [1994] 1 AC 130 .... 24, 47, 125, 140, 144, 160, 161, 163, 180
East End Real Estate Pty Ltd v C E Health & Casualty & General Insurance Ltd (1991)
   25 NSWLR 400 60
Elf Enterprise (Caledonia) Ltd v London Bridge Engineering Ltd (1997)
   Times, 28 November 139
Elf Enterprise (Caledonia) Ltd v London Bridge Engineering Ltd [2000]
   Lloyd's Rep 581 133
Ellesmere Brewery Co v Cooper [1896] 1 QB 75 124
Equitable Fire & Accident Office [1907] AC 96 .... 30, 31, 32, 69, 71, 72
Equity Syndicate Management Ltd v Glaxosmithkline plc [2015]
   EWHC 2163 (Comm), [2016] Lloyd's Rep IR 155 .... 16, 37
Evans v Marine Medical Care Inc 87 DLR (4th) 173 (1992) 29, 33
Evans v Maritime Medical Care Inc 1991 CanLII 2478 (NS CA) 109
Exall v Partridge (1799) 8 TR 308 40

FAI General Insurance Co Ltd & Fletcher and Speno Rail Maintenance v
   Hamersley Pty Ltd (2003) 23 WAR 291 56
Fairchild v Glenhaven Funeral Services Ltd [2002] UKHL 22, [2003] 1 AC 32 45,
   169–181, 186, 188, 190, 191, 192, 194, 195, 197, 198, 199, 202, 203, 205
Family Insurance Corp v Lombard Canada Ltd [2002] SCJ No 49,
   2002 SCC 48 .... 23, 109
Family Insurance Corp v Lombard Canada Ltd 1999 Can LII 6253 108
Farm Bureau Mut Ins Co v Ries 551 NW 2d 316 (Iowa 1996) 13
FBI Foods Ltd – Aliments FBI Ltée v Glassner 86 BCLR (3d) 136 209
Federation Insurance Ltd v Wason (1987) 163 CLR 303 72
Fish & Fish Ltd v Sea Shepard UK [2015] UKSC 10, [2015] AC 1229 207
Fisk v Masterman (1841) 8 M & W 165 26
Fitzgerald v Lane [1987] 1 QB 781 178
Fleetwood v Charnock (1629) Nelson 10 118
Friend v Brooker [2009] HCA 21 209

Gale v Motor Union Insurance Co [1928] 1 KB 359 .... 35, 48, 51, 132
Gardiner v Moore [1969] 1 QB 55 209
Gebhardt v Saunders [1892] 2 QB 452 117
Gillyngham v Watergate (1380) CP 40/477 117
GIO v Crowley [1975] 2 NSWLR 78 .... 147, 149, 152, 154, 158
GIO Australia Ltd v P Ward Civil Engineering Pty Ltd (2000) NSWSC 371 84
GIO General Ltd v Insurance Australia Ltd (t/as NRMA Insurance) [2008] ACTSC 38,
   (2008) 15 ANZ Insurance Cases 61–761 .... 13, 132, 142

TABLE OF CASES

GIO (NSW) v QBE Insurance Ltd (1985) 2 NSWLR 543 .... 11, 127, 135
GIO (NSW) v Royal Exchange Assurance of London (1965) 82
    WN (Pt 1) (NSW) 468 142
Godin v London Assurance Co (1758) 1 Burr 489, 97 ER 419 5, 9, 13, 14, 16, 20, 23, 24,
    126, 133, 138, 145, 147
Goldman v Southern Union General Insurance Co of Asia Ltd [1930] SASR 275 72
Goldstein v Salvation Army Assurance Society [1971] 2 KB 291 19
Graves v Traders and General Insurance Co 241 So 2d 116 107
GRE Insurance Ltd v QBE Insurance Ltd [1985] VR 83 .... 74, 104, 147, 154, 155, 158
Greater Northern Ins Co v Mount Vernon Fire Ins Co 798 NE 2d 167
    (NY 1999) 48, 49
Gregg v Scott [2002] EWCA Civ 1471, [2003] Lloyd's Rep Med 105;
    on appeal [2005] UKHL 2, [2005] 2 AC 176 185
Grupos Torras SA v Al-Sabah (No 5) [2001] Lloyd's Rep Bank 36 209

Hampton v Minns [2002] 1 WLR 1 130
Hebdon v West (1863) 3 B & S 579 .... 18, 147
Henderson v Henderson (1843) 3 Hare 100 209
HIH Casualty & General Insurance Ltd v FAI General Insurance Co Ltd
    (1997) 9 ANZ Ins Cas 61–358 .... 87, 88, 91, 93, 148, 152
HIH Casualty & General Insurance Ltd v Pluim Construction Pty Ltd
    [2000] 11 ANZ Insurance Cases 61–477 .... 65, 83, 100, 101
HIH Claims Support Ltd v Insurance Australia Ltd (2011) 280 ALR 1 .... 117, 120
Hills Flooring Ltd v WH Foote & Co Ltd (1985) 3 ANZ Insurance
    Cases 60–646 (NZHC) 133
Hole v Harrison (1675) 1 Ch Cas 246 126
Home Insurance Co of New York v Gavel (1927) 3 DLR 929, (1928) 30
    LI LR 139 .... 30, 69, 70, 71, 72
Hordern v Commercial Union Assurance Co (1884) 5 LR (NSW) 309 72
Horwell v London General Omnibus Co Ltd (1877) 2 Ex D 365 211
Humphries v The Proprietors "Surfers Palms North" Group Titles Plan 1955
    (1994) 179 CLR 597 99

IEG v Zurich Insurance plc UK Branch [2015] UKSC 33, [2016] AC 509 .... Xx, 169
Investor Compensation Scheme Ltd v West Bromwich Building Society
    [1998] 1 WLR 896 .... 20, 47, 200
Ionides v Pender (1874) LR 9 QB 531 15

Jameson v Central Electricity Generating Board [2000] 1 AC 455 209
Jetstar Airways Ptd Ltd v Free [2008] VSC 539 .... 112, 113
John v Rawlings (1984) 36 SASR 182 .... 11, 127, 158
Johnson v Wild (1890) 44 ChD 146 121
Jones v Medox Inc 430 A 2d 488 (DC 1981) 48, 49

Kempton v National Fire Insurance Co 136
Koursk, The [1924] P 140 .... 207, 208

Lacey v Hill (1874) LR 18 Eq 182 126
Lambert Leasing Inc v QBE Insurance Ltd [2015] NSWSC 750 62

TABLE OF CASES

Lamb-Weston Inc v Oregon Auto Ins Co 219 Or 110, 341 P 2d 110,
  76 ALR 2d 485 (1959) 104, 107
Land v United States Fidelity and Guaranty Co 78 F 3d 187 13
Lavin v Toppi (2015) 316 ALR 366 124
Lawson v Wright (1786) 1 Cox Eq Cas 275 126
Layne & Bowler (Australasia) Pty Ltd v Pearson Machine Tool Co Ltd
  (unreported, 25 November 1984) 148
Legal & General v Drake Insurance [1992] QB 887, [1991] 2 Lloyd's
  LR 43 .... 20, 23, 24, 47, 159–163, 180
Limit (No 3) Ltd v ACE Insurance Ltd [2009] NSWSC 514, (2009) 15
  ANZ Insurance Cases 61–823 .... 127, 147, 163
Lister v Romford Ice and Cold Storage Co Ltd [1957] AC 555 217
Lloyd v Dimmack (1877) 7 Ch D 39 126
Lodrigue v Montegut [1978] AMC 2272 (ED La 1977) 106
London Assurance Co v Sainsbury (1783) 3 Dougl 246 219
Lonpac Insurance Bhd v American Home Assurance Co [2011] SGHC 257 .... 21, 22
Loyst v General Accident, Fire and Life Assurance Corp [1928] 1 KB 359 48
Lumbermen's Underwriting Alliance v Axa Pacific Insurance Co 57 BCLR (4th) 293 108
Lumley General Insurance Ltd v QBE Insurance (Aust) Ltd [2008]
  VSC 216 .... 152, 218

M & S Fashions Ltd v Bank of Credit and Commerce International SA
  (In Liquidation) [1993] 3 WLR 220 124
Macclesfield Corp v Great Central Railway [1911] 2 KB 528 117
Mahoney v McManus (1981) 180 CLR 370, (1981) 36 ALR 545 .... 120, 207, 210
Manitoba Assurance Co v Whitlam (1903) 34 SCR (Can) 191 .... 70, 73
Manufacturer's Mutual Insurance Ltd v National Employer's Mutual General Insurance
  Association Ltd (1990) 6 ANZ Ins Cas 61–038 .... 148, 149
Mason v Sainsbury (1782) 3 Doughl 61 219
Mathie v The Argonaut Marine Insurance Co Ltd (1925) 21 Ll LR 145 .... 14, 15, 23
Maxwell v Jameson (1818) 2 B & Ald 5 117
McConnell v Lynch Robinson [1957] NI 70 211
McFarlane v Daniell (1938) 38 SR (NSW) 337 99
McFarlane JA and Commercial Union Association Co Ltd v Hayden [1977]
  1 Lloyds LR 1 52
McGeough v Stay N' Save Motor Inns Inc 116 DLR (4th) 108
McGhee v National Coal Board [1973] 1 WLR 1 .... 176, 177
McKenzie v Dominion of Canada General Insurance Co (2007) 86 OR (3d) 419 167
Merryweather v Nixon (1799) 8 TR 186 212
Metropolitan Properties Co (Regis) Ltd v Bartholomew
  (1996) 72 P & C R 380 124
Miller v National Farmers Union Property and
  Cas Co 470 F 2d 700, 701 (8th Cir) (1972) 104
Milos Equipment Ltd v Insurance Corporation of Ireland 47
  BCLR (2d) 296 151
Milverton Group Ltd v Warner World Ltd [1995] 2 EGLR 28 124
Monksfield v Vehicle & General Insurance Co Ltd [1971] 1 Lloyd's
  Rep 139 .... 24, 144, 145, 159, 163
Morgan v Price (1849) 4 Exch 615 .... 13, 14, 19

Morgan v Seymour (1638) 1 Ch Rep 120 118
Morris v Ford Motors Co Ltd [1973] QB 792 217
Moss v Penman 1993 SC 300 140
Moule v Garrett (1872) LR 7 Exch 101 210
Muirhead v Forth and North Sea Steamboat Mutual Insurance Co [1894]
 AC 72 19
Mutua v Foreign and Commonwealth Office [2012] EWHC 2678, (2012) 162
 NLJ 1291 207

Nanyang Insurance Co Ltd v Commercial Union Assurance plc [1996] 1
 SLR(R) 441 .... 33, 41
National Employers Mutual General Insurance Association Ltd v Haydon
 [1979] 2 LI R 235, [1980] 2 Lloyd's Rep 149 .... 37, 51, 77 78, 132, 164, 197
National Farmers Union Mutual Insurance Society Ltd v
 HSBC Insurance (UK) Ltd [2010] EWHC 773 (Comm),
 [2010] 1 CLC 557 .... 3, 46, 102, 104
National Mutual Fire Insurance Co Ltd v Insurance Commissioner 26 [1985]
 VR 811 135
National Protector Fire Insurance Co Ltd v Nivert [1913] AC 507 72
Nationwide Building Society v Dunlop Haywards (DHL) Ltd and
 Cobbetts (A Firm) [2009] EWHC 254 (Comm), [2010] 1 WLR 258 215
New Zealand Municipalities Co-operative Insurance Co Ltd v
 South British Insurance Co Ltd (unreported, 29 July 1983) 144
Newby v Reed (1763) 1 Wm Bl 416 .... 13, 19, 20, 128, 155
Newland v Nominal Defendant [1983] 1 Qd R 514 (FC) 134, 135
Newy v Reed (1763) 1 Wm Bl 416 14
Nicholas & Co v Scottish Union and National Insurance Co 165
Nicholas v Wesfarmers Currangh Pty Ltd [2010] QSC 447 .... 59, 61
Nichols & Co v Scottish Union and National Insurance Co (1885) 14 R
 (Ct of Sess) 1094 .... 132, 164
Nisner Holdings Pty Ltd v Mercantile Mutual Insurance Co Ltd [1976]
 NSWLR 406 .... 5, 54, 68, 144
North British & Mercantile Insurance Co Ltd v London Liverpool &
 Globe Insurance Co (1877) 5 Ch D 569 .... 9, 13, 14, 24, 128, 131,
 133, 138, 143, 145, 149, 155, 164, 167
North British & Mercantile Insurance Co Ltd v
 Public Mutual Insurance Co (NZ) (1935) 54 NZLR 678 .... 144, 145, 149
Norwich Winterthur Insurance (Aust) v State
 Government Insurance Office (1982) 149 CLR 327 135

O'Kane v Jones [2004] 1 Lloyd's Rep 389, [2005]
 Lloyd's Rep IR 174 .... 24, 156, 163, 165
Ocean Accident and Guarantee Corporation v Williams (1915) 34
 NZLR 924 144
Oceanbulk Shipping & Trading SA v TMT Asia Ltd [2010]
 3 WLR 1424 200
Offley and Johnson's Case (1583) 2 Leo 166 .... 118, 126
Offshore Logistics Services v Mutual Marine 462 F Supp 485
 (1978) 107

TABLE OF CASES

Pacific Employers Insurance Co v Non-Marine Underwriters
(1939) 71 DLR (4th) 731 164
Pandurevic v Southern Cross Constructions (NSW) Pty Ltd (No 3)
[2012] NSWSC 1601 152
Parker v National Farmers Union Mutual Insurance Society Ltd [2012]
EWHC 2156 (Comm), [2013] Lloyd's Rep IR 253 111
Parr's Bank Ltd v Albert Mines Syndicate [1900] 5 Com Cas 116 140
Pendlebury v Walker (1841) 4 Y & C Ex 424 123
Performance Cars Ltd v Abraham [1962] 1 QB 281 208
Peter v Rich (1629/1630) 1 Chancery Reps 34 .... 118, 126
Petrofine (UK) Ltd v Magnaload Ltd [1984] QB 127 24
Phillips v Syndicate 992 Gunner [2003] EWHC 1084 (Comm),
[2004] Lloyd's Rep IR 426 .... 45, 169, 196, 203, 204, 205
Pickering v Marsh 7 X II 192 123
Portavon Cinema Co Ltd v Price & Century Insurance Co Ltd [1939]
4 All ER 601, [1939] 65 Ll L Rep 161 .... 5, 9, 133, 166
Post Office v Norwich Union Fire Insurance Society Ltd
[1967] 2 QB 363 186
Pratt v Aigaion Insurance Co SA [2009] 1 Lloyd's Rep 225 47
Promet Engineering (Singapore) Pte Ltd v Sturge (The Nukila) [1997] 2
Lloyd's Rep 147 179
Prudential Insurance Co v IRC [1904] 2 KB 658 3

Qantas Airways Ltd v Aravco Ltd (1996) 185 CLR 43 99
QBE Insurance Ltd v AMP Workers' Compensation Services (NSW)
Pty Ltd [2000] NSWSC 1070 147
QBE Insurance Ltd v Fortis Insurance Ltd [1999] VSC 212 144
QBE Insurance Ltd v GIO (NSW) (1986) 4 ANZ Ins Cas 60 11
QBE Insurance Ltd v GRE Insurance Ltd (1983) 2
ANZ Insurance Cases 60–533 152

Rainy Sky SA v Kookim Bank [2011] UKSC 50, [2011] 1
WLR 2900 .... 169, 189, 200
Randal v Cockran (1748) 1 Ves Sen 98 219
Rathbone Brothers plc v Novae Corporate Underwriting [2014]
EWCA Civ 1464, [2014] WLR(D) 488 .... 17, 44
Renehan v Leeuwin Ocean Adventure Foundation Ltd (2006) 17 NTLR 83 99
Reynolds v Wheeler (1861) 30 LJ (CP) 350, 10 CB (NS) 561 126
Rogers v Davies (1777) 2 Park (8th edn) 601 .... 13, 14, 19
Rothwell v Chemical & Insulating Co Ltd [2007] UKHL 39, [2008]
1 AC 281 .... 201, 202
Royal Brompton Hospital NHS Trust v Hammond [2000]
Lloyd's Rep PN 643 214
Royal Brompton Hospital NHS Trust v Hammond (No 3) [2002]
UKHL 14, [2002] 1 WLR 1397 .... 211, 212, 216
Ruaro v Ferrari [2007] FCA 2022 99

Samancor Ltd v Mutual & Federal Insurance Co Ltd (Case Number 565/03) 213
Scholefield Goodman & Sons Ltd v Zyngier [1986] 1 AC 562 125

TABLE OF CASES

Scottish Amicable Heritable Securities Association Ltd v
   Northern Assurance Co (No 2) (1886) 18 LR Ir 132
Scottish Amicable Heritable Securities Association v
   Northern Assurance Co (1883) 11 R 287 ..... 14, 140, 165
Seagate Hotel Ltd v Simcoe & Erie General Insurance Co
   (1981) 27 BCLR 89 ..... 52, 109
SHC Capital Ltd v NTUC Income Insurance Co-operative Ltd
   [2010] SGHC 224 ..... 39, 162, 163
Sickness & Accident Assurance Association Ltd v General Accident Assurance
   Corp Ltd (1892) 19 R 977, (1892) 29 ScLr836 ..... 141, 144, 147, 155
Sienkiewicz v Grief (UK) Ltd [2011] UKSC 10, [2011] 2 AC 229 ..... 169, 191, 203
Simcoe & Erie General Insurance Co v Kansa General Insurance Co
   (1994) 93 BCLR (2d) 1 (BCCA) 107, 108
Sims v Foster Wheeler Ltd [1966] 1 WLR 1508 216
Sims v Scottish Imperial Ins Co (1902) 10 SLT 286 18
Sinochem International Oil (London) Co Ltd v Mobil Sales and Supply Corp
   [2000] 1 Lloyd's Rep 339 110
Snowdon, Re, ex p Snowdon (1881) 17 Ch D 44 ..... 122, 126
Sobrany v UAB Transtira [2016] EWCA Civ 28, [2016] RTR 18 37
South British Insurance Co Ltd v Norwich Winterthur Insurance (NZ) (1982)
   2 ANZ Insurance Cases 60–499 127
Spalding v Tarmac Civil Engineering Ltd [1967] 1 WLR 1508 216
Speno Rail Maintenance Australia Pty Ltd v Metals &
   Minerals Insurance Pte Ltd 20 (2009) 253 ALR 364 ..... 54, 55, 56, 67, 79
State Farm Mutual Auto Insurance v Bogart 717 P 2d 449, 451 (Ariz) (1986) 104
State Fire Insurance General Manager v Liverpool and London and
   Global Insurance Co Ltd [1952] NZLR 5 ..... 49, 51, 80, 132
State Government Insurance Commission v Switzerland Insurance Australia Ltd
   (t/a a Federation Insurances) [1995] SASA 5490 11
Steadfast Insurance Co Ltd v F & B Trading
   Co Ltd (1971) 125 CLR 578 ..... 54, 68, 69, 70, 73, 74, 136
Stirling v Forrester (1821) 3 Bli 575 ..... 118, 120, 126
Stolberg v Pearl Assurance Co Ltd (1971) 19 DLR (3d) 343 57
Stratti v Stratti [2000] NSWCA 358 ..... 210, 218
Strech v State Insurance General Manager (1984) 3
   ANZ Insurance Cases 60–577 ..... 82, 133, 145
Structural Polymer Systems Ltd v Brown [1999] CLC 268 ..... 37, 132
Swain v Wall (1642) Rep Ch 149 ..... 119, 123, 126
Sydney Turf Club v Crowley (1971) 1 NSWLR 324, [1972] 126
   CLR 420 ..... 5, 148, 218, 220

Tai Ping Insurance Co Ltd v Tugu Insurance Co Ltd [2001] 2 HKC 401 ..... 23, 158
Talbot v Berkshire County Council [1994] QB 290 208
TCB Ltd v Gray (1987) 3 BCC 503 124
Tip Top v State Insurance (2002) 7 NZBLC 103 134
Toussaint v Martinnant (1787) 2 TR 100, 100 ER 55 118
Transfield Pty Ltd v National Vulcan Engineering
   Insurance Group Ltd [2002] NSWSC 830 ..... 56, 63
Travelers Insurance Co v J Carpenter 411 F 3d 323 (2006) 13

TABLE OF CASES

Trenton Cold Storage Ltd v St Paul Fire & Marine Insurance Co
(1999) 11 CCLI (3d) 127; on appeal (2001) 146 OAC 348 .... 37, 167
Trenton Works Lavalin Inc v Panalpina Inc (1994) 126 Nova Scotia Reports
(2d) 287 220
Trident General Insurance Co Ltd v Mc Niece Bros Pty Ltd (1988) 165 CLR 107 .. 83, 95
Trustees Executors Ltd v QBE Insurance (International) Ltd
(2010) 16 ANZ Ins Cas 61–874 20
Tucker v Bennett (1927) 60 OLR 118 117
Turner v Davies (1796) 2 Esp 478 123
Tyrie v Fletcher (1772) 2 Cowp 666 25

Underhill v Horwood (1804) 10 Ves 209 .... 118, 124
Union Marine Insurance Co Ltd v Martin (1866) 35 LJ CP 181 .... 15, 16

Vero Insurance Ltd v QBE Insurance (Australia) Ltd [2011] NSWSC 593 58
Viger v Geographical Services Inc 277 [1972] AMC 2113 106

Walker v Bowry (1924) 35 CLR 48 130
Ward v National Bank of New Zealand (1883) 8 App Cas 755 123
Wawanesa Mutual Insurance Co v Co-op Fire & Casualty Co
(1980) 119 DLR (3d) 188 128
Weddell v Road Transport & General Insurance Co Ltd [1932] 2 KB 563,
(1931) 41 Ll L Rep 69 .... 36, 37, 41, 48, 51, 78, 108, 132, 148
Weld-Blundell v Stephens [1920] AC 956 211
Western Australian Bank v Royal Insurance Co (1908) 5 CLR 533 .... 74, 145, 166
Westminster Fire Office v Glasgow Provident (1888) 13 App Cas 699 164
White & Tudor LC (6th edn) Vol 1, p 122 118
Whitham v Bullock [1983] 2 KB 81 .... 209, 210
Whiting v Burke (1871) 6 Ch App 342 124
Williams v North China Insurance Co (1876) 1 CPD 757 .... 23, 24
Wilsher v Essex Area Health Authority [1988] AC 1074 .... 176, 177
Wolenberg v Royal Co-operative Collecting Society (1915) 84 LJKB 1316 .... 14, 18
Wolmershausen v Gullick [1893] 2 Ch 514 .... 118, 126, 130
Wooldridge v Norris (1868) Law Rep 6 Eq 410 126
Work-Cover Qld v Suncorp Metway Insurance Ltd [2005] QCA 155 151
WorkCover Queensland (2001) 11 ANZ InsCas 61–489 63

Yates v Whyte (1838) 4 Bing NC 272 219

Zurich Australian Insurance Ltd & Minerals Insurance Pte Ltd [2007] WASC 62, (2007)
209 FLR 247 .... 59, 60, 61, 65, 67, 147, 157
Zurich Australian Insurance Ltd v Metals & Minerals Insurance Pte Ltd [2009] WASCA
31, [2009] HCA 50 (2009), 240 CLR 391 .... 57, 79, 87–103
Zurich Insurance (Singapore) Pte Ltd v B-Gold Interior Design & Construction Pte Ltd
[2008] 3 SLR(R) 1029 22
Zurich Insurance Co v Shield Insurance Co [1988] IR 174 .... 135, 137
Zurich Insurance plc UK Branch v International Energy Group Ltd [2012]
EWHC 69 (Comm); on appeal [2015] 2 WLR 1471 .... 193–195, 197–198,
203, 205

TABLE OF LEGISLATION

Asbestos Industry Regulations 1931, SI 1931/1140 170

Bubble Act 1720 .... 4, 12, 110

Civil Liability (Contribution) Act 1978 .... 6, 211, 212, 217
s1(1) 196, 212, 213, 215
s2(1) 120, 216
s2(2) 216
s3 .... 206, 208
s6(1) 212, 215
s7(3) 216
Compensation Act 2006 .... 192, 196, 205
s3 .... 185, 204
s3(2) 186
s3(2)(a) 204

Earthquake Commission Act 1993 (NZ) .... s 18
.... 20, 21
s19 20
s20 20
s22 20
s30(1) 20, 21
s30(2) 21
s30(3) 21
Employer's Liability Act 1880 185
Employers' Liability (Compulsory Insurance) Act 1969 .... 183, 199–202
s1(1) 199
Employers' Liability Act 1880 185
Evidence Act (Cap 97, rev edn 1997) (Sing) .... s 93
.... 22
s94 22

Fair Trading Act 1999 (Aus) s32W
.... 112–114
s32X 112–114
Financial Services and Markets Act 2000 111
Fire Life Insurance Duty Act 1782 4

Insurance Contract Act 1984 (Aus) 6, 70, 100
s8 111
s9 64
s11(9) 95
s11(11) 94
s13 .... 82, 111
s14 111
s21 82
s34 111
s35 111
s36 111
s37 111
s37A 111
s37B 111
s37C 111
s37D 111
s37E 111
s38 98
s42 111
s43 .... 98, 111
s44 111
s45 .... xxi, 7, 53–56, 62, 63, 67, 72–78, 82–86, 92–98, 101, 103, 107, 110, 111, 222
s45(1) 7, 51, 56, 58, 60, 63, 67, 68, 73, 76, 81–83, 92, 96–103, 107
s45(1)(b) 102
s45(2) 7, 51, 65, 66, 67, 73, 81, 82, 88,

91, 94, 100, 102, 110
s46 76
s46(1) 64
s48 .... 83, 95, 96
s52 .... 98, 111
s53 .... 98, 111
s54 100
s56(1) 95
s69 111
s76 .... 7, 74, 75, 82, 110
s76(1) 74, 75
s76(2) 75
Insurance Law of the PRC
(China) art.56 149

Law Reform (Married Women
and Tortfeasors) Act 1935
s6(1) 211, 212
s6(1)(c) 211
Limitation Act 1980 130
s5 121
s10 121

Marine Insurance Act 1906 .... 9, 13
s16 10
s27(2) 10
s27(3) 10
s27(4) 10
s28 10
s32 9
s32(1) 14
s32(2) 10
s32(2)(a) 10
s32(2)(b) 10
s80 24
s80(1) 24, 148, 149, 156
s81 196
s82(a) 26
s82(b) 26
s83 26
s84(1) 26
s84(2) 26
s84(3) 26
s84(3)(b) 26
s84(3)(c) 26
s84(3)(e) 26
s84(3)(f) 26, 27

s88 25
s89 25
s90 25
Marine Insurance Act
1908 (NZ)
s33 11
s33(1) 11
s33(2)(a) 11
s33(2)(b) 11
s33(2)(c) 11
s33(2)(d) 11
Marine Insurance Act
1909 (Aus)
s38 11
s38(2)(a) 75
s38(2)(d) 75
Merchant Insurers
Bill 1693 4
Motor Vehicles (Third Party Insurance)
Act (Aus) 142
Motor Vehicles (Third Party Insurance)
Regulations (Aus) 142

Public Health (London)
Act 1891
s4(1) 117

Road Traffic Act 1972
s148 160
s149 160
s151 162
Road Traffic Ordinance
1958 (Mal)
s74(1) 34
s75(1)(b) 34
s80 34
s80(1) 34, 35

Supreme Court of Judicature
Act 1873 207
Supreme Court of Judicature Act
1875 207

Trade Practice Act 1974
(Cth) (Aus)
s68 99
s68(1) 99

Trade Practices Amendment (Australian
 Consumer Law)
 Act 2010 (Aus) 112, 114
 s12BG(1) 114

Unfair Contract Terms Act 1977 111
Unfair Terms in Consumer Contracts
 Regulations 1999, 1999/2083 111
 reg 6 111
 reg 8 111

Workers Compensation Act 1951
 (Aus) 133
Workers' Compensation Act 1990
 (Qld) (Aus) 64
Workmen's Compensation
 Act 1897 185
Workmen's Compensation
 Act 1900 185
Workmen's Compensation Act 1906 185
Workmen's Compensation Act 1925 185

Part A

CHAPTER 1

An overview
Double insurance

1.1 Background: the theory of double insurance

1.1.1 Problems with double insurance

There is always the risk of fraud when an assured takes out an insurance policy. An assured can take out numerous insurance policies and make claims under all policies. Insurers have implemented mechanisms to prevent an assured receiving more than he is entitled to. A question is whether the use of exclusion or limitation clauses in the policies to prevent recovery is justifiable. This book examines the history, development of the law of insurance and the factors the courts consider when deciding such issues – for example, whether there is sufficient protection for an assured when double insurance arises, and under what circumstances does an insurer have to pay out under the insurance policy. The cases do not provide any firm guidance. In some cases, the trial judge may find that the facts do not give rise to double insurance. However, on appeal, the appeal court may find that there is double insurance. This clearly illustrates the complexities of double insurance, and the difficulties the courts face when trying to provide principles or guidelines on double insurance.[1]

1.1.2 Insurance premiums

The general principle is that an assured can only recover the amount which he is entitled to for the loss suffered. The law is unclear as to the order in which the claim from the insurers is to be made. A contract of insurance has been defined as a contract involving two parties, the insurer and an assured. The insurer receives a premium, and in return for the premium, the insurer will pay a sum of money on the happening of an event for which the assured has obtained insurance cover.[2] Some form of consideration is usually required, but not in every situation.[3]

---

[1] Although in *National Farmers Union Mutual Insurance Society Ltd v HSBC Insurance (UK) Ltd* [2010] EWHC 773 (Comm), Gavin Kealey QC, sitting as Deputy High Court Judge, tried to provide some guidance.
[2] *Prudential Insurance Co v IRC* [1904] 2 KB 658 at 663.
[3] *Prudential Insurance Co v IRC* [1904] 2 KB 658 at 663.

1.1.3 Development of the insurance industry

The law relating to insurance developed with the needs of the insurance industry. The earliest written form evidencing indemnity type insurance transaction, such as marine insurance, was seen in the first text of insurance in 1488.[4] The earliest policy of insurance was in 1547.[5] The first decision on marine policies that the court decided was in 1588. The court specialising in hull cases was introduced in 1601.[6] The history of fire insurance dated back to the Great Fire of Great London which happened in 1666 and the first property insurer was formed in 1680. The Fire Life Insurance Duty Act 1782 was introduced and fire policy cases reached the courts by the eighteenth century.

1.1.4 Regulation of the insurance industry

Regulation of the insurance market started in 1576. The Chamber of Assurance was established in 1601, due to merchants taking out insurance policies covering the same risk. This led to the introduction of the requirement for registration of marine policies.[7] However, underwriters were not in a position to pay out for loss suffered where there was destruction of merchant ships, as illustrated in the case of the Battle of Lagos.[8] As a result, the Merchant Insurers Bill 1693 was introduced to provide some form of protection to an assured.[9] This was strongly opposed by creditors. The legislation was therefore not implemented.[10]

Next came the introduction of the South Sea Company in 1711. The South Sea Company agreed to assume a substantial proportion of the national debt and, in return for its shares, the company would get exclusive trading rights in the Americas.[11] This led to speculative and fraudulent trading.[12] As a result of this, the Bubble Act 1720, was permitted, under the Act of Parliament or Royal Charter, and was passed to provide some form of control.[13] The Bubble Act specifically applied to marine insurance, which at the time was dominated[14] by Royal Exchange Assurance and London Assurance.[15] The effect of the Bubble Act[16] made it difficult for new companies to be set up. There had to be some

---

4 de Santanerna, *On Insurance and Merchants' Bets* (1488).
5 *Ibid.*
6 *Colinvaux's Law of Insurance* (11th edn 2016), paras 1–6.
7 *Colinvaux*, paras 1–6.
8 *Ibid.*
9 *Ibid.*
10 G. Clayton, *British Insurance* (1971), pp. 53–54.
11 *Colinvaux*, paras 1–6.
12 *Ibid.*
13 *Ibid.*
14 It had done so for almost a century.
15 *Colinvaux,* paras 1–6.
16 This piece of legislation, it was thought, was not successful when it was introduced. Prior to that, there was no regulation of the finances of marine insurers, and protection for non-life insurance did not come into effect until 1909.

form of protection when a loss was sustained. The vast majority of the policies at the time were marine and non-life insurance, which was not indemnity insurance.[17] Property insurance was only in its infancy. The market was dominated by Lloyd's underwriters handling marine insurance cases. It was only later that there was the development of mutual societies which were organised by shipowners. The mutual associations would provide support to their own members when losses were suffered, and money was taken from a common fund. If the money in the funds were not sufficient, the society would call for more money from members.[18]

1.1.5 Attempt to define double insurance

In 1758 Lord Mansfield CJ[19] attempted to define double insurance. The concept of double insurance was to provide protection to an assured by allowing him to make a claim for a loss he has suffered by insuring the same subject matter, covering the same loss with numerous insurers. There were many reasons why an assured would take out insurance with numerous insurers. For example, (1) to deal with the situation where one insurer becomes insolvent, (2) where insurance is taken out by another on the assured's behalf without his knowledge,[20] (3) where the assured himself may have taken out two policies without knowing,[21] (4) the assured may have forgotten to cancel previous policies, or (5) where the insurer wishes to increase the amount of his coverage.[22]

1.1.6 Requirements of double insurance

There are certain requirements that have to be satisfied before there is double insurance. One key requirement is that the insurance taken out must cover the same property. It is unclear whether it has to be on identical property or whether it would be sufficient if another policy in effect covers a substantial part of the property already assured.[23] The general position is that double insurance occurs when two insurance policies cover the same risk which gives rise to the claim.[24] Further, the policies must cover the same interest and the same assured.

---

17 The categories of insurance are as follows: (1) marine insurance; (2) fire insurance; (3) life insurance; and (4) accident insurance. These classes are distinguishable according to the manner in which the assured has suffered a loss due to the specified event. There are contracts which do not fall within the category of indemnity, such as life insurance, personal accident insurance and sickness insurance. The earliest types of insurance were marine, life and fire, as a result of increase in business between parties and countries. The principles regarding contribution and subrogation also developed and were accepted as part of the legal structure.
18 *Colinvaux*, paras 1–6.
19 *Godin v London Assurance Co* (1758) 1 Burr 489.
20 *Portavon Cinema Co Ltd v Price and Century Insurance Co Ltd* [1939] 4 All ER 601.
21 *The Sydney Turf Club v Crowley* (1972) 126 CLR 420.
22 *Nisner Holdings Pty Ltd v Mercantile Mutual Insurance Co Ltd* [1976] NSWLR 406.
23 *MacGillivray on Insurance Law* (11th edn 2011), 23-003. There is no case law on this point.
24 *Bovis v Commercial Union Assurances* [2001] 1 Lloyd's Rep 416, 418.

1.1.7 Type of clauses

Insurers limit liability by relying on the following clauses: (1) excess clauses; (2) exclusion clauses; and (3) rateable proportion clauses. An insurer will only have to pay out the excess amount not covered under the first policy when there is an excess clause. An exclusion clause excludes payment. A rateable proportion clause will make an insurer liable up to a certain proportion of the loss. It is common for an insurer to rely on a combination of the clauses to avoid the policy.

1.1.8 Uncertainty

The law relating to double insurance is unclear. The courts have attempted to provide some guidance, but have been unsuccessful. In some cases, where the same type of clause exists in both policies, such as excess or escape clauses or rateable proportion clauses, the courts have held that they are self-cancelling and an insurer must contribute equally to the assured.

1.1.9 Contribution

Once double insurance has been established, the next issue is contribution. This usually arises where one insurer has paid out for the loss in full and seeks contribution from the other insurers. The courts have devised the following three methods of calculation: (1) the "maximum liability" test, (2) the "independent liability" test and (3) the "common liability" test. The application of these formulae can lead to very different results in terms of contribution. This has led to uncertainty. The court however will adopt whichever method leads to a fair, just and equitable result. The cases have established that the Civil Liability (Contribution) Act 1978 does not apply to double insurance. The principles of equity developed from the principles of co-surety cases, and the principles of tort and equity apply to double insurance.

1.2 Different approaches: possible solution

The approach adopted in other jurisdictions could provide some assistance. The Australian legislative approach to double insurance could be a possible way forward, with some amendments. This would require similar legislative provisions to be implemented in England.

1.2.1 Australian legislation

The Australian legislation gives an assured more protection. The Australian Law Reform Commission in its Report No 20 considered the authorities in England dealing with the clauses. It concluded that the authorities in this area were "difficult to follow and impossible to reconcile". As a result of the Law Reform Commission's Report, specific legislation in the form of the Insurance Contracts Act

1984, was implemented. Under s45, any "Other insurance" is void, unless it fell within the two exceptions provided for under s45(1) and s45(2) of the legislation.

Section 45(1) deals with situations where the contract of insurance was not a contract of insurance required to be effected by or under law, including the law of a state or territory. Section 45(2) provides that s45(1) does not apply where some or all of the loss is not covered by a contract of insurance that is specified in the first-mentioned contract. This provides protection to an assured. The assured will immediately be entitled to recover for his loss once he has identified an insurer to make a claim. Section 76 of the Act has similar effect. Once the legislative provision has been satisfied and an assured has been paid out, the issue of contribution arises.

1.2.2 Should the Australian position be followed?

However, the Australian legislation is not perfect. It does not expressly provide that for the clause in the insurance policy to be excluded from the provisions of the legislation, it would have to be established that the clause is a true excess clause. The cases in Australia are yet to deal with the specific issue of a true excess clause.

CHAPTER 2

General principles

2.1 The history of double insurance

2.1.1 The Chamber of Assurance

Double insurance arises where an assured takes out numerous insurance policies with different insurers to cover the same loss to ensure recovery for the loss which may arise in future. Therefore, where an assured has an interest in a subject matter for which he has an insurable interest, under common law,[1] he can approach any insurer who has provided cover. The insurer must however insure the same assured, insure the same subject matter already assured and the risk assured must cover the same interest.[2]

The reason for multiple insurance is the likelihood of insolvency of the insurer with whom the policy has been taken out with. If there was insolvency of the insurer, this would have the consequence that other insurers or a sole insurer might bear the whole of the loss. This would, it could be argued, be considered unfair. The main concern of an insurer is the possibility of fraud by the assured.

In 1657, the Chamber of Assurance was established to handle mercantile transactions, and played a crucial role in the early development of insurance. These transactions took place in Lombard Street, London. The main purpose of the Chamber of Assurance was to register policies and assist parties to settle disputes. The system of registration prevented or reduced an assured taking out numerous policies of insurance on the same subject matter.

2.1.2 The Marine Insurance Act 1906

The Marine Insurance Act 1906 has international application. The concept of insurance first developed in marine insurance. The statutory definition of double insurance can be found in statute in the form of s32 Marine Insurance Act 1906.[3]

---

1 *Godin v London Assurance Co* (1758) 1 Burr 489, *Albion Insurance Co Ltd v Government Insurance Office* (NSW) (1969) 121 CLR 342.

2 *North British & Mercantile Insurance Co Ltd v London Liverpool & Globe Insurance Co* (1877) 5 Ch D 569, 583; *Portavon Cinema Co Ltd v Price* [1939] 4 All ER 601, *Co-operative Bulk Handling Ltd v State Government Insurance Commission* (1990) 3 WAR 145; *Boys v State Insurance General Manager* [1980] 1 NZLR 87, 91, 94.

3 (1) Where two or more policies are effected by or on behalf of the assured on the same adventure and interest or any part thereof, and the sums assured exceed the indemnity allowed by this Act, the assured is said to be over-assured by double insurance. (2) Where the assured is over-assured by double insurance – (a) The assured, unless the policy otherwise provides, may claim payment from the insurers in such order as he may think fit, provided that he is not entitled to receive any sum in

2.1.2.1 The Marine Insurance Act: United Kingdom

Section 32(2) of the Marine Insurance Act 1906 covers situations where an assured is overassured by double insurance.[4] This section deals with situations giving rise to a valued[5] or unvalued policy,[6] where the subject matter is the same and has been overvalued.

A valued policy is a policy which specifies the agreed value of the subject-matter (Marine Insurance Act 1906 s27(2)). An unvalued policy is one which does not specify the value of the subject matter but, subject to the limit of the sum assured, leaves the insurable value to be ascertained subsequently: s28 Marine Insurance Act 1906.

Section 32(2)(b) is based on the case of *Bruce v Jones*.[7] Therefore, where you have a valued and an unvalued policy, and the loss suffered is covered in full under the unvalued policy, the assured can only make a claim against the valued policy first, and not for the full sum but only for the difference. In the case of *Bruce v Jones*, there were several valued policies of insurance which were effected upon the same vessels which had been valued differently and where, upon a total loss, the assured would receive only a certain amount under some of the policies. In another policy he would only be allowed to recover the difference between the amount received and the agreed values under that policy. The owner of the ship took out four insurance policies where the agreed values of the ships was in the sum of £3,000, £3,000, £5,000 and £3,200 and upon a total loss would receive under the three former polices the sum of £3,126.13s.6d. The shipowner sued under the latter policy. The court considered that between the assured and the underwriter of that policy, the value of the ship was £3,200 and so the assured was only entitled to recover the difference between the sum fixed as the value of the ship and £3,126l.13s.6d.

---

excess of the indemnity allowed by this Act; (b) Where the policy under which the assured claims is a valued policy, the assured must give credit as against the valuation for any sum received by him under any other policy without regard to the actual value of the subject-matter assured; (c) Where the policy under which the assured claims is an unvalued policy he must give credit, as against the full insurable value, for any sum received by him under any other policy: (d) Where the assured receives any sum in excess of the indemnity allowed by this Act, he is deemed to hold such sum in trust for the insurers, according to their right of contribution among themselves.

4 Under s32(2)(a) the assured, unless the policy otherwise provides, may claim payment from the insurers in such order as he may think fit, provided that he is not entitled to receive any sum in excess of the indemnity allowed by this Act; (b) where the policy under which the assured claims is a valued policy, the assured must give credit as against the valuation for any sum received by him under any other policy without regard to the actual value of the subject matter assured; (c) where the policy under which the assured claims is an unvalued policy he must give credit, as against the full insurable values, for any sum received by him under the policy and (d) where the assured receives any sum in excess of the indemnity allowed by this Act, he is deemed to hold such sum in trust for the insurers, according to their rights of contribution amongst themselves.

5 Where there is no fraud, it will be conclusive of the insurable value of the subject matter as to whether the loss is total or partial (see s27(3) Marine Insurance Act). A value fixed by the policy is not conclusive for the purpose of determining whether there has been constructive loss (s27(4) Marine Insurance Act 1906).

6 Also see s16 Marine Insurance Act 1906.

7 (1863) 1 H & C 769 which overruled *Bousfield v Barnes* (1815) 4 Camp 228.

2.1.2.2 The Marine Insurance Act: other jurisdictions

Identical provisions can also be found in New Zealand (s33 Marine Insurance Act 1908) and Australia (s38 Marine Insurance Act 1909). However, in Australia it only applied to marine insurance. Under s33 where there are two or more policies which have been taken out by the assured on the same adventure and interest or part of it and where the sum that he has assured exceeds the indemnity which is allowed by the Act, he is considered to be overassured by double insurance.[8] Where this is the case, the assured can claim payment from the insurers in any order he thinks fit, unless the policy provides differently or the Act states that he is not entitled to receive any sum in excess of the indemnity.[9] Where it is a valued policy, credit must be given against the valuation for sums which he has received under any other policy, without regard to the actual value of the subject matter assured.[10] If it is an unvalued policy, he must also give credit, as against the full insurable value, for sums that he has received under any other policy.[11] In England, where the assured has received any sum which is in excess of the amount permitted under the Act, he will be deemed to hold this sum in trust for the insurer, according to the rights of contribution among themselves.[12] The same wording can be found in s38 of the Marine Insurance Act 1909.

In Australia, for example, similar principles can be found in *Albion Insurance Co Ltd v GIO (NSW)*[13] where Menzies JJ stated:

> There is double insurance when an assured is assured against the same risk with two independent insurers. To insure doubly is lawful but the assured cannot recover more than the loss suffered and for which there is indemnity under each policy. The assured may claim indemnity from either insurer. However, as both insurers are liable, the doctrine of contribution between insurers has been evolved ... There is no reason why the doctrine should not apply to insurance against liability to third parties and there is every reason in principle that it should. The doctrine however only applies when each insurer insures against the same risk, although it is not necessary that the insurance should be identical. Thus one insurer may insure properties A and B against fire and the other insurer may only insure property A against fire. Again, one policy may be for a limited amount and the other may be for an unlimited amount.

---

8 Section 33(1) Marine Insurance Act 1908.
9 Section 33(2)(a) Marine insurance Act 1908.
10 Section 33(2)(b) Marine Insurance Act 1908.
11 Section 33(2)(c) Marine Insurance Act 1908.
12 Section 33(2)(d) Marine Insurance Act 1908.
13 (1969) 121 CLR 342. This approach has been followed in other cases such as *John v Rawlings* (1984) 3 ANZ Ins Cas 60–564; *Boy v State Insurance General Manager* [1980] 1 NZLR 87; *Australian Eagle Insurance Co Ltd v Mutual Acceptance (Insurance) Pty Ltd* [1983] 3 NSWLR 59 (CA); *GIO (NSW) v QBE Insurance Ltd* (1985) 2 NSWLR 543 and *QBE Insurance Ltd v GIO (NSW)* (1986) 4 ANZ Ins Cas 60. Further see the judgment of Kitto J who stated that what resulted in the right of contribution was the simple fact that each contract was a contract of indemnity and covered the identical loss that the same assured sustained. This was because the assured only received one satisfaction. In *State Government Insurance Commission v Switzerland Insurance Australia Ltd (Trading as a Federation Insurances)* [1995] SASA 5490, at para. [14], the full court of the Supreme Court of Australia confirmed that this was the correct approach and even went as far as saying that there could be no doubt that this was the law.

One policy may cover the risk of a whole voyage and the other may cover only part of the voyage. Differences of this sort may affect the amount of contribution recoverable but they do not bear on the question whether or not each insurer has assured against the same risk so as to give rise to some contribution. The element essential for contribution is that, whatever else may be covered by either of the policies, each must cover the risk which has given rise to the claim. There is no double insurance unless each insurer is liable under his policy to indemnify the assured in whole or in part against the happening which had given rise to the assured's loss or liability.

2.1.2.3 The Bubble Act 1720

Before, due to the large number of marine insurance policies, the main source of insurance policies derived from individual underwriters, where there were no controls over the transactions, and which lead to failure to comply with terms, leading to default.[14] In 1720, the introduction of the Bubble Act prevented the formation of insurance companies except two insurance companies with Royal Charters. The two insurance companies were the Royal Exchange Assurance and the London Assurance,[15] which only got support from the Crown after paying off the King's civil debt.[16] The introduction of the Bubble Act in 1720, was a device used to prevent or restrict the formation of companies to raise capital, and unless there was authorisation by an Act of Parliament or Royal Charter.[17] However, there was no express prohibition in the Bubble Act preventing an individual from providing marine insurance services.[18] As a result, due to the demand for insurance policies, Lloyd's Coffee House developed and first opened in 1688, although insurance cannot be shown to have been written at Lloyd's until 1720. In 1730, Lloyd's was soon recognised as the hub of marine underwriting and dominated shipping insurance.[19]

Before the introduction of the Bubble Act 1720, there were over 150 merchants who had marine policies valued in the millions.[20] The law developed at the time to grant a marine insurance monopoly to two chartered insurers.[21] The importance of marine insurance was more prevalent during the time of the war, and although the two chartered companies who had priority due to the Bubble Act, Lloyd's underwriters wrote the overwhelming majority of the risks placed and by 1812 had secured some 95% of the market.[22]

---

14 *Colinvaux*, para. 11–074.
15 At the time it was also called the Royal Exchange and London Assurance Corporation Act 1719.
16 Ron Harris, "The Bubble Act: Its Passage and Its Effects on Business Organization" (1994) 53(3) *Journal of Economic History*, 610–617, 613.
17 Gurses, *Marine Insurance Law* (2nd edn 2017), p. 2.
18 *Ibid*.
19 *Gurses*, p. 3.
20 *Colinvaux*, paras A1–7.
21 *Ibid*.
22 *Ibid*.

2.2 The concept of double insurance

The development of the concept of double insurance is illustrated in earlier marine insurance cases such as *Newby v Reed*,[23] *Rogers v Davies*,[24] *Bousfield v Barnes*,[25] *Morgan v Price*[26] and *Bruce v Jones*.[27] The courts in *North British Insurance v London, Liverpool & Globe Insurance*[28] saw an extension of those principles to other types of liabilities.[29]

The principle of "double insurance"[30] has been called different things in different countries, such as dual insurance[31] or stacking.[32] Stacking is more accurately defined as placing losses in the policy year which is of most advantage to the assured or reassured. The principles of double insurance can also be found in various jurisdictions such as England, Australia, Canada, Germany, the People's Republic of China, Singapore and the United States for example. The scope and wordings in these jurisdictions vary, as some provisions can be found in legislation.

The Marine Insurance Act 1906 was adopted more or less verbatim in Australia, New Zealand, Hong Kong, Singapore and Canada. In Australia, however, the Act does not apply to contracts governed by Insurance Contracts Act 1984, which include non-marine, and consumer marine.

The basic principle is that it will apply when two or more insurers cover the same type of policy, which means that each policy must indemnify the same loss against the same assured.[33] In England, the definition was given legislative

---

23 (1763) 1 Wm Bl 416.
24 (1777) 2 Park 8th edn, 601.
25 (1815) 4 Camp 228.
26 (1849) 4 Exch 615.
27 (1863) 1 M & R 769.
28 (1877) 5 Ch D 569.
29 In these cases there were numerous marine policies which were under individual underwriters, who did not have financial control.
30 *Collyear v CGU* [2008] NSWCA 92. Also see *Godin v London Assurance Co* (1758) 1 Burr 489. In the article "Insurance between Neighbours: *Stannard v Gore* and Common Law Liability for Fire" (2013) 25(2) J Environmental Law 305, Jenny Steel noted that although there was a duty to insure your neighbor, this would create double insurance in the sense that both parties are well advised to insure, this was not double insurance in the technical sense. This was because, for example, the victim's fire insurance, if called upon to pay, would have a subrogation claim against the tortfeasor, so the loss would lie entirely with the tortfeasor (or the tortfeasor's public liability insurers).
31 So called in Australia. See *GIO General Ltd v Insurance Australia Ltd t/as NRMA Insurance* [2008] ASTSC 38.
32 So called in America. Staking denoted the availability of more than one policy providing reimbursement of the losses of the assured. See *Breaux v American Family Mutual* 553 F 3d 447 (6 Cir 2009) and *Farm Bureau Mut Ins Co v Ries* 551 NW 2d 316 (Iowa 1996). Also see *Travelers Insurance Co v J Carpenter*, 411 F 3d 323, at §[30]–[37] (20 June 2005), where the United States Court of Appeals, Second Circuit, dealt with a provision in Vt Stat Ann Tit 21 §624(e)(2003) dealing with workers' compensation insurer's right to reimbursement of proceeds of an unassured/underassured motorist policy. This section governed dual liability, in a third-party action, and prevented double recovery. The court had to decide how the prohibition on "double recovery" in §624(e) was defined. *Bogart v Twin City Fire Insurance Co* 473 F 2d 619 §[8] (9 March 1973)(dealing with stacking cases in Texas) and *Land v United States Fidelity and Guaranty Co* 78 F 3d 187, at §[13] (25 March 1996) (dealing with aggregation or stacking of multiple policies in Mississippi).
33 *GIO General Ltd v Insurance Australia Ltd t/as NRMA Insurance* [2008] ASTSC 38.

effect due to the enactment of s32(1) of the Marine Insurance Act 1906. There was obviously a need to give protection to an assured, by the implementation of legislation. There is nothing to prevent an assured from taking out numerous polices, as insurance contracts are essentially contracts of indemnity. However, an assured cannot recover more than his full indemnity.[34]

2.3 Cases on double insurance: is there double insurance?

2.3.1 North British Insurance v London, Liverpool & Globe Insurance

The cases illustrate the difficulty in identifying whether double insurance arises. In *North British Insurance v London, Liverpool & Globe Insurance*, grain had been assured by two companies, Rodocanachi and Co and Barnett and Co, with two separate underwriters against any loss or damage by fire which had been assured. There was a specific provision that:

> if at the time of any loss or damage by fire happening to any property hereby assured, there be any other subsisting insurance or insurances, whether effected by the assured or by any other person, covering the same property, the company shall not be liable to pay or contribute more than its rateable proportion of such loss or damage.

Mellish LJ[35] stated that:

> Now I do not know of any English cases on the subject of contribution as applied to fire policies; but I can see no reason why the principle in respect of contribution should not be exactly the same in respect of fire policies as they are in respect of marine policies, and I think if the same person in respect of the same right insures in two offices, there is no reason why they should not contribute in equal proportions in respect of a fire policy as they would in the case of a marine policy. The rule is perfectly established in the case of a marine policy that contribution only applies where it is an insurance by the same person having the same rights, and does not apply where different person insure in respect of different rights. The reason for that is obvious enough. Where different persons insure the same property in respect of their different rights they may be divided into two classes. It may be that the interest of the two between them makes up the whole property, as in the case of a tenant for life and remainderman.

2.3.2 Mathie v The Argonaut Marine Insurance Co Ltd

There is no requirement at common law for an assured to inform his insurer of other policies taken out, unless there is a change in the character of the risk,

---

34 *Morgan v Price* (1849) 4 Exch 615; *Godin v London Assurance Co* (1758) 1 Burr 489; *Newy v Reed* (1763) 1 Wm Bl 416; *Rogers v Davis* (1777) 2 Park's Marine Inscc (8th edn) p. 601; *North British and Mercantile Insurance Co v London, Liverpool and Global Insurance Co* (1877) 5 ChD 569,CA; *Scottish Amicable Heritable Securities Association v Northern Assurance Co* 1883 11 R (Ct of Sess) 287 and *Wolenberg v Royal Co-operative Collecting Society* (1915) 84 LJKB 1316. Also see *Bruce v Jones* (1863) 1 H & C 769. This is the position no matter how many policies the assured has taken out.
35 (1877) 5 Ch D 569, 583.

which amounts to a fraud. In *Mathie v The Argonaut Marine Insurance Co Ltd*,[36] the House of Lords heard an appeal involving insurance of a cargo of coal sailing on the vessel named *Selene*, which sailed from Delagoa Bay to Bombay. The *Selene* had become a total loss at sea. The hull had been assured for £26,000 by a time policy. The respondent took out insurance of £6,000 on freight or anticipated freight for the intended voyage. In addition to this £4,000 was taken out for disbursements. The value of coal dropped on the voyage to Delagoa Bay, and no business had been entered into. This resulted in the respondent failing to obtain freight for the vessel. The respondent purchased additional coal on his own account and payed extra premium, so as to obtain an extension of the risk. The respondent entered into failed negotiations in reducing his insurances on hull. However, he obtained further insurance on the coal cargo for £6,000 from the appellants. The appellant argued, *inter alia*, on appeal that there was misrepresentation[37] and gross over-valuation and concealment of the over-valuation. Lord Buckmaster[38] summarised the issue before the court as follows:

> the question and the only question which arises in this appeal is whether the respondent was bound to make a disclosure to the underwriters with whom he effected an insurance on cargo on his ship of the fact that he had already effected an insurance for freight which in the circumstances was higher than the freight that he could possibly earn.

The House of Lords relied on *Ionides v Pender*,[39] which was referred to by the judge who stated:

> As I understand it, in order to find out whether existing insurances ought to be disclosed when a fresh insurance is taken out one has to consider this: of course one must take the figures, but one has to consider whether the discrepancy between the assured value and the actual insurable value is of such a nature as to change the character of the risk from a business rise to a speculative risk.

2.3.3 Union Marine Insurance Co Ltd v Martin

However, not in all cases where there is an overlap in the policies will there be double insurance. In *Union Marine Insurance Co Ltd v Martin*[40] the court considered the intention of the parties and concluded that the first policy terminated when the second policy came into force. The court stated that there will be no double insurance even where an overlap is of a minor nature.[41]

---

36 (1925) 21 Ll LR 145.
37 That there had been misrepresentation in that the valuation of £6,000 was stated to represent cost, insurance and profit only, whereas in fact such valuation included a considerable sum in respect of freight.
38 (1925) 21 Ll LR 145, 146.
39 LR 9 QB 531.
40 (1866) 35 LJCP 181.
41 *Union Marine Insurance Co Ltd v Martin* (1866) 35 LJCP 181. In *Union Marine Insurance* the court looked at the intention of the parties and concluded that the first policy terminated when the

2.3.4 Godin v London Assurance Co

In *Godin v London Assurance Co*,[42] there was a dispute as to whether there was double insurance. The court had to decide "whether the plaintiff ought to recover his whole loss, or only half". In *Godin*, Mr Amyad and Company of London sent a ship from London to Meybohm. Amyad and Company took out an insurance policy first with private insurers for £1,100,[43] which was signed by several private underwriters. Mr Amyad then assured £800[44] and £900[45] with other private insurers. The total sum assured was £2,800.[46] Under the instructions of Meybohm, who endorsed the bill of lading to Mr John Tamzen in Moscow, an application for further insurance was made to the defendants, the London Assurance Company.[47] The defendants were made aware of the existence of the other insurance. The goods and ship were lost. It was argued that the insurers should pay the whole amount, as the insurers received a premium for the whole risk. The court[48] commented: "Insurance was considered as an indemnity only, in case of a loss: and therefore the satisfaction ought not to exceed the loss. This was calculated to prevent fraud; lest the temptation of gain should occasion unfair and willful losses." The court went on to say "the law certainly says that he ought not to recover doubly for the same loss, but be content with one single satisfaction for it". It was argued that the indorsement of the bills of lading transferred Meybohm's interest in all policies. Therefore, Tamesz had the right to Mr Amyand's policy, and as Tamesz was the assignee of Meybohm, he was the *cestui que trust* of it. Tamesz could recover the money assured. The court held[49] that "Tamesz, the assured, has a right to recover his whole loss from the defendant, upon the policy now in question, by which they are bound to pay the whole."

2.3.5 Union Marine Insurance Co Ltd v Martin

There have been situations where the courts have concluded that the facts do not give rise to double insurance. In *Union Marine Insurance Co Ltd v Martin*,[50] a vessel from Bombay to Calcutta was assured for a period of 30 days once it had been moored in Calcutta. The owners of the ship then effected another policy with the same insurer, for the period at and from Calcutta to Bombay. During the continuation of the risk, which both policies had assured for, the vessel was lost

---

second policy came into force. See *Equity Syndicate Management Ltd v Glaxosmithkline plc* [2015] EWHC 2163 (Comm) (a motor policy covering an employee driving a hire car) where the court held that there was no double insurance.
42 (1758) 1 Burr 489.
43 On the ship, tackle and goods, at and from London to St Petersburg, and at and from thence back again to London.
44 On goods only, and was only at and from St Petersburg to London.
45 On goods only, and at and from the south to London.
46 £2,300 was on goods and £500 was on the ship.
47 For £2,316.
48 (1758) 1 Burr 489, 491.
49 (1758) 1 Burr 489, 495.
50 (1866) 35 LJ CP 181.

in Calcutta. Insurers had paid the owners for the total loss under the second policy. The monies payable under the first policy had not been deducted. The court held that the second policy was in substitution for the first. The original insurers were liable on the second policy.

2.3.6 Rathbone Brothers plc v Novae Corporate Underwriting Ltd

In *Rathbone Brothers plc v Novae Corporate Underwriting Ltd*[51] the court had to consider liability insurance. PEV, the second plaintiff, was a personal trustee of the Walker Trust. NHTC, which was subsequently acquired by Rathbone, the first plaintiff, administered the trust. NHTC then changed its name to Rathbone Trust Company Jersey Ltd and employed PEV. An instrument of release and indemnity was entered into with PEV, which permitted Rathbone and Rathbone Trustees to claim an indemnity from PEV for any liabilities arising from the performance of his services. PEV then became a consultant for Rathbone Trustees, and stopped working full-time. A consultancy agreement provided for indemnity for PEV for certain liabilities. Rathbone took out insurance for its subsidiaries, which consisted of Rathbone Trustees, AIG and the defendant's excess insurers. The first layer of responsibility would be covered by AIG. The excess would be covered by the excess insurers. A claim was brought by beneficiaries of the Walker Trust for breach of professional duties and fiduciary duties. The excess policy (clause 5.14) provided: "Insurance provided by this policy applies excess over insurance and indemnification available from any other source." Burton J had to decide whether PEV was an assured person under the PI excess policy, and whether there was double insurance, which arose from the indemnity or D & O policy. The judge stated that PEV came under the definition of an assured person, and that there was no double insurance. The Court of Appeal agreed that there was no double insurance. Elias LJ[52] considered the meaning of "available from any other source" and stated:

> 56. It seems to me that if the insurers can take advantage of an indemnity given by one co-assured to another, this would significantly undermine the protection afforded by the policy. Employers frequently give indemnities to directors and employees for liabilities arising out of their negligent conduct. A major reason for taking out insurance is to protect against the risks of incurring liability as a consequence of such negligence. In my judgment, that would be obvious, both to the insurers and to the assured. It would frustrate the purpose of professional indemnity insurance to interpret the policy so as to exclude the insurers from liability in the very circumstances where that insurance is most likely to be needed. In my judgment, it would require very clear language to treat the indemnity granted by the assured company to be the primary source of cover ahead of the insurance for which the assured company has paid. The commercial understanding would be that the insurers receive the premium to meet precisely that kind of liability.
>
> . . .

---

51 [2014] WLR(D) 488.
52 [2014] WLR(D), at §[56]–[57].

57. It would be clear that any other insurance cover would be from a source independent of Rathbone plc and the other assured companies. In my view it is reasonable to construe the clause so that the non-assured indemnification also needs to come from some external source. Again, therefore, I am in agreement with the judge below on this point.

...

63. Liability policies will not habitually give a free-standing coverage for defence costs even where the liability itself is not assured, and in my view there would need to be very clear provision in the policy to that effect in order for the argument to succeed. This is supported by the decision of the Court of Appeal in *Astra Zeneca Insurance Co v XL Insurance (Bermuda) Limited* [2013] EWCA Civ 1660, reported at [2013] Lloyd's Rep IR 290 para. 72 where Christopher Clarke LJ observed that in respect of non-marine liability insurance at least, the right to recover defence costs must, absent clear wording to the contrary, depend on some free-standing entitlement under the policy. That was a claim where no liability could be established but precisely the same principle must apply where no liability is covered. As Mr Kendrick pointed out, liability insurers generally have no interest in defeating claims for which they would not be liable under the policy.

2.3.7 Conclusion

Therefore, there must be more than one policy which is valid, and which covers the same interest. The policy must not exclude the risk[53] or be a policy which does not cover the risk. However, the insurance policies do not have to be identical. The policies could cover different subjects and different risks, in addition to the risk which are covered in common. A common liability to indemnity of the same assured for the specific loss must be present.

2.4 Recovery from insurers

2.4.1 An assured's right of recovery

If the assured decides to make a claim from one insurer in full, he cannot seek to recover from another insurer.[54] In *Wolenberg v Royal Co-operative Collecting Society*,[55] the Court emphasised that where there were numerous policies taken out with different insurers to cover funeral expenses, and if one of the insurers pays out in full to cover funeral expenses which were assured, no claim can be made against any of the other insurers who have not paid under the policies.

---

53 *Body Corporate 74246 v QBE Insurance (International) Ltd* [2015] NZHC 1360 (16 June 2015), where the plaintiff's property was damaged by separate events in 2007. On 22 February 2011 and 13 June 2011 the Canterbury earthquakes occurred. QBE were the plaintiff's insurers of its property from 4 September 2009 to 4 September 2010. Allianz Insurance which provided cover over the building for 12 months starting from 4 September 2010 which was also on risk, at the time of the 2010 earthquake, and gave rise to double insurance.

54 *Hebon v West* (1863) 3 B & S 579 and *Sims v Scottish Imperial Ins Co* (1902) 10 SLT 286. Where double insurance by an assured will be treated as being "one insurance", therefore he then cannot seek recovery from the other insurer.

55 (1915) 84 LJKB 1316.

Furthermore, the assured cannot seek to recover the premium paid, unless there has been fraud or where there is a mistake of fact. This was followed in *Goldstein v Salvation Army Assurance Society*.[56]

In *Bruce v Jones*,[57] a marine insurance case, the court[58] considered valued policies. The court concluded that if the ship is valued at an amount which is higher than that of the policy, the assured should only be able to recover, the difference between the sum which the assured has already recovered and the value of the ship under the present policy. The interests of the insurer and assured should be balanced. The choice as to which insurer the assured decides to claim against for the recovery of the loss is not determined in any particular manner. An assured can choose to claim any amount from the insurer as he thinks fit.[59]

In *Bousfield v Barnes*,[60] the court considered *Muirhead v Forth and North Sea Steamboat Mutual Insurance Co.*[61] In *Bousfield v Barnes*, a ship was assured against all risks except those undertaken by the government which was valued at £6,000. The policy was subscribed for £600. Another policy was then taken out with London Assurance, insuring the ship for £6,000, after being valued at above £8000. London Assurance only paid to the plaintiff £6,000 when the ship was wrecked, and which had been subscribed. The defendant argued that the action could not be permitted, as the plaintiff had received the full amount of the sum valued by the policy. Lord Ellenborough[62] stated:

> I think the valuation in this policy is only conclusive in settling a loss upon it between the assured and the underwriters who have subscribed it, without taking into consideration what has been transacted between the assured and third persons. If a total loss happens, these underwriters shall not pay more than the amount of the valuation; and if there be a partial loss, the valuation regulates the amount of the average contribution. I will likewise take care that the assured does not recover upon the whole more than the real value of the subject matter assured. But I think it is not enough for the underwriters on a particular policy to shew that the assured has received from another quarter the amount of the valuation in that policy, unless this amounts in point of fact to a complete indemnity. In the present case the ship assured is proved to have been worth above £8000. The plaintiff has received only £6000 from the London Assurance. He has therefore an interest of £2000 to which he may apply the policy on which the action is brought. That policy is only subscribed for £600. Therefore, when the whole of that sum has been paid, he will still be a loser to the amount of £1400 by the total loss of his vessel.

The court found in favour of the plaintiff.

---

56 [1971] 2 KB. 291.
57 (1863) 1 H & C 769.
58 Pollock CB.
59 *Newby v Reed* (1763) 1 Wm Bl 416; *Rogers v Davies* (1777) 2 Park (8th edn) 601; *Bousfield v Barnes* (1815) 4 Camp 228; *Morgan v Price* (1849) 4 Exch 615; and *Bruce v Jones* (1863) 1 M & R 769.
60 (1815) 4 Camp 228.
61 [1894] AC 72.
62 (1815) 4 Camp 228, 229, 230.

2.4.2 Conclusion

The courts were keen to ensure that the insurers are not defrauded as a result of an assured taking out numerous policies and where claims were made for loss suffered under such policies. If payment has been made to the assured, it is for the insurer to ask the other insurers to pay their portion which has been paid out by the insurer under the first policy.[63]

2.5 Interpretation of policy wording in double insurance clauses

The wording in insurance policies may limit or exclude liability. In Australia, the legislature has gone so far as to conclude that all such clauses would be void, except in very limited circumstances.

2.5.1 Contractual and legislative exclusions

In *Body Corporation 398983 v Zurich Australian Insurance Ltd*[64] the court had to interpret the national disaster damage clause in the policy. This case looked at contractual exclusion or limiting of liability, and the legislative provision dealing with situations where there was double insurance. The clause had the effect of limiting the amount which was payable by Zurich for natural disaster damage where there was cover provided under statute. The clause stated that "the Insurers liability will be limited to the amount of loss in excess of the Natural Disaster Damage Cover". The court stated that when interpreting the contract, the meaning intended by the parties to that contract had to be considered. This is to be done on an objective basis, by looking at what a reasonable and properly informed third party would consider the parties to have intended. This would include the background knowledge that would reasonably be available to the parties at the time. The courts would generally look at the plain and ordinary meaning of the contract and will only displace it where there were strong grounds to persuade the court that something had gone wrong regarding the contractual language that has been used that would justify this course.[65] These principles were the same as those which would apply to insurance contracts.[66] Therefore double insurance arose in the present case because the statutory cover and the Zurich policy both would respond to the body corporate's loss in relation to the Salisbury apartments. Section 30(1)[67] of the Earthquake Commission Act 1993 contained

---

63 *Newby v Reed* (1763) 1 Wm Bl 416; *Davis v Gildart* (1777) 2 Park's Marine Inscc 8th edn, p. 424; *Godin v London Assurance Co* (1758) 1 Burr 489; *Legal and General Assurance Society Ltd v Drake Insurance Co Ltd* [1992] QB 887, CA. Also see *Austin v Zurich General Accident and Liability Insurance Co Ltd* [1945] KB 250.

64 [2013] NZHC 1109.

65 The cases referred to were *Vector Gas Ltd v Bay of Plenty Energy Ltd* [2010] 2 NZLR 444 at [19], [61]; *Investors Compensation Scheme Ltd v West Bromwich Building Society* [1998] 1 WLR 896 at 912–913; and *Chartbrook Ltd v Persimmon Homes Ltd* [2009] 3 WLR 267 at paras [14]–[15].

66 *Trustees Executors Ltd v QBE Insurance (International) Ltd* (2010) 16 ANZ Ins Cas 61–874.

67 This section states that where on the occurrence to any property of natural disaster damage against which it is assured under any of ss18–20, or s22, of this Act, the property is also assured against that damage under any contract or contracts made otherwise than under this Act, the insurance

an "other insurance" clause which provided damage which exceeded the cover of the contract under the insurance contract and any deductibles. The Zurich policy also contained "other insurance" clauses,[68] GC09 and MD15. The Zurich policy would respond only after all other cover had been exhausted under the GC09 policy. However, by virtue of s30(3)[69] the clause would be defeated. The parties agreed that s30(2) applied,[70] which provided that subsection (1) of the section shall not apply with respect to any contract of insurance made otherwise than under this Act to the extent that the contract provides for cover in the excess of the amount to which cover is provided under this Act. The court had to decide whether the body corporate could recover and whether its entitlement would be the same if s30(2) applied[71] or would be less.[72] The court held that the wording in MD15 was specifically added to trigger s30(2). The words "will be limited to" emphasised that the cover under the policy is only cover in excess of the statutory cover. Therefore s30(2) would not be triggered. It was unnecessary for the court to read the wording of clause MD15 to make sense of the clause.[73] The definition of "loss" in clause MD15 bore its ordinary meaning of being deprived of something or of the diminution of possession resulting from a change in conditions. This would have to be the actual loss.

2.5.2 Interpreting clauses: Singapore High Court

Courts in other jurisdictions have attempted to provide guidance when interpreting clauses in policies. In *Lonpac Insurance Bhd v American Home Assurance Co*[74] the Singapore High Court was asked to consider whether extrinsic evidence could be admitted to help assist the court to construe the annual policy which had been issued. The primary issue was whether the annual policy also covered the plaintiff's claim, which could result in double insurance. The extrinsic evidence which Lopac sought to adduce was in the form of affidavits from employees of the group and its insurance broker. The decision of the assistant commissioner was to refuse the production of extrinsic evidence. The plaintiff argued that the facts of *Lonpac Insurance Bhd v American Home Assurance Co* were similar to

---

of the property under this Act (to the amount to which it is so assured) shall be deemed to be in respect of so much of that disaster damage as exceeds the sum of – (a) the total amount payable under that contract or those contracts in respect of that natural disaster damage; and (b) the proportion of the natural disaster damage to be borne by the assured person under the conditions applying to the insurance of the property under the Act. This section was similar to s18 Earthquake and War Damage Act 1944 (EQWD Act).

68 GC09 and MD15.

69 Subsection (3) states that notwithstanding anything to the contrary in any contract whereby any property is assured against natural disaster damage otherwise than under this Act, where the property is or has at any time also been assured against that natural disaster damage under any of the ss18–20, or s22, of this Act, the contract shall have effect in all respects as if the property were not and had never been assured under this Act.

70 If it did not, and in absence of MD15, then Zurich's policy would have to respond first.

71 Which was the body corporate's argument.

72 As was contended by Zurich.

73 It could be argued that if the court were to do this, this would go beyond the intention of the parties.

74 [2011] SGHC 257, at para. [1].

those in *China Insurance Co (Singapore) Pte Ltd v Liberty Insurance Pte Ltd* where the reason for the production of extrinsic evidence was to show that the assured had taken out the second policy only because they were told to do so by their insurance broker and after they were informed that their first policy did not cover liability to workmen injured while onboard the vessel.

In *China Insurance Co (Singapore) Pte Ltd v Liberty Insurance Pte Ltd*, Phang JC was of the view that such extrinsic evidence was relevant, admissible and persuasive in the defendant's favour.[75] He concluded that, even assuming that a comparison of the policies alone was insufficient to determine the case in the defendant's favour, the production of the extrinsic evidence would clearly have accomplished this. Phang JC went on to conclude that there was no double insurance as the two policies covered different risks. In a detailed analysis[76] by the court, it was held that extrinsic evidence could be admissible to explain the risks intended to be covered under the policy between Lonpac and REL.

It could be argued that the position adopted in Singapore would be helpful where there is a dispute by the parties as to the policy terms, apart from those as expressly stated in the documents itself. Although the decision in *Lonpac Insurance Bhd v American Home Assurance Co* related to two insurance companies, it could be argued that the same principles would apply to an insurer and assured position. However, to adopt this approach where the claim is made years later may be problematic. This is because it would be difficult to locate witnesses to provide witness statements or the insurance company itself could have gone into liquidation. Therefore, a better alternative could be to rely solely on the documentation produced as a result of the discussions between the parties to ascertain their intentions, and to adopt an objective test.

2.6 Contribution as a general concept

There are two aspects to double insurance. First, an assured cannot recover more than his indemnity but he can choose which policy to claim under and,

---

75 The Court of Appeal in *Zurich Insurance (Singapore) Pte Ltd v B-Gold Interior Design & Construction Pte Ltd* [2008] 3 SLR(R) 1029 which stated that the remarks of Phang J with regard to the admissibility of extrinsic evidence was *obiter*. The court however in *Lonpac Insurance Bhd v American Home Assurance Co* considered that it was wrong to suggest that the Court of Appeal in *Zurich* confined *China Insurance* to its facts.

76 The Evidence Act (Cap 97, rev edn 1997), s93 (which states that when the terms of a contract or of a grant or of any other disposition of property have been reduced by or by consent of the parties to the form of a document, and in all cases in which any matter is required by law to be reduced to the form of a document, no evidence shall be given in proof of the terms of such contract, grant or other disposition of property or of such a matter except the document itself, or secondary evidence of its contents in cases in which secondary evidence is admissible under the provisions of this Act), s94 (when the terms of any such contract, grant or other disposition of property, or any matter required by law to be reduced to the form of a document, have been proved according to s93, no evidence of any oral agreement or statement shall be admitted as between the parties to any such instrument or their representatives in interest for the purpose of contradicting, varying, adding to, or subtracting from its terms subject to the following provisions) and the case of *China Insurance Co (Singapore) Pte Ltd v Liberty Insurance Pte Ltd* [2005] 2 SLR(R) 509.

second, the insurer who pays the claim under the policy is then entitled to seek contribution from the other insurers.[77]

The origins of contribution began when the Courts of Equity had to decide the control and direction of the cause of action arising under deeds or contracts, and not with the creation of independent and separate causes of action.[78] If the assured has assured the same subject matter covering the same loss with a few insurers under the doctrine of double insurance,[79] then the insurer who has paid out[80] can seek contribution from other insurers who have also provided cover. This is due to the equitable doctrine of contribution[81] which only applies to insurers.[82] Matters within the realm of equity include situations where (1) a legal remedy was not available and where the equitable remedy was more efficient, or (2) the procedure in equity was more favourable to the parties. The approach taken by the Courts of Chancery allowed for an adjustment of parties' rights by bringing all interested parties before it, to avoid multiplicity of suits. Contribution, it was said, would fall within this category.[83] Contribution is not based on contract, even though it could be modified by contract. Contribution is based on the principles of natural justice.

---

77 John Lowry and Philip Rawlings, *Insurance Law: Doctrines and Principles* (2nd edn 2005).
78 *Legal and General Assurance Society Ltd v Drake Insurance Co Ltd* [1991] 2 Lloyd's Law Reports 44, per Gibson LJ.
79 These principles can also be seen in the UNCTDA Model Clauses on Marine Hull and Cargo Insurance, cl 10.5. which deals with co-insurance. Clause 10.5.1 provides that where two or more insurers are liable under this insurance, each insurer is liable only for his proportion of the claim, which is the proportion that his subscription bears to the sum assured, and shall on no account be held jointly liable with his co-insurers. In *Tai Ping Insurance Co Ltd v Tugu Insurance Co Ltd* [2001] 2 HKC 401, Stone J concluded that there was double insurance based on (1) both policies cover the loss of the goods by theft/robbery; (2) both polices cover the same interest; (3) both policies were in force at the time of the loss; and (4) both the policies were legally enforceable at the time.
80 *Williams v North China Insurance Co* (1876) 1 CPD 757.
81 This is based on the principle of equity: *Godin v London Assurance Co* (1758) 1 Burr 489. In *Mathie v Argonaut Marine Ins Co* (1925) 21 LI LR 145 it was stated that under common law the assured is not required to disclose to the insurer that he has previously taken out insurance with another insurer which covers the same risk, unless there is a degree of over-insurance which is likely to give rise to fraud.
82 This is the position for co-insurers and the equitable doctrine of contribution is confined to indemnity insurance and operates to prevent the assured from being unjustly enriched: John Lowry and Philip Rawlings, *Insurance Law: Doctrines and Principles* (2nd edn 2005) p. 270. Also see *Caledonia North Sea Ltd v BT plc* [2002] Lloyd's Rep IR 261; *Family Insurance Corporation v Lombard Canada Ltd* [2002] SCJ No 49 where Bastarache J stated as follows:

> It is a well-established principle of insurance law that where an assured holds more than one policy of insurance that covers the same risk, the assured may never recover more than the amount of the full loss but is entitled to select the policy under which to claim indemnity, subject to any conditions to the contrary. The selected insurer, in turn, is entitled to contribution from all other insurers who have covered the same risk. This doctrine of equitable contribution among insurers is founded on the general principle that parties under a coordinate liability to make good a loss must share that burden pro-rata. It finds its historic articulation in the words of Lord Mansfield CJ in *Godin v London Assurance Co* (1758) 1 Burr 489, 97 ER 419 at 420: If the assured is to receive but one satisfaction, natural justice says that the several insurers shall all of them contribute pro-rata, to satisfy that loss against which they have all assured.

83 *Legal and General Assurance Society Ltd v Drake Insurance Co Ltd* [1991] 2 Lloyd's Law Reports 43 and *Halsbury's Laws of England* (4th edn 1976) Vol. 16 (Equity) at para. 1214, referred to in *Drake*.

Therefore, payment by one person liable will release the others from the principal demand and they are required to contribute as a return for this benefit. This only applied where all the parties are liable to a common demand,[84] and was an equitable right. This required someone who has taken a premium to share the burden of meeting the claim.[85]

In *Godin v London Assurance Co*[86] Lord Mansfield stated, "If the assured is to receive but one satisfaction, natural justice says that the several insurers shall all of them contribute pro-rata to satisfy that loss against which they have all assured." This position has been codified in legislation in the Marine Insurance Act 1906, s80 which provides that:

> Where the assured is over-assured by double insurance, each insurer is bound, as between himself and the other insurers, to contribute rateably to the loss in proportion to the amount for which he is liable under the contract. If any insurer pays more than his proportion of the loss, he is entitled to maintain an action for contribution against the other insurers, and is entitled to maintain an action for contribution against the other insurers, and is entitled to the remedies as a surety who has paid more than his proportion of the debts.

Under s80(1) an insurer will have to contribute rateably to the loss in proportion to the amount he is liable to pay under the policy contract.[87]

The following requirements must be satisfied for contribution to arise: (1) the policy must be in force at the time of the loss; (2) the policy must not be void; and (3) the risk must attached.[88] The apportionment of the loss will be done according to various rules of practice that have been adopted more or less uniformly by the different insurers.[89] It is different in practice where a distinction is drawn where the policies are "specific", which means that they would not be subject to average.[90]

---

84 *Halsbury's Laws of England* (4th edn 1976) Vol. 16 (Equity) para. 1252.
85 *Legal and General Assurance Society Ltd v Drake Insurance Co Ltd* [1991] 2 Lloyd's Law Reports 43.
86 (1758) 1 Burr 489. Also see *American Surety Co of New York v Wrightson* (1910) 16 Com Cas 37.
87 *O'Kane v Jones* [2005] Lloyd's Rep IR 174, *American Surety Co of New York v Wrightson* (1910) 103 LT 663, *Williams v The North China Insurance Co* (1876) 1 CPD 757; *Boag v Economic Insurance Co Ltd* [1954] 2 Lloyd's Rep 581, *Legal and General Assurance Society Ltd v Drake Insurance Co Ltd* [1991] 2 Lloyd's Law Reports 44 (where there were two instruments covering same loss but differing in scope), *Eagle Star Insurance Co Ltd v Provincial Insurance plc* [1993] 2 Lloyd's Law Report 143 (where the second insurer repudiated for breach of warranty or misrepresentation), *Drake Insurance plc v Provident Insurance plc* [2004] Lloyd's IR 277, *Monksfield v Vehicle and General Insurance Co* [1971] Lloyd's Rep 139 (assured failed to give notice of potential claim, whether second insurer was liable to contribute after payment by the first insurer). Also see decision in *Legal and General Assurance Society Ltd v Drake Insurance Co Ltd* [1991] 2 Lloyd's Law Reports 43, *Godin v London Assurance Co* (1785) 1 Burr 489, *Petrofine (UK) Ltd v Magnaload Ltd* [1984] QB 127, *North British and Mercantile Insurance Co v London, Liverpool and Global Insurance Co* (1877) 5 Ch D 569 (meaning of "covering the same property").
88 *Halsbury's Laws of England* (4th edn 1976) Vol. 16 (Equity) para. 539.
89 Hardy Ivamy, *General Principles of Insurance Law* (6th edn 1993), p. 523.
90 *Ibid.*

2.7 Premiums

2.7.1 Return of premiums when the insurer refuses to pay

The issue of return of premiums is uncertain and complex. For example, is an assured entitled to claim a rateable return of his premium from each insurer, in a manner representing the amount by which he is over-assured by double insurance?[91] In most cases the insurer has the upper hand. An assured has to accept the terms of the policy to get cover.

The issue of the return of premiums was raised in *Tyrie v Fletcher*[92] where the court had to decide whether a proportionate part of the premium ought to be returned or not. The court decided to approach the case from general principles applicable to all policies of insurance, and approached the case from two angles. The first was where the underwriter has received premium for running the risk of indemnifying the assured and, whatever cause, if he does not run the risk, the consideration, for which the premium or money was put into his hands, fails and therefore the premium has to be returned. The second was if the risk of the contract of indemnity has commenced, there shall be no apportionment or return of the premium. The court accepted the latter approach. The court held that no premium should be returned once the risk was entire. In *Tyrie*, the plaintiff, who was the assured, sued the defendant, an underwriter for the return of part of the premium paid out. The plaintiff argued that the premium ought to be returned as the compensation estimated for the risk of 12 months was much more than adequate to the risk actually run in the case, which was only two months. Furthermore, from the nature of the insurance, both parties knew that risk was divisible and that, if it ceased before 12 months, the whole of the premium would not be retained by the defendant. This argument was put forward on the basis that, where there was a suitable compensation for a given risk, the risk had turned out to be different from what was expected. The defendant argued that, as soon as the ship sailed from the port in London, the policy attached for the whole time it was assured against. There was no calculation of the premium per month, but it was one entire gross sum of 91% stipulated and paid for 12 months. Therefore, the contract was entire, without any intention or thought of division, or apportionment. The defendant also argued that the position would be different where the risk did not attach and would therefore result in the return of the premium. One entire indivisible risk would not warrant the return of the premium.

2.7.2 Legislative framework of the return of premium

The principles in *Tyrie* can now be found in legislation under ss88–90 of the Marine Insurance Act. There are exceptions where the premiums are in fact returnable. These include where (1) the consideration has totally failed and there

---

91 *Colinvaux's Law of Insurance in Hong Kong* (2nd edn 2010), para. 11.040.
92 (1772) 2 Cowp 666.

has been no fraud or illegality on the part of the insurer or his agents;[93] (2) to the extent that any part of the premium proportionate to an apportionable part of the consideration has totally failed;[94] (3) where the policy is void, or is avoided by the insurers from the commencement of the risk as long as there is no fraud or illegality;[95] (4) where the assured has no insurable interest and the policy was not effected by way of gaming or wagering;[96] (5) to the extent of a proportionate part of the premium, where the assured has over-assured under an unvalued-policy[97] or where he has over-assured by double insurance[98] or where the policy contains a stipulation for the return of premium on the happening of a certain event, and that event happens.[99] Under s82(a),[100] where the premium is recoverable, the assured can seek recovery of it from the insurers. Under s82(b),[101] if it has not been paid, it shall be retained by the insurer or his agent.

2.7.3 Position of premiums prior to legislation

Prior to legislation being implemented, in the case of *Fisk v Masterman*[102] the issue for the court was whether the underwriters were bound to return part or all of the premiums and, if they were required to return the premiums, in what proportion and upon what principle should the calculations be made. A return of premiums was permitted in the event of double insurance. The court held that the assured was entitled to a return of premium on the amount of the over-insurance to which the underwriters who subscribed to the policies, when the vessel had arrived safely, were to contribute rateably in proportion to the sum assured by them respectively. No return of premium prior to that date could be returned. In *Fisk*, insurance was taken out on a cargo by sea by five policies and further insurance was taken out on six different policies. All the policies together exceeded the amount of the value of the subject matter assured, but the former policies did not. The court referred to *Marshall on Insurance*[103] and stated that the court was

---

93 Marine Insurance Act 1906 s84(1), (3)(b).
94 Marine Insurance Act 1906 s84(2).
95 Marine Insurance Act 1906 s84(3).
96 Marine Insurance Act 1906 s84(3)(c).
97 Marine Insurance Act 1906 s84(3)(e).
98 Marine Insurance Act 1906 s84(f).
99 Marine Insurance Act 1906 s83.
100 Marine Insurance Act 1906.
101 Marine Insurance Act 1906.
102 (1841) 8 M & W 165.
103 3rd edn, p. 649 which stated:

> All the underwriters upon policies in which the effects are assured beyond their value, must bear any loss that may happen, and repay a part of the premium, in proportion to their respective subscriptions, without regard to the priority of their dates. If by several policies, made without fraud, the sum assured exceed the value of their effects, these several policies will in effect, make but one insurance, and will be good to the extent of the true interest of the assured; and in case of loss, all underwriters on the several policies shall pay according to their respective subscriptions, without regard to the priority of their dates. And it follows from thence that all underwriters on the several policies would be equally bound to make a return of premium for the sum assured above the value of the effects, in proportion to their respective subscriptions.

not at liberty to distinguish between the two insurances and therefore the return must be made on both policies at rateable proportions.

There are exceptions to the common law principle that premiums remain indivisible when risk attaches. When this happens, the premium will not be returned. This can now be found in s84(3)(f) which permits a proportionate part of the several premiums to be returned to the assured where the assured is over-assured through double insurance. Section 84(3)(f) provides:

> Where the assured has overassured by double insurance, a proportionate part of the several premiums is returnable: Provided that, if the policies are effected at different times, and any earlier policy has at any time borne the entire risk, or if a claim has been paid on the policy in respect of the full amount assured thereby, no premium is returnable in respect of that policy, and when double insurance is effected knowingly by the assured no premium is returnable.

This section will only apply where the policies are effected at different times, and any earlier policy has at any time borne the entire risk; or if a claim has been paid on the policy in respect of that policy. When double insurance is effected knowingly by the assured, no premium is returnable. In practice this may extend to cases of property and liability policies as such policies usually state the limited circumstances in which any part of the premium is to be returnable.[104]

---

104 *Colinvaux*, para. 11.077.

CHAPTER 3

Effect of double insurance on claims

3.1 The rights of an assured

3.1.1 Restriction by insurers of assureds' rights

Insurers typically seek to limit assureds' rights under insurance contracts by limiting liability or excluding liability entirely. The common law recognised the legitimacy of such clauses. A typical scenario was where an assured purposefully destroys the assured property and seeks to recover against two insurers under separate insurance contracts. To guard against this, standard protections include: (1) requiring the assured to disclose any existing insurance contract over the same property or subject matter; (2) restricting the assured from taking any other insurance over the property while the policy is in force (breach of which results in automatic termination of the policy); and (3) including a term in the policy that would have the effect of converting the policy into an excess insurance. These insurance contracts would include one or more of the following clauses: (1) exclusion clauses, (2) rateable proportion clauses and (3) excess clauses. Another technique adopted by insurers would include in the insurance contract "Other insurance" clauses to exclude paying out on an assured's loss.[1]

3.2 Effect of "other insurance" clauses

"Other insurance" clauses are included in insurers' standard form policies. Such clauses may: (1) absolve an insurer from liability should other insurance covering the same risk be in existence or taken out during the period of cover (unless the insurer is notified in writing of that other insurance); (2) restrict the insurer's liability to the loss in excess of that covered by the other insurance; or (3) restrict the insurer's liability to a rateable proportion of any sum payable in the event of any loss. These clauses are designed to cover situations where the assured has effected two policies against the same risk. The policy of the law endorses such clauses on three grounds: (1) they protect insurers from fraudulent over-insurance, (2) they facilitate the investigation of claims, and (3) they allow the insurers to seek contribution where appropriate from another insurer.[2] Such clauses will usually be worded as follows:

---

1 *Evans v Maritime Medical Care Inc* (1992) 87 DLR (4th) 173.
2 The Measure of Indemnity under Property Insurance Policies (1983) 2 Canta LR 103.

[A] The assured shall give notice in writing to the insurer of any insurance or insurances already effected, or which may subsequently be affected, covering the rest hereby assured, and unless such notice be given and the particulars of such insurance or insurances be stated in or endorsed on this policy by or on behalf of the insurer before the occurrence of any loss or damage, all benefit under this policy shall be forfeited.

[B] If other insurance exists which applies to a loss or would have applied if this policy did not exist, this policy will be considered excess insurance and the insurer is not liable for any loss or claim until the amount of such other insurance is used up.

[C] If other valid insurance with any other insurance covering a loss also covered by this policy, other than insurance that is specifically stated to be in excess of this policy, the insurance afforded by this policy shall be in excess of and shall not contribute to such other insurance. Nothing herein shall be construed to make this policy subject to the terms, conditions and limitations of the other insurance.[3]

3.3 Combination of clauses in policies

Sometimes insurers will include a combination of such clauses in the policy, which, together, may leave the assured without any cover for the loss suffered. The first policy may have the effect in law of exempting the insurer's liability, or of limiting, or postponing it.[4]

3.4 Complexities of double insurance illustrated

This section illustrates the complexities that can arise when an assured takes out double insurance against the same risk under separate contracts of insurance. In *Equitable Fire & Accident Office*,[5] the respondents effected two policies of insurance against fire with the appellant company for stock in trade and other goods in a shop owned by the respondents. Liability was denied on two grounds. One of the grounds raised at trial was that the policies had become null and void by reason of the respondents omitting to give notice of additional insurance taken out with the respondents, without consent. The trial judge permitted recovery of the value of the assured goods which had been destroyed or damaged by fire. It was common ground that the respondents had not obtained the appellant's consent before entering into the second insurance contract. Each policy pertaining to the goods contained the following clauses: "No additional insurance on the property hereby covered is allowed except by the consent of this company indorsed hereon. Breach of this condition will render this policy null and void." One of the conditions indorsed in the policy stated:

> 12. The assured must, at the time of effecting the insurance, give notice to the company of any insurance or insurances already made elsewhere on the property hereby

---

3 Derrington and Ashton, *The Law of Liability Insurance* (2nd edn 2005), pp. 675, 676.
4 *Home Insurance Co of New York v Gavel* (1928) 30 Ll LR 139.
5 [1907] AC 96.

assured, or any part thereof, and on effecting any insurance or insurances during the currency of this policy elsewhere on the property hereby assured, or any part thereof, the assured must also forthwith give notice to the company thereof so that the particulars thereof may be indorsed on the policy, and unless such notice be given, the assured will not be entitled to any benefit under this policy, and on the happening of any loss or damage, the assured shall forthwith declare in writing, to the company, all other insurances effected by him, or by any other person, on any of the property, and the giving of such notices at the respective times aforesaid shall be a condition precedent to the recovery of any claim under this policy.[6]

The effect of the clauses would forfeit the cover of an assured for failure to inform the insurer of the existence of any additional insurance taken out over the same goods. The respondents had taken out a second policy over the goods but it was discovered that the premium had never been paid. The trial judge held that, as no premium had been paid, the parties must have treated the insurance contract as having no effect in law. No claim had been made under it, and it was unlikely that any claim would be made in the future. The contract specifically made payment of the premium a condition precedent before the policy became unenforceable, and provided that the insurer would bear no liability under it where the premium remained outstanding.[7]

On appeal to the Privy Council, Lord Davey, explained:[8]

It is plain from the language of the condition that it applies as well to the first premium as to any renewal premium, or indeed it may be said that it applies primarily to the first premium. The instrument must be read as a whole for the purpose of ascertaining the intention of the parties, and effect, so far as possible, must be given to every part of it. Their Lordships are of opinion that the 11th condition[9] qualifies and restricts the engagement of the company and converts what would otherwise be an absolute engagement into a conditional one, and that the words "having paid" to the company are common form words or words of style for expressing the consideration for the company's engagement which would become accurate when that engagement became effective. The Judicature Act provides that where the rules of law and of equity differ the rules of equity shall prevail. It is familiar law that in equity a vendor was never held to be estopped by a statement in the conveyance that the purchase-money had been paid, or even by an indorsed receipt for the money signed by him, so as to exclude the enforcement of the vendor's lien. Their Lordships think that in any case the parties should not be held in equity to be estopped as between themselves from shewing that the consideration had not in fact been paid. But in the present case they think that the condition read with the operative part of the instrument negatives any such estoppel; for the only meaning which can be given to the words is that the consideration must be not only expressed to be paid,

---

6 [1907] AC 96, 98.
7 [1907] AC 96, 99.
8 [1907] AC 96, 100.
9 And the 11th indorsed condition was in the following words:

This insurance will not be in force until, nor will the company be liable in respect of any loss or damage happening before the premium, or a deposit on account thereof, is actually paid, and no such payment or deposit and no payment in respect of the renewal of this policy shall be good unless a printed form of receipt for it, issued from the office of the company and signed by one of the company's authorised officers or agents, shall have been given to the assured.

but actually paid. Their Lordships cannot treat the fact of the executed policy having been handed to the respondents as a waiver of the condition or attach any importance to the circumstance. What was handed to the respondents was the instrument with this clause in it, and that was notice to them, and made it part of the contract that there would be no liability until the premium was paid. It is not a question of conditional execution, but of the construction of what was executed.

The decision in *Equitable Fire & Accident Office* represents a gloss on the law applying to double insurance contracts generally. The policy entered into with the appellant was not avoided by failure to give notice of another insurance policy covering the same risk. Under the terms of the policy, the contract of insurance never became effective as the premium had not been paid. If the second policy is not effective at the time when the insured incurs the loss, it will not have the effect of contravening the clause in the first policy, and will not invalidate it.

3.5 Policy considerations

There are competing policy considerations which leave the justification for double insurance clauses in doubt. On the one hand it might be argued that, if the assured agrees to the inclusion of clauses in the policy limiting or excluding liability, such clauses should be permitted. However, on the other hand there are cases where the assured ostensibly agrees to the terms of the policy, but the assured may not have read or fully understood the terms. In such cases where an assured has paid the premiums under the policy, arguably he ought to be protected for any loss regardless.

3.6 A comparison: the Australian position

In Australia, the insurance market differs slightly from the insurance market in the United Kingdom. The Australian insurance market is more of a consumer market with little in the form of re-insurance. The Australia market covers life, health and property but, unlike the United Kingdom, not marine insurance. Nevertheless, the issues that have arisen in Australia often involve commercial policies similar to those found in the United Kingdom.

3.7 Types of clauses

As mentioned above, insurers use various clauses to exclude or limit liability when an assured takes out double insurance in the form of escape clauses, excess clauses and rateable proportion clauses. An escape clause excludes all liability of the insurer if an event occurs which is stated in the policy as having such effect. This usually includes situations where the assured has taken out double insurance. In contrast, an excess clause excludes only partial liability. An insurer will be liable to cover only the excess where there is another policy in existence. The policy containing the excess clause recompenses for the loss remaining after payment is made under the other insurance policy. The third clause is the rateable proportion clause. This clause limits the insurer's liability to paying a proportional rate for the loss the assured suffers. It is common for insurers to draft their policies so as to ensure that their indemnity liability will be as limited as possible.

3.8 Uncertainty of such clauses

The uncertainty caused by the clauses can be remedied if the wording is not absolute in one policy. In the Canadian decision of *Evans v Marine Medical Care Inc*.[10] there were two policies in existence – one was a group hospital policy and the other a motor liability policy. The former excluded cover if there was another contract in existence which covered the same loss. The latter policy excluded any liability if there was a hospital policy in force. The Supreme Court of Nova Scotia looked at the wording of the two policies to ascertain whether or not either or both policies were absolute. The court concluded that the hospital plan was not absolute but conditional upon payment being made under some other policy. This was in contrast to the motor liability policy. The policy's escape clause was operative only where sums were actually payable under another policy. Here the insurer under the motor liability policy incurred no liability. Where the wording of the two policies is clear, as was the case in *Evans v Marine Medical Care Inc*, there is no problem in identifying which policy is the excess policy.

3.9 Concurrent "escape" clauses

3.9.1 Absolute escape clauses

3.9.1.1 *Bankers & Traders Insurance Co Ltd v National Insurance Co Ltd*
An insurance policy with an absolute escape clause can exclude liability by shifting the loss to other insurers. In *Bankers & Traders Insurance Co Ltd v National Insurance Co Ltd*,[11] the Privy Council had to decide upon the liability of insurers to satisfy a judgment obtained by third parties in a road traffic accident. Here, third parties were run into and knocked down by a motor vehicle owned by Mr Kwang Shi Ching, but driven by Mr Ko Beng Lai. The third parties sued the driver. Mr Ko was assured with National Insurance Co Ltd. The policy contained the following clause: "The company will indemnify . . . the assured whilst personally driving a private motor car . . . not belonging to him and not hired to him under a hire purchase agreement." Kwong was assured with Bankers & Traders

---

10 87 DLR (4th) 173 (1992). *SHC Capital Ltd v NTUC Income Insurance Co-Operative Ltd* [2010] SGHC 224; *Nanyang Insurance Co Ltd v Commercial Union Assurance plc* [1996] 1 SLR(R) 441 and *Bankers & Traders Insurance Co Ltd v National Insurance Co Ltd* [1985] 1 WLR 734. Also see *Chui Man Kwan v Bank of China Group Insurance Co Ltd* [2008](DCMP 211/2008, unreported), where cover was converted to an excess policy where another policy is present has the same effect, if no similar provision is present. In *Chui Man Kwan*, the wording in Tugu policy was as follows (this was an excess clause):

> If at the time of any claim under this policy there is any other insurance indemnifying any person or assured who are entitled to be indemnified under this policy, this policy is not to be called upon in contribution and, subject to the policy limits of indemnity, is only to pay any amount if and so far as not recoverable under such other insurance.

11 [1985] 1 WLR 734 (an appeal from the Federal Court of Malaysia to the Privy Council).

Insurance Co. Ltd. Its policy contained the following clause: "The company will indemnify (a) any authorised driver who is driving the motor vehicle provided that such authorised driver . . . is not entitled to indemnity under any other policy."

I THE ISSUES

The third parties sued both insurers as they were uncertain which company was at risk. Under s80 Road Traffic Ordinance 1958 an insurer is required to satisfy judgments against persons who are assured in respect of third-party risks. The court had to decide[12] (1) which insurer was on risk at the material time of the accident, and had to satisfy the judgment sum and costs and (2) whether the insurer on risk at the time of the accident could seek contribution from the other insurer for 50% under condition 7 of the insurance policy.

The wording of s80(1)[13] suggests that the only policy which was at risk at the time was the driver's policy.

II THE DECISION OF THE COURTS

The trial judge held that the driver's insurance policy was at risk at the time and had to satisfy the judgment against Ko. However, on appeal, the court explained:

> As *this car* was assured with the second defendants, [the owner's insurers who are the appellants in this appeal] it is their policy which was on risk ... The decisive factor which is the subject matter of the insurance is the specified motor car. It is because of the use of the motor car that an insurance is required.

Their lordships focused on the wording of s80. The Federal Court on the other hand took into account ss74(1) and 75(1)(b) of the Ordinance. This resulted in the Federal Court drawing the inference that:

> it was the legislative purpose of the Ordinance to require that, in all cases where there were in existence more than one policy of insurance, the insurers of the vehicle's owner are to satisfy the third party's judgment and that exclusions of cover contained in the owner's policy are to be disregarded. This view was reinforced by the use of the definite article in the references to the vehicle which are to be found in section 74(1) and section 75(1)(b) of the Ordinance.[14]

The legislation under s80(1) was clear, and Ko had been issued with a certificate of insurance under his policy. The liability to the third party was covered under

---

12 [1985] 1 WLR 734, 736E.

13 If, after a certificate of insurance has been delivered under subsection (4) of section 75 of this Ordinance to the person by whom a policy has been effected, judgment in respect of any such liability as is required to be covered by a policy under paragraph (b) of subsection (1) of section 75 of this Ordinance (being a liability covered by the terms of the policy) is given against any person assured by the policy, then notwithstanding that the insurer may be entitled to avoid or cancel, or may have avoided or cancelled, the policy the insurer shall, subject to the provisions of this section, pay to the persons entitled to the benefit of the judgment any sum payable thereunder in respect of the liability, including any amount payable in respect of costs and any sum payable in respect of interest on that sum by virtue of any written law relating to interest on judgments.

14 [1985] 1 WLR 734, 737E–G.

the driver's policy. Judgment had been entered where Ko was held liable, and he was the person named as the assured under the policy. There was no double insurance in this case.

3.9.2 All policies containing absolute clauses

Where all the policies contain absolute clauses excluding liability, an assured will find himself without any protection. This first arose in *Gale v Motor Union Insurance Co.*[15] This case involved double insurance, where the risk was covered by two different insurers. The plaintiff, Gale (G), took out a policy for his car with Motor Union Company. A clause in the policy extended coverage to persons driving the car with his consent. It stated:

> Section A. The company shall indemnify the assured or (subject to the provisions of clause 6) any relation or friend driving with the assured's consent against the payment of all sums which they shall become legally liable to pay for compensation in respect of accidents caused by any motor vehicle belonging to the assured and described in the above schedule (*a*) to any third person (including passengers in the car), but excluding any person in the service or household of the assured or of the person driving the car: (*b*) to any property oranimal belonging to a third person. . . . . Provided always that the due observance and fulfilment of the conditions and qualifications indorsed on this policy shall be a condition precedent to any liability of the company under this policy.[16]

There was an additional clause, which provided:

> Condition 6. The extension of the indemnity to friends or relatives of the assured is conditional upon such friend or relative being a licensed and competent driver and not being assured under any other policy.
>
> Condition 10: If at the time of the happening of any accident, injury, damage or loss covered by this policy, there shall be subsisting any other insurance or indemnity of any nature whatsoever covering the same, whether effected by the assured or by any other person, persons or firm, then the company shall not be liable to pay or contribute to any such damage or loss more than a rateable proportion of any sum or sums payable in respect thereof for compensation.

Loyst (L), who drove the plaintiff's car, was involved in an accident. L had a policy under Accident Corporation which had similarly worded provisions.[17] L drove

---

15 [1928] 1 KB 359.
16 [1928] 1 KB. 359, 360.
17 The policy (*inter alia*) contained the following provisions:

> The corporation will, subject to the terms, conditions and limitations contained herein and of any indorsement hereon, indemnify the assured his executors and/or administrators in respect of any car described in the schedule against . . . Clause 2 (1) All sums which the assured shall become legally liable to pay in respect of any claim by any person (including passengers in the car) for loss of life or accidental bodily injury or damage to property (including animals) caused by through or in connection with such car and in addition the law costs payable in connection with such claim when incurred with the consent of the corporation. (2) The assured will also be indemnified hereunder whilst personally driving a car not belonging to him provided the assured's own car is not in use at the same time, and provided that there is no other insurance in respect of such car whereby the assured may be indemnified.

G's car with his consent. Damages were recovered from L personally as a result of the collision. Both companies denied liability. Each plaintiff[18] then claimed against the insurers. The matter went for arbitration, where "for the plaintiffs it was contended that one or the other of the policies covered Loyst, who should be indemnified by the one so far as he was not by the other". Furthermore, when considering condition 5 and condition 10 of Accident Corporation and Motor Union Company's policy respectively, the two insurers were liable to contribute rateably toward the full indemnity.[19] Motor Union Company argued that where a policy extended the right of indemnity to a person other than the person to whom the policy was issued, a strict interpretation must be adopted. Both companies could not be liable. Accident Corporation argued that if one insurer was liable, then the other was not. Rateable contribution did not apply. The arbitrator stated:

> that the liability of one insurer excluded liability of the other, and that the conditions in both policies as to rateable proportions did not apply; that Loyst satisfied the requirements of condition 6 of the Motor Union Company's policy, and that therefore Gale, as trustee for Loyst, was entitled to be indemnified by the Motor Union Company in respect of all pecuniary loss suffered by Loyst in consequence of the collision of April 4, 1925. Loyst's claim against the Accident Corporation failed. The question for the Court was whether the award was correct in law.

Roche J[20] held that both companies were liable rateably, as the material clauses should be read together, explaining and qualifying each other. The clauses found in the motor car risks policy first provided that if the risk was covered by another policy the insurer will not be liable and, second, where two policies covered the risk, then the insurers were liable to pay rateably. Both clauses should be read together, and the second clause qualified the first. The judge went on to say that the position would be different if the policy did not have a rateable proportion clause but stood alone as an exclusion clause. If that was the case, neither insurer would be liable equally. An assured will therefore have no protection.

3.9.3 Self-cancelling clauses ineffective

3.9.3.1 *Weddell v Road Traffic and General Insurance Co Ltd*

This problem was remedied by the court in the case of *Weddell v Road Traffic and General Insurance Co Ltd*,[21] where self-cancelling clauses were held inef-

---

The following was among the conditions indorsed on the policy:

> Condition 5. If at the time of the occurrence of any accident loss or damage there shall be any other indemnity or insurance subsisting whether effected by the assured or by any other person the corporation shall not be liable to pay or contribute more than a rateable proportion of any sums payable in respect of such accident, loss or damage. . . . the due observance and fulfilment of the provisions and conditions of this policy. . . . shall be a condition precedent to any liability of the corporation to make any payment under this policy.

18 Gale as trustee for L and L on his own behalf.
19 £120 in the case of the A B C car, and £150 in that of the Morris Cowley.
20 This was a special case stated by the arbitrator.
21 [1932] 2 KB 563.

fective, as such clauses do not cancel out each other. They should be construed as excluding from the category of co-existing cover any cover which is expressed to be itself cancelled by such co-existence. In such situations, both companies are liable and subject to any rateable proportion clause present.

In *Weddell*, a policy was issued to the respondents, Road Transport and General Insurance Co Ltd. The policy holder was Justin Weddell. The clause in the policy provided:

> If at any time any claim arises under this policy there is any other existing insurance covering the same loss, damage or liability the company shall not be liable. . . . to pay or contribute more than its rateable proportion of any loss, damage, compensation, costs or expense. Provided always that nothing in this condition shall impose on the company any liability from which but for this condition it would have been relieved under the provisions of section II of this policy.

Another clause provided that the company would indemnify the assured where there was injury or damage caused by or through or in connection with any motor car which was provided for in the Schedule. The policy extended cover to an assured's relative or friend, who drove the car for social, domestic or pleasure purposes with the assured's general knowledge and consent, provided that such relative or friend is not entitled to indemnity under any other policy. Weddell's brother, Laurens Weddell, was also assured with another insurer, Cornhill Insurance Co Ltd. Under that policy indemnity was provided against all sums which he became legally liable to pay by way of compensation. It further provided that, "The indemnity granted. . . . is hereby extended to cover the assured while driving any private motor-car not belonging to him for pleasure or professional purposes if no indemnity is afforded the assured by any other insurance." Laurens Weddell injured Frederick Ward while driving his brother's car. Laurens Weddell failed to give notice to Cornhill Insurance Co Ltd, which resulted in Cornhill repudiating liability. Frederick Ward brought a claim for damages. The arbitrator found that Road Transport and General Insurance Co Ltd were liable to indemnify Lauren Weddell against one-half of all sums which he would be liable to pay under the action. The judge confirmed the arbitrator's decision. This decision rejects the notion that the clauses would cancel out each other. Each insurer will be liable.

This was reaffirmed in *Structural Polymer Systems Ltd v Brown*.[22]

3.9.3.2 Extension of the principle of *Weddell* in excess clauses

In *National Employers Mutual General Insurance Association Ltd v Haydon*,[23] Templeman LJ extended the principle in *Weddell* to cases where two policies contained excess clauses. In *Haydon* a firm of solicitors were sued for professional negligence. There were two "claims made" policies, the NEM's Professional

---

22 [1999] CLC 268. See also *Trenton Cold Storage Ltd v St Paul Fire & Marine Insurance Co* (1999) 11 CCLI (3d) 127; *Equity Syndicate Management Ltd v Glaxosmithkline plc* [2016] Lloyd's LRIR 155; *Sobrany v UAB Transtira* [2016] EWCA Civ 28.
23 [1980] 2 Lloyd's Rep. 149, 156.

Indemnity Policy (the NEM Policy) and the Law Society's Professional Indemnity Insurance (the Master Policy). The solicitors were assured under the NEM Policy which required notification to be given. The NEM Policy consisted of clause (i) under the heading "General Exceptions to All Sections", and clause 3[24] under the heading "Conditions". The Master Policy contained two clauses, clause 2 and clause 5. Clause 2[25] contained an indemnifying provision and clause 5[26] contained a provision limiting the insurer's liability. Neither of the policies contained a rateable proportion clause. Stephenson LJ stated that the case turned on the construction of the two policies looked at as a whole and the general exception (i) in the NEM Policy and general exclusion 5(b)(iii) in the Master Policy. He considered the approach adopted by the trial judge at first instance, who was of the view that this was a "classic case of double insurance", which resulted in contribution from the defendants on a 50% basis. He also considered that there was no distinction between the exclusion clauses in the two policies, even though the Master Policy was narrower than the NEM Policy – although he went on to say that both exception clauses and exclusion clauses were drafted in a strict sense in form and in substance. Further, even if the exclusion clause was not drafted in the strict sense, it would still be difficult to distinguish them. He went on to apply the principle in *Weddell's* case and that the policies should be looked at independently. The exclusion clause would cancel out each other, resulting in both insurers becoming liable and a contribution claim could be made. This would have been the position if each policy was liable but for the presence of the exclusion clauses in the policies. He therefore found for NEM.

However, the two clauses, the Court of Appeal considered, were clearly distinguishable from each other. The claim was only covered by the NEM Policy and not by the Master Policy. The label given to the clauses was not important and the policies had to be read as a whole. When notice was given to NEM by the solicitors on 24 March 1976, NEM bore the risk completely unless indemnity was covered by the other policy. The Master Policy only provided cover after 24 March and not before that date. Therefore "the assured is or would but for the existence of this Policy be entitled to indemnity under any other Policy" did not apply. However due to the effect of clause 3, even though notice was given on 24 March, it was deemed to have been made during the existence of

---

24 If during the period of insurance the solicitor became aware of and gave notice to, the insurance company of an occurrence which might subsequently give rise to a claim, then subsequent claims arising would be deemed to have been made during the subsistence of the policy.

25 Clause 2:

> On the terms and conditions herein contained the insurers shall indemnify the Assured against all loss to the Assured whensoever occurring arising from any claim or claims first made against the Assured or the Firm during the Period of Insurance in respect of any description of civil liability whatsoever incurred in connection with the Practice.

26 Clause 5 sets out the general exclusions, of which (b) is the relevant exclusion:

> "(b) This insurance shall not indemnify the Assured in respect of any loss arising out of any claim: ...
> (iii) in respect of any circumstance or occurrence which has been notified under any other insurance attaching prior to the inception of this Certificate."

the policy. The solicitors were not assured under the Master Policy. The Court of Appeal held that there was no double insurance because the Master Policy did not cover losses occurring during its currency. The Master Policy was not an exclusion clause because it tried to prevent liability from ever arising. Although some authors have commented that the distinction between clauses prevents liability from arising, and a clause which excludes accrued liability, is too fine to be justified, and the approach taken by Lloyd J should be the correct approach.[27]

3.10 Has the *Weddell* principle been followed in other jurisdictions?

The above principles have been followed[28] in other jurisdictions such as Singapore. The case of *SHC Capital Ltd v NTUC Income Insurance Co-operative Ltd*[29] involved two insurance companies, SHC Capital Ltd ("SHC") and NTUC Income Insurance Co-operative Ltd ("NTUC"). Both provided workmen's compensation insurance. SHC sought a declaration that NTUC was liable for a payout made pursuant to a workmen's compensation policy. A workman, Omar, employed by EIN Engineering and Construction, was seriously injured, when struck by a mobile crane operated by Ng Kia Soong. The premises where the accident happened was owned by Pan United Concrete Pte Ltd (Pan-United), which had engaged Simei Engineering & Trading (Simei) as its main contractor.[30] Simei then engaged EIN Engineering & Trading and Construction (EIN) as its sub-contractor. Simei also engaged Huo Hin Trading Co Pte Ltd (Hup Hin), which employed Hock Swee Seng Construction and Transportation (Hock Swee). Omar sued for negligence claiming damages for personal injury from (1) Pan-United as occupier of the premises; (2) EIN as his employer; (3) Simei as the main contractor; and (4) Hock Swee as the owner and operator of the mobile crane which was involved in the accident. Interlocutory judgment was entered by consent for 90% of the total liability, with damages to be assessed. After they were assessed, SHC paid for EIN and Simei's liabilities, which made no apportionment between EIN's and Simei's respective liabilities, even though Omar was an employee of EIN and not Simei's. The court had to decide: (1) whether Simei and/or EIN were both double assured at the relevant time; (2) whether NTUC properly excluded its liability to indemnify Simei and/or EIN under its contingent liability clause in its policy and (3) whether, if NTUC was liable to indemnify Simei and/or EIN under the NTUC policy, SHC's right to seek a contribution or reimbursement had now been excluded by its voluntary payment. The court held that the words in

---

27 *Colinvaux*, para. 11–092.
28 *Principles of Insurance Law* (6th edn 2005), p. 1233.
29 [2010] SGHC 224.
30 The project involved the collection of several dismantled structures from another site and delivered these structures to the premises.

PART A

the operative clauses of the NTUC[31] and SHC[32] policies covered the same type of risk, which was the risk of a claim by the assured's own employee arising from personal injuries sustained in the course of his employment by the assured. There was double insurance in respect of liability for injuries of their employees, as the NTUC policy applied to Simei and EIN because the wording of the policy covered "all tiers" of sub-contractors and the cross-liability clause. Further, Simei and EIN were assured under the SHC policies. Both NTUC's policy and SHC's policy was issued to EIN regarding EIN's liability to Omar. The court adopted the principles applied in the United Kingdom.[33] The High Court went on to explain:

31

WITNESSETH that if any workman in the Assured's employment shall sustain personal injury by accident or disease caused during the Period of Insurance and arising out of and in the course of his employment by the Assured [Pan-United and subsidiaries, subsequently extended to all tiers of sub-contractors, which includes EIN and Simei] in the Business, the Society will subject to the terms exceptions conditions and warranties, and any memorandum if applicable, contained herein or endorsed hereon (all of which are hereinafter collective referred to as the Terms of the Policy) indemnify the Assured against all sums for which the Assured shall be liable to pay compensation either under the Legislation or at Common Law, up to $10,000,000 any one claim or series of claims arising out of any one event and will in addition pay all costs and expenses incurred by the Assured with the written consent of the Society.

(emphasis added)

32

WITNESSETH that if any workman in the Assured's employment shall sustain personal injury by accident or disease caused during the Period of Insurance and arising out of and in the course of his employment by the Assured [EIN or Simei] in the Business, the Company will subject to the terms exceptions conditions and warranties, and any memorandum if applicable, contained herein or endorsed hereon (all of which are hereinafter collective referred to as the Terms of the Policy) indemnify the Assured against all sums for which the Assured shall be liable to pay compensation either under the Legislation or at Common Law, and will in addition pay all costs and expenses incurred by the Assured with the written consent of the Company.

(emphasis added)

33 At para. [36] where it was stated:

The right of contribution exists as between co-insurers who have assured the same assured against the same risk, in respect of the same subject matter: *MacGillivray on Insurance Law Relating to All Risks Other Than Marine* (11th edn 2008) at para. 23–001. Thus, when two insurers are liable for the same loss, the insurer called upon to make payment may have the right to seek payment from the other insurer: *MacGillivray* at para. 23–032. The concept of contribution is similar to another concept known as reimbursement, save for a slight difference. In the case of contribution, it is essential that both the plaintiff and defendant are jointly and/or severally liable to the same third party in respect of the same debt: see *Moule v Garrett* (1871–1872) LR 7 Ex 101 at 104; *Bonner v Tottenham and Edmonton Permanent Investment Building Society* [1899] 1 QB 161 at 178 and Mitchell, *The Law of Contribution and Reimbursement* (2003) at para. 1.06. In the case of reimbursement, the plaintiff and defendant do not need to be jointly and/or severally liable to the third party in respect of the same debt. It would suffice if the plaintiff is compellable or compelled under the law or by necessity to discharge the defendant's debt and was not acting officiously in so doing: *Halsbury's Laws of England* (4th edn reissue) Vol. 40(1) at para. 63; *cf* Goff and Jones, *The Law of Restitution* (7th edn 2007) at para. 15–001 which states that the plaintiff must have been compelled by law to make a payment in order to obtain reimbursement. An example of a claim in reimbursement is where a surety who was called upon to pay a sum of money on the default of the principal debtor or some other person who is principally liable makes a claim against the principal for a full indemnity: *Halsbury's Laws of England*, Vol. 40(1) at para. 65. Another example may be found in *Exall v Partridge* (1799) 8 TR 308, where the claimants' goods which were on land leased to the defendants, were seized by the landlords in distress of rent. The claimant, having paid rent to obtain the release of goods, successfully obtained recoupment (another word for reimbursement) from the defendants.

15 However, an insurer may seek to exclude its liability by way of indemnity to its assured or by way of contribution to another insurer, who has assured the same assured person in respect of the same risk. One method of achieving this end is to provide that an insurer is not liable if the policy holder has been assured for the same risk under another policy. Such an exclusion clause has been construed in *Bankers & Traders Insurance Co Ltd v National Insurance Co Ltd*[34] where a car owner allowed a friend to drive his car, and in the course of doing so, the friend injured a third party. The car owner had an insurance policy insuring against any liability to third parties caused by any driver driving his car, with the owner's consent. In the car owner's policy, there was a clause which provided that the car driver would be indemnified for third party risks provided that he (*i.e.* the car driver) was "not entitled to indemnity under any other policy." On the facts of that case, the friend who was then driving the car also had a policy of insurance which assured him against liability to third parties caused while driving a private car not belonging to him. The third parties brought an action against both insurers claiming payment. The Privy Council (on appeal from the Federal Court of Malaysia) held that by virtue of the exclusion clause in the car owner's policy, the policy containing an exclusion clause was *not on risk at the time of the accident*. Therefore, the full burden of the indemnity must be borne by the driver's insurers.

16 Similarly, in *Nanyang Insurance Co Ltd v Commercial Union Assurance plc* [1996] 1 SLR(R) 441, two insurers had assured the same assured against the risk of accidents in the course of work. In Commercial Union Assurance Plc's insurance policy, it excluded its liability to indemnify the assured if it had any other policy of indemnity or insurance in respect of the same risk, unless the loss suffered by the assured was higher than the "amount which would be payable under such other indemnity or insurance had this policy not been effected." The loss sustained by the assured was $63,023.28, which was lower than the upper limit of policy issued by Nanyang Insurance Co Ltd. The court held that the Commercial Union Assurance Plc's exclusion clause had rendered it not liable. There was no double insurance and Nanyang Insurance was legally obliged to indemnify the assured for 100% of his loss. Thus, although Nanyang Insurance had already limited its liability to no more than its rateable proportion (i.e. 50–50 in the event of double insurance), its rateable proportion clause did not operate.

17 However when both insurers exclude liability in their respective contracts with the assured person in the event of double insurance, then, the exclusion clauses cancel each other out, with the net effect that both insurers share liability equally as amongst themselves. In *Weddell v Road Transport & General Insurance Co Ltd* [1932] 2 KB 563, Rowlatt J said the following while construing two third-party motor insurance contracts containing exclusion of liability clauses (at 567–568):

> In my judgment it is unreasonable to suppose that it was intended that clauses such as these should cancel each other (by neglecting in each case the proviso in the other policy) with the result that, on the ground in each case that the loss is covered elsewhere, it is covered nowhere. On the contrary, the reasonable construction is to exclude from the category of co-existing cover any cover which is expressed to be itself cancelled by such co-existence, and to hold in such cases that both companies are liable, subject of course in both cases to any rateable contribution proportion clause which there may be.

3.11 Escape clause against excess clause

In some cases, one policy may contain an escape clause and another policy may contain an excess clause. There are no authorities in the United Kingdom which

---

34 [1985] 1 WLR 734.

deal with this. In such a situation, the two clauses will not be self-cancelling due to the existence of the second policy providing for an excess clause. It would be undesirable for an assured to have no protection if the clauses were to cancel each other out. If, for example, an assured takes out Policy A, which contains an escape clause and, at the same time, takes out Policy B, which contains an excess clause, it can be said that Policy B will provide cover. The issue of cover becomes more significant when there are more than two policies in existence with such clauses, where different events happen during different policy years, and where there are different types of policy cover.[35]

The courts in New Zealand have held that in cases where policies contain an escape clause and an excess clause, they are self-cancelling. In *Commercial Union Assurance Co of NZ Ltd v Murphy*[36] a house was completely damaged in a fire. The first plaintiff, Mr Murphy, was a concrete contractor, who was assured by Guardian Royal Exchange Assurance Co Ltd (Guardian Company), the second plaintiff, for projects commenced by Mr Murphy. The first defendant was Lockhead and Hansen Ltd. The second defendant was Commercial Union. The issue was whether Commercial Union was liable to Mr Murphy for $7,115.80 only, as the excess over the amount which was paid to Mr Murphy by Guardian Company or alternatively liable for $67,115.80, which was the amount for the reinstatement of the house. Guardian Company issued a cover note of $60,000 for the assured projects when Mr Murphy started work on them. The court looked the policy as a whole, and terms in the memorandum, when considering the scope of cover under each policy. The building contract entered into between Mr Murphy and Lockhead and Hansen was partly oral and partly written. The written part was a Master Builders Federation Standard Form which stated:

> Clause 10 (ii) The Builder shall at all times from the commencement of the works until the said works are taken over by the Owner keep the same assured to their full insurable value in the joint names of the Owner and the Builder and the Mortgagee (if any) against loss or damage by fire and such fire insurance indemnity policy shall be extended by an "Extraneous Risks Endorsement" as commonly used in New Zealand.

As a result of this clause, the builder then took out a Contract Works Policy with Commercial Company which contained the following clauses:

35
> The following is an extreme example of the issue in the context of liability insurance. In year one the assured may be covered on an events basis in respect of harmful acts occurring during the currency of the policy. In year two the assured may have switched his cover to injuries occurring, so that he is protected against injury suffered during the currency of the policy even though arising from an act in an earlier year. In year three he may have switched again, this time to claims made cover under which any claim made against the assured during the currency of the policy is assured. If the assured commits a negligent act in year one, which results in injury to the claimant in year two and leads to a claim in year three, then each of the policies is potentially required to respond. If each policy contains an escape or excess clause, the cases would indicate that those clauses are void. If that is right, then of course further issues arise as to how contribution is to operate – if at all – in such a case.
>
> *Colinvaux*, para. 11–093

36 [1989] 1 NZLR 687, an appeal from the judgment of Quilliam J (1987) 4 ANZ Insurance Cases 74,883.

Condition 7. This insurance does not cover any loss, destruction, damage or liability which is assured by or would, but for the existence of this Policy, be assured by any other policy or policies, except in respect of any excess beyond the amount which would have been payable under such other policy or policies had this insurance not been effected.
...
Memorandum 3. The insurance by this policy extends to include the interest of any Employer of the Assured in respect of any contract to which this insurance applies but only to the extent to which the Employer's interest is required to be assured jointly with that of the Assured by terms of any contract entered into between the Employer and the Assured.

When this policy was issued, Guardian Company was not notified about the Commercial Union policy before the fire.[37] The trial judge held that condition 7 could be disposed of by relying on the position that the Guardian Company payment to Mr Murphy was *ex gratia*, as Guardian Company had not been notified under the contract. Commercial Union was required to pay the whole amount of $67,115.80. On appeal, it was held that the intention of the parties to the Commercial Union insurance policy was important. The court stated:

It seems to us that the proper inference is that the builder and the owner intended that the full risk should be borne by the insurers selected by the builder; it was fortuitous that insurance taken out by the owner happened to remain in place also. The supervening agreement was that insurance should be the responsibility of the builder. We do not think that the standard condition 7 in the Commercial Union policy can have been evolved with any eye to such a case, although in its literal language and considered in isolation it could apply.[38]

Mr Murphy was entitled to cover under the Commercial Union policy. Clause 10(ii) in the building contract did not fall within the issue of double insurance.

3.12 Concurrent "excess" clauses

An excess clause has the same effect as an escape clause. If two policies each contain an excess clause, the clauses will be self-cancelling, and both insurers will be liable. If Policy A has an excess clause, and Policy B does not contain a similar clause, the excess clause in Policy A is effective. In *Austin v Zurich General Accident and Liability Insurance Co Ltd*,[39] the plaintiff, Austin, was driving a car belonging to Aldridge, with his consent. At the time of the accident, Aldridge and Nicholson were passengers. The executrices of the passengers brought an action against the plaintiff. The plaintiff's insurers, Bell Assurance Association, settled

---

37 Clause 3 of Mr Murphy's Guardian policy provided:

INSURANCE WITH OTHER COMPANIES. 3. The Assured shall give notice to the Company of any insurance or insurances already effected, or which may subsequently be effected, covering any of the property hereby assured and unless such notice be given and the particulars of such insurance or insurances be stated in or endorsed on this Policy by or on behalf of the Company before the occurrence of any loss or damage, all benefit under this policy shall be forfeited.

38 [1989] 1 NZLR 687, 690.
39 [1945] KB 250.

the claim. A claim was then brought[40] against Zurich, who had issued a policy to Aldridge. The policy was effective and covered third-party claims arising out of accidents causes by or through or in connection with his car. This policy also extended to persons driving the car with the assured's permission. Liability was denied by Zurich who claimed that notification had not been given in accordance with the policy. The Zurich Policy contained certain limitations. One of the terms provided that the person indemnified would not be entitled to indemnity if any other policy existed. The general condition in the policy also stated that the company would not be liable[41] to pay or contribute more than its rateable proportion of any loss, damage, compensation, costs or expense. The Bell policy provided that if there was other indemnity or insurance, the underwriters will not be liable to pay or to contribute, except in excess of the sum actually recovered or recoverable under such indemnity or insurance. Tucker J[42] considered the facts of the present case to be indistinguishable from the decision in *Weddell's* case and held that liability to indemnify should be shared by the companies equally.

An excess clause in a professional indemnity policy which operated as an excess clause does not apply to an assured's D & O policy. The issue in *Rathbone Brothers plc v Novae Corporate Underwriting*[43] was whether PEV, the second plaintiff and the personal trustee of the Walker Trust, had to ensure that it had exhausted all remedies which were available to them before claiming against the insurer. The court had to consider when a policy which contained an excess clause would not apply. The court went on to state that if the policy provided for indemnification from a policyholder or a co-assured, the clause which provided that "insurance provided by this policy applies excess over insurance and indemnification available from any other source" did not apply. However, this would not be the case if there was clear wording permitting the assured to obtain indemnification from an external source. The Court of Appeal went on to explain that where the policy was a D&O policy, no cover for the loss would be provided where there was "other insurance" – for example, where the policy covered defence costs.

3.13 Rateable proportion clauses

The effect of a rateable proportion clause[44] limits the insurer's liability to the amount as stated in the insurance policy, where there is another insurance policy

---

40 Austin endorsed the following term on counsel's brief:

I agree to the below-mentioned terms and I agree either to assign to the Bell Assurance Association such rights as I may have against the Zurich Insurance Co., and/or to allow them in my name to proceed against the said Zurich Insurance Co., to recover the whole or any part of the said sums for the benefit of the said Bell Assurance Association.

41 Except under s6.
42 In the Court of Appeal in *Austin v Zurich* [1945] KB 250.
43 [2014] EWCA Civ 1464 (CA).
44 "If at the time of any claim . . . there shall be any other insurance covering the same risk or any part thereof the company shall not be liable for more than its rateable proportion thereof."

in effect. The assured is at a greater risk where other insurers become insolvent. The assured therefore will have to bear the risk himself.[45]

Problems arise when polices are not concurrent but respond to the same loss. This is what happened in *Phillips v Syndicate 992 Gunner*,[46] a case involving an asbestos-related disease claim. This was the first time an insurer challenged liability on a proportionate basis, as previous claims had all been settled on a full liability basis. The deceased contracted malignant mesothelioma after being exposed to asbestos dust, during the time he worked for his employers, which was not a period of continuous employment. The insurer, who challenged the requirement to pay the balance of a judgment debt, argued that its liability only corresponded to the proportion which their period of insurance bore to the total period of the employee's employment. The defendant insurers were only insurers for part of the deceased's employment. The insurers relied on the standard "rateable proportion" clause which frequently appeared in employer's liability policies[47] and which provided:

> If at the time any claim arises under this policy there be any other insurance covering the same liability the Underwriters shall not be liable to pay or contribute more than their due proportion of any such claim and costs and expenses in connection therewith.

Eady J stated:[48]

> The plain purpose of the provision is to give the insurer the right to pay a "rateable proportion" in cases of double insurance (i.e. two or more policies covering the same risk at the same time). I can see no basis in authority, or on the construction of the language, for treating it as embracing *successive* policies of insurance.

Eady J considered that it was necessary to look at the nature of the risk which was covered by the policy in question. In the present case, the context which gave rise to the legal liability was the continuous failure to provide protection to the employee from asbestos fibres over a period of time. The question "is always whether the legal liability at the time it is established is such as to fall within the scope of the risk assured against".[49] An insurer had to indemnify the employer in full, as rateable proportion clauses do not apply to consecutive policies. Further, the court rejected the argument that it was necessary to imply a rateable proportion clause in successive policies to enable the contract to have business efficacy. Some authors have commented that this reasoning is correct, as liability of an insurer is based on individual exposure, and that claims arising in different years

---

45 *Colinvaux*, paras 11–095.
46 [2004] Lloyd's Rep IR 426. This came after *Fairchild v Glenhaven Funeral Services Ltd* [2002] 3 WLR 89.
47 The defendant relied on condition 6 of the employer's liability policy or that there was an implied term in the contract which could be read in by reason of custom and practice or business efficacy.
48 [2004] Lloyd's Rep IR 426, para. [22].
49 [2004] Lloyd's Rep IR 426, para. [18].

are different acts of negligence.[50] This case is however easily distinguishable, as it is not a case of double insurance and is case specific.

3.14 Clauses in combination: excess or escape clauses against rateable proportion clauses

3.14.1 National Farmers Union Mutual Insurance Society Ltd v HSBC Insurance (UK) Ltd

It is common for policies to contain a combination of clauses. An excess clause in a policy results in the policy only having to satisfy a claim where another policy in existence has been exhausted. Where an excess clause is present in one policy and another policy has a rateable proportion clause, the rateable proportion clause will not be triggered because there is no other policy in effect. The same applies where there is an escape clause in one policy and a rateable proportion clause in another. Deputy Judge Gavin Kealy QC provided some useful guidance on the interpretation of such clauses and their effect when in combination in cases where there was double insurance.

The two of the preliminary issues considered in *National Farmers Union Mutual Insurance Society Ltd v HSBC Insurance (UK) Ltd*[51] were (1) whether on a true construction of the entirety of the HSBC policy it did not provide cover to the buyers for damage due to the fire, because on a true construction of the entirety of the NFU Mutual policy it provided cover and there is no conflicting clause in that policy which cancels it; and (2) whether on a true construction of the entirety of the NFU Mutual policy that policy, under general conditions, only contains a general pro rata clause where there is other insurance covering the same damage.

There were two insurers, National Farmers Union Mutual Insurance Society ("NFU"), which assured the buyers, and HSBC Insurance (UK) Ltd ("HSBC"), which assured the sellers. The parties exchanged contracts for the sale of The Old Hall, the property which was the subject matter of a trust. A fire broke out between the dates of exchange of contracts for sale and completion. The sellers were paid the full purchase price on completion, and suffered no loss. Therefore, they did not claim under their policy with HSBC. The buyers made a claim and were indemnified by NFU. NFU then sought contribution from HSBC. The key terms of HSBC's building policy were set out in section one.[52] The HSBC policy also contained claims applicable to the whole of the insurance.[53] The NFU policy contained a number of standard sections of cover for a wide variety of risks.

---

50 *Colinvaux*, paras 11–096.
51 [2010] 1 CLC 557.
52 The insurance covers the buildings for physical loss or physical damage. It did not pay out if the building was assured under any other insurance.
53 Claims under condition 2 stated:

OTHER INSURANCE. We will not pay any claim if any loss, damage or liability covered under this insurance is covered wholly or in part under any insurance except in respect of any excess beyond the amount which would have been covered under such other insurance had this insurance not been effected.

There were also a number of general clauses.[54] The question which arose was whether there was double insurance. NFU argued that the HSBC's policy provided buildings cover to the buyers against the risk of damage to the buildings. HSBC argued that since the buyers were covered by another insurance policy for the building, on the construction of their policy, their liability was limited to that of an excess insurer attaching in excess of the cover provided to the buyers under the NFU policy. Judge Kealey QC, on an analysis of the construction of the wording of the clauses, concluded that the HSBC policy was subject to the exception that an indemnity would not be provided if the buyers had taken out their own building insurance which covered the same risk as the HSBC policy. The buyers did so here. As a result, the NFU policy regarding the "other insurance" provision was not triggered. NFU was liable to pay the full extent without pro rata apportionment, subject only to the indemnity limit for buildings cover in that policy. Judge Kealey QC held that there was only one policy covering the buyer for the fire and damage to The Old Hall, which therefore did not trigger the "other insurance" policy in the NFU policy. The buyers were not assured at the same time by the NFU and HSBC policies. Therefore, there was no double insurance.

3.14.2 The principles and approach adopted in NFU

The court first stated the principles of double insurance and the rules for contribution.[55] The judge further explained that it was the objective contextual background against which the policies were to be construed and one should not speculate about the real intention of the parties. He discussed (1) escape/exclusion clauses; (2) rateable proportion clauses; and (3) excess clauses, and the decided cases. Although he concluded that the authorities and well-established principles were of limited value in providing a clear consensus of analytical approach, he confined it to the facts of the present case.[56] He did not find the decision in *Weddell* of much help due to the different in wording of the clauses.[57] He discussed Roche

---

54
    If when you claim there is other insurance covering the same accident, illness, damage or liability, we will pay our share. This does not apply to an accident or illness assured under the Accident to the family or Personal accident and illness sections of your policy, or under the Contents section – "Additional insurance".

55 *Eagle Star Insurance Co Ltd v Provincial Insurance plc* [1994] 1 AC 130, 138, *Legal and General Assurance Society Ltd v Drake Insurance Co Ltd* [1992] QB 887, *Investor Compensation Scheme Ltd v West Bromwich Building Society* [1998] 1 WLR 896, *Pratt v Aigaion Insurance Co SA* [2009] 1 Lloyd's Rep 225.

56 [2010] 1 CLC 557.

57 Although commenting that Rowlatt J was stating that in the context of this case an "escape" clause includes in the category of co-existing cover any insurance that does not contain an equivalent escape clause. He went on to observe that such provision in each policy which Rowlatt J was dealing with only operated as secondary cover, present only in the absence of primary cover, although concluding that this was not a recognised principle. According to this analysis, NFU cover would be

J's analysis in *Gale v Motor Union Insurance Co*[58] and *Loyst v General Accident, Fire and Life Assurance Corp*,[59] and stated:[60]

> There is a suggestion in the penultimate sentence of the passage above, taken from Roche J.'s judgment, that, if there had been no "rateable proportion" provisions in the policies, the effect of the "escape" provisions in both policies would have been to deprive Mr. Loyst of an indemnity altogether. I venture to doubt whether this is what Roche J. meant but, if it is, it would be inconsistent with the subsequent authorities, including Weddell and, in my view, would be wrong. The conclusion he reached is, however, entirely consistent with the subsequent authorities on the basis that the "escape" provisions in both policies cancelled each other out such that the "rateable proportion" provisions in each policy remained in full force and effect, and applied.

He further went on to differentiate the analysis in *Gale* on the basis that the rateable proportion clause in the NFU policy only took effect if there was no other insurance covering the same damage which was already covered by the NFU policy. He then went on to consider the decision of Tucker J in *Austin v Zurich General Accident & Liability Insurance Co Ltd*,[61] which followed *Gale* and *Weddell*. Tucker J, when dealing with excess and rateable proportion clauses, stated that the facts of the case were indistinguishable from that of *Weddell* and should be followed. Tucker J concluded that indemnification of 50% by the company was not applicable. Gavin Kealey QC disagree with the views of Tucker J, and explained that the effect of both policies containing escape clauses meant that they cancelled out each other. Each insurer was liable to pay rateably. In *Weddell* only one of the policies[62] contained an escape clause but the other policy[63] did not contain either an escape clause or rateable proportion clause. This did not however mean that the latter policy was liable to pay out 50% or liable under some rateable proportion. Gavin Kealy QC was of the view that, if it were not for the condition precedent, Cornhill would be 100% liable, subject only to such monetary limit of indemnity as the policy provided. This he said was contrary to the decision of *National Farmers Union*.

In *Austin*, the Bell policy contained an escape clause and the Zurich policy contained a rateable proportion clause, after the escape clauses in both polices had been cancelled out. Gavin Kealey QC disagreed that this would result in both the policies agreeing to pay its assured 50% of the assured's loss, if covered by other insurance. He considered the correct conclusion would be that the Zurich policy would indemnify to the extent of its limit, without contribution from

---

primary cover and the HSBC would be secondary cover, which would mean that HSBC's cover was not available to them.

58 An escape clause in both the Bell and Zurich Policy. An excess clause in the Bell policy and a rateable proportion clause in the Zurich policy.
59 [1928] 1 KB 359.
60 At para. [38].
61 [1945] KB 250.
62 The road transport policy.
63 The Cornhill policy.

the Bell policy, above which excess cover would be made by the Bell policy.[64] Although concluding that the wording was materially different from the decision of *Austin*, he went on to say that even if one were to treat the rateable proportion clause in the NFU clause as the same as the excess clause in the HSBC policy, and if they were in competition or conflict, the conclusion would be the same as that reached by Tucker J.[65]

Gavin Kealey QC commented that these authorities provided no guidance to the case at hand and went on to consider the decisions in New Zealand and Australian instead. He looked at the Australian Law Commission Report No 20 which referred to the English cases, and which subsequently resulted in the enactment of s45 of the Insurance Contracts Act. He was of the view that more assistance was to be gained from the New Zealand case of *State Fire Insurance v Liverpool & London Global Insurance*.[66] In *State Fire*, the plaintiff and the defendant were both insurance companies. The plaintiff's policy provided for indemnity to the board, a local body. However, there was an endorsement which provided as follows:

> It is hereby agreed and declared that the indemnity provided by this Policy No 285502 is extended to include indemnity in respect of the legal liability of the Assured's Officers subject however to the proviso that if the Assured's Officers are otherwise indemnified in respect of their legal liability the indemnity under this policy in respect of the legal liability of the Assured's Officers shall not apply until the full amount of the indemnity otherwise provided has been applied as far as it shall go in satisfaction of the liability.

In addition to the above, there was an endorsement in the form of a condition 12 which stated:

> Other Insurance on the Risk. – (a) Should the Assured at any time during the continuance of this Policy have, effect or maintain any contract with any other Insurer indemnifying him against the risk described in this Policy or any part thereof, except with the permission in writing of the General Manager, then this policy shall become null and void. (b) If, at the time of any injury being sustained, any other insurance is existing with any other Insurer, covering the risk of the liability, and whether such insurance is in the name of the Assured or in that of any other person, the General Manager shall be liable under this Policy only proportionately to the total liability of all the Insurers in respect of the risk under which the liability of the General Manager arises.[67]

---

64 This was the alternate argument that HSBC raised and on which Gavin Kealy QC relied from US judgments such as *Greater Northern Ins Co v Mount Vernon Fire Ins Co* 798 NE 2d 167 (NY 1999) and *Jones v Mexdox Inc* 430 A 2d 488 (DC 1981) App at 489, 491–494.

65 He looks at the authorities in the US courts: *Great Northern Ins Co v Mount Vernon Fire Ins Co* 798 NE 2d 167 (NY 1999) and *Jones v Medox Inc* 430 A 2d 488 (DC 1981) App at 489, 491–494. Although he referred to US cases and was referred to US case, he considered that the US authorities provided little assistance.

66 [1952] NZLR 5. In *State Fire Insurance* there were two policies. The first policy contained an excess clause and a rateable proportion clause. The second policy contained a rateable proportion clause only.

67 [1950] NZLR 867, 868.

In *State Fire* the court drew a distinction between the clause in the state policy and concluded that the rateable proportion clause should be subordinate to the indemnity provision, and any inconsistency was to be decided in favour of granting primacy to the indemnity clause and the excess provision within it. This approach resulted in coverage operating as excess to the board's. Hutchinson J stated that the case was not one where it had to reconcile the clause to ensure that an absurd result does not occur, unlike the English cases. He stated that the court was dealing with resolving the conflict between the clauses giving indemnity in the state policy and the contribution provision in that policy. Therefore, the rateable contribution should be subordinate to the clause giving indemnity because of the endorsement on the state policy which is a special provision, unlike the rateable proportion clause which is a general clause. The state policy would only be invoked after the rights of the Globe policy have been exhausted. This was due to the state policy being considered as an excess policy.

Gavin Kealey QC adopted the same approach when deciding the present case by concluding that the qualified extension of buildings cover to the buyers is not itself further qualified by the generally applicable claims conditions in HSBC's policy. The former was a special provision taking precedence over the latter to the extent of any conflict between the two. Further, the latter was subordinate to the former so far as the existence of liability was concerned. The NFU policy covered the buyers without qualification for the risk of loss or damage to the buildings of The Old Hall by fire. Therefore, no buildings insurance covering the same risk was extended to cover the buyers and, as a result, no double insurance was present.

CHAPTER 4

Legislative reform of double insurance

4.1 "Other insurance" clauses – Australian legislation barring double insurance exclusion clauses

The English authorities were discussed in the Commission's Report[1] and considered "difficult to follow and impossible to reconcile". There were numerous issues and areas of concern which were identified. Legislation was considered a way to give sufficient protection. There is specific legislation in Australia prohibiting the inclusion of clauses limiting or excluding liability where there is double insurance. The effect of the legislation is to make such clauses void, unless the insurance contracts fall within the exceptions under s45(1) or (2) of the Insurance Contracts Act 1984.[2] The double insurance provision in the policy becomes void not the entire insurance contract. Should the United Kingdom enact similar legislation? If not, can the common law position be developed in a similar fashion to that of s4?

4.2 Australian Law Reform Commission, Report on Insurance Contracts, Report No 20 (1982)

4.2.1 Terms of reference

The Australian Law Reform Commission, Report on Insurance Contracts, Report No 20 (1982) carried out an extensive review of the problems which arose in double insurance. The terms of reference of the Australian Law Reform Commission looked at (1) the bargaining power between insurer and assured; (2) the need for contract of insurance to strike a fair balance between the interests of insurer and assured; (3) the desirability of ensuring that the manner in which insurance contracts are negotiated and entered into is not unfair; and (4) the desirability of ensuring that there are no unfair provisions in insurance contracts.[3] The Commission dealt with these issues in four stages: (1) before the contract; (2) during the contract; (3) cancellation and renewal of the contract; and (4) when a claim is made. In particular, what rules should apply where there is double insurance?

---

1 *Gale v Motor Union Insurance Co* [1928] 1 KB 359, *Weddell v Road Transport and General Insurance Co Ltd* [1932] 2 KB 563, *Austin v Zurich General Accident and Liability Insurance Co Ltd* [1945] KB 250, *State Fire Insurance General Manager v Liverpool and London and Global Insurance Co Ltd* [1952] NZLR 5 and *National Employee's Mutual General Insurance Association Ltd v Haydon* [1979] 2 Ll R 235.
2 Section 45 Insurance Contract Act 1984.
3 Australian Law Reform Commission Report Terms of Reference.

4.2.2 The guiding principles

The guiding principles that were considered for the proposals were the need to strike an appropriate balance between the economic costs and benefits. This was consistent with the views of the Campbell Committee whose recommendations were designed to improve the operation of the insurance market by ensuring that the assured was provided with sufficient information.

4.2.3 Major recommendations

There were some major recommendations.[4] It was thought that there should be regulations for standard cover and any variation should be brought to the attention of the assured. Apart from regulations, the laws relating to misleading conduct should also be continued. When determining the assured's duty to disclose, it was considered that the test should be what the assured knew, or what a reasonable person in the assured's circumstances would have known, to be relevant to the assessment of the risk. It was suggested that a similar approach should be followed for misrepresentation. The law currently requires that disclosure[5] of material facts should be made by both the insurer and assured, with regard to the risk covered and whether one would be able to make a claim under the policy.[6] The court[7] stated in *Banque Keyser Ullman SA v Skandia (UK) Insurance Co Ltd* that matters that a prudent assured would take into account when deciding whether he should place the risk with that insurer would be considered material.

Another concern was fraud which is a common occurrence in insurance contracts. Where there were attempts of fraud by an assured, it was considered that the court should ensure that the loss suffered by the assured would not be seriously disproportionate to the harm caused by the fraud. Further, "other insurance" clauses should be ineffective unless they fell within a certain category. Other recommendations included that the assured should be entitled to choose whichever insurer he wished to make a claim against, and it was then up to the insurer to seek contribution from the other insurers.[8] The Report pointed out that if an assured has made a claim in good faith, they should be entitled to recover the loss from the insurer. If an insurer was to reject the claim, this would be of serious concern.[9] It went on to conclude that a system which persistently disappoints the reasonable expectations[10] of the assured can hardly claim to represent a fair balance between the competing interest of the assured and the insurer.[11]

---

4 For example, the assured should be entitled to a copy of the policy.

5 It should be noted, however, that the Consumer Insurance (Disclosure and Representations) Act 2012, which considers disclosure provisions, and which has been dealt with in the draft bill 2014, only concerns the disclosure by the assured and does not affect this point.

6 *Banque Keyser Ullman SA v Skandia (UK) Insurance Co Ltd* [1990] 1 QB 665, 770–772.

7 [1990] 1 QB 665, 722.

8 Summary of ALRC Report.

9 The Australian Law Report Commission Report, at para. [19].

10 *Seagate Hotel Ltd v Simcoe & Erie General Insurance Co* (1981) 27 BCLR 89 (CA), *McFarlane JA* and *Commercial Union Association Co Ltd v Hayden* [1977] 1 Lloyds LR1.

11 Background of ALRC Report.

4.3 Australian Law Reform Commission: the draft legislation

4.3.1 Existing problems

There was no guarantee that an assured would receive payment under the policy when a claim is made. The balancing of interest between the assurer and the assured seemed to be disproportionate. It was thought that the inclusion of a term in the policy warning the assured of the consequences of making a claim twice under the policy did not assist in the reduction of the assured's fraudulent intentions. The insurer could include the requirement that the assured provide details of the presence of other insurance. This would also allow for the assured to obtain more details of the likelihood of over-insurance occurring. An insurer should be permitted to exclude liability where there is a genuine excess policy present.[12]

4.3.2 The draft legislation

The Australian Law Reform Commission Report attempted to draft legislation which made the provisions limiting or excluding liability of an insurer void. The draft legislation was attached to the Report.[13] Section 46 of the draft legislation was adopted in its entirety and subsequently became s45, which is as follows:

> **"Other insurance" provisions**
>
> (1) Where a provision included in a contract of general insurance has the effect of limiting or excluding the liability of the insurer under the contract by reason that the assured has entered into some other contract of insurance, not being a contract required to be effected by or under a law, including a law of a State or Territory, the provision is void.
>
> (2) Sub-section (1) does not apply in relation to a contract that provides insurance cover in respect of some or all of so much of a loss as is not covered by a contract of insurance that is specified in the first-mentioned contract.

The rationale[14] for the section was to remove the uncertainty caused by the clauses.

4.4 Combination of limiting or exclusion clauses

The Australian Law Reform Commission, Report on Insurance Contracts, Report No 20 (1982) looked at the problems where there was a combination of clauses. It was concerned[15] with the uncertainty caused to an assured when the clauses

---

12 Paragraph 148 of explanatory memorandum in ALRC Report.
13 Appendix A.
14 Paragraph 147 of explanatory memorandum to Bill.
15 Page 177 of the Report. In the People's Republic of China, for example there is statutory requirement for notification in art 41 Order of the President of the People's Republic of China (No 11) where the assured or the proposer may change the beneficiary by written notice to the insurer. The insurer shall endorse the change on the policy or other insurance certificate or attach an endorsement slip to the insurance contract or insurance certificate upon receipt of the notice. Change of the beneficiary by the proposer is subject to the assured's consent.

appeared in combination such as exclusion clauses, excess clauses or pro rata clauses, which would in some cases result in the assured without any protection[16] when a loss is suffered. Such clauses would not have any effect on layered polices where each policy is for a discrete range of the total risk and where there is no overlap. The Commission was of the view that "other insurance" clauses should therefore be rendered ineffective. An assured should be able to collect payment from one assured and it was then for the insurer to seek contribution from other insurers.

4.5 Cover note

The courts have held that if the first policy[17] was a cover note,[18] there would not be double insurance. The earlier cases[19] held that an assured could claim under a second policy. This resulted in an assured having insufficient protection under the second policy by reason of insufficient cover or a refusal to pay under a claim. This occurred where the term of the policy required notification of the existence of another policy or "other insurance" which may be in existence, and the assured failed to give such notification.

4.6 "Other insurance" provisions: Insurance Contracts Act 1984 s45

4.6.1 The application of s45

The wording of s45 will only apply to contracts of general insurance. If the effect of the provision is to limit or exclude the insurer's liability on the ground that the assured has entered into some other contract of insurance, that specific provision will be void. Section 45 will be triggered when, at the time an insurance contract is entered into, there is other insurance in existence. It does not matter whether the other insurance contract was entered into before or after the contract of general insurance. The section does not apply to provisions which have been entered into by third parties on behalf of the insurer or by naming the insurer as a beneficiary. It would be possible to sever the underlying insurance clause. It should be noted that this will not be the position for all cases, as was held in *Speno Rail Maintenance Australia Pty Ltd v Metals & Minerals Insurance Pte Ltd*.[20]

4.6.2 Time "other insurance" entered into

It should not matter when the "other insurance" policy was entered into. It would be fair on both parties[21] if no distinction is made, especially where such policies

---

16 There was no protection against fraud as such.
17 See also *Deaves v CLM Fire and General Insurance Co Ltd* (1979) 23 ALR 539 where the principles in *Steadfast Insurance Co* were followed.
18 *Steadfast Insurance Co Ltd v F & B. Trading* (1971) 125 CLR 578.
19 *Nisner Holdings Pty Ltd v Mercantile Mutual Insurance Co Ltd* [1976] 2 NSWLR 406.
20 (2009) 253 ALR 364. Also see *Austress-PSC Pty Ltd and Carlingford Australia General Insurance Ltd v Zurich Australian Insurance Ltd* delivered 1 May 1992.
21 Although it could be said more so for an assured.

are entered into without the assureds' knowledge by a third party. Although the wording of the policy specifically makes reference to "at the time an insurance contract is entered into", the timing should not matter as the insurer or the assured himself may not know of the existence of other insurance contracts. Although fairness should be a factor taken into consideration, more protection should be given to the assured due to the vulnerable position the assured usually finds himself in.

4.6.3 Severance

A possible option for the courts is severance. However, it may be difficult for the courts to identify in which type of cases severance should be permitted. The courts therefore have made a distinction between a beneficiary and an assured. In *Speno*, there was a contract between Speno and Hamersley, which provided that Speno would be solely liable for, and had to indemnify Hamersley against, any common law liability for personal injury to Speno's employees. There was also a requirement under the contract that Speno would arrange liability insurance to cover Hamersley's interest as principal. This insurance policy was taken out with Zurich. Two employees were injured under the Speno-Hamersley contract due to the negligence of Hamersley. In the District Court, Speno was held liable to indemnify Hamersley, which totalled some $1.26 million. Zurich however indemnified Hamersley this amount, and then sought contribution from Hamersley's own insurers, Metals & Minerals Insurance Pte (MMI) on the basis that Hamersley was doubly assured. MMI then commenced proceedings against Speno claiming that it was entitled to rights which were held by Hamersley against Speno under MMI's obligation to contribute. Zurich claimed that the underlying insurance clause in the Hamersley policy was void due to the operation of s45(1) Insurance Contracts Act. MMI argued that the underlying insurance clause in the Hamersley Policy meant that there was no insurance because it was Speno who entered into the policy with Zurich. It was further argued by MMI that the relief sought was not available in equity.[22]

The trial judge held that as s45(2) did not save the underlying insurance clause in the Hamersley Policy, MMI could not rely upon it because this section does not apply to "other insurance" clauses where such clause has not been effected by the person who has already been indemnified by the insurer claiming contribution. The trial judge held that the MMI policy resulted in an excess layer policy where insurance was entered into on Hamersley's behalf or when it entered into insurance on its own behalf.

If the assured is making a claim as beneficiary, s45 does not apply. It can be seen that the courts have drawn a distinction between a beneficiary and an assured, when deciding issues when there is co-insurance present, and where the policy was named or identified. The legislation, however, does not make such a

---

22 See para. [57] of judgment.

distinction. An assured would not be able to rely on s45 to void a clause, if he is a named beneficiary, if such a distinction was made.

4.7 Severance

Section 45 permits severance. Another issue raised in *Speno* was whether severance was excluded under s45(1),[23] where a provision made the term ineffective by seeking to deny or limit liability where there is double insurance. The court held that severance was permitted. This was the intent of the legislature. To permit severance would provide flexibility to the courts when deciding cases and when balancing the rights and interests of the parties.

4.8 Meaning of "the assured" – any difference from "any assured" or "an assured"?

The court draws a distinction between "an assured" and "the assured" in the wording of the policy. In *Transfield Pty Ltd v National Vulcan Engineering Insurance Group Ltd*[24] the sub-contractors and the principal contractor made claims for indemnity. The question was whether the policy had to indemnify the sub-contractors if a claim was made by the principal contractor, Transfield, who were all assured under the policy. The judge preferred the approach where each party is to be considered as a separate entity in the same manner as if a separate policy had been issued to each of them, as stated in the cross-liability clause. He noted that the way the insurers had drafted the policy would ensure that a claim could not be made under section C where it could not be made under section B, where damage was caused to property owned by the assured. He went on to state that any doubt should be resolved in favour of the assured.[25] For the exclusion clause to have the effect required by the insurer, the words in the policy would have to read either "any assured" or "an assured" rather than "the assured" in the exclusion clause. He looked at the purpose of the policy and noted the practical difficulties with issuing separate policies. It was sufficient to issue one policy which contained a cross-liability clause, and the relevant parties could each be assured by a policy which responded to any particular claim made by a party.

On appeal, Santow JA[26] had to decide if the policy had to respond where property damage was sustained due to the assumed negligence of another, or whether the exclusion clause as drafted applied. Santow JA held that if there was

---

23 At trial, Zurich was successful in its claim for contribution from MMI, by arguing that Hamersley was doubly assured. MMI then appealed this decision. The issue which the court had to decide was whether, by virtue of s45(1), the underlying insurance clause in the Hamersley policy was void.

24 [2002] NSWSC 830. This accords with *Re FAI General Insurance Co Ltd & Fletcher and Speno Rail Maintenance v Hamersley Pty Ltd* (2003) 23 WAR 291.

25 *C E Heath Underwriting & Insurance (Aust) Pty Ltd v Edwards Dunlop & Co Ltd* (1992–1993) 176 CLR 535 at 541–542.

26 With whom Ipp JA and Young CJ in Eq agreed.

a cross-liability clause in a policy, the meaning of "the assured"[27] should refer to the assured who is looking for coverage. This would extend the scope of the policy to claims between assureds.

Courts in other jurisdictions have adopted different approaches. For example, in *Stolberg v Pearl Assurance Co Ltd*[28] the Supreme Court of Canada held that the wording of the policy should be applied in light of its factual situation. The exclusion clause must be looked at together with the indemnity clauses.[29] The words "the assured" or "assured party" used in the policies are immaterial and refers to the assured entity who has incurred a liability and who is seeking indemnity under the policy.[30]

4.9 Meaning of "entered into": does it include non-party assured?

4.9.1 Zurich Australian Insurance Ltd v Metals & Minerals Insurance Pte Ltd

In *Zurich Australian Insurance Ltd v Metals & Minerals Insurance Pte Ltd* ("Zurich"),[31] the High Court discussed the background to the legislation and the meaning of the term "entered into". The issue was whether the assured had "entered into" a contract within the meaning of s45. It held that s45 does not negative the "other insurance" clause in the policy, if the second policy entered into only names the assured as a beneficiary. In *Zurich* there was a contract entered into between Hamersley and Speno. Speno's insurance policy required Speno to indemnify Hamersley and itself against claims made by employees involved in an accident, and to name Hamersley as an assured. This policy was taken out with Zurich. In addition to this policy, under Hamersley's own contract with Metals & Minerals there was an "other insurance" clause. Under this policy, Speno was named as the beneficiary and not the assured. The wording of the policy taken out by Hamersley with Metals & Minerals Insurance Pte Ltd provided for "other insurance", which was drafted as follows:

> UNDERLYING INSURANCE Underwriters acknowledge that it is customary for the Assured to effect, or for other parties (including joint venture partners, contractors and the like) to effect, on behalf of the Assured, insurance coverage specific to a particular project, agreement or risk.
>
> In the event of the Assured being indemnified under such other Insurance effected by or on behalf of the Assured (not being an Insurance specifically effected as Insurance excess of this Policy) in respect of a Claim for which Indemnity is available under this Policy, such other Insurance hereinafter referred to as Underlying Insurance, the Insurance afforded by this Policy shall be Excess Insurance over the applicable Limit of Indemnity of the Underlying Insurance but subject always to the terms and conditions of this Policy.

---

27 Unless a different intention can be shown.
28 (1971) 19 DLR (3d) 343.
29 This approach has been followed in Hong Kong in the case of *Dragages et Travaux Publics (HK) Ltd v RJ Wallace* [2004] 1 HKC 478, 489 at para. [23].
30 [2004] 1 HKC 478, 489 at para. [25].
31 [2009] HCA 50 (2009), 240 CLR 391.

> In the event of cancellation of the Underlying Insurance or reduction or exhaustion of the Limits of Indemnity thereunder, this Policy shall: (i) in the event of reduction pay the excess of the reduced underlying limit (ii) in the event of cancellation or exhaustion continue in force as underlying insurance but subject always to the terms and Conditions of this Policy.

The draft Insurance Contracts Bill proposed by the ALRC did not define the term "entered into". Section 48,[32] which the ALRC recommended to be included into the legislation, made it permissible for a non-party to a general contract who is specified or referred to in the contract to also be covered, and able to recover from the insurer. As there was no distinction made in the Report or Explanatory Memorandum between double insurance including a non-party and where the assured is named, the court was of the view that the words "entered into" did not include a non-party assured. Under s45(1) Speno had not "entered into" the contract. The court held that non-party would not come within the definition of "entered into". The court did not draw a distinction. It could be said that to provide a definition of "entered into" would place an unnecessary restriction on the courts when deciding whether a case would fall within the definition of "entered into".

4.9.2 Vero Insurance Ltd v QBE Insurance (Australia) Ltd

Interpreting the wording of such clauses has proven difficult. This was illustrated in *Vero Insurance Ltd v QBE Insurance (Australia) Ltd*.[33] The issue was whether a sub-contractor who had a contract of insurance with a particular insurer had entered into a contract with that insurer. In *Vero*, an employee was injured during work for a contractor, Priceright Construction Pty Ltd (Priceright), which was employed by Barclay Mowlem Construction (BMC). Vero indemnified BMC and sought contribution from QBE on the basis of double insurance as the same risk was assured. QBE claimed that it was not liable to contribute due to the exclusion clause, arguing that it would not be liable to indemnify if there existed a more specific insurance cover. The Supreme Court agreed with the referee's decision and concluded that BMC had not "entered into" a contract of insurance with Vero. Vero's policy was "effected by" the contractor.[34] The contractor in this case was not a party to Vero's policy. The contractor was treated as a "non-party assured" and did not come within the definition of "named assureds" under Vero's policy. Therefore, s45 did not apply and contribution could not be sought.

---

32 Entitlement of named persons to claim (1) Where a person who is not a party to a contract of general insurance is specified or referred to in the contract, whether by name or otherwise, as a person to whom the insurance cover provided by the contract extends, that person has a right to recover the amount of the person's loss from the insurer in accordance with the contract notwithstanding that the person is not a party to the contract. (2) Subject to the contract, a person who has such a right: (a) has, in relation to the person's claim, the same obligations to the insurer as the person would have if the person were the assured; and (b) may discharge the assured's obligations in relation to the loss. (3) The insurer has the same defences to an action under this section as the insurer would have in an action by the assured.
33 [2011] NSWSC 593.
34 As this was done through the department's agency and broker at the time.

Einstein J pointed out that this should be the correct approach and refused to depart from the referee's decision, unless the referee had come to his conclusion based on a wrong approach or the parties did not have sufficient opportunity to argue the points before the referee. As neither of these factors were present, the court concurred with the referee's decision.

It is unclear whether such principles apply only to sub-contractor situations, construction insurance policies or whether it has a general application.[35] The cases suggest that if an insurer specifies wide categories of named assureds in such policies, this would limit their rights for contribution, as these insurers can now rely on "other insurance"[36] clauses in the other policies to limit or exclude liability. It is likely that insurers will now devise ways to draft the insurance policies in terms more favourable to themselves. An assured who is not a party to the original insurance contract will not be covered if the insurer confines the category of persons who are treated as an assured for the purpose of the policy in a restrictive manner. It is unclear whether a named assured would fall within the category of a contracting party where there are "other insurance" clauses.

4.10 The term "other insurance"

4.10.1 What is considered to "enter into"?

The decision in *Zurich Australia Insurance Ltd* was revisited by the Supreme Court of Queensland. The court shed some light on s45, the use of the words "other insurance" in contracts, and whether s45 renders other insurance clauses void. The court held that a liberal approach should be adopted when interpreting s45. When considering the words "entered into", one looks at the policy which the party was relying on to activate the "other insurance" clause. In *Nicholas v Wesfarmers Currangh Pty Ltd*[37] the plaintiff, an employee, brought proceedings against Wesfarmers Currangh Pty Ltd ("Currangh"), the operator of the mine, and *G & S Engineering Services Pty Ltd* ("G & S Engineering"), his employer. A liability policy providing indemnity was assured with QBE by Currangh. G & S Engineering also took out a policy with Brit. Currangh made a claim against Brit which was refused on the basis that the "other Insurance" clause in its policy limited its liability, as the QBE policy was not a policy "entered into" by Currangh but by Currangh's parent company, Wesfarmers Ltd ("Wesfarmer"), whose

---

35 These policies are usually known as "floater" or "open cover policy".
36 In this case the "other insurance" clause read as follows:

> The Liability of the Insurer to indemnify the Assured . . . shall not extend to any of the following: . . . Liability for which a separate insurance protection has been effected by the Named Assured . . . except as provided for by Memorandum 6.1 . . .[which provided that QBE would indemnify any losses that were not recoverable under, or in excess of, the separate insurance].

37 [2010] QSC 447. In an article written by Michael Ball J "Double Insurance and Contribution" at para. [8], he was of the view that it was appropriate to extend the meaning of "entered into" to encompass those circumstances as suggested by McMeekin J.

benefit extended to Currangh.[38] The QBE policy had a similar clause to Brit. Brit stated that the QBE 386 policy was "valid and collectible insurance" and that condition 5[39] acted as an excess policy above the 386 policy. Brit placed considerable emphasis on the decision in *Zurich*. It argued that Currangh was a non-party beneficiary and therefore s45(1) did not apply. The court distinguished Zurich on it facts. The question, it was said, was of a broad application. McMeekin J stated at para. [27] that:

> If a company enters into a contract of insurance on behalf of the group of companies, of which it is the parent company and the others its wholly owned subsidiaries, does it enter the contract of insurance, at least so far as s45(1) is concerned, on behalf of each company independently, or does it act merely as the subsidiaries' agent, or is it the only party "entering into" the contract? If the characterisation in either of the first two alternatives was accepted then the method of entering into the contract of insurance would satisfy the precondition triggering the application of s45(1).

The applicant's argument was preferred. The entering into the contract of insurance with QBE by Wesfarmers should be seen as an entering into that contract by Currangh within the meaning of s45(1).[40] McMeekin J commented that his decision was straightforward and based on two reasons. The first was the characterisation of the relationship between Wesfarmer and Currangh as being one of principal and agent due to the payment by Currangh to Wesfarmer of a significant proportion of the premium paid to QBE. If this view is incorrect, it would be appropriate to extend the meaning of "entered into" to cover Wesfarmers actions, otherwise it would encourage the mischief which the legislation wanted to prevent. Second, Currangh did not become an assured by some form of extended definition of assured person. It was a named assured under the QBE policy. He stated that the legislation intended the "commercial convenience and practice" to be taken into account, through the use of agents, and that in the long title to the Act, a fair balance should be struck between the interest of insurers, the assured and other members of the public, so as to enable terms included in contracts to operate fairly. He did not think that it was appropriate to make the working of the clause dependent on whether one acted through an agent, or on one's behalf, when effecting insurance.[41]

---

38 Currangh stated that the matter could be resolved by answering: (1) Is the "other insurance" clause (condition 5) in the Brit insurance policy void by reason of the operation of s45(1) of the Act and (2) If that condition is not void: (i) does it, on its proper construction, exclude QBE 386 policy from the category of "valid and collectible insurance"; (ii) should the Brit policy be construed as if the condition did not exist?"
39 "5. Other Insurance – Where allowable by law, this Policy is excess over and above any other valid and collectible insurance and shall not respond to any loss until such times as the limit of liability under such other primary and valid insurance has been totally exhausted."
40 [2010] QSC 447, para. [29].
41 Paragraph [32], and reference was made to Gleeson CJ in *East End Real Estate Pty Ltd v C E Health & Casualty & General Insurance Ltd* (1991) 25 NSWLR 400 at 404.

McMeekin J distinguish *Zurich*'s case[42] on the basis that *Zurich* was not an agency situation, and that the decision should only be confined to its own facts.[43] The Supreme Court was of the view that a more extended meaning should be given to the words "enter into", taking into consideration the mischief that the legislation was trying to prevent. This was because the relationship between Wesfarmer and Currangh was one of principal and agent. Even if this was not the case, the court was still willing to conclude that, due to the relationship between Currangh and Wesfarmer, the entering into the policy by the head company on behalf of itself and one of its subsidiaries is an entering into the contract of insurance by the subsidiary.

4.10.2 Extension of Nicholas v Wesfarmers Currangh Pty Ltd to beneficial third parties

The above analysis is a departure from the decision in *Zurich* to now cover beneficial third parties. It seems that the court in *Zurich, Currangh and Wesfarmer*, had left open the possibility of extending the meaning of "enter into" to include cases where there exists some sort of close relationship, such as (1) a parent and subsidiary, or one where there is a relationship of (2) agent and principal, between the beneficiary and the party effecting the contract, which would treat the beneficiary as having "entered into" the contract itself. The court rejected the argument put forward by Brit that two preconditions would have to be satisfied for s45 to operate: (1) that Currangh had entered into the QBE 386 policy and (2) Currangh was a contracting party to the Brit policy. The court held that as Currangh was an existing subsidiary and ascertainable, the existing relationship would not be altered by the situation where Wesfarmers purported to act for others who were not ascertainable and could not at the time have given authority.[44] He explained that Wesfarmers' actions in entering into the QBE 386 policy was undertaken as agent for Currangh, so far as the policy put QBE on risk for Currangh's potential claims, and therefore Currangh had "entered into" the QBE 386 policy.[45]

The approach adopted by McMeerkin J was to avoid a situation where the insurer could circumvent s45. McMeerkin J's broad analysis was based on the principles of whether there was an agency[46] and whether there was consent or not, despite the lack of direct evidence, such as an agency agreement.[47] It was fundamental that Currangh paid for the insurance and payment to Wesfarmers leaned strongly towards Wesfarmers not acting on its own behalf in obtaining the insurance but acting on behalf of Currangh.[48] Further, there was an arrangement

---

42 (2009) 240 CLR 391.
43 Paragraph [35].
44 Paragraph [47].
45 Paragraph [48].
46 Paragraph 37.
47 Paragraph 42.
48 Paragraph 38.

of mutual consent in effecting the QBE policy.[49] The court did not have to decide the issue of double insurance where there was no agency relationship and where no consent was given.[50]

4.10.3 The proper approach of the courts

Section 45 will only apply where the assured was party in both insurance contracts. This was held in *Lambert Leasing Inc v QBE Insurance Ltd*.[51] This was reaffirmed[52] by the New South Wales Court of Appeal. The reasoning of the court was that s45 will apply if Lambert, had entered into the policy. In this case, the QBE policy had not been "entered into" because he was named under "additional assureds", with 19 other persons, which clearly indicated that he was a third-party beneficiary of the policy. Therefore, s45 did not apply. Further, Rein J[53] rejected the distinction given by McMeekin J at para. [85] held that:

> In my view the fact that a subsidiary falls within the definition of the assured in a policy schedule is not determinative as to whether that subsidiary is a party to the contract. There is no clause in the Global Policy . . . and no indications which make it clear that Lambert was a contracting assured as opposed to an entity to whom the policy cover was intended to extend. No correspondence between SAAB or its brokers on the one hand, with Global on the other, or between Lambert and SAAB, was sought to be put in evidence.

The approach adopted by the court should be a balanced one. There should not be a distinction drawn between an employee, employer, contractor, parent company,[54] subsidiary and agency relationships. Commercial convenience, practice and certainty can be achieved by the court adopting a consistent approach. The mischief provided for by the legislation should be prevented.

4.11 An easier way out? No double insurance

It is easier for the court to conclude that double insurance does not arise on the facts of the case. In *Australasian Medical Insurance Ltd v CGU Insurance Ltd*,[55] the insurers issued a policy which covered the risks of QML, a partnership

---

49 Paragraph 38.
50 *Sutton on Insurance Law* (4th edn 2014), para. 19.102.
51 [2015] NSWSC 750, per Rein J.
52 [2016] NSWCA 254. The court did not have to deal with the issue of subsidiary, in light of its ruling.
53 In *Sutton on Insurance Law* (4th edn 2014), at para. 19.107, it was stated:

> The authors of this work suggested, in commenting on the reasoning in Nicholas that the conclusion was correct. That was so because, as a matter of law, a co-insurance arrangement entered into by one policyholder on behalf of others gives rise to a binding co-insurance as regards any co-assured who has authorised the insuring policyholder to insure on his behalf.

54 However, for a parent and subsidiary situation it will be very difficult to ascertain the exact relationship, due to the way the companies are structured. Such uncertainty will lead to parties trying to avoid the application and effects of s45.
55 [2010] QCA 189.

of pathologists, who were assured under a professional indemnity with AMIL. CGU were insurers who had issued a policy risk which covered certain risks associated with the conduct of QML's pathology practice. AMIL indemnified QML when a claim was made against the partners and argued that CGU's policy covered the same risk. AMIL further argued contribution as between co-insurers. AMIL claimed that the special condition excluding liability was void due to the effect of s45. The court held that as QML suffered no loss, due to indemnification by AMIL, who did not seek to structure the claim as one of subrogation but instead in its own right as co-insurer, it was therefore an unnecessary party to the action. Further, s45 did not apply. The policies covered different risks. The parties had no intention for CGU's policy to cover the practitioners at QML because they had their own policies which covered them. Therefore there was no double insurance.

The courts will adopt a liberal interpretation when it comes to the meaning of "enter into" under s45. This is consistent with the intention of the ALRC. The purpose of s45 was to ensure that the assured is provided with protection when making a claim. If parties want to exclude the effects of s45, parties have to draft the exclusion clauses carefully, where the contracting party is effecting the contracts for the benefit of other parties. The ALRC did provide two exceptions where the protection did not apply. The first situation is where the other insurance is compulsory, either by or under law, including the law of the state or territory.[56] The second situation is where primary and excess layers are involved.

4.12 The exceptions under s45

4.12.1 Exception 1: not being a contract of insurance required to be effected by or under a law, including the law of a state or territory

4.12.1.1 Public liability insurance

The wording of s45(1) states that an insurer is allowed to exclude or limit its liability where the contract is a contract of general insurance, if the contract is required to be effected by or under a law, such as the law of a state or territory. Other insurance which is compulsory by law will not be void. The issue in *WorkCover Queensland*[57] was whether the insurers, Royal & Sun Alliance Insurance Australia Ltd, under a public liability insurance policy were liable to indemnify the head contractor, Barclays Mowlem Construction Pty Ltd (Barclay Mowlem) against its liability where an employee of a sub-contractor was injured. The employee claimed against the sub-contractor and the construction company. WorkCover contended that there was double insurance. It agreed it and the lead insurer should be liable to indemnify Barclay Mowlem, and was liable to pay Barclay Mowlem under the policy issued under s46(1) of the Workers'

---

56 Section 45(1) ICA.
57 (2001) 11 ANZ InsCas 61–489. This decision was not followed in *Transfield Pty Ltd v National Vulcan Engineering Insurance Group Ltd* [2002] NSWSC 830.

Compensation Act 1990 (Qld).[58] Three policies were issued at the time. The lead insurer argued that under clause 8 (other insurance) of its policy, coverage provided was only for excess over and above that which is recoverable under the other valid and collectible insurance. Wilson J held that Barclay Mowlem, as an employer, was required to effect the policy, to which WorkCover had agreed to provide indemnity under the policy. It was a policy that Barclay Mowlem was "required to be effected by or under a law".

4.12.1.2 Conclusion

The intention of the ALRC was to permit an insurer to exclude liability where there was workers' compensation insurance or compensation for death or injury arising out of the use of a motor vehicle. This was consistent with s9 of the Insurance Contracts Act 1984.[59] The court concluded that the Royal policy did not need to indemnify Barclay Mowlem, due to its exclusion clause.[60] If this was not correct, liability would be excess cover only[61] by not being found void by s45(1).

4.12.2 Exception 2: s45(2) Subsection (1) does not apply where some or all of the loss is not covered by a contract of insurance that is specified in the first-mentioned contract

This subsection raises interesting issues regarding excess layers of cover and the court's approach when interpreting s45(2). The ALRC discussed the effects of "other insurance" clauses which fell into three categories. These included excess, exclusion and rateable proportion clauses. It was of the view that all these clauses should be held to be ineffective as they had no purpose to serve. Instead, where the assured has assured his risk with numerous insurers he should be able to recover the whole loss from any insurer covering the risk. It is then for that insurer to seek contribution from the other insurers. This way, the assured has more protection.[62]

When discussing the exceptions to the legislation, the summary of recommendations[63] emphasised that a true excess liability policy to cover an assured's liability which is over and above that covered by another insurer, which has been specifically identified in the excess policy, will not be void under the section.[64]

---

58 Section 46(1) provides:

> If an employer uses the labour of a worker whose services are lent or hired to the employer by another, cover under a policy maintained by the employer extends to indemnify the employer against legal liability existing independently of his Act to pay damages in respect of injury to the worker arising out of or in the course of work for which the worker's labour is being so used.

59 That it did not apply to a contract entered into for the purpose of a state law relating to workers' compensation or compensation for death or injury arising out of the use of a motor vehicle. See paras [14] and [15] of judgment. Also see para. 54 the ALRC Summary of Recommendation.

60 Clause 3(a).

61 In accordance with clause 7, clause 8 and endorsement 3 of the policy.

62 See ALRC para. 289.

63 Paragraph [54].

64 Also see para. 148 of the Explanatory Memorandum.

Section 45 therefore does not apply to a layered policy covering certain, more specific types of total risk and where there is no overlapping of such risks.

4.13 The meaning of "specifically" under s45(2)

There are two main types of policy which deal with other insurance: (1) where the assured places an obligation on the assured to notify the insurer of existing or subsequent insurances covering the same risk; and (2) where there is no such obligation on the assured but where it will exclude or qualify liability of the insurer in the event of other insurance.[65]

4.13.1 HIH Casualty and General Insurance Co v Pluim Construction Pty Ltd

The recommendation itself does not define "specifically" under s45(2).[66] Guidance can however be found in *HIH Casualty and General Insurance Co v Pluim Construction Pty Ltd*,[67] where *Austress-PSC Pty Ltd and Carlingford Australia General Insurance Ltd v Zurich Australian Insurance Ltd*[68] was considered.

In *HIH Casualty & General Insurance Ltd*, HIH argued that (a) the CU Construction Policy should respond to Constructions claim for indemnity on the basis that HIH's policy was dealing with principal-arranged insurance[69] which permitted HIH to escape its liability under its own policy provided that CU was impaled under the CU policy; and further, (b) there was double insurance which gave rise to contribution between the insurers.[70] These arguments were rejected. CU and Construction accepted the claim for indemnity,[71] but argued that they were not liable. Reference was made to the exclusion clause under clause 6(b). The trial judge held (1) that CU's Construction Policy did not respond as Construction's claim fell within exclusion clause 6(b), and (2) that HIH could not rely upon condition 7 of its own policy which was rendered void by s45(2). The CU Construction Policy was not specified in the HIH Policy. Mason P[72] found that there was no basis for reading unexpressed words into the policy. The words "in respect of which insurance is required by virtue of any legislation relating to motor vehicles" qualified the words "any Vehicle or any attachment to any Vehicle" at the start of sub-clause (b). It was "perfectly understandable" why the drafter of the clause did not pay attention in identification of the persons upon

---

65 See Australian Law Reform Commission, *Report on Insurance Contracts*, Report No 20 (1982), pp. 172–174, paras 280–281.
66 In *Zurich Australian Insurance Ltd & Minerals Insurance Pte Ltd* [2007] WASC 62, it suggested that this may be by name, description or by name.
67 (2000) 11 ANZ Ins Cas 61–477.
68 Delivered on 1 May 1992 QDC 2052/91, unreported decision of Judge Robin QC, DCJ of the Queensland District Court.
69 "The other insurance" exclusion.
70 (2000) ANZ Ins Cas 61–477, para. 18.
71 Although contingently upon HIH filing in its remaining claim.
72 With members of the New South Wales Court of Appeal agreeing.

whom such requirement lay.[73] He agreed with the trial judge's conclusion that the CU Construction Policy did not have to respond to Construction's claim. He went on to consider the significance of condition 7. The issue that had to be determined was whether the words "the policy of insurance provided by the Principal" in condition 7 was sufficient to "specify" the CU policies within s45(2). Manson P[74] held that it was not of sufficient specificity to satisfy s45(2), as it was too general.

The decision of *Austress-PSC Pty Ltd and Carlingford Australia General Insurance Ltd v Zurich Australian Insurance Ltd*[75] was considered[76] and, in particular, the provision "any other Policy of Indemnity or Insurance in favour of or effected by or on behalf of the Assured applicable to such Occurrence". Mason P stated:

> to be construed as requiring reference to "other insurance" to be specific, as opposed to a description in general words capable of extending to the other insurance, if the provision under examination is to survive being struck down by sub-s.(1). It seems to me the underlying notion is that the assured and the insurer have tailored their own bargain to take account of the impact of other contracts.

Mason P concluded that it was unnecessary to seek a definitive meaning of the sub-section, and the exception in s45(2) should be construed narrowly. On the facts[77] of the case before him, Mason P stated that the wording did not identify any particular policy with any particular insurer. Further, the type of insurance the proprietor had to take out was described in the building contract in the broadest generality, with no reference being made to conditions or exclusions. He concluded that the HIH policy was not in form or in substance a type of layered policy or excess insurance. The use of the words "a policy of insurance", which was stated to be "principal-arranged," only emphasise the "futurity, contingency and lack of relevant specificity". The use of the words "a policy of insurance" was held to lack the requirements necessary to fall within the exceptions of s45(2), as "specified".[78] Professor Sutton's interpretation of what would be sufficient for there to be compliance under s45(2)[79] was preferred, which stated as follows:

> where contract A provides cover in relation to a loss that is not covered by contract B and contract B is specified in contract A. In that case, the section has no application

---

73 (2000) ANZ Ins Cas 61–477, para. 26.
74 He agreed with the trial judge.
75 1 May 1992 QDC 2052/91.
76 Analysis of Robyn QC DCJ.
77 Condition 7 of the HIH policy which stated:

> PRINCIPAL-ARRANGED INSURANCE. In the event of the named Assured entering into an agreement with any other party (who for the purpose of this clause is called "the Principal") pursuant to which the Principal has agreed to provide a policy of insurance which is intended to indemnify the named Assured for any liability arising out of the performance of the Works then the Company(ies) will (subject to the terms and conditions of this Policy) only indemnify the names Assured for such liability not covered by the policy of insurance provided by the Principal.

> Also see clause 6(b).

78 (2000) 11 ANZ Ins Cas 61–477, para. 45.
79 *Insurance Law in Australia* (3rd edn 1999).

to contract A. What constitutes specification is not defined but it must mean that contract B need not be precisely named but must be sufficiently described so as to be capable of identification, and the requirement of specification makes it clear that only true excess liability policies are intended to be exempted from the operation of s45(1).

Further academic text was also referred to at paras [40] and [41] of his judgment:

> 40 Derrington and Ashton, The Law of Liability Insurance (1990) take a slightly narrower view of s45(2), stating (at p378) that:
>
>> The position under the Insurance Contracts Act 1984 is that a provision of this type which has the effect of limiting or excluding the liability of the insurer is void, except for an "excess" policy in respect of another policy which is specified in the policy containing the condition. Accordingly, even that form of condition which made the policy containing it an excess policy in the event of other insurance, and which was so effective in the past, is ineffective unless it specified the other insurance.
>>
>> Because of the purpose of s45, it is most probable that the specification of the policy to which it is to be an excess is so general that it would not meet the requirement of sub-s(2) which would except it from the general avoidance which sub-s(1) visits upon conditions relating to other insurance [sic]. Otherwise, the scope of the section is obviously intended to be far-reaching by its reference to the result, so that it may well be found to apply to all such conditions and provisos except those in an excess policy that is related to a specific and named policy.
>
> 41 Kelly and Ball, Insurance Legislation Manual (3rd edn 1995) suggest at p132 that "specified" means that the actual contract must be identified in the excess policy – otherwise the excess policy would not be a "true excess policy".

Applying this reasoning to the wording of the CU Construction Policy, he considered that it would not satisfy the requirement of being "specified". He went on to say, "that it could be possible that a clearly defined class of insurance such as "X's standard Construction Policy with an excess of Y" would suffice. He reserved his position on the likely possibilities.

4.13.2 Conclusion

Therefore, the policy has to be "specified" in the other insurance for it to be a true excess clause. A narrow approach would afford more protection to the assured. A similar approach was followed in *Zurich Australian Insurance Ltd v Metals & Minerals Insurance Pty Ltd*[80] where the court found that the clause in the Hamersley policy was not saved by s45(2) due to the Zurich policy not being specified as required by s45(2).[81] Mason P commented that the wording used in the policy lacked specificity. He did not identify the exact wording that should

---

80 (2007) 209 FLR 247.
81 Also see *Speno Rail Maintenance Australia Pty Ltd v Metals & Minerals Insurance Pte Ltd* where the court came to a similar conclusion and found that the MMI policy was not a genuine excess layer as the other policies were not specific enough.

be adopted when dealing with a "principal-arrangement". It would be difficult to do so, as circumstances are usually case specific. Cases should be dealt with on a case-by-case basis. There must be flexibility. The courts' restrictive approach should not be taken too far and the contractual intention of the parties should be taken into account.[82] Further, due to the way companies are structured, it may be a requirement of the parent company that the subsidiary obtains local cover while the parent company takes out a "top and drop" policy.[83] A head contractor may also adopt a similar approach. The underlying objective of protecting an assured seems to be achieved where a more strict approach is adopted by the courts. This could have the opposite effect as the insurer may use other methods to try and get around this problem.[84]

4.14 Requirement for an assured to notify the insurer: validity of s45(1)

4.14.1 Notification clause

In some cases an assured can only recover under the second policy if there is non-compliance with notification provisions. Therefore, the issues which have to be resolved are whether inclusion of a notification clause in the policy has the effect of making the clause void under s45(1) and, if so, whether the saving provision under s45(2) will be triggered. In *Nisner Holdings Pty Ltd v Mercantile Mutual Insurance Co Ltd*[85] both policies required notification, where there was other insurance in effect. The assured however failed to notify the first insurer of the second policy, the court held that the second policy was not an excess policy, and the first policy could be avoided. Further, that where there is a failure to notify, the most that the assured can recover in terms of losses is only the amount that is assured under the second policy. The second policy is additional cover which would only, if effected, cover an assured up to the increased value of the premises over and above that of the first policy. The Supreme Court concluded that there was double insurance in this case. The assured was only able to recover the amount provided for under the second policy.

4.14.2 Steadfast Insurance Co Ltd v F&B Trading Co Pty

In *Steadfast Insurance Co Ltd v F&B Trading Co Pty*[86] the High Court of Australia had to consider a forfeiture provision in a policy where there was a condition in both policies that notice had to be given of other insurance. The court held that the mere fact that a policy provides for conditions upon breach which

---

[82] *Sutton on Insurance Law* (4th edn 2014), para. 19.110.
[83] A top and drop policy will take effect as an excess cover and which drops down to take the place of the primary cover after it has been exhausted.
[84] See http://taglaw.com/files/DoingBusinessGuides/DoingBusinessinAustralia(ConstructionLiability).pdf (last visited at 19 May 2012) for an interesting discussion on the devices used to limit recovery.
[85] [1976] 2 NSWLR 406.
[86] (1971) 143 CLR 578.

results in the company escaping liability did not mean that no insurance had been effected. In *Steadfast*, a policy which covered loss for damage to property was renewed by Steadfast. The policy contained a clause which required that notice be given if any insurance or insurances had been effected. Failure to give notice would result in forfeiture of all benefits under the policy. A cover note was obtained before loss had occurred with Queensland. No notice of this cover note was given to Steadfast. The court reaffirmed the Supreme Court's view that no forfeiture was permitted due to the failure to notify as the cover not did not fall within the meaning of Steadfast's policy that the insurance with Queensland had been "effected". The nature and operation of the condition which was not fulfilled had to be taken into account. The second policy did not attach, there was no breach of the first policy requiring notice. This is the correct approach where there is clear evidence that the policy has not been effected. The wording of s45[87] covers cases where there is "other insurance" present and notification of such policies should be made by the assured.

In *Steadfast Insurance Co Ltd v F & B Trading Co Pty*, Menzies J correctly pointed out the well-established principle that where there is a term of an insurance policy which has provisions for forfeiture of benefits, it shall be construed strictly against the insurer.[88] That insurance will only be effected when the act attaches risk of loss to another insurer.[89] Menzie J referred to the Privy Council decision of *Equitable Fire and Accident Office Ltd and The Ching Wo Hong*[90] where the appellant denied liability on the basis that the policies that were entered into had become null and void, due to the failure on the part of the respondents to give the company notice of an additional insurance which had been taken out by the respondents with Western Assurance Company, without the consent required under the wording of the policy. This was a condition indorsed in the policies. Prior to the fire, a policy had been executed by the director of Western Company in favour of the respondents. The premium was never paid under this policy. The court stated that the issue was whether the policy executed by the Western Assurance Company became effective,[91] where the premium was not paid either wholly or partially. Lord Davey looked at the plain language of the condition. He held that it would apply to the first premium as to any renewal premium. The whole instrument must be looked at to ascertain the intention of the parties and the effect of the document.[92] Therefore the condition qualified and restricted the engagement of the company. This converted what would have otherwise been an absolute engagement into a conditional one. The words "having paid" which is used in the policy is usually expressed as the consideration for the company's engagement which would have become accurate when the engagement became

---

87 Insurance Contracts Act 1984.
88 *Steadfast Insurance Co Ltd v F & B Trading Co Pty* (1971) 125 CLR 578.
89 *Equitable Fire and Accident Office Ltd v The Ching Wo Hong* (1907) AC 96 and *Home Insurance Co of New York v Gavel* (1927) 3 DLR 929.
90 [1970] AC 96.
91 [1970] AC 96 at p. 99.
92 [1970] AC 96 at p. 100.

effective. The court was of the view that consideration must actually be paid and not just expressed to be paid. The clause was clearly expressed in the instrument that notice was required, and it was clear that no liability would attach until the premium had been paid. The court held that it was not conditional execution. The key factor is what was executed.

4.14.3 Home Insurance Co of New York v Gavel

The Canadian decision of *Home Insurance Co of New York v Gavel* had similar wording to s45, which was referred to in *Steadfast Insurance Co Ltd v F & B Trading Co Pty* was the Canadian decision of *Home Insurance Co of New York v Gavel*.[93] This case dealt with a statutory condition in the policy namely, the ninth statutory condition in the first schedule to the Fire Insurance Policies' Act RSNS, 1923 c.211. The wording differed from that of s45,[94] and specifically dealt with fire insurance. The statutory condition stated:

> The insurer is not liable for loss if any prior insurance with any other insurer, unless the insurer's assent to such prior insurance appears in the policy or is endorsed thereon, nor if any subsequent insurance is effected with any other insurer, unless and until the insurer assents thereto, or unless the insurer does not dissent in writing two weeks after receiving written notice of the intention or desire to effect the subsequent insurance, or does not dissent in writing after that time before the subsequent or further insurance is effected.

The issue on appeal was whether any subsequent insurance had been effected within the meaning of the condition. The respondents argued that the policy never attached and as a result there was no insurance which was effected, and relied on *Equitable Fire and Accident Office Ltd v The Ching Wo Hong*. The appellant relied on the decision of the Supreme Court of Canada in *Manitoba Assurance Co v Whitla*.[95] The assured wanted to abandon his insurance against a fire policy with his existing insurers Manitoba Assurance Co, and wanted to effect the same with another insurance company Royal Insurance Co. He contacted the agent of Royal Insurance Co, who sent him the application form and request for payment of premium. An interim receipt was then issued to the assured which provided insurance until the issue of a policy. The head office of the assured's insurer was sent the application form and premium with the agent's report. The wording of the interim receipt required that written assent of the company had to be obtained where there is prior insurance, or there would be non-liability.[96] The property assured was destroyed by a fire. The interim policy was in force at the time and

---

93 [1927] SCR 481.
94 Insurance Contracts Act 1984.
95 (1903) 34 Can SCR 191 at p. 206.
96 The statutory condition provided: (8). The company is not liable for loss if there is any prior insurance in any other company, unless the company's assent thereto appears herein or is indorsed hereon, nor if any subsequent insurance is effected in any other company, unless and until the company assents thereto or unless the company does not dissent in writing within two weeks after

the assured had not abandoned his policy with his original insurers. There was a provision in Royal Insurance Co's policy which provided that where there was another policy taken out without the company's consent that policy would lapse. Claims were brought against both insurers.[97] Sedgwick CJ was of the view that there was only one question of fact and stated:[98]

> Were there two policies valid on their face and actually subsisting at the same time on the same property in question? Did Bourque as a matter of fact take a subsequent insurance with the Royal, without the knowledge and consent of the appellant company upon the property assured by them? To these questions there is room for but one answer.
>
> Not only had Bourque applied for and obtained from the Royal a further insurance upon the property upon which he held an insurance in the appellant company, but after the fire he immediately notified the Royal and filed his claim with them, and subsequently through his assignees took an action against them for the amount of his interim receipt.
>
> . . .
>
> Now whether that insurance was valid or not cannot be determined in this case so as to bind the Royal were it necessary to do so. And the question is not whether Bourque intended to doubly insure or not. Did he in fact doubly insure? We have nothing to do with his intentions.

Where there was effecting of new insurance, without the assent required, the insurance company could exercise its right to void the policy. He reaffirmed the previous authorities as to whether the second insurance policy voided the first policy. In *Home Insurance Co of New York v Gavel*, the court, on reviewing the cases, concluded that Sedgwick CJ's conclusion and the Canadian cases were no longer binding. The English decision of *Equitable Fire and Accident Office Ltd v The Ching Wo Hong* was preferred. The issue was whether, "any subsequent insurance was effected with any other insurer"[99] was within the meaning of the statutory condition. Here, the policy with the appellant's insurance company North Company, never attached, due to the express wording in the statutory condition, i.e. "the insurer is not liable for loss if there is any prior insurance with any other insurer". Therefore, if there was such prior insurance, the condition applied, and no insurance under the policy was effected.[100] The condition of the policy did not contemplate a subsequent contract of insurance, but a subsequent insurance which was effective.[101] He stated that the attempt to now vivify the contract so as to relieve the appellant from liability must fail.[102]

---

receiving written notice of the intention or desire to effect the subsequent insurance, or does not dissent in writing after that time and before the subsequent or further insurance is effected.
97 The assured assigned his rights to the plaintiff.
98 (1903) 34 Can SCR 191 at p. 199.
99 [1927] 3 DLR at p. 913.
100 [1927] 3 DLR at p. 913.
101 [1927] 3 DLR at p. 913.
102 [1927] 3 DLR at p. 913.

4.14.4 Should a more stringent approach be adopted?

The court will apply a much more stringent approach and find against the insurer[103] where there are two policies in place and there is a notification requirement. In such cases, one has to consider how such provisions are drafted. This is consistent with the intention of the ALRC that the assured should be protected.

4.14.5 Policy terminates before loss

An assured can be left without any cover if the policy terminates before the loss.[104] There can be situations where the wording under Policy 1 provides for notification under the policy, and where Policy 2 only becomes effective when there is notification of Policy 1. Policy 2 may be terminated at some later stage.

4.15 The Canadian position

In Canada, the risk does not attach where a policy taken out is not considered effective. Both s45 and the statutory provision under the ninth statutory condition in the first schedule to the First Insurance Policies' Act, RSNS, 1923, c 211 cover situations where there will be a voiding of the policy. The Canadian provision expressly states that the insurer is not liable if there is prior insurance with another insurer, unless certain requirements are present. In these situations, consent has to be obtained. The Canadian position is that where there is another policy which has been taken out but not effective, and where there was a requirement in the policy to notify of subsequent insurance, as the risk never attached, the subsequent insurance without consent had not been breached.

The position would be different where there were two policies and the latter policy gave notice and the other did not.[105] According to *Home Insurance Co of New York v Gavel*[106] the second policy would be "abortive". It would be unnecessary to consider the issue of whether there was double insurance. Therefore, the subsequent insurance policy must be effective. It would not be sufficient to void the first insurance policy on the basis that the previous insurer had not been notified.

4.16 The correct approach

The wording in s45 Insurance Contracts Act 1984 would cover situations where notification is required, as the phrase "by reason that the assured has entered into some other insurance" is used. It has been suggested that a notification clause

---

103 *Federation Insurance Ltd v Wason* (1987) 163 CLR 303; *Goldman v Southern Union General Insurance Co of A'asia Ltd* [1930] SASR 275; *Hordern v Commercial Union Assurance Co* (1884) 5 LR (NSW) 309 and *National Protector Fire Insurance Co Ltd v Nivert* [1913] AC 507.
104 *Equitable Fire & Accident Office Ltd v The Ching Wo Hong* [1907] AC 961 (PC).
105 *Sutton on Insurance Law* (4th edn 2014), para. 19.115.
106 (1928) 30 Ll LR 9.

would not "survive" due to s45(1) and would not be assisted by s45(2), unless specific reference to them is made in the first-mentioned contract.[107] The wording of the legislation, however, indicates that such clauses would make the clause in the contract completely void. It can be argued that this approach is drastic and a less drastic approach should be adopted.

4.17 Proposed legislative provision

A more balanced approach should be adopted. A suggested legislative provision can be drafted as follows:

> (1) Where a provision included in a contract of general insurance has the effect of limiting or excluding the liability of the insurer under the contract by reason that the assured has entered into some other contract of insurance, not being a contract required to be effected by or under a law, including a law of a State or Territory,[108] all benefit under the policy shall be forfeited, unless the insurer's assent is provided for in the policy for any previous insurance or is endorsed therein by the insurer; and
> (2) where the subsequent policy is an effective policy at the time the previous policy is entered into.

The above proposed legislation would see the courts adopting a wider interpretation of the words "all benefit under this policy shall be forfeited" as indicated by the court in *Steadfast Insurance Co Ltd v F & B Trading Co Pty*. Menzie J was of the view that although, literally speaking, they related to forfeiture of existing benefits, to prevent any risk from attaching, the company could not be held liable for the loss upon the happening of the risk. The courts could conclude that such forfeiture would apply to any loss whether present or future.

Failure to give notice under the second policy, by either stating or indorsing the particulars in or on the policy,[109] subject to the question waiver, resulted in the second insurer being not liable to pay out under the policy, due to the condition on which its liability attached not being fulfilled. This is what happened in *Deaves v CML Fire & General Insurance Co*[110] where Gibbs J moved away from the decision in *Steadfast*, and allowed the second insurer to rely on the forfeiture provision. In *Deaves* the assured had a fire insurance policy with the Queensland State Government Insurance Office. They then attempted to cancel the policy. Subsequently they arranged for further insurance with the respondents. CML did not notify the respondent's representatives. Further there was no endorsement made on any policy of the presence of other insurance.

---

107 *Sutton on Insurance Law* (4th edn 2014), 19.100.
108 Depending on whether such states or territories exist.
109 The CML Policy.
110 [1979] HCA 12. The court interestingly rejected the Canadian cases which had similar provisions which resulted in the assured being able to recover stating that they represented a substantial departure from accepted canons of constructions. This was due to the uncertainties caused if such an interpretation was adopted. See *Manitoba Assurance Co v Whitlam* (1903) 34 SCR (Can) 191, *Australian Agricultural Co v Saunders* (1875) LR 10 CP 668.

The majority[111] decision of the High Court agreed that there was a breach of the requirement under the policy that written notification be given. He accepted the appellant's argument that the fact that a cover note only was issued raised an additional question of whether the cover note itself was to be covered under the requirement of condition 3, or at least to that part of the condition which required written notice to be given. Further once the question was answered in the affirmative the fact that the second contract was in the form of a cover note was immaterial.[112] He went on to state that *Steadfast's* decision was authority for the proposition that unless the Queensland State Government Insurance Office's insurance had been cancelled, the failure to give notice in writing of that insurance to the respondents, and to state or endorse the particulars in or on the CML policy, entitled the consequence, subject to any question of waiver, that CML was not liable under its policy.[113] This would mean that no insurance had been subsequently effected. This was the distinguishing feature from *Steadfast's* case.[114]

4.18 Effects of s76 Insurance Contracts Act 1984

If the insurer knows that the assured has not disclosed certain information which is within his knowledge, the insurer cannot take advantage of it.[115] The problem that arises, is that an assured may not himself be aware of the existence of other insurance.[116] The cases[117] have clearly established that an assured is only required to notify of the existence of other insurance if he is aware of it. If the policy has been renewed without him knowing, or if it was not reasonable for him to be aware that it has been renewed, there is no breach for the failure to notify.

Section 45(1) will apply to "other insurance" clauses which has the effect of making such clauses void. If the insurer seeks to exclude the application of such provision, he must ensure that it has been "specifically" referred to in the policy. If legislation such as s45 were to be passed in English law, the original purpose for which "other insurance" clauses were adopted, which was to detect fraud and allow for contribution amongst insurers,[118] can still be achieved.

The ALRC suggested that with the implementation of s45, the assured will be protected as he will be paid immediately.[119] Once a claim has been made against

---

111 Gibbs ACJ, Stephen and Mason JJ (with Jacobs and Murphy JJ dissenting).
112 23 ALR at p. 551.
113 23 ALR at p. 551.
114 This view was followed by the Supreme Court of Victoria in *GRE Insurance Ltd v QBE Insurance Ltd* [1985] Vic Rp 9 by Anderson J.
115 *Australian Agriculture Co v Saunders* (1875) LR 10 CP 886.
116 For example, an assured may take out travel insurance himself for a trip he is about to go on. Without his knowledge, his employer may then take out insurance for him. The assured when he opens a bank account may have the benefit of an insurance policy being taken out on his behalf under some promotion the bank provides. Here you have a situation where the assured would not be in a position to notify his insurers of the existence of the other policies.
117 *Western Australian Bank v Royal Insurance Co* (1908) 5 CLR 533.
118 *Davjoyda Estates Pty v National Insurance Co of NZ Ltd* (1965) 69 SR (NSW) 381.
119 Section 76(1) Insurance Contracts Act 1984.

one insurer, the insurer will then have to go on to seek contribution from the other insurers.

Under s76 of the Insurance Contracts Act 1984[120] the insurer will have to indemnify the assured fully but only up to the extent of the loss he has suffered.[121] The provision does not permit an assured receiving an indemnity above that which he is entitled to under the policy.[122] This is the position at common law.[123] If it is later realised that the assured received an amount which is more than he is actually entitled to under the policy, he shall be treated as holding the sum that he has received in excess on trust for the insurers.[124] Section 76(1) will only apply in cases of double insurance, where the loss arises out of the same risk, covering the same interest and on the same subject matter.[125] The liability has to be actual and not potential.[126]

4.19 Section 45 and its impact on excess clauses, exclusion clauses and rateable proportion clauses and when the clauses work in combination

4.19.1 Recommendations of the ALRC

The Australian Law Reform Commission, Report on Insurance Contracts, Report No 20 (1982) put forward its recommendations under the heading "Conclusion," at para. 289. The Commission was concerned with the effect of "other insurance" clauses on the "interests of the assured". The Commission focused on how the clause working individually and/or in combination affected the assured. The law as it stood at the time was considered as lacking in protection for the assured. The Commission was of the view that the methods used by the insurers to limit their liability, by using the clauses either standing alone or in combination to do so, created uncertainty and compromised the assureds'[127] position.

---

120 (1) When two or more insurers are liable under separate contracts of general insurance to the same assured in respect of the same loss, the assured is, subject to subsection (2) entitled immediately to recover from any one or more of those insurers such amount as will, or such amounts as will in the aggregate, indemnify the assured fully in respect of the loss; (2) nothing in subsection (1) entitles an assured: (a) to recover from an insurer an amount that exceeds the sum assured under the contract between the assured and that insurer; and (b) to recover an amount that exceeds, or amounts that in the aggregate exceed, the amount of the loss; (3) Nothing in this section prejudices the right of an insurer or insurers from whom the assured recovers an amount or amounts in accordance with this section to contribution from any other insurer liable in respect of the same loss.

121 Section 76(1) Insurance Contracts Act 1984.
122 Section 76(2) Insurance Contracts Act 1984.
123 Also see s38(2)(a) Marine Insurance Act 1909.
124 Section 38(2)(d) Marine Insurance Act 1909 which provides that: "Where the assured receives any sum in excess of the indemnity allowed by this Act, he is deemed to hold such sum in trust for the insurers, according to their rights of contribution amongst themselves."
125 *Sutton on Insurance Law* (4th edn 2014), para. 19.80.
126 *Ibid.*
127 Australian Law Reform Commission, *Report on Insurance Contracts*, Report No 20 (1982) para. 289.

The suggested draft legislation proposed by the Commission was adopted in whole without changes or discussion, although the original section was under s46. There is no suggestion in the recommendation as to what the wording of the proposal form should be.

The Commission considered the effect of the clauses used in double insurance by insurers to limit liability. The original use of such clauses was to prevent fraud by an assured by taking out numerous policies. The use of such clauses to prevent such fraud has not been successful.[128] If fraud is detected, an insurer can refuse to pay out under the policy. The Commission went on to say that, at most, the effect of all the clauses were to act as a disincentive.[129] The Commission was of the view that a possible solution which would achieve the same result was to ask appropriate questions in the proposal form or claim forms. A request in the proposal form for details of other insurance would allow the insurer to see if there was any over-insurance. This would then give the insurer a chance to decide whether they wanted to accept the policy or not.[130]

It is doubtful whether adding such wording in the proposal form would solve the problems that arise with double insurance. The main problem which still remains is that an assured himself may be unaware of the presence of "other insurance". Further, the failure to notify under policy could lead to different results depending on the type of policy which has been taken out and the wording used in the policy, for example whether it is a bare condition or a condition precedent. In such situations an insurer can still rely on the wording of the policy to exclude or limit liability.

The Commission stated in its report that there was no substantial justification[131] for the inclusion in the policy of such "other insurance" clauses. Although the wording in the report stated that there is no "substantial" justification,[132] one has to consider whether justification would have to be substantial or if, as long as there was some justification, it would be sufficient for such clauses to be included in the insurance policy. The Commission further stated that the "reasonable expectation"[133] of the assured would be defeated in such cases.

4.20 True excess liability in a policy

4.20.1 Limits on recommendations

Under the heading "Limits on Recommendations", the Commission stated[134] that the recommendations would have no effect on layered policies in co-insurance

---

128 *Ibid.*
129 *Ibid.*
130 *Ibid.*
131 *Ibid.*
132 *Ibid.*
133 *Ibid*, para. 53.
134 *Ibid*, para. 290.

LEGISLATIVE REFORM OF DOUBLE INSURANCE

where each policy is for a discrete range of the total risk and where no overlap occurred. There is no double insurance in such cases.

4.20.2 Exemptions: true excess clause

The following exemptions were discussed:

> First, it should be made clear that the issue of a true excess liability policy to cover the assured's liability over and above that covered by another insurance which is specifically identified in the excess policy is not effected. Secondly, insurers should be able to restrict the scope of the cover afforded by a policy in order to excluded liability which is also covered by an insurance (whether or not then in existence) which is made compulsory by statute such as workers compensation insurance or motor vehicle third party insurance.[135]

Although the first exception was considered, the wording was not specifically included in the legislation under s45.[136] Therefore if legislation were to be devised for the United Kingdom which is based on the Australian model, the wording of the first exception could be included. The new legislation could be worded as follows:

> (1) Where a provision included in a contract of general insurance has the effect of limiting or excluding the liability of the insurer under the contract by reason that the assured has entered into some other contract of insurance, not being a contract required to be effected by or under a law, the provision is void,[137] unless it is a true excess liability policy.

4.20.2.1 National Employers' Mutual General Insurance Association Ltd v Haydon

The position is not clear regarding claims made liability policies.[138] The decision in *National Employers' Mutual General Insurance Association Ltd v Haydon*[139] considered a "true excess" clause. Lloyd J stated that there were many different kinds of exclusion clauses, and there was "no sensible distinction" between the two exclusion clauses. It did not matter how wide the wording of the policies was drafted. In that case the Master Policy clause was drafted in a much narrower

---

135 *Ibid*.
136 This would seem to give priority to excess clauses, although the wording used by the Commission was "true excess clause", which suggests that priority should be given to excess clauses. This will still cause problems however when you have a situation where there are a combination of the clauses, such as a combination of excess clauses or a combination of all the other type of clauses. The Commission did not consider or deal with the situation where there were rateable proportion clauses or escape clauses, in the way they dealt with situations under true excess clauses.
137 Deleting the words "including a law of state or Territory".
138 A claims made policy is where the insurer is liable to meet all claims made against the assured during the currency of the policy, although the policy also permitted the assured to notify circumstances likely to give rise to a claim within the policy period and thereby bring those within the scope of the cover: see *Colinvaux*, para. 21–007.
139 [1980] 2 Lloyd's Rep 149.

way than the NEM Policy clause, even though both were exclusion clauses. He was of the view that, as long as the clause limited cover, it should, and would, be treated as an exclusion clause, even though by looking at the wording in the policy, it could not be treated as such in a "strict sense". He preferred to look at the substance rather than the form of the clauses. He interpreted the wording of the NEM Policy by using the natural construction of the language in the clause.

The Court of Appeal reversed the decision of Lloyd J. Stephenson J stated[140] that the principles in *Weddell v Road Transport and General Insurance Co Ltd*[141] applied. He disagreed that there was double insurance on the facts of the case, but went on to say that if those two were indistinguishable in their effect as was stated by Lloyd J, the court should invoke the equitable principle of contribution between co-insurers.[142] This would avoid the absurdity and injustice of holding that a person who has paid premiums for cover by two insurers should be left without insurance cover because each insurer has excluded liability for the risk against which the other has indemnified him.[143] He correctly went on to state[144] that it did not matter whether the clauses were rightly labelled exceptions or exclusions. What had to be considered was what in each case was covered by the policies when read as a whole, which included the wording of the clauses.[145] Bridge LJ agreed that the principles of *Weddell* should apply as this produces the only just and sensible result.[146] He went on to agree with Rowlatt J's observation that an absurd result would occur if one was allowed to say that in such circumstances that whichever policy one looked at it is always the other which is effective. To adopt such an approach would permit insurers to use this method to escape liability and the assured would be left without cover.[147] It did not depend on any general principle of law, but upon the true construction of the policies applied to the relevant circumstances.[148]

The analysis and interpretation of clause 5(b)(iii) of the Master Policy, by the Court of Appeal, was that the clause did not try to

> exclude liability consequently on the risk excluded being covered by another policy but on its face excluded liability absolutely for claims arising from past occurrences which had been notified under any other assurances and there was no reason why the exclusion of the claim covered by the clause should not be effective.[149]

He then went on to deal with the issue of contribution and concluded that the policies should be looked at independently, which resulted in the clauses cancelling

---

140 [1980] 2 Lloyd's Rep 149, 152.
141 (1931) 41 Ll L Rep 69.
142 [1980] 2 Lloyd's Rep 149, 152.
143 [1980] 2 Lloyd's Rep 149, 152.
144 [1980] 2 Lloyd's Rep 149, 153.
145 [1980] 2 Lloyd's Rep 149, 153.
146 [1980] 2 Lloyd's Rep 149, 154.
147 [1980] 2 Lloyd's Rep 149, 154.
148 [1980] 2 Lloyd's Rep 149, 154. This may be correct, but some general principles of law could provide guidance.
149 [1980] 2 Lloyd's Rep 149, 153, 155 and 156.

out each other, and each insurer would be liable to pay out for the loss suffered. Therefore, contribution should be permitted.

Section 45 Insurance Contracts Act 1984 clearly states that provisions that have the effect of "limiting or excluding the liability" of the insurer clearly refers to the clauses in the insurance which have been used by the insurers to either prevent the assured from recovering completely or permitting recovery by the assured but the amount which can be recovered would be limited.

4.20.2.2 *Zurich Australian Insurance Ltd v Metals & Minerals Insurance Pte Ltd*

The discussion and analysis of the Supreme Court of Western Australia[150] provides assistance on how to analyse s45. The Supreme Court of Western Australia dealt in some detail with the wording and effect of s45 in *Zurich Australian Insurance Ltd v Metals & Minerals Insurance Pte Ltd*.[151] Zurich brought proceedings to claim contribution from Metals & Minerals Insurance Pte Ltd (MMI) on a rateable proportion for monies paid out by Zurich, as MMI was liable to indemnify Hamersley for liability owed to Nolan and Oatway[152] (employees of Speno who entered into an agreement with Hamersley) under Hamersley's policy. The liability owed by MMI was the same as the liability under the Zurich Policy. Zurich had indemnified Hamersley. Hamersley was therefore doubly assured. Zurich could claim contribution which was to be calculated on either a maximum liability method or the independent actual liability method basis.

MMI denied liability arguing that, given the "special clause" in the Hamersley Policy, which provided that where Hamersley was indemnified under insurance coverage which was effected on Hamersley's behalf by the third party, the Hamersley Policy would then be treated as excess insurance over the applicable limit of indemnity of the underlying insurance policy. Further it argued that Hamersley was not doubly assured and, as a result, Zurich was not entitled to contribution. Zurich relied on s45 to argue that, the "special clause" relied on was void. MMI refused to make contribution and argued that due to the Hamersley Policy and its wording, the Hamersley Policy only acted as an excess policy over the limit of indemnity under the Speno policy. There was no co-ordinate liability as originally argued.

Zurich relied on the established principles in *Albion Insurance Co Ltd v Government Office of NSW*[153] that an assured who insures his interests with two insurers is only entitled to receive the amount of his loss. Once it could be established that the independent insurers were liable, the doctrine of contribution would then arise. The majority in *Albion Insurance Co Ltd* stated: "It seems to us that it is not the principle but the application of the principle which has given rise

---

150 209 FLR 247.
151 (2009) 240 CLR.
152 See *Speno Rail Maintenance Australia Pty Ltd* per Malcom CJ (at 306), per Ipp J (at 309) and per Wheeler J (at 324).
153 [1969] HCA 55.

to the problems that now falls for decision." The Supreme Court agreed with MMI's argument that if there was no obligation for MMI and Zurich to indemnify Hamersley, there can be no entitlement to contribution.[154] MMI requested the court to take into consideration the effect of the underlying insurance clause. The "underlying clause" provided that if the assured was indemnified under such other insurance effected by or on behalf of the assured, which was not an insurance specifically effected as insurance excess of this policy, where indemnity is available for a claim, such other insurance, which is referred to as the underlying cause, would then be treated as excess insurance over the applicable limit of indemnity of the underlying insurance, and would be subject to the terms and conditions of the policy. This in effect meant that the Hamersley Policy operated as an excess policy over the limit of indemnity which had been provided under the Speno Policy. Hamersley's Policy would only be called upon until the limit of Zurich's liability of $2 million had been reached. This situation would not arise here because the amount that would have to be indemnified would only be below $2 million. Therefore, MMI did not have to pay contribution.

The Supreme Court went on to consider the decision in *Australian Eagle Insurance Ltd v Mutual Acceptance (Insurance) Pty Ltd*.[155] The policy contained a heading called "general exclusion",[156] which contained similar wording to the Hamersley Policy. In *Australian Eagle Insurance Ltd*, the decision in *State Fire Insurance General Manager v Liverpool and London and Globe Insurance Co Ltd*[157] was considered. Hutchinson and Cooke JJ considered what would fall within the definition of "excess" clause, and looked at the clause according to its terms, rather than how it was described, because of the difficulty in reconciling the principles of double insurance where there were such "excess" clauses. The correct approach would therefore be that an excess policy would only be called upon once the assured's own insurer paid out first for the loss that had been suffered by the assured. Only then would the "excess" clause fall under an "obligation" to indemnify.

The court viewed the principles as laid down in the New Zealand decision more favourably than the English authorities. The lack of consistency with the wording was noted in *Zurich* where the case of *Re Calf & Sun Insurance Office*[158] was discussed and where Johnson J noted that the relevant wording of the underlying insurance clause in the Hamersley Policy, even though not exactly the same, was "sufficiently similar" to the wording of the "excess" clause in *State Fire Insurance General Manager*. To do so would allow the court to reach the same conclusion as to "its effects". She went on to state that the natural meaning of the wording of the underlying insurance clause in the Hamersley Policy would have the same effect.

---

154 Paragraph [27].
155 (1983) 3 NSWLR 59.
156 Unlike "Underlying Insurance".
157 [1952] NZLR 5.
158 [1920] 2 KB 366.

According to Johnson J, in determining whether the Hamersley policy was a "true excess" liability policy, would depend on whether the underlying insurance clause offends s45(1) and, if so, whether it would fall within the saving provision under s45(2). MMI argued that the Hamersley Policy was not a true excess of loss policy because of the general wording used, which lacked definition, and failed to avoid the mischief that was provided for under s45. The court disagreed with the suggestion by Zurich that the meaning and purpose of s45 was plain.

The words "the assured has entered into some other contract of insurance" raised considerations as to the way in which an assured can be covered by another insurance contract and whether it could be said that in all cases the assured "entered into" the other contract of insurance.[159] The court reviewed the history behind the legislation and was of the view that the doctrine of contribution developed to prohibit an assured from obtaining or retaining a double benefit. She went on to say that the solution to the problem of double insurance was to rely on "excess" clauses,[160] and also acknowledged that in some situations the assured may not be aware of the existence of double insurance. However, there were, in her view, less potentially onerous methods of overcoming the risk of double insurance arising.

The Australian Law Reform Commission (ALRC) considered whether the clause as drafted achieved the aim as envisaged by the ALRC and whether the clause was capable of being construed as creating a prohibition on all "other insurance" provisions.[161] The case of *Austress-PSC Pty and Carlingford Australia General Insurance Ltd*,[162] which dealt with s45 was considered in some detail – in particular, the underlying insurance clauses, and situations with multiple parties. In *Austress-PSC*, Robin DCJ was of the view[163] that s45(2) did not apply on the facts of the case. Section 45(2) must be construed as requiring the reference to "other insurance" to be specific, as opposed to a description of general words which were capable of extending to the other insurance. This would ensure that the clause is not struck down by s45(1). Here the second plaintiff entered into a CIC policy where it would indemnify AW Edwards Pty Ltd (AW) and its subsidiaries. This included the first plaintiff, Austress, who was a contractor and who entered into an agreement to supply and install rock anchors with Remm Pty Ltd, regarding the construction of the Myer Centre. The defendant (Zurich) had also issued a policy of insurance for the construction of the Myer Centre (Zurich Policy). Under a sub-contract, Austress became legally obligated to indemnify Remm and legally liable to the council for damage and the cost of rectification works. The first plaintiff made payment to Remm and the council. No contribution was made by Zurich which covered Remm only and which only covered liability for an amount in excess of $100,000. There was an excess clause in the

---

159 Paragraph [38].
160 Paragraph [40].
161 Paragraph [50].
162 DCT of Qld; 1 May 1992 per Robin DCJ.
163 Paragraph [6].

CIC policy.[164] Zurich claimed that s45(1) applied and the clause was void. Robin DCJ concluded that s45 applied[165] and limited liability by the words "indemnity or insurance . . . effected by or on behalf of the Assured". Further,[166] reference to "other insurance" must be specific and not a description in general words. He disagreed with the suggestion that an assured who benefits under the policy, but not named in the policy, would have "entered into some other contract of insurance". He referred to *Stretch v State Insurance General Manager*[167] and commented that it would be simple for the draftsman to have included the words "by whomsoever effected" if that was the intention. These words were not included in the legislation and should not be read into the legislation.[168] Instead, an extended meaning should be applied to include agreements to extend or vary the contract in the case of life insurance contracts and to extend the meaning of any other contract of insurance to making an agreement to renew, extend or vary the contract. Further, reinstatement of any previous contract of insurance should be included as well.[169]

Johnson J agreed with Zurich's argument[170] and stated:

> Zurich maintains that, when you look at the ALRC Report and consider what is sought to be achieved by prohibiting underlying insurance clauses, nothing could be plainer than that all of these kinds of provisions were to be avoided, including those that created an excess policy where the assured benefited from a policy taken out or entered into by another. I accept that to be the case, particularly because an assured may be unaware of such a policy. Zurich emphasised that the Court is entitled to have regard to what the ALRC says because of s15AA of the Acts Interpretation Act 1901 (Cth).[171]

Zurich further argued that one should also look at the wide-ranging changes to the law of insurance in sections which can be found in the legislation: such as s21 on non-disclosure; s13 by implying a term into contracts of insurance whereas previously it had operated as a principle of law; s76 with respect to contribution between insurers; and s48 third party beneficiary right to recover.[172]

Johnson J stated that the following clause and wording would be an example of the level of specification needed to fall within the exception of s45(2):

> "Insuring Agreement A – Combined Public and Products Liability," in particular to the "Exclusions" which include the following paragraph:

---

164 Providing that Carlingford would not be liable in respect of the occurrence except for any excess beyond the amount payable under another policy of indemnity or insurance "in favour of or effected by or on behalf of the Assured applicable to the occurrence".
165 Paragraph [5].
166 Paragraph [6].
167 (1984) 3 ANZIC 60–577 at 78, 467–6B.
168 Interestingly Johnson J did not agree with the analysis that s11(9) when applied to the words "the entering into of a contract of insurance" was limited to those entered into by the parties to that contract.
169 Paragraph [58].
170 Paragraph [68].
171 Paragraph [68].
172 Paragraph [75].

> Notwithstanding this Exclusion (1) this Insuring Agreement (A) shall indemnify the Assured in accordance with the terms, conditions and endorsements of the Overseas Employers' Liability Insurance issued by American Home Assurance Company Policy Number MG69898 Limit of Indemnity A$5,000,000 (the Underlying Insurance) with which this Policy shall run concurrently;
> PROVIDED THAT
> Underwriters shall be liable only for sums in excess of the Limit of Indemnity provided by the Underlying Insurance.[173]

Johnson J did not accept that an underlying insurance clause, which did not specify the other insurance to the degree as shown above, would not fall within s45(2), and therefore allowed for some flexibility on the part of the insurer.[174]

Zurich referred to *HIH Casualty & General Insurance Ltd v Pluim Construction Pty Ltd*[175] where, although the wording of the policy was different in form, it was suggested that the court could consider the intention behind the clause. The issue was whether it would be sufficient if there was similar intention in such cases for the same principles to apply. This becomes significant in cases where there are numerous and varied sub-contractors who are required to arrange public liability insurance to include the principal's interest and indemnify the principal against personal injury claims made by the sub-contractor's employees.[176]

In *HIH Casualty & General Insurance Ltd* the effect of s45(1) was to void condition 7 as it was too general and not sufficient enough to fall within s45(2). Mason P commented that there was no substantial justification for such "other insurance" clauses, on the basis that all of these types of clauses would have the effect of, as the ALRC stated, defeating the reasonable expectations of the assured. Further, all such clauses should be rendered ineffective.[177] Zurich argued that there was no difference "in substance" between the clauses that MMI relied on and the HIH policy. Emphasis was placed on "futurity, contingency and lack of specificity", and it was argued that the Hamersley Policy did not have specificity or identification "sufficient" to avoid the mischief that Parliament had intended.

MMI argued that the wording, "by reason that the assured has entered into some other contract of insurance" in s45, had the effect of limiting or excluding the liability of the insurer. This was based on (1) the express wording used in s45(1); (2) the distinction between a party to an insurance contract and a person who benefits from a contract;[178] (3) the distinction of the provision in s48 of the Insurance Contracts

---

173 Paragraph [78].
174 Paragraph [80].
175 [2000] 11 ANZ Insurance Cases 61–477.
176 Condition 7 of HIH's policy was headed "PRINCIPAL-ARRANGED INSURANCE" and was in the following terms (at [30]):

> In the event of the named Assured entering into an agreement with any other party (who for the purpose of this clause is called "the Principal" pursuant to which the Principal has agreed to provide a policy of insurance which is intended to indemnify the named Assured for any liability arising out of the performance of the Works then the Company(ies) will (subject to the terms and conditions of this Policy) only indemnify the names Assured for such liability not covered by the policy of insurance provided by the Principal.

177 Paragraphs [35]–[36].
178 Relying on *Trident General Insurance Co Ltd v McNiece Bros Pty Ltd* (1988) 165 CLR 107.

Act;[179] and (4) the rational of the ALRC recommendations.[180] MMI further argued that s45 only applied to certain contracts. The wording of s45 covered general insurance. The term "liability" was a "key" word. There were two ways of looking at the word "liability": (1) it meant a potential or contingent liability, on the first issuing of the insurance contract by the insurer; and (2) it refers to "actual liability", which is incurred when the event which has been assured against occurs, and the insurer then is called upon to satisfy that obligation to indemnify.[181] MMI argued that Professor Sutton's view that one looked at the potential liability as opposed to the actual liability should not be followed. Reliance was placed first on the structure of the provision, which used "limiting or excluding the liability of the insurer under the contract by reason that the assured has entered into some other contract of insurance". Second, the use of "has entered into" and not "or may enter into" in the past tense was used as justification for this. Third, the words that were used were "has the effect of limiting or excluding" and not the use of "limit or excludes" suggested that one looked at the effect of the provision in the circumstances which have accrued. Fourth, the use of the words "by reason that" are words of causation, which means that they are questions of fact to be dealt with in retrospect.

The judge commented that a more natural meaning of the words should be adopted because, when it came to legislative drafting, there could be different ways of saying the same thing.[182] The judge applied a more technical approach in reaching her conclusion. This was as a result of MMI arguing that the underlying insurance clause could be read in a distributive sense, by looking at a clause which related to contracts entered into by the assured and a clause relating to contracts which have been entered into on behalf of the assured. MMI argued that the clause was drafted in an economic expression, where both situations should and could be read into the Insurance Contracts Act.[183]

The judge stated that, read in this way, the provision was void in so far as it concerned contracts effected by the assured, not in so far as it concerned contracts entered into on behalf of the assured.[184] However, she agreed that the clause could be read distributively. The Hamersley Policy operated as an excess policy in two situations: (1) where Hamersley had effected or entered into another insurance policy covering the same risk and (2) where another insurance policy covering the same area of risk had been effected by Hamersley. Section 45(2) should be interpreted to give the words of the section their natural meaning where an assured has either entered into another contract of insurance covering the same risk or where the assured has the benefit of third-party insurance which covers

---

179 Relying on *CE Health Casualty & General Insurance Ltd v Grey* (1993) 32 NSWLR 25 at 43–46; *GIO Australia Ltd v P Ward Civil Engineering Pty Ltd* (2000) NSWSC 371 at [11]; s11(9) and s56 of the IC Act.
180 Paragraph 92.
181 This is assumed on payment of the premium and once the contract has been entered into.
182 Paragraph [103]. Although it could be said that the main intent of the legislature should and must not be overlooked.
183 Paragraph [136].
184 This approach however is difficult to understand due to the precise wording of the legislation.

the same risk. These situations clearly have the effect of limiting or excluding the liability of the insurer under the policy due to its effect of converting a policy which indemnifies the assured for the whole of the loss to a policy which insures for any excess over the applicable limit of indemnity of the underlying insurance policy. Such policies would be void if they were entered into by the assured.[185]

The Judge having correctly identified the effect, approach and intent of the Act and legislation,[186] went on to explain:

> 142. Nevertheless, in my view, the only way in which to achieve that result is to give to the expression "the assured has entered into" and the words of which it is comprised, a meaning they simply do not have; that is, I believe I can achieve that interpretation only by manipulating the English language to confer a meaning that is inconsistent with the natural and proper meaning. The Concise Oxford Dictionary definition of "enter into" is to "engage in (conversation, agreement, inquiry etc.); to bind oneself by (recognizances, treaty, contract)." When one considers the words "enter into" in the phrase "the assured has entered into," it is evident that it involves the assured himself carrying out the activity and, in the relevant context, being the party to the insurance policy. I do not accept that the particular words employed are consistent with the arrangement involved in the Speno Policy, notwithstanding the status of Hamersley under that agreement as an assured. Further, I am not persuaded that it is appropriate to adopt any of the "devices" suggested by either party to achieve the particular result. Therefore, I accept the construction determined by Robin DCJ in Austress-PSC Pty Ltd and Carlingford Australia General Insurance Ltd (supra) although for different reasons.
>
> 143. The final issue with respect to subsection (1) is whether, as MMI submits, the underlying insurance clause can be read in a distributive sense with the result that so much of the clause which does not offend s45(1) remains valid. For the reasons to which I have already referred, while I accept that the underlying insurance clause does address two different circumstances, it is the case that, as Robin DCJ noted, the clear words of s45(1) is that it is the provision which is void; the provision being the underlying insurance clause in the Hamersley Policy. As I have already noted, I accept that this is a technical result which arises simply because of economical drafting. However, it remains the case, as I have noted, that the available material indicates that it was the ALRC's recommendation, which to all intents and purposes appears to have been accepted by the legislature (although it does not appear to have been successfully translated into legislation) that all types of "other insurance" clauses should be prohibited. On that basis, although the result is technical, it is not necessarily inconsistent with the intention behind the implementation of s54.
>
> 144. Essentially, I believe that s45(1) requires amendment to achieve the purpose which I accept was intended by the legislature acting on the recommendation of the ALRC.

4.21 Discussion

If the legislature had intended to provide for such a broad definition by including "by whomsoever effected" and to widen the definition as suggested by Johnson J,[187] the legislature would have expressly done so. The wording in the legislation is

---

185 Paragraphs [139], [140] and [141].
186 Paragraph [141].
187 Paragraph [58].

specific to "the contract by reason that the assured has entered into some other contract of insurance". "Assured" must be read as referring to the assured under the policy. Johnson J's approach of a much wider interpretation would give much greater protection to the assured. Otherwise an assured would be unable to recover anything under the policy or would only be permitted to recover a limited amount from the insurer when a claim is made.

It can be argued that it is doubtful whether Johnson J is correct in saying that when a policy is arranged by a third party, that authorisation by the assured of the other insurance policy was a pre-requisite for there to be double insurance. One of the problems of double insurance, which the legislation attempted to prevent, was a situation where a third party may have entered into an insurance contract with an insurer without the assured's knowledge on his behalf. An assured would be left without protection if it was permissible to argue that where there was no authorisation, there was no double insurance. It is questionable whether this was the intention of the legislature. It is highly unlikely that the legislature had intended the legislation to be read in such a complicated fashion. The approach taken by Johnson J was that defining liability in such a way would assist in the proper construction of the provision. She went on to say that if the validity of the provision was under consideration when a claim was made on the policy or the claim was the subject of litigation, the words "or may enter into" would not be needed. This was because at the time of consideration of the provision, the "other contract of insurance" would have been entered into. The section would apply to "other contracts" entered into both before and after the contract with the "other insurance".[188] This approach can only be what the legislature had intended if it was to afford more protection to the assured. To distinguish between liability before and after would limit the scope of s45.

4.22 Severance of void parts in clauses

4.22.1 The Explanatory Memorandum (Insurance Contracts Bill 1984)

4.22.1.1 Types of policy provisions

The Explanatory Memorandum to the Insurance Contracts Bill 1984 lists five situations where double insurance could arise, namely (1) to increase an assured's cover; (2) the assured may not realise that the policies overlap; (3) the assured may forget to cancel the first policy; (4) the assured may be protecting himself from the first insurer's insolvency and (5) to make a profit by claiming twice for the same loss but under the different contracts of insurance. There are two main types of policy provisions which deal with "the insurance" which was stated as follows:[189] (1) those which impose on the assured an obligation to notify the insurer of existing or subsequent insurances affecting the same risk; and (2) where the policy does not place any obligation on the assured but excludes or qualifies the liability of the insurer in the event of other insurance. If the assured

---

188 Paragraph [102].
189 Paragraph [144] Explanatory Memorandum (Insurance Contracts Bill 1984).

fails to notify the insurer then the insurer may deny liability, in the event there is a loss which the assured suffers to the extent that the second insurance is inadequate to cover the loss.

4.22.1.2 Effect of the type of policy provision

The first type of policy stated above allows the insurer to exclude liability completely for a potential claim for losses flowing from a particular event. The second type of policy shifts the cover from one insurer to another insurer.

4.22.1.3 Categories of clauses

The clauses that are used fall into three main categories. The first category is where the provision purports to exclude liability altogether in the event of other insurance. The second category limits the insurer's liability to a rateable proportion of the loss. The assured then has to bring two actions, which may still result in the assured suffering an overall loss if the other insurance policy is insufficient or if the claim against the other insurer is defective. The third type covers provisions which limit the liability of the insurer to any amount by which the loss exceeds the amount recoverable from the insurer. This will then convert a policy into an excess policy without appropriate reduction in the premium.[190]

4.22.2 Should the void clause be severed?

The next issue which was discussed in *Zurich Australian Insurance Ltd v Metals & Minerals Insurance Pte Ltd* was whether there should be severance under s45(1) – that is, whether the whole clause should be found void or whether the specific part which is void should be severed. The court considered the term the "provision". The judge concluded in her analysis that "provision" fell within the meaning of the section and ruled that the whole clause was void. After concluding that the provision was void where the assured himself has entered into the "underlying insurance policy", the judge then went on to say that the only way to reach this conclusion was to give the phrase "the assured has entered into" a meaning it did not have. This analysis can be somewhat confusing, and would require reading into a phrase an intended meaning it did not have.

The ultimate result of the clauses, whether in isolation or in combination, will be to limit or exclude the indemnity which the assured is entitled to obtain after paying premiums. Therefore, the analysis adopted by Johnson J is unnecessary. The whole intent of the legislation is to prevent such clauses from taking effect. The legislation itself provided a saving provision of such clauses under s45(2). A clause in the policy will not be void only where there is a genuine or true excess clause. Further, the use of the words in s45(1) make specific reference to "not being a contract required to be effected by or under a law, including a law of a State or Territory" as situations where such limitations or exclusions would not

---

190 Mason P in *HIH Casualty & General Insurance Ltd* (1997) 9 ANZ Ins Cas 61–358 at para. 34 and ALRC para. 281.

be void. Paragraph 290 of the ALRC suggests that, in general, the whole clause will be void unless they fall within this exception. The ALRC stated:

> **Limits on Recommendation**
>
> 290. It should be emphasised that these recommendations would have no effect on layered policies in the field of co-insurance where each policy is for a discrete range of the total risk and where no overlap occurs. In addition, two exceptions should be made to the recommendation in the preceding paragraph. First, it should be made clear that the issue of a true excess liability policy to cover the assured's liability over and above that covered by another insurance which is specifically identified in the excess policy is not affected. Secondly, insurers should be able to restrict the scope of the cover afforded by a policy in order to exclude liability which is also covered by an insurance (whether or not then in existence) which is made compulsory by statute, such as workers compensation insurance or motor vehicle third-party insurance.

4.22.3 *Is there sufficient protection for the insurer?*

The Explanatory Memorandum considered the mechanisms used by insurers to protect themselves. These were listed in para. 289:

> 289. The Commission is concerned with the effect of "other insurance" clauses on the interests of the assured. Assureds are detrimentally affected by uncertainty over the effects of individual provisions and combinations of different provisions. More important is the fact that some "other insurance" clauses have the effect of limiting the insurer's liability to its assured. In such a case, the assured's protection may be compromised or lost. While they affect the interests of assureds in this manner, "other insurance" clauses have little independent value for insurers. To the extent that they are intended as a protection against fraud, they are ineffective. At most, such a clause might operate as a disincentive to claiming the same loss twice under different policies. The same effect could be achieved by a clear warning to the assured that he is entitled to claim, under the policy concerned and under any other insurance, no more than his actual loss. To the extent that "other insurance" clauses are designed to ensure that an insurer becomes aware of the existence of other insurance so that it may claim contribution in the event of a loss, the same aim could be achieved by asking appropriate questions in the proposal and claim forms. A request in the proposal form for details of other insurance would also give the insurer the opportunity of assessing any significant degree of over-insurance and deciding whether to accept the proposal. There is no substantial justification for any of the various types of "other insurance" clause. As they may cause the assured's reasonable expectations to be defeated, all forms of "other insurance" provisions should be rendered ineffective. If more than one insurance is in effect in respect of the same risk, the assured should be entitled to recover the whole of his loss from any one of the insurers, which should then be entitled to obtain contribution from the others.

4.23 Specified in the policy?

4.23.1 *Parties specifying terms in contracts*

The next issue the Court of Appeal dealt with in *Zurich Australian Insurance Ltd v Metals & Minerals Insurance Pty Ltd* was the way parties specify things in contracts, and whether the Zurich Policy was sufficiently specified so as to fall within s45(2). MMI argued that the parties can specify something in numerous ways.[191] MMI argued that s45(2) effectively allows the parties themselves to choose their own expression. The judge agreed with the whole range of ways in which parties in a given contract might choose to specify something.[192] However, in light of the legislative effect of the section, the judge considered that it was important to look at the term "specified", which would have to identify a specific contract of insurance or class of contract, rather than talk about terms as was the case in the Hamersley Policy, as it is too general, and it simply referred to "insurance coverage" which had been effected by the assured or other parties who are involved, though unspecified, in the projects.

4.23.2 Possible definition of "specified"

The court looked at the literature relied on to define what would come under "specified", but which was undefined in the legislation itself, under s45(2). Reliance was placed on *HIH Casualty & General Insurance Ltd* and the analysis of Mason P, where reference was made to the academic literature.[193]

When dealing with the issue of specificity as required under s45(2), the judge accepted that there were a whole range of ways in which parties in a given contract might choose to specify something. However, if one were to look at the purpose of the section and at the term "specified", it would identify a specific contract of insurance or class of contract rather than specify a contract in the sort of terms that are used in the underlying insurance clause in the Hamersley Policy, which was particularly general due to the use of the words "insurance coverage" effected by the assured or other parties involved in unspecified projects.[194]

The judge then concluded that one would not be able to specify a contract which had not yet come into existence, and as a result precise details could not be provided. She explained that one could go beyond just speaking in general terms of the clauses being considered. What is required is the need to specify the other policy in such a way that it is clearly understood which policy or which group of policies are being referred to and the purpose of the policy. This would have to be sufficiently clear so as to easily identify that the policy which is under consideration was indeed intended to be a true excess of liability under those particular circumstances.[195] She accepted the argument put forward by MMI that, although the form of class referred to in *HIH Casualty & General Insurance Ltd* was more precise, the decision could still be relied upon to suggest that specification by class would be sufficient. Further, that if a contract could not be clearly specified then the class of contract would be sufficient.[196]

---

191 209 FLR 247, at para. 147.
192 209 FLR 247, at para. 147.
193 Paragraphs 150–153.
194 Paragraph 147.
195 Paragraph 155.
196 Paragraph 156.

Dictionary[197] definitions were considered to define the words "specific",[198] "specify"[199] and "specified".[200] The argument put forward by MMI was that one should look at the natural meaning of the term "specify", and three methods were suggested where specification could be identified. These were: (1) specified by name, policy number, parties; (2) by class (according to that of HIH Casualty & General Insurance Ltd); and (3) specified by description. MMI argued that it was sufficient for one to accept that a contract maybe specified by class, which was sufficiently described in the Hamersley Policy, which satisfied the requirement under 45(2). Further, the underlying insurance policy was effected by that party for the benefit of the assured as an identified entity and not just as a member of an unascertained class, as reference was made to a particular principal, and not just any principal. Reference to "not being affected as insurance excess of this policy" narrowed the class. The judge accepted that this proposition would remove one type of "other insurance", but it did not particularly, or sufficiently, narrow the field.[201]

An argument which the judge thought was of considerable force was that of a situation where you were dealing with a small builder and where you were dealing with an entire worldwide organisation where there were subsidiaries. In the latter case it would be difficult to clearly identify the specific policy. It would be difficult to satisfy the requirement under s45(2), if it was a requirement that the name, number, insurer or something more specific was needed. This would be unduly onerous, if not impossible, due to the constant change of contractual arrangements. In this situation what would be required would be to specify the policy to the extent that it could be ascertained whether the policy with the underlying insurance clause was indeed intended to be an "excess" policy.[202]

MMI suggested that a more practical approach was needed and that certain factors should be taken into account. MMI argued that there should be various degrees of specification such as: (1) the number of "primary" assureds named in the policy; (2) the nature and size of the business conducted by those assureds; (3) the territorial application of the policy; (4) the extent to which the primary assureds may be expected to enter into arrangements which provide alternative insurance cover; and (5) the practical difficulties of identifying by name and policy number (i.e. the extent to which it is reasonable to specify a second policy by reference to class).[203] The judge conceded that it would be difficult to identify with any greater specificity than when compared to the class. In such a situation

---

197 *Macquarie Dictionary*.
198 (1) having a special application, bearing or reference; specifying, explicit or definite; (2) specified, precise or particular; (3) peculiar or proper to something, as qualities, characteristics, effects etc.; (4) of a specific or particular kind.
199 (1) to mention or name specifically; (2) to give a specific character to; (3) to name or state as a condition; and (4) to make a specific mention or statement.
200 MMI said that the word "specified" is capable of including "kind" as opposed to something more precise.
201 Paragraph [161].
202 Paragraph [162].
203 Paragraph [163].

it would be necessary to consider the specification to consider the acknowledgement in the underlying insurance clause, and concluded that the Hamersley Policy had insufficiently specified the other insurance contract for it to fall within the provisions of s45(2).[204] Although she agreed with the analysis of Mason P in *HIH Casualty & General Insurance Ltd* that such wording would be broad and as a result it would be inadequate, she did not elaborate further and said that what was required for it to be specified was that the policy must be referred to by name, policy number or insurer. To provide sufficient information concerning the class would be a necessary requirement so that one would be able to identify the policy within that class as providing primary cover, and the policy with the "excess" clause providing cover for loss over and above the limit of the other policy.[205]

She went on to say that the extensive and varied nature of Hamersley's interest was the main reason why there was a need for some greater level of specificity other than the fact that Hamersley entered into arrangements which included joint ventures, sub-contracts and other commercial arrangements for which it was "customary" for insurance coverage to be taken out by other parties. The judge was of the view that this added absolutely nothing about the nature of the insurance to be provided by MMI under the Hamersley Policy.[206]

Interestingly, the judge did not actually identify what she would consider to have been sufficient information for it to fall within the saving provision in s45(2), as she did not find it necessary to do so. She did not consider that it was particularly difficult to consider the various classes of contracts requiring the other party to obtain insurance to Hamersley's benefit, to specify the criteria in relation to each class of contract. She held that the clause was void and that MMI could not place reliance on s45.[207]

It is clear that although she does not agree with a wide reading of the section, it is not necessary either to identify a particular policy. She suggested a half way point, where it would be enough to provide sufficient information concerning the class to identify the policies within the class as providing the primary cover.

If her analysis is to be followed, this would still leave the assured and the insurer in an uncertain position, because it is unclear what would be considered to be "provide sufficient information". It will be difficult to characterise what particular information should be provided. The words "customary" in the underlying policy is extremely wide.

4.23.3 *The Appeal: Court of Appeal*

Speno appealed,[208] and MMI cross-appealed on the following issues (a) whether one had to look at the actual effect of the provision, as opposed to the proper

---

204 Paragraph [164].
205 Paragraph [165].
206 Paragraph [167].
207 Paragraph 169.
208 209 FLR 247.

construction of the provision; (b) the effect[209] of s45 was to make the whole underlying clause in the insurance policy void; (c) the Hamersley policy was drafted in a way which sufficiently specified the other insurance contract for s45(2) to apply.[210] The decision of the court[211] was given by Beech AJA. The matters not challenged[212] on appeal were (a) the Hamersley Policy was an excess policy[213] due to the underlying insurance clause; (b) s45(1) applied where an assured had entered into other insurance when it is a party to the other insurance policy,[214] and does not apply where a third party has taken out other insurance to which it is a beneficiary ; and (c) where Hamersley itself effected or entered into another insurance policy which both covered identical risks, the s45(1) provision would be engaged, and the provision would be held to be void.[215]

4.23.3.1 Whether s45 should be read as to actual effect or potential effect?
Speno and MMI on the other hand argued that a grammatical and textual context should be adopted to say that s45 should be read as to its "actual effect". This was rejected. Beech AJA was of the view that s45 should be read as to its "potential effect" and not its "actual effect". He stated:

> 86. ... If, and only if, the effect of that provision is to limit or exclude the insurer's liability on the ground that the assured has entered into some other contract of insurance, the provision will be void. In that regard, if an "other insurance" provision in the contract of general insurance has the effect that where, at the time that a claim arises, the assured has entered into another insurance contract, the section will be engaged. It does not matter whether that other insurance contract was entered into before or after the contract of general insurance. I agree with the trial judge's observations to this effect at [102].
> 87. The reference in s45 to a provision that "has the effect of limiting or excluding" rather than "limits or excludes" does not seem to me to support the actual effect construction of s45. As Zurich submits, the "effect" of a provision is an apt form of expressing what appears from the terms of the provision on its true construction. Moreover, the reference to a provision that "has the effect of . . ." is apt to capture notice provisions of the kind referred to in the ALRC Report [280], as well as capturing the second type of clause described in [281]. As I have said, I think that the ALRC Report reveals that both types of clause were intended to be rendered void by s45.
> 88. The causal connection inherent in the words "by reason" seems to me to be a neutral factor in the choice between the actual effect and potential effect approaches. Whichever approach is taken, the question will need to be determined whether the relevant provision has the effect of limiting or excluding "by reason that . . .". On the potential effect construction, that question is determined by reference to the effect of the clause on its proper construction. On the actual effect construction, it is determined by reference to the events that have happened.

---

209 Which is to either limit or exclude the liability of the insurer.
210 209 FLR 247 at [165], [168].
211 Martin CJ and McLure JA agreeing with Beech AJA.
212 209 FLR 247, at para. [61].
213 209 FLR 247 at [139].
214 209 FLR 247 at [142].
215 209 FLR 247 at [131], [136], [137] and [143].

89. On the potential effect approach, the validity of a provision in a contract of general insurance is determined by reference to the proper construction of the provision. Consequently, it is capable of being ascertained immediately. Moreover, the answer to the question of whether the provision is valid will not vary according to subsequent circumstances. By contrast, on the actual effect approach, the validity of the provision cannot be finally determined at any given point in time prior to when a particular claim is made. It is only when a claim is made that the assessment can finally be made, for the purposes of that claim, of whether the provision has the relevant effect. The latter seems to me to be a less desirable outcome, and one that is less likely to have been intended by the legislature.

4.23.3.2 Whether the Speno Policy was specified in the Hamersley Policy under s45(2)?

The court dealt with the argument advanced by Speno and MMI:

116 Speno and MMI submitted to the trial judge, and submit to this court, that the definition of the class of policy or policies in the first paragraph of the underlying insurance clause was sufficient to mean that that class or classes of policies had been "specified" for the purposes of s45(2), having regard to: (a) the many (22) assured under the Hamersley Policy; (b) the worldwide application of the policy; (c) the immense business interests operated by the individual assureds; (d) the specific acknowledgment that it was customary for the various assured, or for other parties on their behalf, to effect insurance coverage specific to a particular project, agreement or risk; and (e) the burden involved in listing each policy providing underlying insurance in relation to each project, agreement or risk, of each of the assured.

117 The trial judge did not accept that submission. In my opinion, her Honour was correct in so concluding, essentially for the reasons which her Honour gave.

118 Her Honour's reasons in relation to s45(2) may be summarised as follows: (a) in deciding whether a policy has been specified within the meaning of s45(2), account must be taken of the purpose of s45: [147], [165]; (b) a policy of insurance need not be individually identified by name, but may sufficiently be specified by class: [147], [156] and [165]; (c) to engage s45(2) it is necessary to specify the other policy or policies in such a way as to make it clearly understood which policy or group of policies are being referred to and to make the purpose of such policy or policies known. The specification must make it clear that the policy under consideration was intended to be a true excess of liability insurance contract in the circumstances: [155]; (d) as to MMI and Speno's submission that the number of primary assured in the policy, the nature and size of their businesses, the scope of territorial application and various other matters made it impracticable, if not impossible, to identify by name, number, insurer or some other more specific way those other insurance contracts, those matters are the very factors which require a greater level of specificity than what is set out in the underlying insurance clause in order for the relevant policy to be "specified" for the purpose of s45(2): [162], [164] and [167]; and (e) considering the purpose of s45(2), and bearing in mind that the requirement that the other insurance policy be specified is designed to ensure that the relevant clause is a "true excess" clause, the underlying insurance clause did not sufficiently specify the other insurance contract for it to be saved by s45(2): [165] and [169].

The court also noted the reference by the trial judge to the case of *HIH Casualty & General Insurance Ltd v Pluim Construction Pty Ltd*,[216] and was in agreement

---

216 [2000] NSWCA 281.

with the analysis of Mason P that the exception in s45(2) should be construed narrowly.[217] The ALRC Report was considered, where the Report concluded that the other insurance provision should not apply where the policy was a true excess liability policy, and the other insurance was specifically identified.[218]

Therefore, Beech AJA stated, "in order that an excess policy be 'specified' for the purposes of s45(2), the specification must contain sufficient information to enable the identification of a specific primary policy to which the excess policy is intended to be secondary".

The court stated that adequate specificity would be required of the other insurance clause or the courts would not treat the policy as a true excess policy.[219]

4.23.4 The Appeal: High Court of Australia

On appeal[220] the High Court did not consider it necessary to consider her honour's analysis regarding s45(2). The High Court considered two questions:[221]

> The first question in this appeal, brought by Zurich Australian Insurance Ltd ("Zurich"), is whether s45 applies to provisions which purport to exclude or limit liability where the assured is not a party to the other contract of insurance but is named in it as an assured person. The second question is whether the section renders void an entire clause of an insurance contract which includes a provision to which the section applies notwithstanding that the clause may include other provisions to which it does not apply.

On appeal it was not challenged that s45(1) did not avoid an "other insurance" provision in an insurance policy where such provision related to another insurance to which the assured is not a party but where he is a named non-party beneficiary, although the High Court considered that this was a question of law central to the determination of the appeal.[222] It was argued that the appeal should be upheld on the ground that s45(1) of the Insurance Contracts Act 1984 operated in such a way that the phrase "the assured has entered into some other contract of insurance" applied to the situation where a person had the benefit of a contract of insurance even though they were not a party to that contract of insurance himself or herself.[223]

The High Court went through the legislative history of s45. It identified that before legislation had been enacted, there were a bewildering variety of laws which governed insurance contracts. These were common law and imperial, state and Commonwealth statutes.[224] These were repealed when the Act came

---

217 [2009] WASCA 31, at paras [119]–[123].
218 [2009] WASCA 31, at para. [126].
219 [2009] WASCA 31 at para. [130].
220 (2009) 240 CLR 391.
221 As stated by French CJ.
222 (2009) 240 CLR 391, at paras [8] and [28].
223 (2009) 240 CLR 391, at para. [10].
224 This was repealed when the Act came into effect.

into effect. The High Court then went on to deal with the statutory framework of s45, by referring to other legislation[225] within the Act and cases. The expression "entered into" was considered to be critical to the constructional question raised by the appeal.[226] Section 11(9) of the Insurance Contracts Act provided a non-exhaustive definition.[227]

The ALRC did not provide a specific definition of what would fall within "entered into". The Australian, Senate, Insurance Bill 1983, stated that the intent of the Bill was to impose on the insurer and assured such obligations before the contract is entered into and would apply to situations where they renew, extend, vary or reinstate an existing contract and where they were to make a new contract. Section 11(11) Insurance Contracts Act provides "where a provision of this Act requires anything to be done before a particular contract is entered into, it is sufficient compliance with that provision if that thing is done at the time when the contract is entered into".

Section 48 was also considered. It covered the position where a party who is not party to the contract of general insurance that has been specified or referred to in the contract as a person which the insurance policy has extended to cover, has the right to recover the amount of loss suffered under the contract.[228]

The question of construction which had to be decided was whether the words "entered into" had the effect of limiting the application of s45 to "other insurance" provisions which affected contracts of insurance to which the assured was a party. The ordinary meaning of "take upon oneself (a commitment, duty, relationship, etc.), bind oneself by, or subscribe to, an agreement"[229] was adopted by the court which was reflected in s11(9) and other sections. The court considered s48, and s56(1) of the Act, and concluded that it did not deem a non-party assured as a party to the contract and therefore could not receive the benefits either contractually or in equity. The court stated:[230]

> Section 48 confers a statutory right of recovery upon a non-party referred to or specified in a general contract of insurance as a person assured or to whom cover extends. It does so directly. Its enactment predated the extension, by the decision of this Court in *Trident General Insurance Co Ltd v McNiece Bros Pty Ltd*, of common law rights of recovery for non-party assured persons under an insurance policy.

225
  Subject to subsection (10), a reference in this Act to the entering into of a contract of insurance includes a reference to: (a) in the case of a contract of life insurance – the making of an agreement by the parties to the contract to extend or vary the contract; (b) in the case of any other contract of insurance – the making of an agreement by the parties to the contract to renew, extend or vary the contract; or (c) the reinstatement of any previous contract of insurance.
  Also see *Akai Pty Ltd v People's Insurance Co Ltd* (1996) 188 CLR 418 at 424, s8(1), (2), s9, s11(9) Insurance Contracts Act.

226 (2009) 240 CLR 391, at para. [18].
227 (2009) 240 CLR 391, at para. [18].
228 Although s48(3) could be relied upon by the insurer. Section 56(1) was also discussed which covered fraudulent claims. And s76 which covered the right of contribution between insurers.
229 (2009) 240 CLR 391 at para. [23].
230 (2009) 240 CLR 391, at paras [24] and [25].

Section 48 does not deem such a person to be a party to the insurance contract thus attracting the rights conferred on a party. It does not purport to confer contractual or equitable rights upon such a person. There is therefore no basis in s48 for assimilating the position of a non-party assured to that of a person who has "entered into" a contract of insurance within the meaning of s45(1).

Section 56(1), dealing with fraudulent claims, distinguishes between such claims made "under a contract of insurance" and claims made "under this Act . . . by a person who is not the assured under a contract of insurance." Section 76, which is to be read with s45, confers an entitlement upon an assured to proceed against two or more insurers who "are liable under separate contracts of general insurance to the same assured in respect of the same loss." The condition of entitlement is the liability of the insurer, which may arise as a matter of contract or pursuant to s48.

As a result of this analysis the court did not accept Zurich's suggestion of amending s45, which was drafted as follows:

> Where a provision . . . has the effect of limiting or excluding the liability of the insurer under the contract by reason that the assured [including a person entitled under s48] has entered into [an arrangement giving it cover under] some other contract of insurance . . . the provision is void.[231]

The High Court did not agree that this was the proper approach. This would clearly narrow the intent and extent to which s45 would operate. If it was the intent of the legislature for such a construction to be adopted, the wording of the legislation would have specifically included this. There would however be situations where the assured was unaware that he is a non-party to a contract but may benefit in some way under the contract. The assured therefore may receive limited indemnity or be completely excluded from recovering for the loss that he has sustained. The High Court was aware of the mischief of s45, as French CJ, Gummow and Crennan JJ stated as follows:

> The text of the provisions of the Act with which s45 must be read points inexorably to the conclusion that s45 is only concerned with "other insurance" provisions affecting double insurance where the assured is a party to the relevant contracts of insurance. It does not allow room for a construction which would include a non-party assured among the ranks of those who have "entered into" the relevant contract. The inclusion of persons not parties to the relevant contract would be inconsistent with the ordinary or any plausibly extended meaning of "entered into" in relation to contracts. In so saying, it must be acknowledged that the purpose of s45 as appears from the ALRC Report and the relevant Explanatory Memorandum is not so confined as to indicate such a construction. There is no distinction made in the Report or the Explanatory Memorandum between "other insurance" provisions purporting to affect double insurance which includes non-party insurance, and double insurance where the assured is a party to the relevant contract. The most that can be said is that the Report seems to have proceeded upon the assumption that the problem of "other insurance" clauses arose in cases in which the assured was a party to both contracts. However, notwithstanding the generality of the mischief to which s45 was directed, the words "entered into" are not capable of encompassing a non-party assured."

---

231 (2009) 240 CLR 391, at para. [26].

However, even though noting the lack of distinction made in the Explanatory Memorandum and the ALRC, and acknowledging the way the ALRC proceeded in its analysis, the High Court still chose to conclude that the words were not capable of including a non-party assured.

This was consistent with the trial judge's analysis. The issue in dispute was whether the whole clause would be considered void, or would only the underlying insurance clause of the offending part of the clause be considered void. The court stated that, "Notwithstanding the want of any challenge to the primary judge's construction, its correctness is a question of law central to the determination of this appeal."[232] The next issue which the High Court had to decide was severance, and the meaning of the term "provision". The High Court looked at the analysis of the primary judge and the reference made to the case of *Austress-PSC Pty v Zurich Australian Insurance Ltd*.[233] The court stated:

> His Honour's reasoning in that case did not extend beyond the proposition that he could not detect any legislative intention in s 45(1) "that the provision be saved so far as it may have other effects." That approach, with respect, begged the question about the proper construction of the word "provision" in s 45(1).

4.23.4.1 The meaning of the word "provision"

The court was of the view that the meaning of the word "provision" in s45(1) had to be considered, and agreed with the description of Lord Simonds, in *Berkeley v Berkeley*,[234] that "It may mean a clause or proviso, a defined part of a written instrument. Or it may mean the result ensuing from, that which is provided by, a written instrument or part of it." The court stated that it was clear that the former definition was correct. Reference was made to the *Oxford Dictionary*.[235] The court went on to say:

> The important element of that definition is that a provision provides "for some particular matter." The fact that there may be more than one provision for a particular matter in one numbered clause of a contract is an accident of drafting. The inclusion in one clause of two statements of rights or liabilities in the form "if X, then Z" and "if Y, then Z" has the same effect as the inclusion of those statements in two separate numbered clauses. Each statement is a provision of the contract. There is no requirement to construe s 45(1) so that its operation depends upon accidents of paragraphing or numbering in contracts of insurance. The Underlying Insurance clause contains two statements each specifying a circumstance in which the Hamersley Policy will be reduced to an Excess Insurance policy. Each is properly regarded as a "provision" of that insurance contract. The question whether a clause of an insurance contract may contain a "provision," within the meaning of s 45(1), with different elements so intertwined that neither can be regarded as a distinct "provision," does

---

232 (2009) 240 CLR 391, at para. 27. As a result, counsel for Zurich applied for leave to amend the grounds of appeal. However, due to the finding of the court, the challenge made was unsuccessful.
233 Unreported, 1 May 1992.
234 [1946] AC 555 at 580.
235 2nd edn (1989), Vol. 12 at 719. Each of the clauses or divisions of a legal or formal statement, or such a statement itself, providing for some particular matter; also, a clause in such a statement which makes an express stipulation or condition; a proviso.

not arise in this case. In the result, s 45(1) operates only to render void that part of the Underlying Insurance clause in the Hamersley Policy which relates to double insurance to which the assured is a party.

The High Court was of the view that only the part of the clause which related to double insurance would be void. However, it is questionable whether the High Court's approach is correct. The view as expressed by Johnson J[236] should be the preferred approach. Johnson J took into consideration what would be a fair balance between the interests of the insurers, assureds and other members of the public even though it may not fully overcome the problems identified by the ALRC. However, her approach would strike a fair balance between competing interest.[237]

This raises issues such as the likely implications of the High Court decision and whether this decision provides sufficient guidance as to the mechanism of s45. The decision of the High Court suggests that where you have a situation where a non-party, for example a principal, is named in an insurance policy but is not a party to the contract with the insurer and, assuming that no consideration has passed between them, the "other insurance" contract will not be void. However, if the principal is actually named in the policy, s45 applies.

4.23.4.2 Severance of the underlying clause

Speno and MMI argued[238] that the trial judge should have severed just the underlying clause which was void, rather than the whole clause. Because the wording in s45(1) stated that the provision was void, therefore parts in the clause which were effected by a third party for the benefit of Hamersley, would not be void. The parties agreed with the trial judge's conclusion that the underlying clause operated when Hamersley effected another policy, and when Hamersley was a named beneficiary in a third-party policy. Zurich argued that to permit severance would be contrary to the purpose of s45.[239]

Beech AJA was of the view that s45(1) was not to be read in a way which excluded severance. The approach adopted by Zurich would lead to some "strange outcomes",[240] especially where there were other matters[241] also stated in the other insurance clause.

The issue which the court had to decide was whether the Court of Appeal erred in failing to find that s45(1) of the Insurance Contracts Act 1984, on its true construction, renders void the whole of the relevant provision of the first respondent's policy of insurance and not just the offending element of it. The Court of Appeal wrongly held that the "other insurance" or "underlying

---

236 Paragraph [42].
237 Paragraph [72].
238 [2009] WASCA 31 at para. [92].
239 [2009] WASCA 31 at para. [94].
240 [2009] WASCA 31 at para. [98].
241 See ss38, 43, 52 and 53 Insurance Contracts Act 1984.

insurance" provision in the first respondent's policy of insurance was capable of being, and should be, read distributively so as to sever elements from that provision and thereby misconstrued, or alternatively misapplied, s45(1) of the Insurance Contracts Act 1984.[242] The court considered s68(1) Trade Practice Act 1974 (Cth) which also contained a provision which had the stipulated effect of voiding that part of the contract. The court agreed with the analysis found in the cases of *Ruaro v Ferrari*,[243] *Renehan v Leeuwin Ocean Adventure Foundation Ltd*[244] and *Qantas Airways Ltd v Aravco Ltd*.[245] In those cases the courts were of the view that s68 avoids a clause in the contract to the extent that the clause is within the description as stated in s68, and "not entirely and for all purposes".[246] Beech AJA stated that an intention to exclude severance cannot be justified by reference to the purpose and object of s45(1).[247] Section 45(1) applies to a policy which the assured has entered into and not when a third party has entered into a contract on behalf of the assured.[248] The intention of the legislation was not to exclude severance,[249] although this was not the case in all cases, as one would also have to look at whether severance is allowed in a contractual context.[250] The court then went on to suggest how the underlying insurance clause[251] could be drafted:

> 110. I accept MMI's submissions that, when this test is applied, the underlying insurance clause can permissibly be severed without affecting the meaning of what remains after severance, in the following way: Underlying Insurance Underwriters acknowledge that it is customary for the Assured to effect or for other parties (including joint venture partners, contractors and the like) to effect, on behalf of the Assured, insurance coverage specific to a particular project, agreement or risk. In the event of the Assured being indemnified under such other Insurance effected by or on behalf of the Assured (not being an Insurance specifically effected as Insurance excess of this Policy) in respect of a Claim for which Indemnity is available under this Policy, such other Insurance hereinafter referred to as Underlying Insurance, the Insurance afforded by this Policy shall be Excess Insurance over the applicable Limit of Indemnity of the Underlying Insurance but subject always to the terms and conditions of this Policy.

This resulted in the underlying insurance clause being severed as shown above and, as a result, there was no double insurance.

---

242 Paragraph 10.
243 [2007] FCA 2022, per Emmett J.
244 (2006) 17 NTLR 83.
245 (1996) 185 CLR 43.
246 [2009] WASCA 31, at para. [105].
247 [2009] WASCA 31, at para. [105].
248 [2009] WASCA 31, at para. [105].
249 [2009] WASCA 31, at para. [106].
250 The court referred to *McFarlane v Daniell* (1938) 38 SR (NSW) 337, 347; *Humphries v The Proprietors "Surfers Palms North" Group Titles Plan 1955* (1994) 179 CLR 597, 604–605.
251 Agreeing with the submission of MMI.

PART A

4.24 Review of the Insurance Contracts Act 1984

A Review of the Insurance Contracts Act was conducted in 2004.[252] The terms of reference were as follows:

> The Review of the operation of the Insurance Contracts Act 1984 (the Act) is to be conducted having regard to the following:
>
> 1. whether the rights and obligations of insurers and assureds (including persons seeking insurance) under the Act continue to be appropriate, including in light of:
>   - product, regulatory and other developments in the financial services industry (particularly the insurance sector) since the Act was enacted; and judicial interpretation of the Act;
> 2. whether any amendments to the Act are required to take into account of the matters set out in item 1, and whether there are any deficiencies in the Act, such as aspects of the relationship between insurers and assureds that are not adequately covered;
> 3. whether any amendments are warranted in order to remove ambiguity and more clearly express the intent of the Act; and
> 4. any other matters relating to the Act which the reviewers consider it appropriate to examine.

In June 2004, a Review of the Insurance Contracts Act 1984 (CTH) was done in consultation with "stakeholders" when the recommendations were drafted. Most of the stakeholders considered that the Insurance Contracts Act "has been generally operating satisfactorily to the benefit of insurers and assureds".

The Review was headed the "Final Report on Second Stage: Provisions other than Section 54".[253] Chapter 8 specifically dealt with limiting the ability to exclude or limit liability because of another contract of insurance. Paragraph 8.1 of the Review stated:

> 8.1 Some provisions in the IC Act operate to curtail the rights and remedies insurers would otherwise have under contract. Issues have been raised about the provisions affecting the ability of insurers to: . . . exclude or limit liability due to another insurance contract (section 45).

After a discussion of the legislation, it went on to deal with the concerns of the stakeholders who were of the view that s45(2) should be clarified due to the uncertainties, such as how much specificity is needed when naming the other insurance covers. The case of *HIH Casualty and General Insurance Ltd v Pluim*

---

252 On 10 September 2003, the Minister for Revenue and Assistant Treasurer, Senator the Hon Helen Coonan and the then Parliamentary Secretary to the Treasurer, Senator the Hon Ian Campbell, announced that we would conduct a review of the Insurance Contracts Act 1984 (IC Act). See Preface of the Final Report on Second Stage: Provisions other than section 54.
253 By Alan Cameron and Nancy Milne.

Constructions Pty Ltd[254] was referred to. Under the heading "Limiting The Ability to Exclude or Limit Liability Because of Another Contract Of Insurance", at paras 8.21–8.25, the Review stated:

> 8.21 Under section 45 of the IC Act a provision in a contract of general insurance will generally be void if it limits or excludes the liability of the insurer because of some other contract of insurance. An exception is where the loss is covered by a contract of insurance that is specified in the first-mentioned contract.
>
> 8.22 Concern has been raised by stakeholders that the meaning of "specified" in subsection 45(2) should be clarified because it is uncertain as to whether other insurance covers have to be precisely named.158 The Law Council of Australia submits that the law needs to be clarified, "in particular it is necessary to signify whether a reference in an excess of loss policy to the underlying insurance solely by reference to a class of insurance is sufficient to invoke section 45(2)".
>
> 8.23 The Review Panel considers a narrow view of subsection 45(2), as taken by Mason P in *HIH Casualty & General Insurance Ltd v Pluim Constructions Pty Ltd*, is consistent with the policy intent.
>
> 8.24 Some submissions argued a wide approach to the subsection 45(2) exception is required because otherwise section 45 operates to discriminate against Australian insurers. The argument is that insurers not subject to the IC Act are able to include valid "other insurance" clauses in their contracts, but Australian insurers cannot due to section 45 (unless they can fall within the subsection 45(2) exception). The Review Panel considers that its proposal regarding clarifying the intended territorial application of the IC Act will address these concerns (see Chapter 1).
>
> 8.25 Accordingly, the Review Panel does not consider a change to section 45 is justified.

The Law Council of Australia then requested that the law needed to be clarified, "in particular it is necessary to signify whether a reference in an excess of loss policy to the underlying insurance solely by reference to a class of insurance is sufficient to invoke section 45(2)".[255]

The Review Panel was of the view that a narrower approach to s45(2) was consistent with the "policy intent." Reliance was placed on the decision of Mason P.[256] It was argued[257] that the current legislation discriminated against Australian insurers. The Review considered, however, that it was unnecessary to change s45.[258]

---

254 (2000) 11 ANZ Ins Cas pp. 61–477.
255 Review of the Insurance Contracts Act 1984 Final Report on second stage: Provisions other than section 54, at para. 8.22.
256 In *HIH Casualty and General Insurance Ltd v Pluim Constructions Pty Ltd* [2002] NSWCA 28.
257 Submissions by (1) Law Council of Australia dated 27 April 2004; (2) Professional Indemnity Insurance Company Australia Pty Ltd dated 21 April 2004; (3) Issue Paper from Consumers' Federation of Australian and (4) Issues Paper from the Australian Medical Association of Australia Limited dated 21 April 2004; and (5) National Insurance Brokers Association of Australia.
258 Reference was made to submissions by the Insurance Council of Australia Limited dated 2004; Law Council of Australia dated 27 April 2004; Phillips Fox dated 21 April 2004; Australian Medical Association of Australia Limited dated 21 April 2004; and Issues Paper from Consumers' Federation of Australia. The Review Panel was of the view that the suggested that the intended territorial application of the IC Act would address these concerns.

4.25 Analysis of the cases

4.25.1 Was the courts' analysis correct?

The Supreme Court, the Court of Appeal and the High Court above focused on ascertaining the underlying policy rather than identifying what is a "true excess" layer, and under what situations would there be a "true excess" layer. In a layered policy, the underlying policy was to be treated as a primary layer. It can be argued that it was therefore unnecessary for the courts to identify the underlying policy as being a member of a class of policies itself being capable of identification, because it was already the primary layer.

4.25.2 True excess clause

Focus should instead be placed on the wording of s45(1)(b) which clearly states, "Subsection (1) does not apply in relation to a contract that provides insurance cover in respect of some or all of so much of a loss as is not covered by a contract of insurance".

As can be seen from the analysis of Johnson J, she was of the view that, when deciding whether the Hamersley Policy was a "true excess", it would depend on whether the underlying insurance clause offended s45(1) and, if so, whether s45(2) would save it. Emphasis was placed on the second part of the wording of s45(2) which states, "that is specified in the first-mentioned contract".

Therefore, the key issue is whether the clause falls within the saving provision of s45(2), and whether that clause is in fact a "true excess" clause. A "true excess clause" has been defined as a policy which has the effect of the policy being excess and treated as over and above any other valid insurance policy, which would only respond to any loss sustained until such time as the limit of liability under such primary and valid insurance has been totally exhausted.[259]

4.25.3 Are the tests adopted by the courts confusing?

The tests laid down by the courts are too complicated and confusing. It is surely not the intention of the legislature that the legislation should be read in such a complicated manner. It is unnecessary to actually provide sufficient information so as to enable the parties to identify the policies within that class providing primary cover. In most cases, if not all cases, the excess layer policy will make absolutely no reference to the underlying policy. Further, the underlying policy, which is the primary layer, may not have been in place at the time, because the assured may not have decided what policy to take out or whether such policies should be taken out.

---

[259] See *National Farmers Union Mutual Insurance Society Ltd v HSBC Insurance (UK) Ltd* [2011] Lloyd's Rep IR 86.

4.25.4 Parent and subsidiary companies: top and drop policies

Top and drop policies are common when one looks at the relationship of parent and subsidiary companies and how policies are to be taken out in such cases. A parent company could take out a policy which has the effect of being a global policy. The parent company then requires the subsidiary to take out a primary layered policy (i.e. the underlying policy) which is to be treated as a local policy. In such cases, the parent company's policy will act as an excess layered policy and only respond once the local policy of the subsidiary company is exhausted. This has been referred to as a "top and drop" policy.[260] It has been said that top and drop insurers are taking only a residual risk and are charging premiums accordingly.[261] The requirement that such a system be in place is usually contractual in nature.

It would be almost impossible for the smooth operation of a company if there was a specific requirement that the primary policy be stated in specific terms. Accordingly, only general terms would be practical.[262] In such situations, like other such excess clause arrangements, the main issue is whether the excess policy is in fact a "true excess" policy. Therefore, the focus should not be on the primary layer, but must be on the excess layer.

4.25.5 How to overcome the practical problem?

It could be argued that s45 should only cover situations where the effect of the clause in the policy was to completely refuse payment to the assured, for example where there is an "escape clauses". Further, clauses such as (1) "excess clauses", where the insurer states that his liability would only be above that of any other policy which is effective at the time, so his liability will only take effect when all the other policies respond, and (2) "rateable proportion clauses," where the insurer will state that the assured can only get a certain proportion of the loss,[263] should not come within s45, because the insurer would still be required to make payment for the loss to the assured and does not completely deny liability. Therefore, such clauses do not completely deny cover to the assured. Further, if there is an excess clause it would be difficult to get around s45(1) by specifying the subsequent policy in the first-mentioned contract.

It can be argued that the way the courts have analysed the effect and mechanism of s45 is unnecessary. If s45 Insurance Contracts Act is adopted in England it would have the effect of holding excess, rateable proportion and exclusion clauses void, unless "specified". Further, the exception should only apply if it is a true excess clause. A better approach would be for the assured to choose which

---

260 *Sutton on Insurance Law* (4th edn 2014), para. 19.110.
261 *Ibid.*
262 *Ibid.*
263 The apportionment was of the assureds' recovery as opposed to permitting the assured from recovering the whole amount. This in turn would postpone the apportionment question to a contribution claim amongst the insurers: see *Sutton on Insurance Law* (4th edn 2014), para. 19.115.

insurer he wants to make recovery from and then it will be for the insurer to seek contribution from the other insurers.[264]

4.26 The effect of the "other insurance" clause – the American position

There are numerous cases in the United States which discuss the issue of double insurance. Although the American position does not provide any guidance to issues raised by Deputy Judge Kealey,[265] it may be worthwhile briefly to mention what the position in the United States is relating to double insurance and whether these principles can be applied in the context of s45.

The problems created by "other insurance" provisions[266] and the ensuing litigation were extensively covered in many law review journals during the 1950s and 1960s. It is interesting to note that some 30 years later the circular riddle of "other insurance" continues to plague insurers, assureds and the courts.[267] For "other insurance" clauses to apply, there must be concurrent policies over the same interest. Its origin comes from policies dealing with property insurance in response to the supposed moral hazard of fraud and carelessness inherent when one's property is over-assured.[268] Such clauses can be found in automobile liability insurance.

4.26.1 The circular reasoning

This issue has still not been resolved by the courts in America, even after some 60 years. It seems that the reason for this is due to the circular reasoning by the courts in trying to provide a solution, which ultimately stems from the wording of the policies used by the insurance industry.[269] An example of this can be found in the leading case of *Lamb-Weston Inc v Oregon Auto Ins Co*.[270] The plaintiff, Lamb-Weston, Inc leased a truck which crashed into a warehouse, which was being driven by its driver on its way to have the brakes repaired. The plaintiff settled its claim with the warehouse owner through a loan receipt fund arrangement

---

264 *GRE Insurance Ltd v QBE Insurance Ltd* [1985] VR 83.
265 *National Farmers Union Mutual Insurance Society Ltd v HSBC Insurance (UK) Ltd* [2010] 1 CLC 557 (Comm).
266 The types of "other insurance" clauses: Excess clauses which provides that liability of the insurer will be limited to the amount by which the loss exceeds the coverage provided by all other valid and collectible insurance. An escape clause avoids all liability for loss when there is other valid and collectible insurance. A pro rata clause states that a pro rata share of the loss, up to the limits of its policy shall be paid by the insurer. An excess escape clause provides that the insurer is liable for that amount of loss exceeding other available coverage and that the insurer is not liable when other insurance has limits equal to or greater than its own.
267 See Linda Kogel Hasse, "Is there a solution to the Circular Riddle? The Effect of 'other insurance' clauses on the public, the courts, and the insurance industry" (1980) 25 SDL Rev 37.
268 *State Farm Mutual Auto Insurance v Bogart* 717 P 2d 449, 451 (Ariz) (1986) and also see "Comment, Concurrent Coverage in Automobile Liability Insurance" (1965) 65 Colum L. Rev 319, 320.
269 *Miller v National Farmers Union Property and Cas Co* 470 F 2d 700, 701 (8th Cir) (1972).
270 219 Or 110, 341 P 2d 110, 76 ALR 2d 485 (1959).

with its carrier, St Paul. Oregon Motor Insurance Company (Oregon), the defendant which assured the truck, refused to pay the plaintiff's claim, even though not disputing the payout by St Paul. The policy contained the following provisions:

> The assured shall not, except at his own cost, voluntarily make any payment, assume any obligation or incur any expense other than for such immediate medical and surgical relief to others as shall be imperative at the time of the accident.
> If the assured has other insurance against a loss covered by this policy the Company shall not be liable under this policy for a greater proportion of such loss than the applicable limit of liability stated in the declaration bears to the total applicable limit of all valid and collectible insurance against such loss.
> No action shall lie against the Company unless, as a condition precedent thereto, the assured shall have fully complied with all the terms of this policy, nor until the amount of the assured's obligation to pay shall have been finally determined either by judgment against the assured after trial or by written agreement of the assured, the plaintiff and the Company.

The policy also contained the following clause:

> The Company shall: (a) Defend any suit against the assured alleging such injury, sickness, disease or destruction and seeking damages on account thereof, even if such suit is groundless, false or fraudulent; but the company may make such investigation, negotiation and settlement of any claim or suit it deems expedient.

The Court of Appeal held that both the defendant and St Paul were equally liable. The court stated that regardless of the nature of the clause used, i.e. either escape, excess or pro rata, these were repugnant and each should be rejected in toto. Justice Perry stated the absurdity of attempting to provide a difference between primary and secondary insurance, and suggested that one must look at the insurance policies to see if there is conflicting "other insurance". If so, the court will nullify them. This would solve the problem of the conflicting clauses, and at the same time safeguard the rights of the policyholder.[271] He stated:[272]

> We are of the opinion that in these later cases the courts have placed this problem in its true perspective by recognizing the absurdity of attempting to assume that where conflicting "other insurance" provisions exist by reason of overlapping coverages of the same occurrence the provisions of one policy must yield to the provisions of the other.
> It may be contended with some slight basis in reason, since the Oregon clause provides for prorating in proportion to the amount of valid insurance then in effect, its liability should be limited in that proportion. Thus, it would pay its prorata share upon that basis as "other valid and collectible insurance" and St. Paul would pay the balance under its excess clause. In this manner some effect is given to the "other insurance" clause of each policy.
> Such a contention leads, however, to a return to the circular reasoning necessary to establish primary and secondary liability, for to sustain this contention such

---

271 Harl H. Haas, "Automobile liability Insurance – Double Coverage and the effect of the 'Other Insurance' clauses" (1959–1961) 1 Willamette LJ 458.
272 At para. 129.

proration can only be given effect by determining the company carrying such "other insurance" clause is a primary insurer with limited liability.

Of course, no difficulty is encountered in reaching a just result under such reasoning if the prorata clause in a policy expresses equal liability with that of another insurer, and, while such a result may be just, we do not believe it can be sustained upon sound reasoning.

4.26.2 Main approaches to resolve the problem

The main approaches used by the courts to resolve the problem of the conflicting "other insurance" clauses are, first, holding the more specific insurer liable to the exclusion of the more general insurer. The courts determine the extent of liability of two concurrent liability insurers by assuming that they are not double insurers at all because of the more specific coverage provided by one. The latter is deemed the primary insurer and the other insurance is secondary in nature only. This approach was criticised as ignoring the "other insurance" clauses of the respective policies, and the courts have resorted to other approaches rather than determining who is the "specific" insurer.[273] Second, holding the insurer of the primary tortfeasor primarily liable.[274] Third, applying the "other insurance" clauses contained in that policy issued subsequent to the other policy. It has been suggested that this approach is ill-fitted as a rational basis for determining liability in automobile cases and was developed as a result of convenience as opposed to reason. The courts have ignored its use, as it is considered immaterial which policy was written first. The only vital issue is that each was in effect at the time of the accident.[275] Fourth, interpreting the clauses' respective policies.[276]

4.26.3 Presence of a combination of the clauses

An escape clause takes priority over a pro rata clause. The case of *Viger v Geographical Services Inc*[277] dealt with combination clauses where there were two policies, a liability policy which contained a pro rata clause and a P & I policy which contained an escape clause. The court gave effect to the escape clause over the pro rata clause. The P & I policy did not have to respond to the loss.[278] However in other parts of the United States the courts have not given priority to escape clauses.[279] Therefore an insurer can avoid liability by including an escape clause in the policy.

---

273 See discussion in Haas, "Automobile liability Insurance – Double Coverage and the effect of the 'Other Insurance' clauses" (1959–1961) 1 Willamette LJ 458, 843.

274 This approach has been rejected due to the difficulty of choosing the primary tortfeasor from among parties to an action.

275 See "Automobile Insurance – Effect of Double Coverage and 'Other Insurance' Clauses" 38 Minn L Rev 838, 847.

276 This approach has been used to resolve the problem of double coverage by looking to the "other insurance" clause in an attempt to reconcile the conflicting clauses.: see "Automobile Insurance – Effect of Double Coverage and 'Other Insurance' Clauses" 38 Minn L Rev 838, 841.

277 [1972] AMC 2113. Affirmed on appeal to the Fifth Circuit Court of Appeal (476 2d 1288).

278 Also see *Lodrigue v Montegut* [1978] AMC 2272 (ED La 1977).

279 *Graves v Traders and General Insurance Co* 241 So 2d 116. Here the Louisiana Supreme Court held that where you have two clauses such as an escape clause and excess clause, they cancelled

4.26.4 Should the American approach be adopted?

Some of the American principles are similar to those found in the English approach and the Australian approach. The use of exclusion clauses was not looked upon favourably and the courts were open to the idea of nullifying such provisions, which is similar to s45, where such clauses were held to be void. Therefore, the suggestion by the courts in *Lamb-Weston Inc* would be consistent with the Australian position of s45(1).

4.27 The Canadian position on double insurance

The Canadian courts have criticised the American position due to the uncertainties caused by the cases. There are no cases in Canada which have decided the issue of escape clauses, excess or pro rata clause. However, where two clauses are in conflict, the court will ascertain the intention of the insurers which is evidenced by looking at the contents of the policies.[280] This was the approach adopted in *Simcoe & Erie General Insurance Co v Kansa General Insurance Co.*[281]

4.27.1 The Canadian solution to avoid the circular approach

On numerous occasions the Canadian court have tried[282] to avoid the circular reasoning adopted where an insurer would argue that if the particular insurer was liable what had to be looked at was whether the other insurance policy would function as the primary policy if the other policy was not in existence. The other insurer would then argue that its policy was excess to the other policy.

---

out each other and, as a result, liability was apportioned. Also see *Offshore Logistics Services v Mutual Marine* 462 F Supp 485 (1978).

280 Hardy Ivamy, *General Principles of Insurance Law* (6th edn 1993), pp. 312–313, where he stated:

> The cardinal rule of construction is that the intention of the parties must prevail. But the intention is to be looked for on the face of the policy, including any documents incorporated therewith, in the words which the parties have themselves chosen to express their meaning. The Court must not speculate as to their intention, apart from their words, but may, if necessary, interpret the words by reference to the surrounding circumstances.

Also see Couch, *Cyclopedia of Insurance Law* (2nd edn 1983), Vol. 16, p. 498: Intent of Insurers as controlling: where it was stated:

> There is authority that the liability of insurers under overlapping coverage policies is to be governed by the intent of the insurers as manifested by the terms of the policies which they have issued. Thus, it has been said that where two or more liability policies overlap and cover the same risk and same accident, the respective liabilities of the insurer must rest upon a construction of the language employed by the respective insurers, and not upon the so-called "primary tortfeasor doctrine" or upon any arbitrary rule or circumstance.

281 (1994), 93 BCLR (2d) 1 (CA) which was affirmed on appeal at (1981) 27 BCLR 89. In this case there were two policies in place which covered personal injury. Both these policies had "other insurance" clauses. One policy contained a pro rata clause and the other an excess clause.

282 (1999) 10 CCLI (3d) 58.

This argument does not resolve the problem of which policy provides primary coverage.[283] McEwan J[284] stated: "Beyond a certain point I do not think it makes much sense to arbitrate what amounts to a kind of drafting 'tag'. The clauses are irreconcilable. Applying the principles set out in the cases the excess clauses are inoperative."

4.27.2 The Canadian approach to "other insurance" clauses

The courts have previously held that where there are "other insurance" clauses, they cancel out each other, and because they cancel out each other, both the policies provide primary coverage, which results in both insurers paying out equally to the applicable limits of each policy or until none of the loss remains.[285] In *Dominion of Canada General Insurance Co v Wawanesa Mutual Insurance Co*, the court was of the view that the insurance companies would need to share liability. Proudfoot J stated that to give effect to the excess clauses of the policies would create an absurd result where no one would pay. She referred to Brown and Menezes, *Insurance Law in Canada*[286] which discussed *Weddell v Road Tpt & Gen. Ins Co*, where both policies had excess clauses. The authors stated as follows:

> This consequence was avoided in the English case of *Weddell v Road Transport & General Insurance Co* where a driver of an automobile was involved in an accident and incurred liability as a result. His liability was assured by a driver's policy and also under the terms of the policy of the owner of the vehicle. Each policy contained a clause denying liability if the risk was covered by other insurance. Rowlatt J considered that "it is unreasonable to suppose that it was intended that clauses such as these should cancel each other. . . .with the result that, on the ground in each case that the loss is covered elsewhere, it is covered nowhere". Accordingly, the judge held that as a matter of construction the category of co-existing cover contemplated by each clause did not include cover "which is expresses to be itself cancelled by such co-existence." the result was that each insurer contributed half the amount of loss as if neither policy contained a double insurance provision. This is a sensible approach.

In *Family Insurance Corp v Lombard Canada Ltd*,[287] two policies were not identical and the court had to decide whether the clauses could be reconciled, by determining the intent of the two insurers as revealed by the content of the policies. Reference was made to *Simcoe & Erie General Insurance Co v Kansa General Insurance Co*,[288] where it was concluded that the clauses were irreconcilable and the excess clauses then became inoperative.

---

283 *McGeough v Stay N'Save Motor Inns Inc* 116 DLR (4th).
284 (1999) 10 CCLI (3d) 58.
285 *McGeough v Stay N'Save Motor Inns Inc* 116 DLR (4th) and *Dominion of Canada General Insurance Co v Wawanesa Mutual Insurance* (1985) 64 BCLR 122 (SC). The above principles were applied in *Lumbermen's Underwriting Alliance v Axa Pacific Insurance Co* 57 BCLR (4th) 293, at [49] and [50].
286 (1982) p. 349 at para. 15:2:11.
287 1999 Can LII 6253 (BC SC).
288 (1994) 93 BCLR (2d) 1 (BCCA) per Hinds J at p. 9.

4.27.3 Ascertaining intention

The court ascertains intention by the means and the extent to which each insurer has sought to limit its liability to the assured when the assured has purchased other policies covering the same risk. The interpretation exercise is done by determining the intentions of the insurers vis-à-vis the assured.[289] In *Family Insurance Corp v Lombard Canada Ltd*,[290] the Supreme Court of Canada, Bastarache J agreed that although it was correct that the intentions of the insurers prevail, the inquiry was of necessity limited to the insurers' intentions vis-à-vis the assured. The entire agreement of insurance contracts was found within the policy itself. Evidence of the intention between the parties must be ascertained by looking at the wording of the policy itself. Where there is a dispute between the insurer and the assured, where the provisions are unambiguous, reference has to be made to the surrounding circumstances. Where the dispute is between insurers, there is no reason to look outside the policy.

If there was no privity of contract between the parties, the unilateral and subjective intentions of the insurers, who were not aware of the existence of the provision in question was irrelevant. In *Family Insurance Corp*, the insurers tried to utilise provisions in their respective policies which contained clauses limiting their own liabilities. Here the owner of a stable and the owner of the horse were sued by Patterson who was injured when he fell from a horse. His claim was settled by the insurers of the owner of the stable, Family Insurance Corporation, under a homeowner/residential insurance policy. The owner was also at the time assured by Lombard Canada Ltd under a Commercial General Liability Policy. The wording of the policies were different, but both contained "other insurance" clauses which claimed to be "excess coverage" to any other insurance coverage held by the assured. The court[291] raised concerns about this area of law. It stated that "the reconciliation of competing and apparently irreconcilable insurance policy provisions has plagued the Court".

4.27.4 Conclusion

The Canadian courts tend to follow the principles developed in England where there would be a cancelling out[292] of the policies. This would result in each insurer being equally liable. This would be a less drastic approach than voiding

---

289 *Family Insurance Corp v Lombard Canada Ltd* 2002 SCC 48. In *Seagate Hotel Ltd v Simcoe & Erie General Insurance Co* (1981) 27 BCLR 89 (CA) where McFarlane JA stated:

> The second matter, which in my opinion is a very important consideration to keep in mind here, is that the court is not asked to interpret a contract made between the appellant and the respondent companies. The issue depends upon the interpretation and the application of two contracts, both insurance policies, the first being a contract between the appellant and the assured and the second the contract between the respondent and the assured.

290 [2002] SCC 48.
291 Bastarache J. He was of the view that this would be a good opportunity for the Supreme Court to clarify the law in this area.
292 However, in *Evans v Maritime Medical Care Inc* 1991 CanLII 2478 (NS CA), the Supreme Court of Nova Scotia considered it unnecessary to resort to the principles as stated by the authors in

such clauses, like Australia. The Canadian courts draw a distinction between an assured and an insurer, and between insurers themselves, when deciding what factors to consider when interpreting the clauses and intent. It could be argued that this distinction would give better protection to an assured.

4.28 Possible solutions to the clauses

4.28.1 Suggested solutions

The following suggestions could provide the solution to the problem of double insurance:

(1) if there is double insurance, regardless of the type of clause used and its wording, all insurers have to indemnify the assured equally;[293] or
(2) follow the Australian position under s45 Insurance Contracts Act 1984 and conclude that all such clauses are void, and provide for exceptions according to s45(2), but that it only applies to true excess clauses.[294]

The United Kingdom could enact similar legislation to that of Australia. Therefore, a policy with an excess or escape clause and another policy with a rateable proportion clause, and the effect that the escape and excess clause prevail over the rateable proportion clause, will be held to be ineffective.[295] This would have the effect of making clauses which limit an insurers' liability, if there is other insurance present, completely void. This will provide certainty and protection to an assured.

4.28.2 Should rights of parties be considered?

It could be argued that the law should be slow to move away from the right of parties to a contract to freely enter into contractual agreements and to decide on contractual terms. Therefore, if the parties choose to include a clause which excludes liability completely, they should be permitted to do so without restrictions being placed by the courts[296] or the legislature.

4.28.3 Other UK legislative protection: are these sufficient?

The Bubble Act 1720, which dealt with commercial transactions, was the first step towards a legislative framework to provide consistency to the insurance

---

Brown and Menezes (see fn 286 above) and instead relied on the clear wording of the policy and held that the MMC policy in that case did not contain an exclusion clause.
293 A common law position.
294 A statutory position.
295 Section 76 Insurance Contracts Acts 1984.
296 *Sinochem International Oil (London) Co Ltd v Mobil Sales and Supply Corp* [2000] 1 Lloyd's Rep 339 at [29].

market. The main concern of consumers was the likelihood of the insurance company closing down or payments under policies not being honoured. This resulted in workmen's compensation, which was introduced in 1897. But there were still problems with the regulation and the development of a consistent structure regarding consumer insurance matters. The Law Reform Committee's Report in 1957[297] contained proposed recommendations, but again these did not go through. The Law Commission recommended reforms in 1980.[298] More resistance was also seen when proposals were put forward in 1980.[299] However, there were some reforms in the form of (1) the Unfair Contract Terms Act 1977, (2) the 1986 Statement of Practice, Insurance Conduct of Business Rulebook,[300] (3) the Insurance Conduct of Business Sourcebook the Insurance Ombudsman Bureau,[301] (4) the Unfair Terms in Consumer Contracts Regulations 1999 and (5) the Financial Services and Markets Act 2000.[302]

The Unfair Terms in Consumer Contracts Regulations 1999 covered consumers contracts and not contracts of insurance. The aim of the Regulations was to ensure fairness, good faith and rights of the parties. The Regulations impacted on the decisions of the Office of Fair Trading and the Financial Services Authority. It has been argued that the Regulations have little application in insurance contracts,[303] because the courts follow established principles in insurance cases.[304] Further the exceptions to the 1999 Regulations[305] are of no relevance in England.

4.28.4 Other Australian legislative provisions

There are legislative provisions in Australia which control policy terms – for example, as mentioned above, s45 Insurance Contracts Act 1984 and other sections.[306] The regulative structure consists of the Australian Prudential Regulatory Authority, which derives its powers from statutes such as the Australian Securities and Investment Commission Act 2001 and Corporations Act 2001. The Financial Ombudsman Service was later set up. There was also the development of the General Code of Insurance Practice which required openness, fairness, and

---

297 Report 5, Cm 62.
298 Insurance law: Non-disclosure and Breach of Warranty (1980) Law Com No 104.
299 Law Com No 104.
300 However, due to the numerous bodies and societies that were set up, each held differing views, which led to decisions being inconsistent and uncertainty.
301 Followed the guiding principle of good insurance practice.
302 Financial Services and Markets Act 2000 gave more recognition to bodies such as the ombudsman.
303 "Unfair Terms in Insurance Contracts: A Solution In Search of A Problem" (2012) 23 Ins LJ 272.
304 *Bankers Insurance Co v South* [2003] EWHC 380 (QB); *Parker v National Farmers Union Mutual Insurance Society Ltd* [2012] EHWC 2156 (Comm); *Direct Line Insurance plc v Fox* [2009] [2010] Lloyd's Rep. IR 324 (QB).
305 For example, regs 6 and 8.
306 For example, ss8, 13, 14, 34–36, 37A–37E, 37, 42, 43, 44, 45, 53, 60 and 52 Insurance Contracts Act 1984.

honesty when dealing with customers.[307] In 2009 there was discussion regarding consumer protection laws and whether more general consumer-based protection should be introduced. This was seen with the introduction of the Trade Practices Amendment (Australian Consumer Law) Act 2010.[308]

4.28.5 The test of fairness

As can be seen from the case of *Jetstar Airways Ptd Ltd v Free*[309] there has been a diversion from the test of unfairness. The courts have focused on "good faith" in determining whether terms contained in a consumer contract are unfair. In *Jetstar Airways Ptd Ltd v Free*, the appeal related to a condition of sale of an airline ticket which was an "unfair term" under Part 2 B of the Fair Trading Act 1999, and which dealt with a question of law. In particular, what is an unfair term under s32W. Under s32X, the court or the tribunal may consider certain matters stated therein. Cavanogh J stated[310] that:

> 3 In my view, the appeal gives rise to two principal legal issues, together with a number of sub-issues. The two principal issues relate to the proper construction of s32W. First, what is the role of the expression "contrary to the requirements of good faith" in s32W? Does it, as VCAT held, merely identify a factor to be taken into account in determining whether a contractual term causes a "significant imbalance in the parties' rights and obligations arising under the contract"? Does it thus play a merely adjectival or subordinate role in the section? Does it play a merely adjectival or subordinate role in another sense, as suggested by the respondent? Or, on the other hand, does it add an extra element to the concept of an unfair term beyond the element of "significant imbalance," as the appellant submits? In any event, what does it mean? Those questions in turn may raise a question about the meaning and effect of the word "significant" in the phrase "significant imbalance." Second, in determining whether "contrary to the requirements of good faith and in all the circumstances" a contractual term causes "a significant imbalance in the parties' rights and obligations arising under the contract" (within the meaning of s32W), what kinds of matters are required or permitted to be taken into account? In particular, to what extent, if any, must or may regard be had to other terms of the contract (especially as to price), to the precontractual conduct of the parties, or to any alternative options available to the consumer at the time of the contract? Must the matter be assessed as at the time of the contract without regard to any subsequent actual events, or may it be assessed as at a later time taking into account any actual detriment to the consumer that has arisen as a result of the existence or operation of the term? As will be seen, I consider that s32X throws considerable light on all of these issues. Other parts of the statutory scheme also need to be considered and I will refer to them in due course. The legislative history and local and overseas authorities are also relevant. In the end, I conclude that VCAT's decision in favour of the consumer in this case was affected by errors of construction of s32W in relation to both of the principal issues just mentioned, and that the decision should be set aside accordingly and the matter

---

307 At para. 1.19.
308 Sections 12BF–12BM.
309 [2008] VSC 539.
310 At para. [3].

remitted to VCAT for reconsideration. But first I turn to the basic facts of the case and to the course of the proceedings below.

The court then went on to discuss the numerous statutory provisions[311] under the legislation, and the English position. The court's conclusion regarding the meaning of "unfair term" was stated as:

> 44. ... the definition of an unfair term might be thought to be circular, as it is impossible to avoid the notion of fairness in determining whether a term causes a significant imbalance in the parties' rights and obligations. However, if the balance of the parties' rights and obligations is thought to be contrary to the requirements of good faith this would be indicative of a *significant* imbalance. There is no separate requirement of "good faith" in consumer contracts; rather "good faith" is a touchstone which might be employed in determining whether a term in a consumer contract is an unfair term.
> 45. It may be that, in practice, the concept of "good faith" provides limited assistance. If it is a principle of fair and open dealing, it provides direction; but it is not a roadmap to a destination. The same goes for the colloquialisms of "playing fair" and "coming clean." In the *Interfoto* case Bingham LJ also suggested that good faith was conveyed by the colloquialism of "putting one's cards face upward on the table"; but, frankly, I think this takes the concept too far.
> 46. In *Esso Australia Resources Pty Ltd v Southern Pacific Petroleum NL (Receivers and Managers Appointed) (Administrators Appointed)* the Victorian Court of Appeal was reluctant to conclude that commercial contracts were of a class that carried an implied term of good faith as a legal incident, although it observed that it may be sometimes appropriate to import such an obligation to protect a vulnerable party from exploitive conduct which subverts the original purpose for which the contract was made. In this context Buchanan JA briefly touched on what might be the content of an implied contractual duty of good faith. This included acting reasonably, not acting capriciously, not seeking to prevent the performance of a contract or withholding its benefits, and not seeking to further an ulterior purpose for [sic] that which a contractual right or power is conferred. Frankly these examples of what might be the content of a duty to show good faith are of limited assistance. This is especially so in light of the detailed guidance provided by section 32X of the FTA, where a host of specific matters are set out which are designed to, and do, guide a court or the tribunal in determining whether a term of a consumer contract is unfair.
> 47. Sir Anthony Mason has said that he thought it probable that the "concept of good faith" embraced no less than three related notions:
>
> 1. An obligation on the parties to co-operate in achieving the contractual objects (loyalty to the promise itself);
> 2. compliance with honest standards of conduct; and
> 3. compliance with standards of contract which are reasonable having regard to the interests of the parties.
>
> In a subsequent and influential article "Contract, Good Faith and Equitable Standards in Fair Dealing" Sir Anthony expanded upon these notions. In relation to the third notion – which might be called a requirement of fair dealing – he observed:
>
> ... within reason and in conformity with the express provisions of the contract, the exercise of power is not [to be] capricious, arbitrary, unconscionable or

---

311 At paras [13]–[23].

unreasonable even to the extent of insisting upon, in an appropriate case, taking account of the interests of the other party.

Although these observations provide some general assistance in understanding the content of "the requirements of good faith" it remains the case that the concept can only play a general adjectival role in determining whether a term in a consumer contract is to be regarded as unfair pursuant to section 32W of the FTA.

48. Finally, I would observe that I would agree with the observation of Professor Beale that the "requirements of good faith" have a procedural aspect and a substantive content. A term in a consumer contract might cause such a significant imbalance in the parties' rights and obligations arising under the contract (to the detriment of the consumer) that the term is unfair even if the term is individually negotiated or brought to the attention of the consumer. On the other hand, there will be other terms in consumer contracts which will not be regarded as unfair if, and only if, individually negotiated; or, if, and only if, brought to the attention of the consumer.

4.28.6 Trade Practices Amendment (Australian Consumer Law) Act 2010

The statutory requirements under s12BG(1)[312] places emphasis on the balances between the parties, their rights and obligations. The Unfair Terms in Insurance Contracts Draft Regulation Impact Statement for consultation, after extensive discussion, concluded that the unfair contract terms legislation was difficult to apply in insurance contracts.[313] This was because it did not provide protection when dealing with regulated policy terms, insuring clauses and exclusions. It had been suggested that an assured's failure to read insurance contracts are not problems of unfairness.[314] However these proposals lapsed when the general elections were announced in 2013.

---

312 Trade Practices Amendment (Australian Consumer Law) Act 2010.
313 See Report dated March 2012.
314 (2012) 23 Ins LJ 272, 286.

Part B

CHAPTER 5

The meaning of contribution

5.1 History of contribution?

5.1.1 Common law contribution

Contribution at common law[1] claims date as far back as 1380.[2] In the early case of *Gebhardt v Saunders*[3] the plaintiff, who was the occupier of the house, sought to recover from the defendants, who were the landlord and owners, for costs and expenses incurred for abating the nuisance which was caused by the structural defect in the drains. The plaintiff had to pay a penalty if there was a default in compliance with the requisitions in the notice issued under s4(1) Public Health (London) Act 1891. Charles J[4] stated:

> In my opinion the ordinary principle of law is applicable to this case apart from the statute, the principle applicable to cases where one man has been legally compelled to expend money on what another man ought to have done, and, without having recourse to s. 11, the plaintiff is entitled to recover from the defendants as having been legally compelled to incur expense in abating a nuisance which the defendants themselves ought to have abated.

There can be relationships where co-ordinate liabilities exist, such as sureties, co-insurers, co-contractors, liabilities under bill of exchange, partners, joint tenants and tenants in common.[5] The basic principles of contribution and reimbursement were summarised in *The Law of Contribution and Reimbursement* as follows:[6]

---

1 There were conflicts between law and equity, in terms of procedural requirements (*Tucker v Bennett* (1927) 60 OLR 118 at 124; [1927] 2 DLR 42 at 47) and substantive differences (*Bonner v Tottenham and Edmonton Permanent Investment Building Society* [1899] 1 QB 161, 174). See Meagher, Gummow & Lehane, *Equity Doctrines and Remedies* (5th edn 2015), paras 10–030, 10–035. In *Albion Insurance Co Ltd v GIO* (NSW) (1969) 121 CLR 342, the court identified the "natural justice" as the generative force which can be found at law and equity. The development of contribution and reimbursement arose in a claimant, defendant and a creditor situation, where the claimant and the defendant are legally liable to the third party, as a result of money paid by the claimant to the third party, or an act which has been performed and where the defendant is also liable.
2 *Gillyngham v Watergate* (1380) CP 40/477 m. 255d. *Albion Insurance Co Ltd v GIO* (NSW) (1969) 121 CLR 342, 350 (the burden must be shared pro rata); *HIH Claims Support Ltd v Insurance Ltd* (2011) 280 ALR 1 at [36], [39].
3 [1892] 2 QB 452. See *Macclesfield Corp v Great Central Railway* [1911] 2 KB 528, 536, 537 where the court held that as the plaintiff paid out as a volunteer by doing the repairs, they could not recover cost which were incurred; *Maxwell v Jameson* (1818) 2 B & Ald 51, 286, where the issue was whether under the circumstances, the action for money paid to the defendant's use could be maintained.
4 [1892] 2 QB 452, 458.
5 *Meagher, Gummow and Lehane*, para. 10–009.
6 Charles Mitchell, *The Law of Contribution and Reimbursement* (2003), at paras 1.01 and 1.03.

1.01 Two parties, who will be described here as the plaintiff and the defendant, are both legally liable to a third party. The law forbids the third party to recover in full from both the plaintiff and the defendant: he may not accumulate recoveries by enforcing his rights against both of them. As between the plaintiff and the defendant, the law also holds that some or all of the burden of paying the third party should be borne by the defendant. Notwithstanding this, however, the law also holds that the third party can choose which of them to sue, and can recover from the plaintiff in full, even though it simultaneously holds that as between the plaintiff and the defendant, the defendant ought to shoulder some or all of the burden of paying him. When the plaintiff pays the third party the effect of his payment is to discharge the defendant's liability to the third party as well as his own liability.

1.03 ... Claims for reimbursement lie when the liabilities owned by the plaintiff and the defendant to the third party are such that the plaintiff is entitled to shift the whole burden of paying the third party onto the defendant. Claims for contribution lie where the plaintiff and the defendant must share the burden of paying the third party, with the result that the plaintiff can shift only part of this burden onto the defendant. However, there is substantially no difference in principle between contribution claims and reimbursement claims, as the basic components of each type of claim are the same, and it is only the quantum of the plaintiff's entitlement which distinguishes them.

The common law principles regarding sureties originated from Scots law[7] and in equity, since cases such as *Fleetwood v Charnock*.[8] A surety can seek contribution from a co-surety or sureties where they are bound jointly, joint and severally,[9] or just severally,[10] regardless of whether the other sureties are aware of the existence of other sureties.[11] This applies whether a surety is compelled to contribute to the debt of another under the same[12] or distinct instrument.[13] For example, in *Offley and Johnson's case*,[14] the court decided that an action could not be brought to seek contribution between sureties.[15]

---

7 DM Walker (ed.), *Institutions of the Laws of Scotland* (1981) 168 and *Institute of the Laws of Scotland* (1751), Vol. 1 237.

8 (1629) Nelson 10, where one surety can seek contribution from another for a debt they are bound jointly. *Peter v Rich* (1629/1630) 1 Chancery Reps 34; *Morgan v Seymour*, 1 Ch Rep 120.

9 *Dering v The Earl of Winchelsea* 2 Bos & P 270; *Clements v Langley*, 5 B & Ad 372; *Underhill v Horwood* 10 Ves 226; *Dunn v Slee* 1 J B Moo 2.

10 *Dering v The Earl of Winchelsea* 2 Bos & P 270.

11 *Coope v Twynam* T & Russ 426; *Stirling v Forrester* 3 Bli 575; *Craythorne v Swinburne* 14 Ves Jun 160. In *Craythorne v Swinburne* (1807) 14 Ves Jun 160, Lord Eldon summarised the decision of Eyre LCB in the decision *Dering v Earl of Winchelsea* (1787) 1 Cox 318, where he stated

> the creditor, who call upon all, shall not be at liberty to fix one with payment of the whole debt; and upon the principle, requiring him to do justice, if he will not, the Court will do it for him.

This was cited in *Wolmershausen v Gullick* [1893] 2 Ch 514, 523; *White & Tudor LC* (6th edn) Vol. 1, p. 122.

12 *Craythorne v Swinburne* 14 Ves Jun 34, 160; *Clements v Langley* 5 B & Ad 372.

13 *Deering v The Earl of Winchelsea* 2 Bos & P 270. These principles were reiterated by Eldon LC in *Craythorne v Swinburne*, 14 Ves Jun 165, 484.

14 (1584) 2 Leo 166.

15 This was permitted later in the second half of the eighteenth century. See *Toussaint v Martinnant* (1787) 2 TR 100 at 105; 100 ER 55 at 57–58.

5.1.2 Equitable contribution

The cases demonstrate that the principles of contribution are not founded on contract but on equity. In *Deering v Earl of Winchelsea*[16] the court considered the issue of contribution amongst sureties. In *Deering v Earl of Winchelsea*, Thomas Deering had to collect duties on behalf of the customs, and had to enter into bonds with three securities to perform his office. Three sureties, Sir Edward Deering, the Earl of Winchelsea and Sir John Rous, executed bonds on a joint and several basis to the Crown. The three sureties entered into securities as follows: (1) Thomas Deering and Sir Edward Deerling, (2) Thomas Deering and Earl of Winchelsea, (3) Thomas Deering and Sir John Rous, each group of surety for £4,000 as penalty, with same conditions for the performance of Thomas Deering's duty as a collector of duties belonging to the customs. The Crown obtained judgment against Mr Deering for amounts which were in arrears. One of the sureties claimed contribution from the others for sums which were recovered against him. Lord Chief Baron stated:[17]

> The real point is whether a contribution can be demanded between the obligors of distinct and separate obligations under the circumstances of this case. It is admitted that if there had been only one bond in which the three sureties had joined for £12,000, there must have been a contribution amongst them to the extent of any loss sustained; but it is said, that that case proceeds on the contract and privity subsisting amongst the sureties, which this case excludes; that this case admits of the supposition that the three sureties are perfect strangers to each other, and each of them might be ignorant of the other sureties, and that it would be strange to imply any contract as amongst the sureties in this situation; that these are perfectly distinct undertakings without connection with each other, and it is added, that the contribution can never be *eodem modo*, as in the three joining in one bond for £12,000, for there, if one of them become insolvent, the two others would be liable to contribute in moieties to the amount of £6000 each, whereas here it is impossible to make them contribute beyond the penalty of the bond.

He went on to state:[18]

> If we take a view of the cases both in law and equity, we shall find that contribution is bottomed and fixed on general principles of justice, and does not spring from contract; though contract may qualify it, as in *Swain v Wall*, 1 *Cha. Rep.* 149.

Eyre CJ,[19] who delivered the judgment of the court, commented:

---

16 (1787) 1 Cox Eq Cas 318, 1184.
17 (1787) 1 Cox Eq Cas 319, 1184.
18 (1787) 1 Cox Eq Cas 320, 1184.
19 2 Bos & P 270., 1276, 1278. Dr Story, in his *Commentaries on Equity Jurisprudence* (A E Randall (ed.), 3rd edn 1920) at § 493, says:

> The claim certainly has its foundation in the clearest principles of natural justice; for, as all are equally bound, and are equally relieved, it seems but just that in such a case all should contribute in proportion towards a benefit obtained by all, upon the maxim *Qui sentit commodum sentire debet et onus*. And the doctrine has an equal foundation in morals, since no one ought to profit by another man's loss, where he himself has incurred a like responsibility. Any other rule would put it in the power of the creditor to select his own victim, and, upon motives of mere caprice or favouritism, to make a common burthen a most gross personal oppression. It would be against equity for the creditor to exact or receive payment

In the particular case of sureties, it is admitted that one surety may compel another to contribute to the debt for which they are jointly bound. On what principle? Can it be because they are jointly bound? What if they are jointly and severally bound? What if severally bound by the same or different instruments? In every one of those cases, sureties have a common interest and a common burthen. They are bound as effectually quoad contribution as if bound in one instrument, with this difference only, that the sums in each instrument ascertain the proportions, whereas, if they were all joined in the same engagement, they must all contribute equally.

5.1.2.1 Co-sureties

The doctrine of contribution is not founded on contract but on the principles of equality of "burthen and benefit",[20] when dealing with a surety situation. The learned authors of *The Law of Restitution*, Goff and Jones,[21] stated that the basis of contribution found in equity was one of unjust enrichment, and not one of contract. It was stated:

> In these circumstances, section 5 [of the Limitation Act 1980] would appear to be inapplicable, unless it could be said that, as soon as the claim lies, a debt arises between the

> from one, and to permit or by his conduct to cause, the other debtors to be exempt from payment. And the creditor is always bound in conscience, although he is seldom bound by contract, as far as he is able, to put the party paying the debt upon the same footing with those who are equally bound. It can be no matter of surprise, therefore, to find that courts of equity adopted and acted upon this salutary doctrine, as equally well founded in equity and morality, at a very early period. The ground of relief does not, therefore, stand upon any notion of mutual contract, express or implied, between the sureties, to indemnify each other in proportion (as has sometimes been argued); but it arises from principles of equity, independent of contract. If the doctrine were otherwise, a surety would be utterly without relief; because he has not, either in equity or at law, any title to compel the obligee to assign over the bond to him upon his making payment, or otherwise discharging the obligation.

And at § 495:

> Originally, it seems to have been questioned whether contribution between sureties, unless founded upon some positive contract between them, incurring such a liability, was a matter capable of being enforced at law. But there is now no doubt that it may be enforced at law as well as in equity, although no such contract exists. And it matters not in case of a debt, whether the sureties are jointly and severally bound, or only severally; or whether their suretyship arises under the same obligation or instrument, or under divers obligations or instruments, if all the instruments are for the same *identical debt*.

Mahoney v McManus (1981) 180 CLR 370, 378; *HIH Claims Support Ltd v Insurance Australia Ltd* (2011) 280 ALR 1 at [39] (where the modern approach to contribution should not be defeated by a technical approach).

20 (1787) 1 Cox Eq Cas 318, 1184. *Stirling v Forrester* (1821) 3 Bligh 575, 596; *Barclays Bank Ltd v TOSG Trust Fund Ltd* [1984] 1 All ER 628, 648a, per Kerr LJ,

> For instance, the rules concerning rights and obligations of contribution in general average were originally based simply on "common principles of justice" (see *Birkley v Presgrave* (1801) 1 East 220 at 227, 229, 102 ER 86 at 88, 89), and these rules were then applied by analogy in laying down the principles of contribution between co-sureties (see *Deering v Earl of Winchelsea* (1787) 1 Cox Eq Cas 318 at 322, [1775–1802] All ER Rep 140 at 143). In my view, the same approach applies here.

American Surety of the New York v Wrightson (1910) 103 LT 663, 665 per Hamilton J. However, if the debtor's obligations has been guaranteed by a surety, which is not payment of money, then the principles of equity do not apply but the court exercises its discretion under the Civil Liability (Contribution) Act 1978, s2(1).

21 7th edn 2009.

parties. However, it may be more persuasive to hold that the equitable doctrine of laches should apply. It is an open question whether equity will then follow the analogy of section 5 of the Limitation Act 1980, when the limitation period is six years, or section 10.

In *Ward v National Bank of New Zealand Ltd*,[22] Sir Robert Collier reaffirmed the principle in *Deering v Lord Winchelsea*:

> It is true that he is entitled to contribution against other several sureties to the same extent as if they had been joint, but the right of contribution among such sureties depends not upon contract but on principles established by Courts of Equity.
> This right of contribution was established in the case of *Deering v Lord Winchelsea* (1), affirmed by Lord Eldon in *Craythorne v Swinburne* (2), and is thus explained by Lord Redesdale in *Stirling v Forrester* (3): The principle established in the case of *Dering v Lord Winchelsea* (1) is universal, that the right and duty of contribution is founded on doctrines of equity, it does not depend upon contract. If several persons are indebted, and one makes the payment, the creditor is bound in conscience, if not by contract, to give the party paying the debt all his remedies against the other debtors. . . . It would be against equity for the creditor to exact or receive payment from one, and to permit, or by his conduct to cause, the other debtors to be exempt from payment. . . .
> In pursuance of this doctrine it has been held that a surety is entitled to the benefit of all securities in the hands of the creditor whether, when he became a surety, he knew of them or not. Thus, in *Pearl v Deacon* (4), where the plaintiff was surety in a promissory note for a sum lent by the defendants to their tenant, and a mortgage was subsequently taken by the defendants on the tenant's furniture for the same debt, they afterwards, under a distress, took the same furniture for arrears of rent. It was held by Sir John Romilly that, inasmuch as the produce of the furniture was first applicable to the payment of the promissory note, the landlords could not, as against the surety, apply it to the payment of their rent, and that the surety was discharged, not, it is to be observed, absolutely, but pro tanto, and the decision was confirmed on appeal. It has been held in other cases that, where the creditor wastes or improperly deals with a security, the surety is released pro tanto. The claim of a several surety to be released upon the creditor releasing another surety, arises not from the creditor having broken his contract, but from his having deprived the surety of his remedy for contribution in equity. The surety, therefore, in order to support his claim, must shew that he had a right to contribution, and that that right has been taken away or injuriously affected.

In *Johnson v Wild*,[23] contribution was claimed by the plaintiff, under the lessee, from the defendants regarding payment the plaintiff had made for rent for a lease which was given in 1878 for a period of 999 years. Chitty J stated, "Co-sureties are liable to the principal demand, either in the whole or in part; and as between the co-sureties, there is not only the common law right of contribution, but there is the equitable right of contribution."[24]

---

22 (1883) 8 App Cas 755, 765; *Duncan Fox & Co v North and South Wales Bank* (1880) 6 App Cas 1 at 12–13.
23 (1890) 44 ChD 146, 150.
24 In *Coope v Twynam* (1823) Turn & R 426, 1166, Eldon LC stated:

> These cases of sureties depend upon nice distinctions in point of fact; *Deering v Lord Winchelsea* settled, that if three persons became sureties for £12,000, each in a separate bond for £4000, there would be a right of contribution between them. That case was much doubted in *Westminster Hall* at the time it was decided; but I believe, upon consideration, it will be found to be quite right. In that

The case of *Re Snowdon, ex p Snowdon*[25] involved an appeal of the adjudication of bankruptcy. The Registrar, in that case, relied on *Craythorne v Swinburne*[26] where it held that a creditor could call upon a surety to pay any part of the debt, and could call on his co-surety to contribute. James LJ[27] stated:

> There is no "legal debt" and there is no "equitable debt," there is no debt so far as either law or equity is concerned sufficient for the purpose of adjudication. The right of a surety who has paid the creditor is to have contribution from his co-sureties, that is to say, all the co-sureties must bear the whole burden of the debt equally. It is impossible to say, when one surety has paid a part of the debt, until the whole debt is paid in respect of which all the co-sureties are jointly liable, what the right to contribution is.

Each creditor shall bear the proportion of contribution due equally. In *Brown v Cork*[28] the court dealt with the relationship between sureties. St Clair Sampson Ltd was part of a group of companies which had entered into a joint and several guarantee for Midland Bank Ltd. Each of the companies in the group guaranteed payments of liabilities of one another, which were cross-guarantees, supported by debentures. The companies encountered financial difficulties and a receiver was appointed. The joint liquidators requested that a separate account should be prepared to ascertain which amounts were due to and from it by way of contribution to or from its co-sureties. It was argued that there should be set off against contribution liabilities and sums due from the companies.[29] Blackett-Ord J held that there should not be set off for inter-company indebtedness. This was appealed. Oliver LJ, on appeal, stated that "the critical question was whether there should be or should not be set-off against claims for contribution other claims for inter-company indebtedness in the distribution to the liquidators of the surplus money in the receiver's hands".[30] He went on to explain that the companies should be treated individually, to identify the indebtedness to be set off against. The respondent argued that an overpaying surety is entitled to take over and to enforce, to the extent of his over-payment, the floating and fixed charges,

---

case it was said by the sureties, we will each give a bond for £4000, but beyond that we will not be liable; it was held however that there was a liability between them as co-sureties. The present case depends upon the question, whether this was really a separate and distinct transaction, or the same transaction split into different parts. If the case of *Deering v Lord Winchelsea* be right, and there was an agreement that *A., B.,* and *C.* should become liable for £1200, each in a bond for £400, there would be a right of contribution between them ; and then it would be a question whether, if the bonds were not given by all, they would be obligatory upon any *1* That would depend upon nice distinctions. It might be waived by subsequent transactions. *December* 3. The *Lord Chancellor* [Eldon] said, that he considered the bonds in this case as distinct obligations, and that it was impossible to apply the doctrine in *Deering v Lord Winchelsea*.

See *Cowell v Edwards* (1800) 2 Bos & P 268; *Craythorne v Swinburne* (1870) 14 Ves 160 at 164.
25 (1881) 17 ChD 44, 45.
26 (1870) 14 Ves 160 at 164.
27 (1881) 17 ChD 44, 46.
28 [1985] BCLC 363, CA (Eng).
29 [1985] BCLC 363g–i, CA (Eng).
30 [1985] BCLC 368c–d, CA (Eng).

which covered the surplus monies in the receiver's hands. Oliver LJ went on to state:[31]

> As I see it, this case really does no more than recognise that the rights of sureties inter se to insist on an equal contribution to the guaranteed debt may be varied by agreement and that that agreement may, and indeed must in the case of a partnership liability undertaken by the partners jointly and severally, be found in the terms of the partnership agreement between them.

There are no principles in law which require a person to contribute to an outlay merely because he has derived a material benefit from it.[32] In *Pendlebury v Walker*[33] it was held that:

> Where several persons are sureties for the payment of one sum of money, though by distinct instruments, and one pays more than an equal share of that sum, he may have contribution from his co-sureties; but if it be arranged by contract, which it may be, that each surety shall be answerable only for a given portion of one sum of money, in such case there is no right of contribution amongst the co-sureties.

5.1.2.2 Guarantor's right

The same principles apply in a guarantor's right to contribution situation.[34] A guarantor can seek contribution from a co-guarantor. Where there are several joint guarantors who were all liable, and one pays the debt, he will then be entitled to bring proceedings against the principal.[35] Where there are several co-guarantors, and one guarantor makes full payment of the debt where there is default by the principal, he is entitled to recover for the excess of his proper share.[36]

In *Macdonald v Whitfield*,[37] in reversing the judgment of the lower court, the court held that directors of a company who mutually agree with each other to become sureties for the bank for a same debt, and under the agreement successively indorse three promissory notes of the company, were entitled and liable to equal contribution and not successively, according to the priority of their indorsements of promissory notes. This right by a guarantor to contribution applies regardless of whether the guarantors are bound severally[38] or jointly and sever-

---

31 [1985] BCLC 372e–f, CA (Eng).
32 [1900] AC 6, 15.
33 (1841) 4 Y & C Ex 424.
34 A surety or a guarantor is also entitled to the benefit of the security given as personal indemnification: see *Swain v Wall* 1 Ch R 149. *Cf Bowditch v Green* 3 Met 360.
35 *Pendlebury v Walker* 4 Younge & Coll 424. *Turner v Davies* 2 Esp. 478 (where one person is induced to become a guarantor).
36 *Cutter v Emery* 37 N H 567 (1859); *Pickering v Marsh* 7 X. II. 192; *Coburn v Wheelock* 34 N Y 440 (1868).
37 (1883) 8 App Cas 733, 750.
38 *Ward v National Bank of New Zealand* (1883) 8 App Cas 755, 765 where Sir Robert P. Collier stated

> But where it is no part of the contract of the surety that other persons shall join in it, in other words, where he contracts only severally, the creditor does not break that contract by releasing another several surety, the surety cannot therefore claim to be released on the ground of breach of contract;

ally.[39] This also applies whether different or same instruments are used, as was illustrated in *Ellesmere Brewery Co v Cooper*,[40] or whether the guarantor knew of the existence of other co-guarantors as illustrated in *Craythorne v Swinburne*[41] and *Whiting v Burke*.[42] In *M & S Fashions Ltd v Bank of Credit and Commerce International SA (In Liquidation)*,[43] Dillon LJ stated "A creditor cannot sue the principal debtor for an amount of the debt which the creditor has already received from a guarantor."

Lavin v Toppi[44] reaffirmed the right to contribution between guarantors. Lavin[45] and Toppi,[46] were directors and equal shareholders of Luxe Studios Pty Ltd, which borrowed money in the sum of $7,768,000 from National Australia Bank. The loan was guaranteed joint and severally by Lavin, a company associated with Lavin, Toppi's husband and Luxe Studios Pty Ltd, which was jointly owned and controlled by Lavin and Toppi. Luxe went into receivership, and the bank turned towards the guarantors for payment, and sued those who did not pay under the guarantee. A property which was used to secure the guaranteed debt was sold and proceeds of the sale which amounted to $4 million was paid to the bank. Lavin counterclaimed on the ground that the guarantee was unenforceable as it was unconscionable. A deed of release and settlement was later entered into where Lavin would pay the bank $1.35 million for the guaranteed debt and $1.73 million for personal loans. The bank covenanted not to sue, provided Lavin paid the settlement sum. The sum was settled. Toppi and her husband used proceeds from the sale of their home to pay the balance of $2.9 million, which discharged the guarantee. They then commenced proceedings against the appellants for contribution being half the difference of the amounts paid by the appellants and the respondents in discharging the guarantee. The judge at first instance was of the view that the court was bound by *Carr v Thomas*.[47] On appeal, the Court of Appeal followed *Carr v Thomas*, and stated that the decision was correct as a matter of principle. The matter was taken further to the High Court of Australia, where the issue was whether a surety who has paid to the creditor a disproportionate amount of a guaranteed debt could seek to recover contribution from the co-surety, where the creditor has agreed to covenant not to sue for payment of the debt, which

---

Canadian Imperial Bank of Commerce v Vopni [1978] 4 WWR 76; *Metropolitan Properties Co (Regis) Ltd v Bartholomew* (1996) 72 P & C R 380, 383; *TCB Ltd v Gray* (1987) 3 BCC 503, 515 (company borrowed money which were secured by debenture, deposit of securities and majority shareholder's personal guarantee).

39 *Underhill v Horwood* (1804) 10 Ves 209, 226. Where there are different sureties and guarantors who are covered by different instruments, and the debt is for eqaul portion, and where the the instruments provided for liability which was separate and distinct, each surety or guarantor would be liable to contribute to the other.

40 [1896] 1 QB 75, 79.

41 (1807) 14 Ves 160, 165, per Lord Eldon LC.

42 (1871) 6 Ch App 342.

43 [1993] 3 WLR 220, 239. In *Milverton Group Ltd v Warner World Ltd* [1995] 2 EGLR 28, 31 it was decided that where there was part payment by a surety of a debt, this would result in a discharge of the principal debtor to the extent of his payment.

44 (2015) 316 ALR 366.

45 The first appellant.

46 The first respondent.

47 [2009] NSWCA 208.

had been guaranteed. The court dealt with the principles of the right to contribution, and agreed with Leeming JS's view that the covenant not to sue did not discharge liability under the guarantee. It avoided the discharge of the liability of one surety operating to release all co-sureties. Liability "remained enforceable by other means such as reliance on rights of recoupment under other securities (if any) between the Bank and the appellants",[48] even though not enforced by legal proceedings. The court followed the decision in *Craythorne v Swinburne*, where it was stated that

> "the creditor, who can call upon all, shall not be at liberty to fix one with payment of the whole debt; and upon the principle, requiring him to do justice, if he will not, the Court will do it for him".[49]

The right of contribution is not applicable between a principal guarantor and a sub-guarantor. In *Eagle Star Insurance Co Ltd v Provincial Insurance plc*,[50] where contribution is determined to the extent of their respective liabilities to the person assured under separate contracts of insurance, it is the "special cut-off point" which requires the position to be judged at the date of the loss. Therefore the liability has to attach before a co-guarantor has to contribute. In *Scholefield Goodman & Sons Ltd v Zyngier*[51] it was held that the term creating the surety depended on the terms of the contract which created the suretyship. In *Scholefield Goodman & Sons Ltd*, Mrs Z covenanted to pay to the bank amounts which were owed to it either by Mrs Z or by Z Ltd, which included amounts arising from any bill of exchange for which Z Ltd might be liable "either primarily or only in the event of any other person failing to duly pay the same". Five bills of exchange were drawn by S Ltd and indorsed by Z Ltd. Z Ltd later dishonoured the bills on maturity. The bills were presented by the bank to S Ltd, who claimed contribution from Mrs Z, after paying the amounts which were owed. A declaration sought by Mrs Z to the effect that S Ltd could not claim relief from Mrs Z or the bank was granted by the trial judge. The Privy Council dismissed S Ltd's appeal. The court looked at the true construction of the bargain between the bank and Mrs Z. Lord Brightman[52] stated:

> There is no reason to suppose that, in a contract between the bank and the surety, the surety desires to confer a benefit on the drawer and to share with him the responsibility for a dishonoured acceptance. Nor is there any reason why the bank should wish to call upon the surety for payment until the parties to the bill have defaulted. As their Lordships have indicated, and as is apparent from *Craythorne v Swinburne*, 14 Ves.Jun. 160, the claim to contribution against a surety must depend upon the true construction of the contract which created the suretyship, because the surety can by such contract limit the scope of his suretyship to whatever extent he pleases. Contribution is founded on the principle that equality is equity, and there is no room

---

48 At para. [40].
49 At para. [44].
50 [1994] 1 AC 130 at 141–142.
51 [1986] 1 AC 562.
52 [1986] 1 AC 562, 574F-H; *Re Denton's Estate, Licences Insurance Corporation and Guarantee Fund Ltd v Denton* [1904] 2 Ch 178, 185, 196 CA.

for the application of this doctrine unless the surety against whom contribution is claimed has placed himself on the same level of liability as the surety who claims contribution from him. It would be possible for a bank guarantee to be so worded that the surety deliberately places himself upon an equal footing with the drawer or indorser of the bill discounted by the bank, but it would produce an irrational result. It is not a construction to be adopted unless the intention is clear, because there is no reason why the bank and the third party who gives the guarantee to the bank should have such an intention. In the instant case there is no such clear intention.

Where a creditor has obtained a judgment, the creditor may seek contribution against co-guarantors.[53] In *Wolmershausen v Gullick*, the plaintiff was the executrix of a surety with four others for a large sum advanced by a bank to a company. The bankers put in a claim as creditors, to obtain the whole amount of the guarantee. The creditor's claim was resisted but a reduced sum was allowed. The plaintiff then sought to claim against the co-sureties for contribution.

5.1.2.3 Co-insurers

The principles regarding co-sureties apply in situations where there are co-insurers. In *Commercial Union Assurance Ltd v Hayden*,[54]

> "The right of co-insurers to claim contributions from each other derives from the principle that where there are two or more sureties for the same debt and one pays more than his due, he can claim contribution from his co-surety: *Newby v Reed* (1763) 1 Wm.Bl. 416."

In *Godin v London Assurance Co*,[55] contribution was permitted between indemnity insurers by Lord Mansfield CJ, when he dealt with a case involving double insurance.

It has been stated that what matters when one looks at contribution today is not so much as to the origins of contribution, that is whether it developed from common law or equity, but the jurisdiction in equity which developed more thoroughly than that at law, and prevails following judicature legislation.[56]

5.2 When does contribution arise in double insurance?

The elements of double insurance must be present before the issue of contribution arises. The fact that there are similarities as to their general nature

---

53 *Wolmershausen v Gullick* [1893] 2 Ch 514; *Re Snowdon, ex p Snowdon* (1881) 17 Ch D 44, 47, CA; *Offley and Johnson's Case* (1583) 2 Leo 166; *Davies v Humphreys* (1840) 6 M & W 153.; *Peter v Rich* 1 Ch Rep 19; *Swain v Wall* (1642) Rep Ch 149; *Hole v Harrison* (1675) 1 Ch Cas 246; *Lawson v Wright* (1786) 1 Cox Eq Cas 275; *Craythorne v Swinburne* (1807) 14 Ves 160; *Antrobus v Davidson* (1817) 3 Mer 569.; *Stirling v Forrester* (1821) 3 Bli 575, 590, 596; *Dering v Lord Winchelsea* (1787) 1 Cox Eq Cas 318; 2 Bos & P 270; *Reynolds v Wheeler* (1861) 30 LJ (CP) 350; 10 CB (NS) 561; *Wooldridge v Norris* (1868) Law Rep 6 Eq 410; *Cruse v Paine* (1868) Law Rep 6 Eq 641; 4 Ch 441; *Bechervaise v Lewis* (1871–72) 7 CP 372, 377; *Lacey v Hill* (1874) LR 18 Eq 182, 191; *Lloyd v Dimmack* (1877) 7 Ch D 398.
54 [1977] 1 QB 804, 809C.
55 (1758) 1 Burr 489; 97 ER 419.
56 Meaher, Gummow & Lehane, *Equity Doctrines and Remedies* (5th edn 2015).

or purpose or extent of rights or obligations[57] would not be enough. In *John v Rawlings*[58] it was stated: "The whole process of reasoning in this area of the law is with respect to the recovery rights as between insurers. Policies of insurance are not kept separate. They are merged as between the insurer and the assured." Where there are two policies which cover property, the first policy providing for a rateable proportion clause, and the latter containing a clause which states that the policy covers the amount in excess of the amount which is payable by any other policy, contribution does not arise.[59] In *Limit (No 3) Ltd v ACE Insurance Ltd*,[60] the Supreme Court of New South Wales had to decide the issue of liability between the primary insurer, ACE and that of an excess insurer, Limit (No 3) Ltd.[61] Here the excess insurer had provided indemnity for the sums which were stated for both policies. In *Limit (No 3) Ltd v ACE Insurance Ltd*. It was held that liability arose after the primary insurer refused to pay. The assured was a joint venture (JV) engaged in the construction of two power transmission cable tunnels. Third parties had made claims against the JV for damage which occurred during construction of the tunnels. The JV conducted repair works and then claimed against their ACE policy, which was refused. As a result, it sought to recover against its excess insurers. The excess insurers paid out, and commenced proceedings to claim contribution against ACE. Rein J stated:[62]

> Given that ACE was on risk from the moment of casualty and Lloyds was only contingently liable on the failure of ACE to indemnify it, I accept that the two insurers were not jointly liable as at the time of casualty. Where one insurer is liable to indemnify and remains liable to indemnify and subsequently another insurer becomes liable there may be some room for argument as to the applicability of *AMP v QBE*, but I proceed on the basis that contribution as a remedy in the insurance context is not available as a remedy for this reason.

Contribution between insurers will exist where there is double insurance if the following factors are satisfied: the policies must cover (1) the same subject matter, (2) the same assured, (3) the same risk, (4) the same period of cover and (5) the same scope. Further (1) the policies which are in existence at the time must respond to the loss when a loss arises, and (2) the insurer is not paying out

---

57 *Albion Insurance Co Ltd v Government Insurance Office* (NSW) (1969) 121 342, 352, per Kitto J.

58 (1984) 36 SASR 182, 184, per Prior J; *Mercer v Petroleum Drilling Services (Aust) Pty Ltd* (1985) 39 SASR 277.

59 *South British Insurance Co Ltd v Norwich Winterthur Insurance* (NZ) (1982) 2 ANZ Insurance Cases 60–499, per White J; (but see *Government Insurance Officer (NSW) v QBE Insurance Ltd* (1985) 2 NSWLR 543 and *Allianz Australia Insurance Ltd v Territory Insurance Office* (2008) 23 NTLR 186). Contribution will apply even though the policies cover different financial limits.

60 [2009] NSWSC 514, per Rein J.

61 A Lloyd's syndicate.

62 At para. [286]. Rein J went on to deal with the second issue which arose, which was whether contribution is available where the party seeking contribution claims entitlement of 100% of the amount. There is a thorough discussion of the cases.

as a volunteer but, due to their legal relationship, is required to pay out on a loss[63] when an event happens.

In practice when dealing with non-marine insurance policies, an assureds' rights are circumscribed by the terms of the policies which will have provisions against double insurance excluding, or limiting, the insurers' liability if other insurers cover the same risk. This results in the assured having little choice but to go to all the insurers to recover for his loss.[64] Another important issue is whether the insurer who has paid out under a claim can then seek contribution from other insurers, and in what order.[65] The principles in *Newby v Reed*[66] which were laid down by Lord Mansfield[67] have been approved and followed.

5.3 Balancing the interest of the insurer and the assured

When balancing the interest between the insurer and the assured, it could be said that both interests are balanced. From the assured's point of view, the benefit of double insurance is the ability to take out numerous insurance policies,[68] and then make a claim against any one of the insurers, for the loss suffered. From the insurer's point of view, once payment has been made to the assured, the insurer can then claim contribution from a particular insurer or all the insurers.[69]

However, methods have been devised that ultimately lead to the insurer not paying out or only having to pay out to a limited extent. This is done by including in the insurance policy clauses or wordings.[70] This deprives the assured of the only potential advantage of double insurance acquired by paying additional premiums (i.e. that of having the choice against which insurer to proceed) and, second, eliminating the multiple debtor situation.[71] The "other insurance" exclusion

---

63 It has been suggested that where there is a rateable proportion clause which limits the plaintiff's liability to 50% of the loss this would be considered as voluntary: see "Double Insurance and payment of another's debt" (1993) 109 LQR 51.

64 See John Dunt and Wayne Jones, *Insurable Disputes* (3rd edn 2011), Chapter 10 "Double Insurance".

65 Where there are two policies which provide cover, one which provides general cover and the other, specific cover, there is no requirement that the specific cover takes priority over the general: *Wawanesa Mutual Insurance Co v Co-op Fire & Casualty Co* (1980) 119 DLR (3d) 188, 192, per McLeod J.

66 (1763) 1 Wm Bl 416.

67 The course of practice was that upon a double insurance, though the assured is not entitled to two satisfactions; upon the first action, he may recover the whole sum assured, and may leave the defendant therein to recover a rateable satisfaction from the other insurers.

68 Of course, assuming the criteria of double insurance is satisfied i.e. the policy covers the same assured, the same interest, the same subject matter and the same peril or risk.

69 Support has been found in *North British & Mercantile Insurance Co v London, Liverpool and Globe Insurance Co* (1877) 5 Ch D 569; *Commercial Assurance Co Ltd v Hayden* [1977] 1 Lloyd's Rep 1, *Bovis Construction Ltd v Commercial Union Assurance Co plc* [2001] 1 Lloyd's Rep 416 and *American Surety Co of New York v Wrightson* (1910) 16 Com Cas 37 (although this was a case dealing with fidelity guarantee). The Australian case of *Albion Insurance Co Ltd v Government Insurance Office of New South Wales* (1969) 121 CLR 342.

70 These include "other insurance" clauses or excess clause, rateable proportion clauses and exclusion clauses.

71 "Double Insurance and Payment of Another's Debt" (1993) 109 LQR 51.

in the policy narrows the choice of insurers to one, as opposed to two or more insurers.[72] For "rateable proportion" clauses the amount to be paid out under that policy will be the proportion as stated in the policy.[73]

5.4 Contribution: common law or statutory?

In *Caledonia North Sea v London Bridge Engineering*[74] Lord Caplan stated that the principle behind contribution was succinctly put by Professor Gloag,[75] as he stated as follows:

> It is a general principle, dependent on equity, that where several persons are liable for the same debt, each, though he may be liable in solidum to the creditor, is liable only for a proportionate share in a question with his co-debtors, and, if he is forced to pay more, has a right of relief against them. This principle, though it has been chiefly illustrated in questions between co-cautioners and insurance companies who have undertaken the same risk, does not depend on any specialty in the law of cautionary obligations or insurance, but proceeds upon a principle of law which must be applicable to all countries, that where several persons are debtors, all shall be equal.

Further he stated that an important factor is that the parties should have undertaken the same risk to the same common creditor. Although noting the distinction between an ordinary contract and a contract of insurance, he concluded that it was clear from the authorities that the contracts which give rise to the joint debt need not be identical. The question was whether the debtors obliged themselves for the same debt in relation to the creditors. Insurance, whatever its special features, is an indemnity to cover losses arising from a particular event. It is difficult to argue that any alternative position should apply.

Generally, contribution is sought where numerous insurers are liable for the same loss suffered by the assured. The issue in *Bovis Construction Ltd v Commercial Union Insurance Co Ltd*[76] was whether contribution was permitted (1) on the basis of the contractual relationship between the parties or (2) permitted due to the equitable principle or (3) permitted under some statutory provisions. Steel J concluded that it was based on equitable principles and the statutory provision, the Civil Liability (Contribution) Act 1978, did not apply. This was to prevent the assured from receiving more than he was entitled to be indemnified for.

In *Austin v Zurich General Accident and Liability Insurance Co Ltd*[77] a technical point arose as to who was the correct party to bring the claim. MacKinnon LJ

---

72 *Ibid.*
73 *Ibid.* The two insurers remain liable, but there is no overlapping liability, and the assured must seek indemnity from both of them. An interesting question was raised in the article:

> Why should the risk of insolvency of one insurer be imposed on the assured when the premium which the other insurer received was calculated on a full liability basis and when the insurer had no right to expect that another party would share the obligation?

74 [2000] Lloyd's Rep IP 249, 257.
75 W Gloag, *The Law of Contract* (2nd edn 1929), p. 206.
76 [2001] Lloyd's Rep IP 321.
77 [1945] KB 250.

was of view that as the claim of Bell, the insurer of the plaintiff, was one of contribution against Zurich on the principle of double insurance, such a claim ought to be brought in the name of the underwriters against the defendant company. It could not be pursued in the name of the assured under the guise of a claim by way of subrogation. Here the court emphasised the distinction between subrogation and double insurance.[78] Confusion can arise when there are more than two policies involved. The principles of subrogation ensure that the assured will not receive more than the indemnity that he is entitled to. Contribution on the other hand prevents any injustice arising between insurers. There have been occasions which have arisen where contribution and subrogation happen at the same time.

5.5 Limitation period for contribution claims

As between co-guarantors, co-contractors, or co-debtors, the statute of limitations runs against the right of contribution of one who has paid more than his share from the time of such payment:[79]

> The guarantor's primary cause of action against a co-guarantor for contribution is for money paid to the debtor's use at his request. Such a claim is treated as one founded on a simple contract, and so the period applicable is one of six years from the date on which the cause of action accrued . . . It is not clear whether the Civil Liability (Contribution) Act 1978 applies to claims between co-guarantors.[80]

Section 10[81] of the Limitation Act 1980 provides that a person has the right to recover contribution for any damage from another person, and can only bring an action after the expiration of two years from the date on which that right accrued.[82] If the claim is a common law claim not covered under the Limitation Act 1980, according to *Hampton v Minns*[83] the six-year limitation period should apply.

---

78 *Caladonia North Sea Ltd v British Telecommunications plc and Others* [2002] Lloyd's Rep IR 261 which stated that they were mutually exclusive.
79 *Halsbury's Laws of England* (4th edn 1976) Vol. 28, para. 875; *Wolmershausen v Gullick* [1893] 2 Ch 514, 528, 529. See also *Davies v Humphreys* (1840) 6 M & W 153, 168, 169, 151; *Walker v Bowry* (1924) 35 CLR 48.
80 *Halsbury's Laws of England* (4th edn 1976) Vol. 20, para. 278.
81 This is under s1 of the Civil Liability (Contribution) Act 1978. Also see *The Law Commission Limitation of Actions* (Law Com No 270).
82 No distinction is made between contribution and reimbursement: see *The Law of Contribution and Reimbursement* (2003), p. 258, 13.11.
83 [2002] 1 WLR 1.

CHAPTER 6

When the right of contribution arises

A THE UK POSITION

6.1 Factors required for contribution in double insurance

The right of contribution in double insurance will only arises where (1) there is double insurance, in that the two policies cover the same assured, the same interest and the same period and are more or less of the same scope; (2) both policies respond to the loss; and (3) the paying insurer has paid under a legal liability and not as a volunteer.

6.2 Same subject matter common to both policies and each policy must cover the same interest in the same subject matter

In the case of *North British and Mercantile Insurance Co v London, Liverpool and Global Insurance Co*[1] Messel J dealt with situations when double insurance arose and stated that clauses in insurance policies should be read in a sensible way. In that case there were two policies in effect. Problems arose due to the drafting of the clauses in the policies, which stated that the insurer would not be liable to contribute more than their rateable proportions if other insurance was present. There was a fire, which broke out destroying some grain, stored with Barnett & Co belonging to Rodocanachi & Co, who had similar policies covering grains stored at different locations. When reading the condition, Messel J stated that as the wharfinger's conditions were not just insuring the assured's property but the property which they were holding on trust or on commission, for which they

---

1 (1877) 5 ChD 569, CA per Jessel MR at 577. In this case, there was a floating policy by the wharfingers (Barnett & Co) which assured against loss and damage by fire of large amounts of grain and seed which was owned by Rodocanachi & Co who were merchants (they issued a merchants' policy) and stored with Barnett & Co. The floating policy was subject to the conditions of average with conditions. The material conditions on the back of the policy were as follows:

> 9. If, at the time of any loss or damage by fire happening to any property hereby assured, there be any other subsisting insurance or insurances, whether effected by the assured or by any other person, covering the same property, this company shall not be liable to pay or contribute more than its rateable proportion of such loss or damage. 10. In all cases where any other subsisting or insurances, whether effected by the assured or by any other person, covering any other property hereby assured, either exclusively or together with any other property on such property in and subject to the same risk only, shall be subject to average, the insurance on such property under this policy shall be subject to average in like manner.

The Supreme Court of Singapore has followed these principles in *China Insurance Co (Singapore) Pte Ltd v Liberty Insurance Pte Ltd* (formerly known as *Liberty Citystate Insurance Pte Ltd*) [2005] 2 SLR 509, at paras [9]–[17] of the decision.

were responsible, this was an important consideration when construing the conditions. The word "property" which was used in the conditions did not mean the actual chattel but the interest of the assured person. The words "covering the same property" in condition 9 did not mean the actual chattel, as it would result in an absurd result. Such wording was included where the same property, that is the subject-matter of the insurance, and the interests were the same.[2] Messel J stated that the condition must be read in a sensible way and that one should not assume that these "great companies", as he called them, intended to entrap their policyholders and to destroy the value of the contract of indemnity by reason of the accidental contract of somebody else, which had no connection with the subject matter of the contract, or with the price paid for the insurance. This can be seen from the development of the cases.[3] Messel J went on to state that it was his duty to make the instrument rational, and to make it a contract such as a person in the city of London would be likely to enter into, and not one which would lead to utter absurdity.[4]

It has to be established that the policy covers the same assured and relates to the same object, for the principles of contribution to apply.[5] The rule will not apply where there are different interests but the subject matter has been assured with numerous insurers.[6] It is essential that each policy must identify the same assured in respect of the same loss.[7] In *GIO General Ltd v Insurance Australia Ltd t/as NRMA Insurance*,[8] Master Harper looked beyond the manner in which the original claim by the injured person was framed,[9] and stated that this was not capable of being determinative of whether dual insurance applied. The case of *GIO General Ltd v Insurance Australia Ltd t/as NRMA Insurance* involved a workers' compensation insurer seeking contribution against a motor vehicle third-party insurer. An employee was injured while driving a truck, and sued his employer for failing to provide a safe system of work. The employer's insurance policy was issued between 2002–2003 financial year under the Workers

---

2 It would never apply to, for example, cases of a tenant for life, or a first mortgagee and second mortgagee, both insuring the same goods.

3 *Gale v Motor Union Insurance* [1928] 1 KB 359; *Weddell v Road Traffic General Insurance Co* [1932] 2 KB 563; *Structural Polymer Systems Ltd v Brown* [1999] CLC 268; *National Employers Mutual General Insurance Association v Haydon* [1980] 2 Lloyd's Rep 149; *Austin v Zurich General Accidental and Liability Insurance Co Ltd* [1945] KB 250 ; *State Fire Insurance General Manager v Liverpool and London and Globe Insurance Co Ltd* [1952] NZLR 5.

4 Although to leave the issue of whether a clause would result in an absurd result to a judge may not be the best alternative as different judges may decide differently.

5 *Nichols & Co v Scottish Union and National Insurance Co* (1885) 14 R (Ct of Sess) 1094; *Scottish Amicable Heritable Securities Association Ltd v Northern Assurance Co (No 2)* (1886) 18 LR Ir.

6 *GIO General Ltd v Insurance Australia Ltd (t/as NRMA Insurance)* (2008) 15 ANZ Insurance Cases 61-761; Anthony A Tarr, Juliet-Anne Tarr and Malcolm Clarke, *Insurance The Laws of Australia* (2010) para. [22.1.3770].

7 *GIO General Ltd v Insurance Australia Ltd (t/as NRMA Insurance)* (2008) 15 ANZ Insurance Cases 61-761.

8 (2008) 15 ANZ Insurance Cases 61-761.

9 Here whether as a claim by an employee against an employer or as a claim against the owner or driver of a motor vehicle.

Compensation Act 1951,[10] and provided for indemnification to the employer on satisfying certain conditions. In addition to employer's insurance policy, third-party insurance was issued between 19 January 2002 and 18 January 2003 to the registered owner of the truck against liability for bodily injury to persons caused or arising out of the use of the truck. The court[11] accepted the wide scope of the traditional third-party policy, and that typical dual insurance cases involved loading or unloading cases where the motor vehicle was stationary. The court stated that, in such cases, it did not matter how the claim was framed against the employer and the vehicle owner, when deciding whether double insurance applied or not.[12] Master Harper went on to explain[13] that "for dual insurance to apply it is essential that both policies indemnify the assured against the same loss".

Although the distinction between insurable interests in the same subject matter[14] may seem easy to comprehend,[15] it is not that straightforward. For example, in *Boag v Economic Insurance Co Ltd*[16] there was a Lloyd's all risk transit policy in place which was issued to cover tobacco and cigarettes which were on transit by motor vehicle from collection of the goods until delivery, including loading and unloading anywhere in England and whilst temporarily off-loaded in the course of transit. There was a fire policy, which was also in place that covered the premises to where the goods were driven. There was a fire at the assured's premises where the lorry was driven. The issue was whether the all risk transit policy came within the definition of the assured's own stock-in-trade at the assured's premises. The court held that it did not, and it was not covered by the fire policy. Therefore, the issue of contribution did not arise.

---

10 Provided that if, during the period of insurance, the employer was liable to pay compensation under that Act to a territory worker, or to pay any other amount in respect of the employer's liability independently of the Act for an injury to a territory worker.

11 Referring to *Australian Iron & Steel Ptd Ltd v Government Insurance Office of New South Wales* (1990) 20 NSWLR 633.

12 The court relied on the decision of the NSW Court of Appeal in *AMP Workers Compensation Services (NSW) Ltd v QBE Insurance Ltd* (2001) 53 NSWLR 35.

13 At para. [32].

14 In *American Surety Co of New York v Wrightson* (1910) 27 TLR 91, where it was stated that the principle of the insurance covering the same subject matter is not confined to property insurance and will apply to any property. Also see *Godin v London Assurance Co* (1758) 1 Burr 489 and *North British & Mercantile Insurance Co* (1877) 5 Ch D 569. In *Elf Enterprise (Caledonia) Ltd v London Bridge Engineering Ltd* [2000] Lloyd's Rep 581 where the court reconfirmed that the law has rejected any attempts to confine contribution to particular categories of insurance. The question ought to be settled on the basis of principle rather than by reference to any rigid classification such as insurance and non-insurance.

15 *Boys v State Insurance Australia Ltd (t/as NRMA Insurance)* (2008) 15 ANZ Insurance Cases 61–761; *Strech v State Insurance General Manager* (1984) 3 ANZ Insurance Cases 60–577 (NZHC) (landlord and tenant); *North British & Mercantile Co v London, Liverpool & Globe Insurance Co* (1877) 5 Ch D 569 (bailor and bailee); *Hills Flooring Ltd v WH Foote & Co Ltd* (1985) 3 ANZ Insurance Cases 60–646 (NZHC); *Portavon Cinema Co Ltd v Price & Century Insurance Co Ltd* [1939] 4 All ER 601; *American Surety Co of New York v Wright* (1910) 27 TLR 91; *Boag v Standard Marine* [1937] 2 KB 113.

16 [1954] 2 Lloyd's Rep 581.

In *Davjoyda Estates Pty Ltd v National Insurance Co of New Zealand Ltd*,[17] the court[18] concluded that there would be double insurance even though there was what seemed to be different rights, which according to the judge was "precisely the same thing" when dealing with a trustee and beneficiary situation. It has been commented[19] that this statement is *obiter* and incorrect, because there was a significant difference in the interest between that held by the trustee and that held by the beneficiary. The burden to insure will be provided for in the trust deed or the will creating the relationship, but problems may arise if the beneficiary sought to become the registered proprietor of the real property subject to the trust.[20]

In *Tip Top v State Insurance*[21] the court held that the policies in effect covered the same subject matter. There were two policies, the first covered property of the assured or any property for which the assured was in some way responsible and the other policy was in the form of a loan receipt which was issued by the bailor's own insurer and which covered the same property.

The above discussion illustrates the problem of identifying whether there is double insurance It is not always clear, as what may be treated as same subject matter in one jurisdiction may differ in another jurisdiction.

6.3 Each policy must cover the same risk

Both policies must cover the same risks.[22] Cases such as *Bovis Construction Ltd v Government Insurance Office of New South Wales*[23] and *Albion Insurance Co Ltd v Government Insurance Office of New South Wales*[24] state that it would be sufficient if the policy covers the risk that has given rise to the claim in more than one policy.[25] In *Albion Insurance Co Ltd v Government Insurance Office of New South Wales*, Barwick CJ, McTiernan and Menzies JJ, in the joint judgment of the court stated:

> The element essential for contribution is that, whatever else may be covered by either of the policies, each must cover the risk which has given rise to the claim. There is no double insurance unless each insurer is liable under his policy to indemnify the assured in whole or in part against the happening which has given rise to the assured's loss or liability ... The matter can, we think, be decided simply enough by inquiring whether payment by one insurer of the policy holder's claim for indemnity

---

17 (1965) 69 SR (NSW) 381.
18 Brereton J.
19 *Sutton on Insurance Law* (4th edn 2014), para. 19.40.
20 Anthony A Tarr, Juliet-Anne Tarr and Malcolm Clarke, *Insurance The Laws of Australia* (2010).
21 (2002) 7 NZBLC 103, 564.
22 See Marine Insurance Act 1906, s32(1); *Arnould's Law of Marine Insurance and Average* (17th edn 2010), p. 1537, para. 32–04; *MacGillivray & Parkington on Insurance Law* (13th edn 2017) para. 25–001.
23 (1967) 121 CLR 342. Also see *Borg Warner (Aust) Ltd v Switzerland General Insurance Co Ltd* (1989) 16 NSWLR 421, Cole J at 428–432; *Baulderstone Hornibrook Engineering Pty Ltd v Gordian Runoff Ltd* (2008) 15 ANZ Insurance Cases 61–780; contrast *Newland v Nominal Defendant* [1983] 1 Qd R 514 (FC), Macrossan J at 522.
24 (1969) 121 CLR 342.
25 Therefore, the policies do not have to be co-extensive.

would provide the other insurer with a defence to a like claim against it. It clearly would, and it would simply because the policy holder had by the payment made been indemnified against the risk assured against. He had received all that he was entitled to receive under both policies so that payment by one insurer would discharge both. Thus, payment by one is made for the benefit of both, and, contribution is equity.

However, in *National Mutual Fire Insurance Co Ltd v Insurance Commissioner*,[26] the Supreme Court of Victoria had to consider the plain, ordinary meaning of the policy or notional contract of insurance under the provisions of a statute to ascertain whether another policy had covered that risk. It would seem that whether the policies cover the same risk bears more heavily on the insurer, as this would mean that the insurer might not be able to seek contribution from other insurers. The cases[27] suggest that there is a development of the test used to ascertain whether the risk has been covered in both policies. The courts do not place emphasis on whether there is temporary or partial overlap under policies, which cover different classes of business, as long as the assured subject matter in question came within each of them.[28]

In the early case of *Australian Agricultural Co v Saunders*,[29] the court[30] was concerned with the issue of whether there was double insurance and whether, on the construction of the policy, the goods were "assured elsewhere". In *Australian Agricultural Co v Saunders*, the assured covered some 3,000 pounds of wool, which were in bales. The wording of the policy stated that the insurance covered the wool against fire, "in any shed, or store, or station, or in transit to Sydney by land only, or in any shed or store, or on any wharf in Sydney, until placed on board ship". At a later stage another policy, which was a marine insurance policy,[31] was taken out as well. This policy covered a shipment of wool, which was transported from Newcastle in New South Wales to Sydney then to London. This policy included "trans-shipment or landing or reshipment at Sydney". The

---

26 [1985] VR 811. See also *Commercial Union Assurance Co of Australia Ltd v Commissioner of Insurance* [1080] VR 443; *Norwich Winterthur Insurance (Aust) v State Government Insurance Office* (1982) 149 CLR 327; *CE Heath Underwriting & Insurance (Aust) Pty Ltd v State Government Insurance Commission (SA)* (1983) 34 SASR 1 (workers' compensation legislation).

27 *Albion Insurance Co Ltd v Government Insurance Office of New South Wales* (1969) 121 CLR 342; *Australian Agricultural Co v Saunders* (1875) LR 10 CP 668; *National Mutual Fire Insurance Co Ltd v Insurance Commissioner* (1985) 3 ANZ Insurance Cases 60–652; *Zurich Insurance Co v Shield Insurance Co* [1988] IR 174; *American Surety Co of New York v Wrightson* (1910) 103 LT 663; *Baulderstone Hornibrook Engineering Pty Ltd v Gordian Runoff Ltd* (2008) 15 ANZ Insurance Cases 61–780; cf *Newland Nominal Defendant* [1983] 1 Qd R 514 (FC), 522; *Government Insurance Office (NSW) v QBE Insurance Ltd* (1985) 2 NSWLR 543.

28 *Australian Agricultural Co v Saunders* (1875) LR 10 CP 668 and *Colinvaux's Law of Insurance in Hong Kong* (2nd edn 2010). Although this approach has not been followed by the English courts and they are of the view that the short-term or coincidental does not constitute double insurance when dealing with the right of contribution.

29 (1875) LR 10 CP 668.

30 By the Court of Exchequer Chamber.

31 The policy term included a clause:

> Lost or not lost at and from the river Hunter to Sydney per ship or steamers and thence per ship or steamers to London, including the risk of craft, from the time that the wools are first waterborne, and of transshipment and landing and reshipment at Sydney.

defendants' policy provided that it was a condition of the policy that if wool was "assured elsewhere", notice of such insurance should be given; if not, this would lead to the policy becoming void. The plaintiffs did not notify the defendants of the new policy. There was a fire at the warehouse in Sydney where the wool was stored for reshipment. There was a claim made by the plaintiffs under the first policy for the loss suffered. The court agreed with the Court of Common Pleas that the plaintiffs were entitled to recover. The court was of the view that the latter policy did not cover the goods that were kept on land, but only covered marine risks. Therefore, the goods did not fall within the meaning of "trans-shipment, landing, and reshipment at Sydney", while it was being stored in the warehouse. Therefore, double insurance did not arise. The goods were not "assured elsewhere".[32] Notice[33] of the second policy[34] did not have to be given. The effect of the judgment was that if there was insurance provided for in other policies it did not mean that they would cover insurances of a different nature, which overlapped in part, and that the phrase should be limited to policies covering the same class of business and the same subject matter.[35]

In the case of *American Surety Co of New York v Wrightson*[36] the plaintiffs were an American insurance company, which issued a policy[37] agreeing to pay an American bank for any loss or damage that occurred out of any loss or damage, caused by the dishonesty of any of its employees, which came within the amount shown in the schedule. Another policy at Lloyd's[38] was taken out which provided that "the underwriters were liable for loss caused by the dishonesty of employees and for loss sustained by the loss or destruction on the owners' premises of bonds, banknotes and owing to fire or burglary". The employee who had been assured misappropriated a sum of $2,869 and the bank claimed full indemnity in the sum of $2,500. The balance of $180 was then claimed under the Lloyd's

---

32 This was held to mean "a specific insurance of the sane risks, and that the words were not satisfied in the case of different policies upon different policies upon different risks, by the mere possibility of one overlapping the other under some possible circumstances".

33 There have been cases where if there is a waiver of notification requirement in one policy, where the policies overlap, there is no double insurance.

34 In some cases, notification of subsequent policies may be a condition precedent, as was the case in *Kempton v National Fire Insurance Co*. This as mentioned above could be problematic for an assured who is unaware of the existence of such insurance. There have been situations where the assured has taken out a subsequent insurance policy but the latter policy never came into existence, and the court has stated that there is no double insurance: *Steadfast Insurance Co Ltd v F & B Trading Co Ltd* (1971) 125 CLR 578. In the United States the general approach of the courts is to favour the insurer and where further insurance is taken out it is likely to lead to the property being destroyed to claim indemnity. In Germany, the German Insurance Contract Act provides that in such situations the assured must inform each insurer of the existence of other insurance, without undue delay. Also see "Commentaries on the Recent Amendment of the Insurance Law of the People's Republic of China Regarding Insurance Contracts from the Perspective of Comparative Law" (2011) 10(4) Washington University Global Studies Law Review 749, 779, 780. It is questionable whether *Saunders* is authority for double insurance, in light of the comments by Pollock B at p. 678.

35 *Colinvaux*, para. 12–094.

36 (1901) 103 LT 663. See also Charles Digby Jess, *The Insurance of Commercial Risks: Law & Practice* (4th edn 2011), para. 20–04.

37 One of the employees was guaranteed up to $2,500.

38 This was for the sum of $40,000.

policy. Both these sums were paid, and it was agreed that under the policies the loss was covered. The only issue was the amount of contribution that was to be apportioned between the insurers. Hamilton J was of the view that there was no double insurance, because the policies were not of the same nature or the same scope. Hamilton J compared the wording of the policies. He concluded that on a reading of the instrument there was great dissimilarity between their scope and their capital. He looked at the headings used under the policy: one was called a security ship bond and the other was called a guarantee. Both policies indemnified National Park Bank of New York against losses to its property caused by certain perils assured against. He considered the coverage under the policy and the time period of the coverage. He noted that the policies covered different items and different periods. The plaintiffs' policy assured against the bad faith and dishonesty of the scheduled employees only, and no other risks. The insurance was for a period of 12 months, commencing 1 June in each year. The other policy covered periods commencing on 18 November of each year, and covered not only the loss to the assureds' property by bad faith and dishonesty but loss caused by their negligence, loss by fire, and covered them locally not merely on their own premises, but if the documents were in transit in their own hands, or in the hands of their clerk or servants throughout the limits of Greater New York. The Lloyd's policy contained a self-renewing clause, stating that any loss occurring was subject to a further premium of a certain per cent. He concluded that the common elements of insuring against loss by dishonesty and bad faith of the employers differed considerably in scope, in terms of the hazard covered and the persons and things bringing those hazards into operation.

This approach suggests that it does not matter whether the policy is accidentally overlapping or not. It could be argued that it is unnecessary for the scope of coverage of the policy to be identical because it would not be possible to apportion any specific part of the premium paid under the wider policy to the subject matter in question.[39]

The courts[40] in *Zurich Insurance Co v Shield Insurance Co Ltd*[41] had to deal with the issue of whether both policies in force covered the same risk. The two policies were a motor insurance policy and an employers' liability policy. Under the motor insurance policy, the plaintiff had to indemnify Q for any negligent driving of Q's motor car and had to indemnify the driver if a person who was driving the motor car was doing so with Q's authority. The defendant under an employers' liability policy was liable to indemnify Q against liability to pay compensation for injury, accident or disease sustained by any employee of Q, arising out of and in the course of his employment with Q. S, an employee, was seriously injured when his motor car, which was owned by Q and in which he was a passenger, collided with a bus. D was driving. D and S were both travelling in the

---

39 *Colinvaux's Law of Insurance in Hong Kong* (2nd edn 2010) p. 417.
40 Supreme Court of Ireland, per Gannon J.
41 [1988] IR 174.

course of their employment. S recovered a substantial sum and Q could claim indemnity from D for the full award. Gannon J stated:[42]

> It is an accepted principle of law that a plaintiff who has recovered full satisfaction in damages from one party cannot also recover the same or any part of that claim from another party equally liable for the same damage. There may not be double satisfaction merely because there is double indemnity. A corollary of this principle is that as between those persons who are liable in damages to compensate the same plaintiff upon the same cause of action the one who discharges the liability in full is entitled in equity by subrogation to recover from the others a contribution of the proportions of what he has paid commensurate with the liability of such others to the same plaintiff.

Gannon J referred to the decision and principles discussed by Lord Mansfield in *Godin ev London Assurance Co.*[43] He went on to explain:[44]

> In the circumstances of double insurance the insurer by whom the claim is discharged in full has an equitable right to require contribution from the other insurers so that the payment is borne fairly by all (*North British and Mercantile Insurance Company v London, Liverpool, and Globe Insurance Company* (1877) 5 Ch D 569). But an insurer who has made payment to the assured under the policy of indemnity is entitled to the benefit of all rights of the assured in respect of the loss for which indemnity was provided, including the right of action against the tortfeasor who has caused the loss. Thus by subrogation the insurer may in the name of the assured recover from the tortfeasor the loss of the assured for which the insurer provided indemnity under the policy. Because the purpose of such right of subrogation is to enable the insurer obtain the benefit of any means whereby the loss or damage may be or may have been diminished this right of subrogation is not limited to pursuing an existing cause of action (See *Castellain v Preston* (1883) 11 QBD 380). Because of the emphasis placed upon this latter aspect I think it desirable to quote from the judgment of Brett LJ in that case at p. 388 at of the report where he says:
>
>> In order to apply the doctrine of subrogation, it seems to me that the full and absolute meaning of the word must be used, that is to say, the insurer must be placed in the position of the assured. Now it seems to me that in order to carry out the fundamental rule of insurance law, this doctrine of subrogation must be carried to the extent which I am now about to endeavour to express, namely, that as between the underwriter and the assured the underwriter is entitled to the advantage of every right of the assured, whether such right consists in contract, fulfilled or unfulfilled, or in remedy for tort capable of being insisted on or already insisted on, or in any other right, whether by way of condition or otherwise, legal or equitable, which can be, or has been exercised or has accrued, and whether such right could or could not be enforced by the insurer in the name of the assured by the exercise or acquiring of which right or condition the loss against which the assured is assured, can be, or has been diminished.

---

42 [1988] IR 174, 177.
43 (1758) 1 Burr 489 at 492.
44 [1988] IR 174, 178, 179.

At pp. 389 and 390 of the report Brett LJ goes on to say:

> And I go further and hold that if a right of action in the assured has been satisfied, and the loss has been thereby diminished, then, although there never was nor could be any right of action into which the insurer could be subrogated, it would be contrary to the doctrine of subrogation to say that the loss is not to be diminished as between the assured and the insurer by reason of the satisfaction of that right.

The court held that while the liability to afford indemnity under each of the policies could arise on the happening of the same event, neither the interest of the assured under those policies nor the risks assumed by the plaintiff and defendant respectively were the same. The liability under the motor policy was Q's vicarious liability as owner of the motor car, for the breach by the driver of a duty owed to the public in general and not for any breach of a duty which was owed by Q to S as his employer. The employers' liability policy covered the liability of Q for breach of its duty to take care in relation to S's safety in the performance of his duties under his employment. As a result, the right to contribution did not arise.

A similar conclusion on incidental overlaps was reached in *Elf Enterprise (Caledonia) Ltd v London Bridge Engineering Ltd*.[45] The claim was for death and personal injuries on the Piper Alpha platform in 1988, where the assured had no right to be indemnified by third parties who had granted the assured the contractual indemnities, which was covered by the insurance policy. If the insurers advanced such a claim it would have to be done by way of a right to contribution from the indemnifier. The defenders were required to make good to the pursuers any loss, which had resulted through the death or injury of any of the defenders' employees. The action was brought on indemnities. Elf Enterprise (Caledonia) Ltd (formerly OPCAL) sought reimbursement of £130 million, which was paid to the families of the men killed in the explosion and fire on the Piper Alpha offshore platform in 1988, and to survivors from contractors who had been engaged by them when operating the platform.[46] The insurance covered the liabilities of the Piper Alpha oil platform for death or personal injuries to persons employed on the platform. There was also a contractual obligation by the contractors to indemnify operators against death or injury to contractors' employees unless caused solely by negligence or wilful misconduct of the operators. The wording of the indemnities varied between the contracts. The general principle was that a party could only recover under the indemnity for the loss incurred. The defenders argued that the plaintiff could not seek compensation twice as they had already been indemnified. This was on the basis that the losses which were covered and the beneficiaries of the insurance and the indemnities were the same. Lord Caplan stated that two indemnifiers were jointly and severally liable, and if

---

45 (1997) Times, 28 November.
46 The court was surprised that the issue of contribution was only raised after 381 days of proceedings, even though it was the fundamental issue in the case.

one had paid out more than his share, he is entitled to seek relief from the other co-obligants on a pro rata share.[47] He stated:[48]

> Where in such a case there were two indemnifiers their liability was joint and several, and if either paid more than his share then he was entitled to relief from his co-obligants to the extent of their pro rata share (*Gloag Contract* (2nd edn) p. 206; *Moss v Penman* (1993 SC 300)), for otherwise the latter would benefit from unjust enrichment.
>
> Unlike a right of subrogation in an action arising out of a delict, such a right of relief resided in the co-obligant directly; see *Sickness and Accident Assurance Association Ltd v General Accident Assurance Corporation Ltd* ((1892) 19 R 977); *Albion Insurance Co Ltd v Government Insurance Office* ((1969) 121 CLR 342).
>
> The question was whether there was any justification in confining the application of those principles to insurance alone. In *Eagle Star Insurance Co v Provincial Insurance* ([1994] 1 AC 130) Lord Woolf had expressed the view that the law of contribution applied to a statutory as opposed to a contractual indemnity. What the pursuers expressly claimed were the subrogation rights of their insurers. They referred to *Darrell v Tibbits* ((1880) 5 QBD 560) which concerned a tenant's obligation to repair the property, where the Court of Appeal had held the landlord's insurers were entitled to be put in the place of the assured.
>
> Contribution among joint debtors liable in respect of the same loss did not seem to have been argued. The pursuers also argued that the question of contribution arose only in the context of insurance and not where collateral indemnities were included in contracts for the provision of services: compare *Scottish Amicable Heritable Securities Association v Northern Assurance Co* ((1883) 11 R 287).
>
> They referred to *Parr's Bank Ltd v Albert Mines Syndicate* ([1900] 5 Com Cas 116) but that was not on all fours with the present case: there the sureties were liable for a predetermined sum, whereas the insurers had accepted liability only for a loss on the sureties defaulting.
>
> Their obligations had been different but here both insurers and contractors were pledged to cover the same loss. Nor on the terms of the policy in *Parr's Bank* could the insurers have been obliged by the sureties to contribute towards any payment made by the latter. What mattered was whether the parties had undertaken the same risk to the same common creditor.
>
> However different the genesis of the contracts, there could be no doubt that the pursuers' insurers and the contractors, if they had any obligations to OPCAL and the participants, had it under contracts of indemnity.
>
> It was clear from the authorities that the contracts that gave rise to the joint debt did not need to be identical.
>
> If a party enjoyed the benefit of two or more indemnities covering the same loss and he recovered his whole loss it was difficult to see on what principle he retained a right to enforce his indemnity against the non-paying indemnifier. His loss had been satisfied.
>
> There was no principle that entitled him to enforce his loss from the indemnifier as there was in the case of a wrongdoer. Perhaps if the indemnities had been granted to cover only facts occasioned by the indemnifier's own negligence some nice questions would arise, but that was not the case here. No one suggested that the defenders had been negligent.

---

47 W Gloag, *The Law of Contract* (2nd edn 1929); *Moss v Penman* (1993 SC 300).
48 (1997) Times, 28 November.

The question ought to be settled on the basis of principle rather than by reference to any rigid classification such as insurance and non-insurance. The law had rejected attempts to confine contribution to particular categories of insurance.

The court went on to say that the right of subrogation was different as the right of relief lay with the co-obligant directly.[49] On the facts of the present case, the court concluded that although the obligations were different, both the insurers and contractors were pledged to have covered the same loss. The insurers were not obligated by their sureties under the terms of the policy in Parr's Bank to contribute towards any payment made by the sureties. The court stated that the issue in the case was whether the parties had undertaken the same risk to the same common debtor. He agreed that the contracts which gave rise to the debts did not have to be identical in nature and, once a party had recovered the whole loss under two or more indemnities covering the same loss, the party would not be entitled to enforce his indemnity against the non-paying indemnifier as he had already satisfied his loss. The insurers of OPCAL and the participants did not have any right of subrogation in respect of the indemnities granted by the defenders. They had no title or interest to sue. The only way open to the insurer was to recover by way of a separate action under contribution.

It has been commented that the above reasoning is flawed[50] as it overlooks (1) the different nature of the two contracts, which would of itself preclude contribution;[51] (2) the consequences that had the contractor paid out first, they could have sought contribution from the insurers even though they were not parties to the insurance contract and had not paid a premium for protection under it; and (3) the long-standing rule applicable to subrogation, namely that payment by the insurers entitles them to the rights of the assured against any third party who is not an insurer covering the same risk by way of double insurance.

The House of Lords,[52] reversing the decision of Lord Caplan, held that the insurers were entitled to exercise rights of subrogation, as the law was settled. Where an insurer had indemnified in full an assured for loss that was covered by a contract of insurance between them, he could enforce, in his own name, any right which was present to the assured. Lord Bingham in the House of Lords stated that the issue was whether, (1) as the operator contended, a subrogated claim properly made in its name by its insurer, who has indemnified it under a policy of insurance, to enforce a contractual right of the operator against the contractor or (2) as the contractor contended, a claim for contribution by one party liable to indemnify the operator against another? The operator's view was preferred.[53]

---

49 He referred to *Sickness and Accident Assurance Association Ltd v General Accident Assurance Corporation Ltd* (1892) 19 R 977 and *Albion Insurance Co Ltd v Government Insurance Office* (1969) 121 CLR 342.
50 *Colinvaux's Law of Insurance in Hong Kong* (2nd edn 2010) p. 418.
51 Their insurable interests were different.
52 *Caledonia North Sea Ltd v British Telecommunications plc* [2002] Lloyd's Rep IR 261.
53 Agreeing with the decision of the judges of the Inner House.

B THE AUSTRALIAN POSITION

The position in Australia[54] was illustrated in *Albion Insurance Co Ltd v Government Insurance Office of New South Wales*,[55] where the court re-affirmed the presence of double insurance where an assured is assured against the same risk with two independent insurers. To insure with two insurers was lawful but an assured could not receive more than the loss suffered and for which indemnity under each of the policies is present. The assured can however choose from which insurer he wishes to seek indemnity.

The High Court of Australia in *Albion Insurance Co Ltd v Government Insurance Office (NSW)*[56] applied the principles as laid down in *Government Insurance Office of New South Wales v Royal Exchange Assurance of London*.[57] The plaintiff was the insurer of A & V Bence Pty Ltd under an employees' indemnity principle where liability of employees was covered under the Workers' Compensation Act under an endorsement for common law liability.[58] The defendant also assured the same company under the Motor Vehicles (Third Party Insurance) Act. Under the Motor Vehicles (Third Party Insurance) Regulations, the third-party policy provided as follows:

> Such insurer hereby agrees that during the period commencing and terminating as shown above, and during any period for which the insurer may renew this policy, the insurer shall insure the owner and any other person who drives the motor vehicle, whether with or without the authority of the owner, against all liability (except a liability referred to in subsection two of section ten of the said Act) incurred by the owner and/or the driver in respect of death of or bodily injury to any person caused by or arising out of the use of the motor vehicle in any part of the Commonwealth of Australia.

At the time of the accident, both policies were current and enforceable. Street J held that none of the exceptions available under the policies applied to the present case. Both the employers' indemnity policy which was issued by the plaintiff and the third-party policy issued by the defendant contained provisions

---

54 Australia has the same requirements for there to be the presence of double insurance: *Albion Insurance Co Ltd v Government Insurance Office (NSW)* (1969) 121 CLR 342 (Barwick CJ, McTiernan and Menzies JJ; *Allianz Australia Insurance Ltd v Territory Insurance Office* (2008) 23 NTLR 186; *GIO General Ltd v Insurance Australia Ltd (t/as NRMA Insurance)* [2008] ACTSC 38.

55 [1969] CLR 342.

56 (1969) 121 CLR 342. In *Commercial & General Insurance Co Ltd v Government Insurance Office (NSW)* (1973) 129 CLR 374, the High Court of Australia re-iterated that the right to contribution between co-insurers which was recognised by the decision in *Albion*, could never amount to a complete indemnity but must be always confined to rateable contribution. This is the equity which can be relied on for rateable contribution.

57 (1965) 82 WN (Pt 1) (NSW) 468.

58

> Subject to the terms and conditions of this Policy it is hereby declared and agreed that the Insurer will indemnify the Employer against liability to pay damages at Common Law or under the Compensation to Relatives Act 1897 as amended, for, or in respect of, personal injury to any employee who is a worker within the meaning of the Workers' Compensation Act, 1926–1954, and who at the time of the injury is in the direct employment of the Employer and is engaged in an employment to which this policy expressly applies.

indemnifying A & V Bence Pty Ltd in respect of liability on its part to pay damages to the employee for injuries. The three-member court[59] agreed that the doctrine of contribution applied to insurance against liability to third parties and stated that it only applied when each insurer insures against the same risk. They do not have to be identical. They provided the following examples where (1) one insurer insures properties A and B against fire and the other insurer only insures property A against fire; (2) one policy may be for a limited amount and the other may be for an unlimited amount; and (3) one policy may cover the risk of a whole voyage and the other may cover only part of the voyage. These differences may only cover the amount of contribution recoverable but do not bear upon the question of whether or not each insurer has assured against the same risk so as to give rise to contribution. The court pointed out that each policy must cover the risk before contribution would arise. The court further explained that double insurance did not arise unless each insurer is liable under his policy to indemnify the assured in whole or in part against the incident, which gave rise to the assured's loss or liability. The court departed from the views of Myers J and concluded that the assured company assured against the same risk with both the plaintiff and the defendant. The court was of the view that the matter could easily be resolved by making enquiries whether payment by one insurer of the policyholder's claim for indemnity would provide the other insurer with a defence to a like claim against it. The answer was that it did, as the policyholder had been indemnified once payment was made to him. The assured had already received the amount he was entitled to under both policies, so that payment by one insurer would discharge both insurers. The reason was that payment made by one of the insurer was beneficial to both of them, and because contribution is an equitable concept.[60] It could be argued that this approach[61] should be adopted by the English courts.

The authors of the textbook *Australian Insurance Law*[62] illustrated how this approach was applied to the decision in the case of *Australian Agricultural Co v Saunders*.[63] It was concluded that if the test as laid down in *Albion Insurance Co Ltd v GIO*[64] (NSW) was to be applied in *Saunders*, the result would be that it would be "inevitable" that there was double insurance present. The authors went on to say that the fire and marine insurance policies, when applying their ordinary meaning of applying to wool in the warehouse awaiting transfer onto a ship, would have provided a defence to the fire insurer, on payment by the insurer.

---

59 Barwick CJ, McTiernan and Menzies JJ.
60 This principle applies to other classes of insurance which were also contracts of indemnity. See *North British and Mercantile Insurance Co v London, Liverpool, and Globe Insurance Co* (1877) 5 Ch Div 569. Although counsel in *Albion Insurance Co Ltd v Government Insurance Office (NSW)* (1969) 121 CLR 342, when referring to the decision in *American Surety Co of New York v Wrightson* (1911) 27 TLR 91 the stated that the comments were *obiter* and did not actually touch upon the issue. Also see *Borg Warner (Aust) Ltd v Switzerland General Insurance Co Ltd* (1989) 5 ANZ Insurance Cases 60–905 and *Compare Newland v Nominal Defendant* [1983] 1 Qd R 514.
61 Barwick CJ, McTiernan and Menzies JJ.
62 AA Tarr, Kwai-Lian Liew and W Holligan, *Australian Insurance Law* (2nd edn 1991).
63 (1875) LR 10 CP 668.
64 (1969) 121 CLR 342.

In *Saunders* the issue arose in the context of a policy term, and not whether there was contribution or not. It was said that the two situations should not be treated in the same way. There was no reason for the rules of contribution to apply in such actions, as the Insurance Contracts Act 1984 removed the effect of the policy terms which restricted coverage preserving the contributions claims.

In *Nisner Holdings Pty Ltd v Merchantile Mutual Insurance Co Ltd*[65] the court's view was followed that where there was incidental overlap, it would not automatically result in double insurance.[66] In Australia contribution will exist between different types of policy even if the overlap between the policies is incidental. This will apply if both insurers are liable for the same loss.[67] In *New Zealand Municipalities Co-operative Insurance Co Ltd v South British Insurance Co Ltd*[68] insurers made a contribution claim. The insurers paid out under a public liability policy for injuries sustained by a cyclist caused by a trench, which had been dug for the Board. The High Court held that the same risk was not covered where one of the polices covered the negligent act of the employees of the board and the other policy covered vicarious liability which did not cover negligent acts of the employees. Therefore, there was no contribution and as a result the second insurer was unable to claim contribution.

6.4 The policies must be in force and valid

An insurance policy must be legal[69] when loss occurs[70] and must not have lapsed.[71] The court in *Sickness & Accident Assurance Association Ltd v The General Accident Assurance Corporation*[72] had to deal with a policy, which was effective when the premium had not been paid. The insurance company indemnified the tramway company for the loss suffered. The insurance company then brought an action under the right of contribution against the other insurance company for the money that had been paid out on the basis that the risk covered was identical. The agreement entered into stated that the policy covered a tramway against accidents, which were caused by their vehicles to third parties for a period

---

65 [1976] 2 NSWLR 406.
66 Although this case was not dealing with the issue of contribution.
67 *Sutton on Insurance Law* (4th edn 2014), para. 19.140.
68 High Court, Christchurch, 29 July 1983 (A165/81).
69 An example used where a policy uses a PPI clause where the production of such a policy itself would be sufficient for proof of interest. Such clauses would not lead to a double insurance situation arising and such clauses will be considered void. This has been provided for by s4 Marine Insurance Act 1906: see John Dunt and Wayne Jones, *Insurance Disputes: Double Insurance* (3rd edn 2011), Chapter 10.
70 See cases such as *Eagle Star Insurance Co Ltd v Provincial Insurance plc* [1994] 1 AC 130; *Sickness & Accident Assurance Association Ltd v General Accident Assurance Corp Ltd* (1892) 19 R 977; *North British & Mercantile Insurance Co Ltd v Public Mutual Insurance Co (NZ)* (1935) 54 NZLR 678; *Monksfield v Vehicle & General Insurance Co Ltd* [1971] 1 Lloyd's Rep 139; *QBE Insurance Ltd v Fortis Insurance Ltd* [1999] VSC 212.
71 *Ocean Accident and Guarantee Corporation v Williams* (1915) 34 NZLR 924, 927–929, per Denniston J.
72 (1892) 19 R 977; *North British & Mercantile Insurance Co Ltd v Public Mutual Insurance Co (NZ)* (1935) 54 NZLR 678 (SC) 683–684.

of 12 months from 24 November 1888 inclusive. This was however subject to the condition that there could be no insurance effected until premium had been paid. An accident occurred on 24 November 1888, before the premium had been paid under the terms of the contract. Lord Low held that the pursuers had the right to sue. The court held there was no attachment to the second policy, as the requirement that the premium had to be paid had not been complied with. There was no double insurance.

Where there is a clause which provides the insurer with the right to repudiate its liability under the policy, as a result of the breach of a condition which was included therein, there will be no right for contribution.[73] This was held in *Monksfield v Vehicle and General Insurance Co Ltd*.[74]

The same principles were applied in Australia. The courts have stated that it would be unfair to the assured where the assured had no knowledge of the existence of other insurance.[75] In New Zealand, the Supreme Court in *North British & Mercantile Insurance Co Ltd v Public Mutual Insurance Co of NZ*[76] applied the English authorities[77] to adopt a broader approach. The court stated that the subject matter of the insurance included that which was common to both the contracts, that is, the use of the trailer with a motor car and the use of the motor car with a trailer. Similar principles were followed in *Commercial Union Assurance Co New Zealand Ltd v Murphy*,[78] *Western Australian Bank v Royal Insurance Co*[79] and *Stretch v State Insurance General Manager*.[80]

---

73 A similar approach can be seen in *Eagle Star Insurance Co Ltd v Provincial Insurance plc* [1993] 2 Lloyd's Rep 143.
74 [1971] 1 Lloyd's Rep 139.
75 *Commercial Union Assurance Co New Zealand Ltd v Murphy* [1989] 1 NZLR 687; *Western Australia Bank v Royal Insurance Co* (1908) 5 CLR 533.
76 [1935] NZLR 678, 683–684.
77 *Godin v London Assurance Co* (1758) 1 Burr 489 (marine insurance), *North British and Mercantile Insurance Co v London, Liverpool, and Globe Insurance Co* (1877) 5 ChD 569 (fire insurance).
78 [1989] 1 NZLR 687, 690 (CA), per Cooke P for the Court.
79 (1908) 5 CLR 533, 571, per Higgins.
80 (1984) 3 ANZ Insurance Cases 60–577.

CHAPTER 7

The rights of an insurer to seek contribution and enforcement

7.1 Contribution: principles of equity

The issue of contribution between insures causes difficulty. The court adopts basic principles of equity, which is one of reason, justice and fairness.[1] The court should and will take into consideration all matters which go towards ensuring a just result.[2] This approach was adopted by Lord Mansfield in *Godin v London Assurance Co*,[3] who stated that the rights of contribution was found in equity and not in contract. He stated:[4] "If the assured is to receive but one satisfaction, natural justice says that the several insurers shall all of them contribute pro rata, to satisfy that loss against which they have all assured."

7.2 Entitlement to contribution

An assured cannot seek to recover more than the loss sustained by him. An assured can choose to recover his loss from any insurer, and it is then for the insurer to seek contribution from the other insurers.[5] In *Australian Eagle Insurance Co Ltd v Mutual Acceptance (Insurance) Pty Ltd*,[6] Priestly JA stated that two questions should be

---

1 *Albion Insurance Co Ltd v GIO (NSW)* (1969) 121 CLR 342, *GRE Insurance Ltd v QBE Insurance Ltd* [1985] VR 83 and *Albion Insurance v GIO* (NSW) (1969) 121 CLR 342. Kitto J stated how he considered the principle should be applied as follows:

> What attracts the right of contribution between insurers, then, is not any similarity between the relevant insurance contracts as regards their general nature or purpose or the extent of the rights and obligations they create, but simply the fact that each contract is a contract of indemnity and covers the identical loss that the identical assured has sustained; for that is the situation in which "the assured is to receive but one satisfaction" . . . and accordingly all that insurances are "regarded as truly one insurance": *Sickness and Accident Assurance Association Ltd v General Accident Assurance Corporation Ltd* (1892) 29 ScLr836 at 837.

Further see *Accident Compensation Commission v Baltica General Insurance Co Ltd* [1993] 1 VR 467, 480.

2 *Government Insurance Office of New South Wales v Crowley* (1975) 2 NSWLR 78 (S Ct NSW Helsham CJ in Eq); *GRE v QBE*, [1985] VR 83 at 103–104, per McGarvie J *American Surety Co of New York v Wrightson* (1910) 103 LT 663 (KBD/Hamilton J).

3 (1758) 1 Burr 489.

4 (1758) 1 Burr 489, 420.

5 *Hebdon v West* (1863) 3 B & S 579; *Commercial & General Insurance Co Ltd v Government Insurance Office* (NSW) (1973) 129 CLR 374, 379–380 (CLR); *Boys v State Insurance General Manager* [1980] 1 NZLR 78 (SC), 92 per Barker.

6 [1983] 3 NSWLR 59, 64 (CA); *Zurich Australian Insurance Ltd v Metals & Minerals Insurance Pte Ltd* (2007) 209 FLR 247; *Limit (No 3) Ltd v ACE Insurance Ltd* (2009) 15 ANZ Insurance Cases 61-823; *QBE Insurance Ltd v AMP Workers' Compensation Services (NSW) Pty Ltd* [2000] NSWSC

asked as to whether an insurer can claim contribution from another insurer where there is double insurance: (1) did the insurers have a common burden, and (2) if the assured was to be paid under both policies, would they be paid twice in respect of the same loss. The law of contribution does not apply if (1) is answered in the negative. If the answer to (2) is no, the rule against double insurance does not operate.

7.3 Policy providing method of apportionment

It must first be established that both insurers are liable for the loss, before identifying which method of calculation should be adopted.[7] The method of apportionment depends on the policy wording. If no such provision exists, it will be divided on a pro rata basis.[8]

An insurer who makes ex gratia payments will not be entitled to recover[9] contribution from the other insurers.

7.4 Methods of calculating insurer's liability for insurance

7.4.1 Maximum potential policy

There are three methods of calculation[10] for contribution: (1) the maximum potential liability, (2) the independent actual liability; and (3) the common liability.

1070. In *Borg Warner (Aust) Ltd v Switzerland General Insurance Co Ltd* (1989) 16 NSWLR 421, 432 per Cole J where he stated that

> In my view it accords with doctrines of equity in the sense of "reason, justice and law" that two insurers should equally contribute to indemnify an employer where the employer has attracted a liability flowing equally from an event occurring within the period assured by each insurer, coupled with a common act of the employer crystallising liability in a given quantum under each insurance policy.

Although see *Manufacturers' Mutual Insurance Ltd v National Employers' Mutual General Insurance Association Ltd* (1990) 6 ANZ Insurance Cases 61–038, per Priestly JA at 76, 965.

7 Although see *HIH Casualty & General Insurance Ltd v FAI General Insurance Co Ltd* (1997) 9 ANZ Ins Cas 61–358, which was a case dealing with settling of third-party claims against an assured.

8 There have been previous discussions as to whether there was a need for a rateable proportion clause in a policy, due to the equitable right of contribution which would usually result in obtaining payment from co-insurers. However, if the clause was different from that found in *Hayden's* case, and similar to the one in *Weddell v Road Transport* [1932] 2 KB 563, the conclusion reached would be different where, if there was double insurance, one insurer's liability would be reduced due to either a breach of condition or because he was insolvent. See also Commercial Union where the wording provided as follows: "If at the time of any claim arising under this Section there shall be any other insurance covering the same risk or any part thereof the Company shall not be liable for more than its ratable proportion thereof." The Lloyd's policy provided: "If any claim covered by this Policy is also covered in whole or in part by any other insurance, the liability of the Underwriters shall be limited to their rateable proportion of such claim."

9 See *Sydney Turf Club v Crowley* [1971] 1 NSWLR 274. Although subrogation may be a possible option in such cases. Also see *Layne & Bowler (Australasia) Pty Ltd v Pearson Machine Tool Co Ltd* (unreported, 25 November 1984) dealing with workers compensation liability and where the court originally stated that the insurer could seek recovery by contribution from other insurers who had also provided cover in respect of injuries which occurred in previous years. However, see *Manufacturer's Mutual Insurance Ltd v National Employer's Mutual General Insurance Association Ltd* (1990) 6 ANZ Ins Cas 61–038 where the courts to the opposite view and considered that the correct approach would be to look at each year separately to which policy covered that particular year.

10 Although see s80(1) Marine Insurance Act which applies to non-marine insurance cases.

These methods of calculation lead to different results. There is no requirement that the court follow one particular method. It is entirely discretionary as to which equitable principles apply.[11] This however causes uncertainty for insurers.[12]

In most cases, insurers are liable for different sums or the sum exceeds the liability of one but not the other.[13] In *North British & Mercantile Insurance Co Ltd v Public Mutual Insurance Co (NZ)*,[14] the court had to determine whether the damages, which had become payable, should be apportioned between two insurers, and on what basis. Smith J stated: "The remaining question is as to the basis of contribution. In the absence of a clear indication to the contrary, I think that the loss must be borne equally." However, problems do arise when there are policies, which cover different kinds of property.

Under the maximum potential liability, the contribution of the insurer having lesser liability is limited to the proportion that its maximum liability bears to the aggregate of maximum liabilities under both policies.[15] The maximum potential liability has been used when dealing with marine insurance policies,[16] although it has been rejected in liability insurance cases.[17]

The case of *Commercial Union Assurance Co Ltd v Hayden*[18] was an appeal against the judgment of Donaldson J on how liability between insurers should be apportioned, where the same risk is covered and the policy itself contained a provision limiting liability to a rateable proportion of any claim. The plaintiffs, Commercial Union Assurance Co Ltd, provided public liability cover for Messrs GT and D Cartwright. There was a limit for £100,000 on any one occurrence. The Lloyd's underwriters also provided public liability cover. A limit of

---

11 *Government Insurance Office of New South Wales v Crowley* [1975] 2 NSWLR 78 per Helsham J at (84–85), although it was not expressly stated it could be seen that the approach taken was of a discretionary nature.

12 But not for an assured as he would have received his share of indemnity for the loss he has suffered.

13 In the People's Republic of China, the law was amended in the form of Insurance Law of the PRC, art.56, which states that in the event of double insurance, the proposer shall notify all the insurers concerned of the relevant information with respect to such double insurance; the total sum of indemnity patments made by all insurers concerned in double insurance shall not exceed the assured value. Unless specified otherwise in the contract, the insurers concerned shall be liable for indemnity payment in proportion to their respective sum assured and the total amount of sum assured; the proposer of double insurance may, with respect to the portion of the total amount of the sum assured which exceeds the assured value, request each insurer to return the premiums pro rata. Further, double insurance has been defined as insurance where a proposer enters into insurance contracts with two or more insurers in respect of the same assured subject matter, the same insurable interest and the same assured event, while the total sum assured exceeds the assured value.

14 (1935) 54 NZLR 678, 684, per Smith J.

15 *Drayton v Martin* (1996) 67 FCR 1, *Commercial Union Assurance Co Ltd v Hayden* [1977] 1 QB 804. See *North British & Mercantile Insurance Co v London, Liverpool & Globe Insurance Co* (1877) 5 Ch D 569, 583(CA), per Mellish LJ; *Commercial Union Assurance Co Ltd v Hayden* [1977] QB 804, 812 (QB) per Cairns LJ, where it was questionable whether the maximum liability approach applied when the policies contained rateable proportion clauses.

16 Hardy Ivamy, *General Principles of Insurance Law* (6th edn 1993) 528–529; Marine Insurance Act 1909, s86(1).

17 *American Surety Co of New York v Wrightson* (1911) 27 TLR 91; *Commercial Union Assurance Co Ltd v Hayden* [1977] QB 804.

18 [1977] 1 QB 804.

£10,000 was taken out for one accident or a series of accidents, which arose out of one event. However, both policies contained a rateable proportion clause, which stated: "If at the time of any claim arising under this section there shall be any other insurance covering the same risk or any part thereof [Commercial Union] shall not be liable for more than its rateable proportion thereof." A personal injury claim was made against Messrs Cartwright, which was settled by Commercial Union, after agreement by both insurers, but subject to without prejudice to the issue of apportionment. There was a dispute as to apportionment. Commercial Union claimed that liability should be shared equally. The Lloyds Underwriter argued that apportionment should be ten-elevenths against Commercial Union and one-eleventh against Lloyd's. Lloyd's argued that the calculation of contribution should be on a "maximum liability" basis. Commercial Union argued that the calculation should be on an "independent liability" basis. The court stated that:

> To ascertain the proportions of contribution by reference to the limits of indemnity would, in my judgment, be an odd way of sharing the "burthen" in equity between insurers; and in cases where there was a limit under one policy but none under another, it would be a difficult judicial task, probably an impossible one, to assess, as counsel for Lloyd's suggested should be done and Donaldson J agreed (I quote from the judgment):
>
> ... the maximum cover which will ever be likely to be provided by the unlimited policy and to compare this figure with the sum specified in the other policies.

The court held that where there are two insurers with differing upper limits for claims, the inference was that they were both accepting the same level of risk up to the lower of the limits and a "rateable satisfaction" would be an equal division of liability up to the lower limits. Under the maximum potential liability method, the contribution of the insurer having the lesser liability is limited to the proportion that its maximum liability bears to the aggregate of maximum liabilities under both policies.[19]

In *Drayton v Martin*[20] FAI General Insurance Co Ltd brought an action against the underwriters for contribution for amounts paid out in settlement to the Draytons, who were former clients of Mr Martin. The Draytons were advised to invest in endowment policies, which were issued by National Mutual Life Association of Australasia Ltd. The Draytons later suffered losses as a result of taking out the endowment policies. A professional indemnity policy was issued to Mr Martin, who was an accountant, as well as an investment adviser. Mr Martin also assured under an Accountant's Professional Indemnity Policy, which was underwritten by the accounting underwriters. Sackville J stated the issue of contribution as follows:[21]

---

19 *Drayton v Martin* (1996) 67 FCR 1 at 37–38.
20 (1996) 137 ALR 145.
21 (1996) 137 ALR 145, 177.

The final issue is the extent of the contribution the accounting underwriters should be required to make to the payment of $292,000 made by FAI in discharge of Mr. Martin's liability to the Draytons. Mr. Williams contended that the appropriate approach was to apply the "maximum potential liabilities test. Under this test, the contribution of the insurer having the lesser liability is limited to the proportion that its maximum liability bears to the aggregate of maximum liability bears to the aggregate of maximum liabilities under both policies.

Sackville J went through the authorities and confirmed that there "is no rule of law that the maximum liabilities test must be applied".[22] He was of the view that the correct approach was that the "amount which has been paid should be borne in proportion to the burden of liability which has been paid should be borne in proportion to the burden of liability which that payment has lifted from the respective insurers."

The result of maximum potential liabilities is that the same proportions will be used for each insurer throughout the range of possible claims, and liability "scaled evenly, in the same proportion to the total amounts of cover, from the smallest possible loss to a loss which equals or exceeds the total of the sum assured".[23] Where there are concurrent polices and the policies do not have rateable proportion clauses, the proportions should be calculated under the maximum liability principle.[24]

7.4.2 Independent actual liability

Under the independent actual liability method, contributions are assessed according to the proportions that the independent liability of each insurer, if it were the only insurer, bears to the total of such independent liabilities.[25] It has been stated that where an average clause is provided for in one or more of the polices, the correct method to calculate contribution is the independent liability method.[26]

The courts have concluded, in some cases, it did not matter which test applied and that liability would be based on 50% apportionment. For example, in *WorkCover Qld v Suncorp Metway Insurance Ltd*,[27] the parties agreed to apportion on a 50% basis, and the liability of each insurer was to indemnify to an unlimited extent for the full amount of damages suffered by the assured. The payment by WorkCover Queensland released Suncorp Metway Insurance Ltd from liability

---

22 (1996) 137 ALR 145, 177.
23 Australian Law Reform Commission, *Insurance Contracts*, Report No 20 (AGPS, 1982) at para. 292, p. 179.
24 *Colinvaux*, 12–123.
25 *Drayton v Martin* (1996) 67 FCR 1, at 37–38; *Commercial Union Assurance Co Ltd v Hayden* [1977] 1 QB 804. Where Policy A provided a formula for sharing liability and another policy, Policy B, was silent as to this, Policy A could not bind the insurers of Policy B. In these situations the courts in Canada have also tended to favour the Independent Liability approach: *Dominion of Canada General Insurance Co v Wawanesa Mutual Insurance Co* (1985), 64 BCLR 122 (SC) This case was approved in *Milos Equipment Ltd v Insurance Corporation of Ireland* 47 BCLR (2d) 296 at 302.
26 *MacGillivray and Parkington*, para. 25–033 *et seq*.
27 [2005] QCA 155.

to the assured for its rateable proportion, as its potential liability was for the full amount of the claim. The contribution should be 50%. In WorkCover Qld, Jerrard JA concluded that there was double insurance between WorkCover and Suncorp, which entitled the Suncorp, as co-insurer to pay an equal contribution to an assured which WorkCover had indemnified. In the present case, an employee of a transport business partnership was injured while driving the prime mover, which was owned and registered under the name of Mr White of the partnership, as required under the Motor Vehicle Insurance Act 1936 (Qld). At the time there were accident insurance policies in effect between WorkCover and the Whites, who made up the partnership. The Whites were entitled to indemnity under this policy. WorkCover took over the proceedings from the employee against the Whites. A compromise was reached and WorkCover paid the employee $632,183.67 together with $40,000 as agreed costs. The trial judge held that there was sufficient identity of the assured which resulted in double insurance. Equality was equity and therefore Suncorp Metway was required to contribute $336,091.83. Jerrard JJ did not favour the argument that Suncorp's contribution should be 50% of Mr. White's indemnified liability.

Another case which adopted the "independent liability" approach was *Government Insurance Office (NSW) v Crowley*,[28] where Helsham J commented that the maximum liability approach would work equitably in most insurance cases when dealing with specific property, but the correct method for calculating contribution between insurers would be by reference to their actual liability, and not their potential or maximum liability. However, in the case of *QBE Insurance Ltd v GRE Insurance Ltd*,[29] a case dealing with specific property, the court chose to apply the independent liability approach when assessing contribution. It has been commented[30] that the independent liability approach is "much more realistic in its results".

In *Guidebook to Insurance Law in Australia and New Zealand*,[31] Thomas stated "each case depends upon its own facts. In each, the court has to decide, as a matter of justice, the amount each insurer is obliged to contribute." To ascertain the correct approach, when the court decides the issue of contribution, it has been stated that the purpose of contribution must be considered.[32,33]

The Australian Law Reform Commission, *Insurance Contracts*, Report No 20,[34] discussed independent actual liabilities as follows:

---

28 [1975] 2 NSWLR 78, 83 per Helsahan J (where the case of *Pandurevic v Southern Cross Constructions (NSW) Pty Ltd (No 3)* [2012] NSWSC 1601 was distinguished).

29 (1983) 2 ANZ Insurance Cases 60–533, decision of the Supreme Court of Victoria.

30 *Commercial Union Assurance Co Ltd v Hayden* [1977] QB 804, 816 (QB); *Lumley General Insurance Ltd v QBE Insurance (Aust) Ltd* [2008] VSC 216: *Drayton v Martin* (1996) 67 FRC 1, Sackville, 37–39; *HIH Casualty & General Insurance Ltd v FAI General Insurance Co Ltd* (1997) 9 ANZ Insurance Cases 61–358.

31 RG Thomas, *Guidebook to Insurance Law in Australia and New Zealand* (1981), p. 228.

32 *Government Insurance Office (NSW) v Crowley* [1975] 2 NSWLR 78, 83 per Helsham; *The Laws of Insurance, Insurance and Income Security*, para. [22.1.3740].

33 *The Laws of Insurance, Insurance and Income Security*, para. [22.1.3740].

34 (AGPS, 1982), at para. 292, p. 179.

On the other hand, under an apportionment according to the total of the independent actual liabilities of the two insurers, their independent liability will be equal and each will bear one-half (and not a relatively small and relatively high proportion respectively) of any loss up to a claim which equals the amount of the policy with the lower limit. The liability under that policy will then equal one-half of the sum which it insurers and its liability will thereafter progressively increase until it reaches the sum assured by that lesser policy, at the stage when the amount of the loss is equivalent to or greater than the total of the sums assured by both policies.

The Report considered the views of insurers and considered, in particular, the views of Cairns LJ[35] and Lawton J[36] in *Commercial Union Assurance Co Ltd v Hayden*. They favoured the application of the independent liability calculation.

The Report at para. [296] identified two problems with the independent actual liabilities test, and stated as follows:

First, questions of contribution only arise when a loss has occurred. At that point, subject to any limitation in the policy, each insurer has an absolute obligation to indemnify the assured against his loss. The only fair method of apportionment is to divide the loss equally between the two insurers up to the lower limit of liability. Secondly, the independent actual liabilities method produces anomalous results. This point can be illustrated by reference to the earlier example, in which the loss was $44000 and the cover given by the two policies, A and B, was $2 000 000 and $40 000 respectively. Suppose the premium paid in respect of policy A was $10 000 and the premium in respect of policy B was $500. If each insurer charges the same premiums, the first $500 paid in respect of policy A would be paid to cover the risk of loss up to $40 000. The remainder of the premium would be to cover the additional risk of loss in excess of $40 000. Each insurer has been paid the same premium in respect of the loss for which it is liable, yet the insurer under policy A bears a disproportionate amount of the loss if the independent actual liabilities method is adopted. The fairest method of apportionment appears to be on the basis of equal independent liabilities. Only on that basis would each insurer bear an equitable proportion of the loss in relation to the premiums each has been paid. The equal actual liabilities test is the only test which appears to be both practical and sound in principle. The Commission recommends that, in the absence of contrary agreement between the affected insurers, losses should be apportioned on the basis of equal independent liabilities.

A The calculations

Maximum potential liability

Example A where the difference between the respective policy is not that great:
Policy A £1000000 Policy B £500000 Loss suffered: 10000
The maximum liability apportionment under both policies = Policy A + Policy B is £1500000
Policy A pays 1000000 × 10000 = 6667
1500000
Policy B pays 500000 × 10000 = 3334
1500000

---

35 [1977] QB 804, 815–816.
36 [1977] QB 804, 822.

Independent actual liability apportionment

The total independent liabilities is 20000.
Policy A pays $\frac{10000 \times 10000}{20000} = 5000$
Policy B pays $\frac{10000 \times 10000}{20000} = 5000$

Example B (where the difference between the respective policy is greater):

Policy A £2000000 Policy B £50000 Loss suffered: £10000
The maximum liability apportionment under both policies = Policy A + Policy B is £2500000
Policy A pays $\frac{2000000 \times 10000}{2500000} = 8000$
Policy B pays $\frac{50000 \times 10000}{2500000} = 2000$

Independent Actual Liability Apportionment

The total independent liabilities is £60000.
Policy A pays $\frac{10000 \times 10000}{60000} = 1667$
Policy B pays $\frac{50000 \times 10000}{60000} = 8333$

7.4.3 Common liability test

This method of calculation requires each party to be liable up to the limits of the lower-valued policy, and surpluses will be covered by the insurer with the higher policy. For example:

Policy A is capped at £100,000 and Policy B is capped at £250,000. If the loss incurred is £100,000, then the liability will be divided equally between them. If the loss is £150000, then the sum will be divided equally between the insurers and the extra amount will be borne by the insurer with the higher policy.

7.5 Where policy does not cover a specific loss but a wide range of events

In *GIO v Crowley*,[37] the court considered that the maximum liability test may do justice and equity where there is some direct bearing between the loss and policy, as opposed to some wider range of events. The amount of insurance cover could not enable one to ascertain in a fair manner the proportion of loss each insurer should bear for the loss in question.

In *GRE Insurance Ltd v QBE Insurance Ltd*,[38] a dispute arose between two insurance companies regarding individual liabilities for damages caused by a fire

---

37 (1975) 2 NSWLR 78.
38 [1985] VR 83.

to certain buildings issued with cover notes. QBE sought contribution from GRE of a rateable proportion of $800,000 to which the latter was liable, the court however ordering GRE pay $373,333.33 together with $111,079.93 interest and costs to QBE. There was a contribution clause (clause 10) in QBE's policy stating that:

> If at the time of any destruction or damage to any property hereby assured, there be any other subsisting insurance or Insurances, whether effected by the Assured or by any other person or persons, covering any of the property, the Company shall not be liable to pay or contribute any more than its rateable proportion of such destruction or damage.

QBE then sued GRE for contribution.[39] The court adopted the independent liability test, stating that there were competing bases.

O'Bryan J held QBE was entitled to contribution from GRE according to the principles based on equity. Each insurer was liable under its particular policy rateable proportions and, if not liable as a matter of equity, QBE would be entitled to recover from GRE in a similar rateable proportion. The Court of Appeal however held that this was the wrong approach. There was no right of contribution where only one insurer is liable.[40] There was no subrogation as the assured had no claim against GRE. Therefore, no cover had been effected at the time of the occurrence of the loss or damage, and there was no right which was capable of being assigned or subrogated to QBE.

GRE v QBD was followed in *William John Drayton, Nancy Mae Drayton, Bruce William Drayton and Ross Drayton v John Leslie Martin, the National Mutual Life Association of Australasia Ltd and Roger Budd Agencies Pty Ltd Fai General Insurance Co Ltd*[41] where the judge adopted the independent liabilities test as there was nothing to suggest that the application of such test would not lead to a just and equitable result.

7.6 Where there is property insurance

In *Commercial Union Assurance Co Ltd v Hayden*[42] Lawton J stated:

> When there are two insurers with differing upper limits for claims, the inference I would draw is that they were both accepting the same level of risk up to the lower of the limits. It this be so, in my judgment, "a rateable satisfaction," to use Lord Mansfield CJ's phrases [in *Newby v Reed* (1763) 1 Wm Bl 4161, would be an equal division of liability up to the lower limit; the burden of meeting that part of the claim above the lower limit would fall upon the insurer who had accepted the higher limit.

---

39 But later amended its claim to add the vendor and the purchaser as plaintiffs and to add a claim based on subrogation.
40 *North British and Mercantile Insurance Co v London Liverpool and Globe Insurance Co* (1877) 5 Ch D 569; *Sickness and Accident Assurance Association v General Accident Assurance Corporation* (1892) 19 R (Ct of Sess) 977; Hardy Ivamy, *General Principles of Insurance Law* (6th edn 1993) p. 526; *Halsbury's Laws of England* (4th edn 1976) Vol. 25, para. 539.
41 [1996] FCA 1504 (24 May 1996).
42 [1977] QB 804, 822F–G.

The Court of Appeal stated[43] that under property insurance the property is assured for a stated sum by an insurer, which represents the value of the property. Where there was under-insurance, the assured could not recover more than the amount assured for under the property. Where there is over-insurance, an assured cannot receive more than the sum assured for. The premiums for such types of insurance differ. The court considered which meaning was more likely to have been intended by reasonable businessmen, and the type of parties involved. It acknowledged that each limit of the liability and premium was fixed without knowledge of the limit under any other policy that was issued or which was going to be issued. The method which provided the most realistic result was the independent liability method. The court was of the view that it would be artificial to use the limits under two policies to adjust liability where claims were within the limits of either policy.

7.7 Where there is marine insurance

However, in *O'Kane v Jones, The Martin P*[44] Deputy High Court Judge Richard Siberry QC stated:

> 260. There has been some discussion of the correct method of apportionment in leading textbooks: see, for example, Arnould, Vol. I, at paras 436–438, and Vol. III (the Supplement), para. 438, O'May, Marine Insurance (1993) pp. 500–502, and Goff & Jones, The Law of Restitution (6th edn 2002) at para. 14–022. In O'May, it is stated that in cargo insurance the method often adopted in practice on valued policies is to deem there to be double insurance only to the extent of the lower assured value -in other words, to adopt the common liability method. It was in the light of the comments in O'May that the learned editors of Arnould withdrew, in Vol. III, their tentative suggestion, in Vol. I para. 439, that the independent liability approach adopted by the majority in *Commercial Union* was likely to be held to be of general application to marine insurance, and substituted the comment that the correct approach must be regarded as an open question in the present state of English law.

He was of the view that the legislation, the Marine Insurance Act s80(1), which provided that in cases of double insurance, each insurer was bound to contribute rateably to the loss in proportion to the amount for which he is liable under his contract, excluded the common liability method and "to that extent at least is not ambiguous".[45] Furthermore, the court concluded that as the end result was the same for both methods of calculation, the court did not have to decide whether the independent liability test or the maximum liability approach was correct.

---

43 [1977] QB 804, 814G–H.
44 [2004] Lloyd's Law Rep 389, 442.
45 [2004] Lloyd's Law Rep 389, 442.

7.8 Criticisms and possible solutions

7.8.1 The Australian Law Reform Commission

These three tests have been applied at the discretion of the courts, where there is no express agreement between the parties. The application of each test has not been straightforward. The Australian Law Reform Commission[46] discussed the problems which arose from the methods of calculating contribution. The view of the Commission was that the independent liability test[47] should be applied in all cases regardless of the nature of the policies and whether the policy contained clauses which modified contribution rights. The consensus was that the maximum liability method was complex and difficult to apply, as the main concern between insurers was that they should be "entitled to know what their rights and liabilities are".

In *Commercial Union Assurance Co Ltd v Hayden*,[48] the court held that the independent liability basis would be a more realistic approach. However, the court acknowledged that it would be problematic to apply, where one insurer's proportion steadily increases, if the loss is larger. The court did not provide a definition of what would be considered as "larger losses".

In *Zurich Australian Insurance Ltd v Metals & Minerals Insurance Pte Ltd*[49] Johnson J considered the authorities of previous decisions when deciding which approach should be used. In Zurich, Zurich argued that the correct approach was the maximum potential liability method. MMI on the other hand argued that the correct approach should be the independent actual liability approach in the case of liability insurance. Johnson J stated that the court is entitled to apply some variant of the two types of approaches if there are particular circumstances, which make it necessary to depart from the principal methods if a just result is to be achieved. He was of the view that as the maximum potential liability method[50] had been rejected on numerous occasions by the courts, in both Australia and Great Britain when dealing with liability insurance, that approach should not be followed. The arguments in favour of the independent actual liability were more compelling. To follow the maximum potential liability would lead to gross distortion of reason, justice and fairness because it would mean that the insurer would be liable for only a small amount of total liability.

---

46 *Insurance Contracts*, Report No 20 (AGPS, 1982) at para. [295] under heading Discussion Paper.
47 The ICA was of the view that the basis for assessment for contribution on the independent liability test was satisfactory. But see the view of the IBCA, which argued that he agreed maximum liabilities basis was established by practice and stated that there was no "valid reason" for the application of the independent liability insurance for all cases. See para. [295] of the Australian Law Reform Commission Report.
48 [1977] 1 QB 804.
49 (2007) 209 FLR 247.
50 The ALRC Report No 20 also aired its dissatisfaction with this approach as well, as lacking any legal or other principle.

Although the application of the maximum potential liability may be an attractive method to adopt as it results in the same proportion throughout the range of possible claims, regardless of the sum of loss claimed, the courts are more likely to apply the independent actual liability method.[51]

In *Tai Ping Insurance Co Ltd v Tugu Insurance Co Ltd*[52] it was argued that the court should not use either the maximum liability test or the independent liability test. Instead, a new approach should be adopted, called the "other interest" approach. This approach takes into account "other interests" of the subject of the policy. In this case, it was the particular loss involving the property of all six companies which was considerably more than the maximum limit of liability under the Tugu/General Accident Policy. Counsel in that case did not put forward any authorities to support this "ingenious and diverting" argument. The court, although agreeing that this was an innovative course, concluded that this could well amount to a recipe for potential inequity in the context of a contribution exercise which looks at equitable principles when looking at the facts of the case. The court correctly pointed out that such an application could lead to a large number of variables arising which would extend beyond the well-known parameters of the maximum liability test and the independent liability basis. The learned judge placed reliance on Professor Bird's analysis of the complexities which could arise, even where there were only two insurers. This is the correct approach especially when you have, as was pointed out by Professor Bird, sums which have been assured which are not the same or the policies have different ranges so it becomes difficult to calculate the ranges.[53]

7.8.2 The draft Insurance Contracts Bill 1982

Clause 77 of the draft Insurance Contracts Bill 1982[54] looked at liability where there were separate contracts of insurance for the same loss suffered. The draft Bill included a formula which insurers objected to. The insurers were of the view that issues of contribution should be left to the insurers. Further a "hands-off" approach was a better approach to adopt when looking at apportionment in general insurance.[55]

---

51 *Government Insurance Office (NSW) v Crowley* [1975] 2 NSWLR 78; *GRE Insurance Ltd v QBE Insurance Ltd* [1985] VR 83. Also see *John v Rawling* (1984) 36 SARA 182 where an employee had died in a trailer accident, where the trailer and the utility were both assured with different insurers, in addition to the workers compensation insurance which was also in existence. Pryor J rejected the argument put forward that each insurer should be liable rateably for the loss according to each insurer's actual liability. He held that each insurer was liable in respect of the same losses equally. It was of no significance that one insurer's liability arose in two contracts.
52 [2001] 2 HKC 401, 406H–I.
53 [2001] 2 HKC 401, 408A–B.
54 In Appendix A.
55 Section 76(3). See *General Accident Insurance Co of Australia Ltd v Sun Alliance Insurance Ltd* (1989) 17 NSWLR 80 (interest payable on contribution).

7.9 Volunteers and the right of recovery

The general principle is that contribution can only be made if both insurers were liable at the date of the loss, and not if liability only arises afterwards. The case which discusses voluntary payment by an insurer when there is double insurance was *Legal & General v Drake Insurance*.[56] The ruling of the trial judge, that the plaintiffs could claim 50% contribution from the defendant, was appealed on the following grounds:

> that the judge erred in (1) holding that the plaintiffs were entitled in equity to contribution from the defendants as co-insurers; (2) holding that the plaintiffs were entitled to such contribution notwithstanding that the defendants were not liable to the assured under the terms of their insurance by reason of his admitted breaches of conditions precedent to any liability of the defendants to indemnify him; (3) declining to follow or apply *Monksfield v Vehicle and General Insurance Co. Ltd.* [1971] 1 Lloyd's Rep. 139 or the relevant passages in the standard text books on insurance law to the same effect; (4) holding that where the assured was not entitled to indemnity from insurer A by reason of matters occurring after the events or accident which gave rise to the claim, but he was entitled to be and was indemnified by insurer B, then insurer B was entitled to contribution from insurer A, who was not entitled to rely on such matters as against insurer B unless insurer B had acted unfairly so as to prejudice insurer A.

The defendants argued that the plaintiffs were only liable to 50% due to double insurance, and that the excess that was paid out was made voluntarily. The court stated that double insurance must exist at the date of the loss beforecontribution arose. A right to repudiate would be a good defence against contribution if the assured had been in breach of a condition prior to the loss.[57] It was further argued that an insurer would not be entitled to contribution where payment was made voluntarily in excess of their liability.

In *Legal & General v Drake Insurance*, the driver of a car was assured under two policies covering different periods. Under both the Drake Policy and the Legal and General Policy, it was a condition precedent that immediate notice in writing be provided if other insurance was entered into. The policies included a rateable proportion clause, which provided:

> If at the time any claim arises under the policy there is any other insurance covering the same loss, damage or liability the society will not pay or contribute more than its rateable proportion if the person making the claim to be indemnified is the policy holder, nor make any payment or contribution if the person claiming to be indemnified is not the policy holder.

The Court of Appeal, re-affirming the principles laid down by Lord Mansfield, stated that an insurer is entitled to recover from another insurer in cases of double insurance, not based on contract but based on equity, and that the burden should

---

56 [1992] QB 887.
57 Citing *Colinvaux's Law of Insurance* (8th ed) (2010).

be shared equally.[58] The court considered the situation where the requirement to give notice was a condition precedent, where the liability of an insurer to indemnify only arose when notice was given, and where notice was not given due to the assured claiming only against one of the insurers.[59] The court was of the view that potential liability would suffice. However, the validity of the claim was an important factor that also had to be considered. Even though parties are permitted either to exclude or modify the right of contribution by contract, they cannot modify or exclude the equitable right to contribution. The Court of Appeal held that the plaintiff could recover only a contribution in respect of Mr Arora but, as contribution was to be made by the plaintiff in excess of his rateable contribution between co-insurers, no claim in contribution could be made. Contribution had to be made but limited to the amount of the rateable proportion clause. A third party who has obtained judgment against an assured in respect of liability, required to be assured under the Act,[60] could enforce the judgment against the insurer, notwithstanding any provision contained in the policy of insurance, such as the rateable proportion clause. Section 148 of the Road Traffic Act 1972 strictly prohibited policy defences. The insurer must exercise his right of recourse to obtain the benefit of monies paid out as a volunteer. In this case, Legal and General Assurance Society Ltd did not do so and were therefore only able to recover 50% from Drake.

7.9.1 Should Legal & General v Drake Insurance be followed?

Legal & General v Drake Insurance has been criticised by academics such as Goff and Jones[61] where the authors commented that: (1) Drake Insurance protest did not magically oblige it to make the payment; (2) the rateable proportion clause was not the subject of litigation in Eagle Star;[62] and (3) even though the

---

58 *Qui senti commodum sentire debet et onus.*
59 See discussion by Nourse LJ who stated at p. 898:

> In the simple case where one of two insurers, who are independently and unconditionally liable to the same assured for the whole of his loss, accepts sole liability for settling the claim, he has an undoubted right of contribution from the other insurer for half the costs of the settlement. There being no contract between the two insurers, the right of contribution depends, and can only depend, on an equity which requires someone who has taken the benefit of a premium to share the burden of meeting the claim. Why should that equity be displaced simply because the assured has failed to give the notice which is necessary to make the other insurer liable to him? At the moment of the accident either insurer could have been made liable for the whole of the loss. Why should he who accepts sole liability for settling the claim be deprived of his right to contribution by an omission on the part of the assured over which he has no control? As between the two insurers the basis of the equity is unimpaired. He who has received a benefit ought to bear his due proportion of the burden. While accepting that a line must be drawn somewhere, I am of the opinion that a denial of the right to contribution in circumstances such as these would be unduly restrictive and indeed inequitable. An attempt to state in general terms where the line ought to be drawn is neither necessary nor desirable. For present purposes it is enough to say that it ought not to be drawn so as to exclude the right to contribution in a case where, at the moment of the accident, each insurer is potentially liable for the whole of the loss.

60 Section 149 Road Traffic Act 1972 (re-enacted).
61 At para. 14–036.
62 *Eagle Star Ltd v Provincial Insurance plc* [1994] 1 AC 130.

insurer was liable to a third party for the whole loss it did not mean that it was entitled to claim contribution from a co-insurer. The authors went on to state that the Court of Appeal's decision could be justified, based on the fact that the defendant insurer had an arbitral award in his favour.

7.9.2 Where both policies contain rateable proportion clauses

The Privy Council in *Eagle Star Ltd v Provincial Insurance plc*[63] had to consider the position where both policies contained rateable proportion clauses. One policy cancelled before the accident and another policy cancelled after the accident. Lord Woolf noted that both parties had an obligation to indemnify third parties under the legislation and concluded that the contractual approach was appropriate as their respective liabilities to the person assured would indicate the scale of the double insurance. The incidence of liability was not the date at which the insurer was discharged from liability. According to Lord Woolf's analysis,[64] both insurers each should contribute to its statutory liability in the same proportion, based on their contractual duty. In this case both insurers had done this.

However, the Court of Appeal in *Drake Insurance Co v Provident Insurance Co*,[65] where the facts were very similar to that of *Legal and General Insurance*, came to a different conclusion. In *Drake Insurance Co v Provident Insurance Co*, it was held that in a co-insurer situation, where the policy contains a rateable proportion clause and one of the insurers does not seek or pursue contribution from the other co-insurer prior to paying the assured or does not check whether a situation of double insurance arises, the court will treat that insurer as a volunteer. In *Drake Insurance Co v Provident Insurance Co*, Drake had a policy with Mrs Kaur who was driving her husband's car and injured Mr Beach. Drake's Policy contained the following clause:

> If at any time any claim arises under this policy, there is any other existing insurance covering the same loss damage or liability the Company shall not be liable to pay or contribute more that its rateable proportion of such claim.

Provident Insurance Co avoided cover, and refused to pay. Drake Insurance Co then decided to pay the motorcyclist's claim and sought equitable contribution on the basis that Drake Insurance Co and Provident Insurance Co were co-insurers. Provident Insurance Co refused to pay on two grounds: (1) it had validly avoided Mr Singh's policy for non-disclosure and (2) relied on a special clause in Drake's Policy. The judge held that the policy could be avoided by the insurer on the ground of non-disclosure where it could be shown that there was material non-disclosure, and the insurer was induced to accept the risk as a result. In the present case, the insurer could not show that the policy could be avoided.

---

63 [1994] 1 AC 130.
64 Although not dealing specifically with the voluntary payment point.
65 [2004] QB 601.

The insurer was a volunteer paying out in full. The insurer was unable to claim contribution. On appeal, Rix LJ stated that it was important to consider the circumstances of the case before a decision could be made on Drake Insurance Co's right to recover contribution. If litigation had preceded the payment by Drake Insurance Co, the voluntary payment point would not have existed and it would not make sense if a sensible settlement which could have been made is not made until litigation proceedings between the parties were concluded. Rix LJ stated:[66]

> Subject to the question of voluntary payment, which to my mind is a separate matter, the Privy Council did not regard the mere existence of the rateable proportion clause as excluding the operation of the equitable rule of contribution. If it had done so, it could not have found in favour of contribution in that case, for it specifically rejected the statutory approach in favour of the contractual approach in the passage I have cited above. If I may respectfully say so, I would agree that the clause does not of itself exclude a right to contribution, seeing that the essence of the clause is to apply a rateable liability as a matter of contract. It would therefore be surprising if it had the effect of prejudicing one insurer who had paid too much. Each insurer has not ceased to insure for the same loss just because it cannot be forced by contract to pay more than its rateable proportion or because the clause in effect requires the assured to involve both his insurers at once in order to obtain a full indemnity. In *Legal and General Assurance Society Ltd v Drake Insurance Co Ltd* [1992] QB 887, 894 Lloyd LJ asked: "But what is a rateable proportion clause other than an attempt by insurers to exclude the equitable doctrine of contribution by a contractual provision intended to achieve the same effect?" But he did not say that the attempt succeeded. Of course, if the assured is forced to involve both his insurers, then there will be no need for contribution and the need for the application of the doctrine is excluded as a matter of fact.

The plaintiffs were able to recover as they were not volunteers. Rix LJ went further and stated that he did not see what difference s151 of the Road Traffic Act[67] should make.

7.9.3 Other jurisdictions?

Similar principles have been followed in Singapore as well. In the case of *SHC Capital Ltd v NTUC Income Insurance Co-operative Ltd*[68] Omar, who was employed as a construction worker, was injured on-site. A claim was made against the developer, the main contractor, and the sub-contractor. There were numerous policies which were each covered by NTUC and SHC. SHC paid out on the claims and the court had to decide whether SHC could recover contribution from NTUC. The court reviewed the different policy clauses. The High Court[69] stated:

---

66 At para. [114].
67 Section 149 of the preceding Act.
68 [2010] SGHC 224.
69 At para. [46].

46 From the foregoing discussion, it is apparent that regardless of the utility of legal compulsion as a touchstone of voluntariness, it is not sufficient to explain every contribution and reimbursement award. Before it was set aside, the arbitral award in Drake Insurance, while binding upon the assured and Provident, did not bind Drake. Drake was thus not compelled by law, but by necessity, in the circumstances, to fully indemnify the assured. Furthermore, the requirement of legal compulsion is difficult to sustain in a case where a plaintiff has freely undertaken his legal liability to its creditor. In double insurance cases, usually, two indemnity insurers would have freely and independently chosen to indemnify the same assured. It would be difficult to justify why either of the insurers would be entitled to contribution using the legal compulsion analysis, since they have both chosen voluntarily to expose themselves to their legal obligations.

The problems arising in *Drake Insurance plc* do not arise in Australia due to the statutory provision of s45 Insurance Contracts Act 1984 which cancels the effects of a rateable proportion clause or other clauses which seek to limit the liability of the insurer.[70]

In *Limit (No 3) Ltd v ACE Insurance Ltd*[71] insurers under an excess layer policy sought 100% indemnity after having paid on the ground that they were on risk. The primary layer insurer denied liability. The Supreme Court of New South Wales held that as the excess layer insurer was not liable at the date of loss, no contribution arose.

7.9.4 Event after loss and insurer denies liability

However, the position in relation to contribution is unclear where there is an event after the loss, and where an insurer claims that they are not liable for the loss suffered, for example where the requirement of notification is necessary but is not complied with.[72]

---

70 See also *SHC Capital Ltd v NTUC Income Insurance Co-operative Ltd* [2010] SHGC 224, although the facts did not raise an issue of contribution as the claimant argued that sole liability rested with the defendant, the court stated that the sole question was whether the claimant paid as a volunteer.
71 (2009) NSWC 514.
72 In Robert Merkin and Jenny Steele, *Insurance and the Law of Obligations* (2013), p. 145:

> To give a simple example, suppose that the assured's business premises are assured by insurer A and insurer B at the date of the loss, and that each policy contains a condition precedent that the assured notifies any claim within 14 days of the occurrence of the assured peril. A fire then occurs and the assured notifies A, but not B, within 14 days. Plainly A is liable to meet the claim, but if A pays and then brings a contribution action against B, B may assert that although it was liable when the fire occurred it ceased to be liable 14 days later so that there is no basis for a contribution claim. The cases on this point are divided, some favouring the view that a contingent contribution claim arises as soon as the fire occurs and crystallizes when A makes payment, whereas others assert that the assured has to have a valid and subsisting claim against B at the date that A makes payment.

The cases which the authors referred to in support were *Legal and General Insurance Society Ltd v Drake Insurance Co Ltd* [1992] QB 887; *O'Kane v Jones* [2004] 1 Lloyd's Rep 389; *Monksfield v Vehicle and General Insurance Co Ltd* [1971] 1 Lloyd's Rep 139; *Eagle Star Insurance Co Municipal Mutual Insurance Ltd* [1994] 1 AC 130; *Bolton Metropolitan Borough Council v Municipal Mutual Insurance Ltd* [2007] 1 WLR 1492.

7.10 Whether incidental overlaps allow for contribution?

Where there is an overlap, all policies must respond to the claim. The policy must be legal and in force at the time of the loss.

There will be no overlap in cases where the policy is a consecutive one.[73] Where different assureds have different interest in the same property, double insurance will not be present. Other cases where double insurance may not be present include situations where each assured insures their own interest. For example, in (1) an owner and bailee of goods, (2) mortgagor and mortgagee, (3) landlord and tenant, (4) employer and contractor[74] (5) where a primary policy and a later excess of loss policy is taken out,[75] or (6) where there is a primary policy and an increased value policy.[76]

7.10.1 Mortgagor and mortgagee

The court in the case of *North British and Mercantile Insurance Co v London, Liverpool and Globe Insurance Co*[77] held that there was no double insurance where each party had assured his own interest.[78] Therefore no pro rata payment was necessary. This principle was re-affirmed in *Boys v State Insurance General Manager*,[79] where the court held that there was no double insurance because the mortgagee who assured the dwelling on an indemnity basis did not know that the mortgagor had taken out further cover for replacement cost additional to the indemnity value under the mortgage policy. It did not matter that the sum recovered would be held on trust for the mortgagor. The parties had therefore assured different interests in the same subject matter.

In *Nichols & Co v Scottish Union and National Insurance Co*,[80] the mortgagee building society rules required that property mortgaged to the building society would have to be assured in the name of the trustees of the society. The member or mortgagor would have to pay premiums. Where an assured loss occurred, the amount received under the policy would be applied to the amount which had been secured under the mortgage deed or spent to repair the damaged premises. This

---

73 *National Employers Mutual General Insurance Association Ltd v Haydon* [1980] 2 Lloyd's Rep 149. The court did not agree with the trial judge's application of *Weddell v Road Transport & General Insurance Co Ltd* [1932] 2 KB 563. He based his decision on there not being co-existing cover.
74 *North British & Mercantile Insurance Co v London, Liverpool & Globe Insurance Co* (1877) 5 Ch D 569, 577 per Jessell MR.
75 *Pacific Employers Insurance Co v Non-Marine Underwriters* (1939) 71 DLR (4th) 731.
76 *Boag v Standard Marine Insurance General Manager* (1984) 3 ANZ Ins Cas 60–577 (HC NZ).
77 (1877) 5 Ch D 569.
78 In that case, under the custom of that particular trade, the wharfingers were liable for any loss arising, regardless of the cause. The wharfingers assured grain in their warehouse with the defendant. The merchants assured the grain with the plaintiff company, which contained an exclusion clause, limiting their liability on the existence of other insurance to a rateable contribution. A fire broke out damaging the goods. The wharfingers paid out. An application was made to the court to ascertain who should be liable.
79 [1980] 1 NZLR 87. See *Westminster Fire Office v Glasgow Provident* (1888) 13 App Cas 699.
80 (1885) 14 R (Ct of Sess) 1094.

was done at the option of the mortgagee. A mill was sold to A & Co by the society. A & Co then mortgaged the property to the society and later assured the property for its own benefit with Y & Co. Loss was suffered and A & Co sued its insurers. The mortgagee's policy provided that if there was any other subsisting insurance cover, the insurer was only liable for the rateable proportion of the loss suffered. The mortgagor's insurers paid the mortgagor a rateable proportion clause under the mortgagor's policy. The mortgagor then sued to recover the balance. The court held that the society had an interest in both parties, as the mortgagee's insurance "in substance, although not in form, was an insurance for the benefit of the mortgagor". This triggered double insurance and the pro rata clause applied.[81]

It has been[82] stated that the better view in circumstances like those in *Nicholas* was that each party insures his own interest and can recover in full against his insurer; since the mortgagor has a contractual right to have the debt paid off by the mortgagee and the mortgagor's insurers will be subrogated to that right after payment by them to the mortgagor. Although neither the mortgagor, nor his insurer, can compel the mortgagee to make any recovery, the overall result would probably be that the loss fell on the insurers of the mortgagee.[83]

If the insurance policies are taken out in the name of a loan company by the proprietors in each case and in the name of the mortgagees in reversion, the courts have held that there will be no double insurance where there are successive mortgages.[84]

This principle can be seen in the case of *Clarke v Fidelity Fire Insurance Co of New York*[85] where the court held that there was no overlapping insurance. In *Clarke*, Clarke assured the house against destruction by fire. A statutory condition was imposed where there was "other insurance". A separate policy was taken out by the mortgagee to insure against his interest in the building. The court held that the homeowner was owner in possession and the mortgagee was the holder of a security to indemnify him against losses on his loan and, as there was no "other insurance", the homeowner could claim for her loss in full.

7.10.2 Landlord and tenant

It is common for insurance to be taken out on the same premises by both a landlord and tenant. The courts have held that as the landlord and tenant had assured their interest separately, the landlord was not entitled to the benefit from the

---

81 Although this decision was doubted in *O'Kane v Jones, The Martin P* [2004] 1 Lloyd's Rep. 389, where the court questioned the correctness of the decision in *Nicholas & Co v Scottish Union and National Insurance Co*. The court concluded that *Nicholas* did not establish the proposition that there is double insurance for the purposes of the Marine Insurance Act if there were different assureds with different insurable interests in the same property, even if one may have to hold all or part of the proceeds of any insurable claim in trust or for the account of the other.
82 *MacGillivray on Insurance Law* (11th edn 2008), p. 666.
83 *Boys v State Insurance General Manager* [1980] 1 NZLR 87.
84 *Scottish Amicable Heritable Securities Association v Northern Assurance Co* (1883) 11 R 287.
85 [1925] OJ No144 (Ont CA).

tenant's insurance contract.[86] In *Andrews v Patriotic Assurance Co (No 2)*[87] the landlord and tenant assured the same building. There was a covenant to repair, but no covenant to insure. A fire broke out. The tenant recovered the loss in full from his own insurers, but did not reinstate the premises due to bankruptcy. The landlord then sought to recover from his insurer, who claimed that liability was only on a pro rata basis.

Where the parties each rely on his own insurers to pay for the loss, double insurance will not arise. Double insurance will be present where an assured does derive a benefit from another's insurance, even though their interest was different. This arose in *Portavon Cinema Co Ltd v Price*,[88] where the plaintiff brought proceedings under two fire insurance policies issued by Lloyd's underwriters. The Lloyd's underwriters were represented by Mr Edward Steane Price and Century Insurance Co Ltd. The plaintiff was a lessee of Empire Cinema. These policies were concurrent at the time in respect of Empire Cinema. The plaintiff claimed under the policy for building, fixtures, furnishings, films etc. The landlords were assured by Woodward Theatres Ltd against loss or damage to Empire Cinema.

7.10.3 Vendor and purchaser

It is common in vendor and purchaser cases for the purchaser to be usually advised to cover the full value of the improvements. The vendor will retain the existing insurance until completion. Two premiums were usually to be paid between the contract stage and stage of completion on one property. In the case of *Davjoyda Estates Pty Ltd v National Insurance Co of NZ Ltd*,[89] which involved a vendor and purchaser situation, where both had insurable interest, even though the risk could pass to the purchaser, the court held that there was no insurance.

There is no overlapping policy where each assured covered his own interest. In *Allianz Australia Workers Compensation (NSW) Ltd v NRMA Insurance Ltd*,[90] a claim was made by workers' compensation insurers against a motor vehicle third-party insurer for contribution. Mr Noel Harris was employed by Trueform Pty Ltd. He was injured while unloading a semi-trailer during the course of his employment. The semi-trailer consisted of a prime mover and trailer owned by Trueform. The plaintiff was Trueform's workers' compensation insurer. The defendant was the authorised insurer of both the prime mover and the trailer. A claim for personal injury was commenced. The court held that where the defendant in proceedings is not the same person assured under the third-party policies, and where the registered owner would not be liable if sued, the claim for contribution must fail.

---

86 *Andrews v Patriotic Assurance Co (No 2)* (1886) 18 LR Ir 355.
87 (1886) 18 LR Ir 355.
88 [1939] 65 Ll L Rep 161.
89 (1965) 69 SR (NSW) 381 (FC). Also see *The Western Australian Bank v The Royal Insurance Co* (1908) 5 CLR 5.
90 [2007] ACTSC 40.

7.10.4 Primary and excess cover

Primary or excess coverage arises where there are numerous insurers. This could result in policies covering different layers of risk. A primary policy will respond first, due to the insurer's liability attaching when the loss assured occurs, when coverage is layered.[91] Any coverage over and above that of the primary policy is known as an "excess" policy. Another type of policy is known as an umbrella policy which includes (1) standard form excess coverage and (2) broader coverage.[92] In such case, there is no double insurance. Therefore, if there is no double insurance, the insurer will have to seek recourse through subrogation,[93] through covenants under the contract[94] or contractually.

---

91 *McKenzie v Dominion of Canada General Insurance Co* (2007) 86 OR (3d) 419.
92 See *Trenton Cold Storage v St. Fire & Marine Insurance Co* (2001), 146 OAC 348 (CA).
93 *North British and Mercantile Insurance Co v London, Liverpool and Globe Insurance Co* (1877) 5 Ch D 569.
94 *Andrews v Patriotic Assurance Co* (1886) 18 LR Ir 355.

CHAPTER 8

Asbestos litigation from an insurance perspective

8.1 Development of mesothelioma: application to double insurance

Mesothelioma operates across long periods and different policies of insurance. There has been discussion[1] as to whether double insurance occurs in asbestos cases and, if so, how contribution would be distributed between the insurers. The issue as to whether double insurance applies to mesothelioma cases is unclear, due to the structure of the policies. This is the first time that the courts have considered the issues of the construction of such polices between different insurers during different policy years, under different forms of liability cover such as liability insurance and personal injuries (i.e. employers' liability and public liability).

It is difficult to identify the defendant insurer, as it is unclear which policy applies. There is no double insurance where the policies are consecutive policies, as double insurance arises only where there are concurrent policies. The issue will be whether there is a single indivisible loss in every year or separate losses in each year.

8.2 Development of mesothelioma cases: the law

It is therefore important to analyse the development of the decisions in this area, such as *Fairchild v Glenhaven Funeral Services Ltd*,[2] *Phillips v Syndicate 992 Gunner*,[3] *Barker v Corus*,[4] *Bolton Metropolitan Borough Council v Municipal Mutual Insurance*[5]; *Sienkiewicz v Grief(UK) Ltd*,[6] *Bolton Metropolitan Borough Council v Municipal Mutual Insurance*,[7] *Rainy Sky SA v Kookmin Bank*,[8] *Durham v BAI(Run off) Ltd*,[9] and *International Energy Group Ltd v Zurich Insurance plc UK*,[10] to attempt to resolve the problems which have arisen.

Parliament was of the view that there should be intervention in the form of legislation, regarding the issue of whether and when liability should be joint or

---

1 *Phillips v Syndicate 992 Gunner* [2004] Lloyd's Rep IR 418.
2 [2003] 1 AC 32.
3 [2004] Lloyd's Rep IR 418.
4 [2006] 2 AC 572.
5 [2006] 1 WLR 1492.
6 [2011] 2 AC 229.
7 [2006] 1 WLR 1492.
8 [2011] 1 WLR 2900.
9 [2012] 1 WLR 867.
10 [2015] 2 WLR 1471.

several in such cases. This was due to the effect of the decision in *Barker v Corus*. The cases developed from the perspective of tort and the issue of causation, when considering the issue of which employer was liable. The legislature was of the view that protection was needed, and laws were enacted[11] in the form of the Compensation Act 2006.

8.3 The impact of mesothelioma litigation

8.3.1 The decision in Fairchild v Glenhaven Funeral Services Ltd: Court of Appeal and House of Lords

It is important to understand the history and medical aspect of the disease of mesothelioma. Lord Bingham summarised the disease in *Fairchild v Glenhaven Funeral Services Ltd*.[12] Since the 1930s the implications of inhaling large quantities of asbestos dust have been studied[13] and understood in greater detail.[14] Lord Bingham stated[15] as follows:

> It has been recognised for very many years, at any rate since the "Report on Effects of Asbestos Dust on the Lungs and Dust Suppression in the Asbestos Industry" by Merewether and Price in 1930 and the making of the Asbestos Industry Regulations 1931 (SR & O 1931/1140), that it is injurious to inhale significant quantities of asbestos dust. At first, attention was focused on the risk of contracting asbestosis and other pulmonary diseases. It is a characteristic of asbestosis that the disease, once initiated, will be influenced by the total amount of dust thereafter inhaled. Thus in the case of asbestosis the following situation may arise. C may contract asbestosis as a result of exposure to asbestos dust while employed by A, but without such exposure involving any breach of duty by A. C may then work for B, and again inhale quantities of asbestos dust which will have the effect of aggravating his asbestosis. If this later exposure does involve a breach of duty by B, C will have no claim against A but will have a claim against B. B will not escape liability by contending that his breach of duty is not shown to have had any causative effect.

He went on to explain:[16]

> From about the 1960s, it became widely known that exposure to asbestos dust and fibres could give rise not only to asbestosis and other pulmonary diseases, but also to the risk of developing a mesothelioma. This is a malignant tumour, usually of the pleura, sometimes of the peritoneum. In the absence of occupational exposure to asbestos dust it is a very rare tumour indeed, afflicting no more than about one person in a million per year. But the incidence of the tumour among those occupationally exposed to asbestos dust is about 1,000 times greater than in the general

---

11 The same outcome should be adopted when implementing legislation similar to that of s45. This specific issue was not discussed in ALCR.
12 [2003] 1 AC 32, 43.
13 In relation to the risk of contracting asbestosis and other pulmonary diseases.
14 Report on Effects of Asbestos Dust on the Lungs and Dust Suppression in the Asbestos Industry by Merewether and Price and the Asbestos Industry Regulations 1931.
15 [2003] 1 AC 32, 42, [6].
16 [2003] 1 AC, 43, [7].

population, and there are some 1,500 cases reported annually. It is a condition which may be latent for many years, usually for 30–40 years or more; development of the condition may take as short a period as 10 years, but it is thought that that is the period which elapses between the mutation of the first cell and the manifestation of symptoms of the condition. It is invariably fatal, and death usually occurs within 1–2 years of the condition being diagnosed. The mechanism by which a normal mesothelial cell is transformed into a mesothelioma cell is not known. It is believed by the best medical opinion to involve a multi-stage process, in which 6 or 7 genetic changes occur in a normal cell to render it malignant. Asbestos acts in at least one of those stages and may (but this is uncertain) act in more than one. It is not known what level of exposure to asbestos dust and fibre can be tolerated without significant risk of developing a mesothelioma, but it is known that those living in urban environments (although without occupational exposure) inhale large numbers of asbestos fibres without developing a mesothelioma. It is accepted that the risk of developing a mesothelioma increases in proportion to the quantity of asbestos dust and fibres inhaled: the greater the quantity of dust and fibre inhaled, the greater the risk. But the condition may be caused by a single fibre, or a few fibres, or many fibres: medical opinion holds none of these possibilities to be more probable than any other, and the condition once caused is not aggravated by further exposure. So if C is employed successively by A and B and is exposed to asbestos dust and fibres during each employment and develops a mesothelioma, the very strong probability is that this will have been caused by inhalation of asbestos dust containing fibres. But C could have inhaled a single fibre giving rise to his condition during employment by A, in which case his exposure by B will have had no effect on his condition; or he could have inhaled a single fibre giving rise to his condition during his employment by B, in which case his exposure by A will have had no effect on his condition; or he could have inhaled fibres during his employment by A and B which together gave rise to his condition; but medical science cannot support the suggestion that any of these possibilities is to be regarded as more probable than any other. There is no way of identifying, even on a balance of probabilities, the source of the fibre or fibres which initiated the genetic process which culminated in the malignant tumour. It is on this rock of uncertainty, reflecting the point to which medical science has so far advanced, that the three claims were rejected by the Court of Appeal and by two of the three trial judges.

The *Fairchild v Glenhaven Funeral Services Ltd* decision was an appeal by employees who had developed mesothelioma over the years due to their working conditions. It was argued that the defendant's breach of duty by failing to protect the plaintiffs from the risk of contracting the disease had led to the employees inhaling substantial quantities of asbestos dust or fibres. The judge was of the view that in two[17] of the three cases in the appeal it was for the plaintiff to establish, on a balance of probabilities, that a particular tortfeasor had exposed that employee to the asbestos dust which had the effect of causing the disease. In the third case,[18] the judge concluded that each of the employers had contributed to the employee being exposed to asbestosis dust and fibres and, as a result, materially contributed to the employees developing the disease. Therefore, liability should be apportioned between the employers. The requirement that the

---

17 Judith Fairchild (the 1st claimant) and Doreen Fox (the 2nd claimant).
18 Edwin Matthews (the 3rd claimant).

employee had to prove that the employer was the one who exposed him to the asbestos dust can, unless the employee has only worked for that employer, prove extremely difficult. To require the employee to do so would put an unnecessary burden on the employee.

8.3.1.1 The Court of Appeal

In the Court of Appeal, two points were raised: (1) whether a plaintiff who suffered from mesothelioma could recover compensation from anyone who had exposed the individual to asbestos dust if he had not been employed by the same employer throughout the period of exposure; and (2) if a plaintiff who is unable to identify a particular employer who is still viable and/or assured, whether he can recover compensation from the occupiers of the premises who exposed him to significant amounts of asbestos dust. The Court of Appeal held that the disease was an indivisible disease triggered on a single unidentifiable event by one or more of the tortfeasors, and it could not be safely concluded, on a balance of probabilities, which of the tortfeasors and which period of exposure could be said to have exposed the employee to asbestosis or the fibres. The element of causation had to be proved to establish the tort. This had not been done. The defendants, and the first two appellants, could not establish causation, and their appeals were dismissed by the Court of Appeal. The Court of Appeal however allowed the appeal of the third appellant. Therefore, the matter was taken further to the House of Lords.

8.3.1.2 The House of Lords

The House of Lords dealt with the issue of causation and modified the principles to take into account policy considerations.[19] Lord Bingham stated[20] that the essential questions which underlined the appeal could be expressed as follows:

> If (1) C was employed at different times and for differing periods by both A and B, and (2) A and B were both subject to a duty to take reasonable care or to take all practicable measures to prevent C inhaling asbestos dust because of the known risk that asbestos dust (if inhaled) might cause a mesothelioma, and (3) both A and B were in breach of that duty in relation to C during the periods of C's employment by each of them with the result that during both periods C inhaled excessive quantities of asbestos dust, and (4) C is found to be suffering from a mesothelioma, and (5) any cause of C's mesothelioma other than the inhalation of asbestos dust at work can be effectively discounted, but (6) C cannot (because of the current limits of human science) prove, on the balance of probabilities, that his mesothelioma was the result of his inhaling asbestos dust during his employment by A or during his employment by B or during his employment by A and B taken together, is C entitled to recover damages against either A or B or against both A and B? To this question (not formulated in these terms) the Court of Appeal (Brooke, Latham and Kay LJJ), in a reserved judgment of the court reported at [2002] 1 WLR 1052, gave a negative answer. It did so because, applying the conventional "but for" test of tortious liability, it could not be held that C had proved against A that his mesothelioma would probably not have

---

19 Jonathan Morgan, "Lost Causes in the House of Lords: *Fairchild v Glenhaven Funeral Services*" (2003) 66(2) MLR 277–284.
20 [2003] 1 AC 32, 40, [2].

occurred but for the breach of duty by A, nor against B that his mesothelioma would probably not have occurred but for the breach of duty by B, nor against A and B that his mesothelioma would probably not have occurred but for the breach of duty by both A and B together. So C failed against both A and B. The crucial issue on appeal is whether, in the special circumstances of such a case, principle, authority or policy requires or justifies a modified approach to proof of causation.

I REDEFINING THE CAUSATION PRINCIPLE?

This case looked at the tort of liability differently and whether the principles were of general application or had redefined causation (that is the "but for" test) to only apply in mesothelioma cases. For example, in personal injury cases the plaintiff is required to prove that a duty is owed, the duty owed has been breached, the plaintiff has suffered a loss or damage, and that the breach led to the damage. Further, but for the breach, the Plaintiff would not have suffered the damage. The Plaintiff has to prove this on a balance of probabilities.[21]

II ISSUES FOR CONSIDERATION BY THE HOUSE OF LORDS

The House of Lords had to consider (1) whether, on the present facts,[22] it should vary or relax the general principles of causation[23] in a situation where there was more than one tortfeasor who could have exposed the victim to the disease, but the victim was unable to identify a particular tortfeasor due to the nature of the disease; (2) what should be the approach adopted where there was a "mechanical application" of the general principles; and (3) whether the result would be appropriate in these sort of cases.[24]

III CONSIDERATION OF VARIOUS JURISDICTIONS

Lord Bingham went through a detailed analysis of all the literature and cases from various jurisdictions, and stated that, although the problem was universal, the approach adopted was not universal.[25] In certain countries the plaintiff would lose his claim based on the test of causation and in others it was common for the plaintiff to succeed.[26] Lord Bingham explained:[27]

> Whether by treating an increase in risk as equivalent to a material contribution, or by putting a burden on the defendant, or by enlarging the ordinary approach to acting in concert, or on more general grounds influenced by policy considerations, most jurisdictions would, it seems, afford a remedy to the plaintiff. Development of the law in this country cannot of course depend on a head-count of decisions and codes adopted in other countries around the world, often against a background of different rules and traditions. The law must be developed coherently, in accordance with principle, so as to serve, even-handedly, the ends of justice. If, however, a decision is given in this

---

21 [2003] 1 AC 44, [8].
22 Which were considered to be of a special nature.
23 [2003] 1 AC 44, [8].
24 [2003] 1 AC 44, [9].
25 [2003] 1 AC 66, [32].
26 [2003] 1 AC 66, [32].
27 [2003] 1 AC, 66, [32].

country which offends one's basic sense of justice, and if consideration of international sources suggests that a different and more acceptable decision would be given in most other jurisdictions, whatever their legal tradition, this must prompt anxious review of the decision in question. In a shrinking world (in which the employees of asbestos companies may work for those companies in any one or more of several countries) there must be some virtue in uniformity of outcome whatever the diversity of approach in reaching that outcome.

IV THE PROPER APPROACH

This approach would ensure a just result, although such a result could lead to a clash of policy considerations.[28]

V PARTIES' ARGUMENTS

The court considered the arguments put forward by the parties. The appellants' argued that the employer was liable even though the damage may not have been caused by him. The risk increased when more tortfeasors were involved but had gone into liquidation or disappeared.[29] The alternative argument put forward placed more emphasis on strong policy arguments which favoured compensating the plaintiff who had suffered substantial and serious harm.

VI LORD BINGHAM'S VIEW

Lord Bingham was of the view that the imposition of such liability on a "duty-breaking" employer was heavily outweighed by the injustice of denying redress to a victim.[30] He stated:

> I am of opinion that such injustice as may be involved in imposing liability on a duty-breaking employer in these circumstances is heavily outweighed by the injustice of denying redress to a victim. Were the law otherwise, an employer exposing his employee to asbestos dust could obtain complete immunity against mesothelioma (but not asbestosis) claims by employing only those who had previously been exposed to excessive quantities of asbestos dust. Such a result would reflect no credit on the law.[31]

In reaching this conclusion, he placed weight on *McGhee v National Coal Board*[32] where Lord Wilberforce stated that:

> the employers should be liable for an injury, squarely within the risk which they created and that they, not the pursuer, should suffer the consequence of the impossibility, foreseeably inherent in the nature of his injury, of segregating the precise consequence of their default.

The House of Lords concluded that if a plaintiff is able to show that conditions (1)–(6)[33] above have been satisfied, he would be entitled to sue both tortfeasors.

---

28 [2003] 1 AC 66, [33].
29 [2003] 1 AC 66, [33].
30 [2003] 1 AC 66, [33].
31 [2003] 1 AC 67, [33].
32 [1973] 1 WLR 1, 7.
33 As posed by Lord Bingham.

He looked at the situation where A and B both expose the employee to the risk, to which he should not have been exposed in the first place, and which they should have protected him from. Emphasis was placed on policy considerations. Therefore, the employee should be entitled to receive full compensation, i.e. 100%. Lord Bingham went on to suggest that it was open to the employer to seek contribution against each other or any other employer liable in respect of the same damage in "the ordinary way".[34]

VII ANALYSIS OF BINGHAM'S VIEW

Lord Bingham seems to suggest that his opinion or conclusion is directed at cases where each of conditions (1)–(6) are satisfied, and to no other type of cases. He went on to say that it would be unrealistic to suppose that the principles which have been laid down in *Fairchild* would not over time be the subject of "incremental and analogical development".[35] He disagreed with Lord Hutton's approach and preferred the view that the ordinary approach of causation should be varied rather than drawing legal inferences which were inconsistent with the proven facts.

VIII LORD NICHOLLS'S VIEW

Lord Nicholls agreed with the other lordships. He considered that the scope of the defendant's liability should be extended due to the "unattractiveness" of the result which would arise if the plaintiff was left without a remedy. The facts of the present case were a good example where policy decisions would warrant a departure from the usual threshold of the "but for" test.[36] Although he noted that considerable constraints would be imposed where there was an attempt to relax the threshold "but for" test of causal connection.[37] There must be good reasons for departing, which must be sufficiently weighty to justify depriving the defendant of the protection of the test which is normally and rightly afforded to him.[38]

IX LORD HOFFMANN'S VIEW

Lord Hoffmann considered it important to deal with the issue of whether causation was a question of fact or a matter of common sense.[39] In his opinion, the causal requirements were just as much a part of the legal conditions for liability as the rules which prescribed the kind of conduct which attracts liability or the rules which limit the scope of that liability.[40] Further he considered that the concepts of fairness, justice and reason were connected with the rules which governed the requirements to conclude that the conduct was tortious.[41] The sig-

---

34 [2003] 1 AC 68, [34].
35 [2003] 1 AC 68, [34].
36 [2003] 1 AC 70, [41].
37 [2003] 1 AC 70, [43].
38 [2003] 1 AC 70, [43].
39 [2003] 1 AC 70, [50].
40 [2003] 1 AC 70, [54].
41 [2003] 1 AC 70, [56].

nificant feature in the present case which would warrant a departure from the long-standing principles were: (1) the duty which specifically required the protection of employees by preventing them being unnecessarily exposed to the risk of a particular disease; (2) the duty which was intended to create a civil right to compensate for injuries which were relevantly connected to the breach; (3) the greater the exposure to asbestos, the greater the risk to contract the disease; (4) except where there has been only one significant exposure to asbestos, medical science cannot prove whose asbestos is more likely to have produced the cell mutation which caused the disease; and (5) the employee has contracted the disease against which the employee should have been protected.[42]

Lord Hoffmann was of the view that a requirement that there be proof of a link between the defendant's asbestos and the disease contracted by the plaintiff would empty the duty of content, unless it was a situation where you had a single employer. He did leave open the possibility of the court on future occasions formulating different casual requirements in these types of cases.

X ANALYSIS OF LORD HOFFMANN'S VIEW

If the above five requirements are present, the next issue to consider is which rule would result in a just result and conform to policy considerations, with regard to common law and statute, to ensure that employees do not contract asbestos-related diseases. He queried (1) whether a rule should be formulated where the employer, in breach of his duty, would be held liable for the injury to the employee for creating a significant risk to the employees' health, even though the physical injury caused could have been caused by someone else; or (2) would a rule apply only where the employee has been subjected to a risk by a breach which is caused by a single employer, where the employee would not have any remedy.[43] After carrying out a balancing exercise, Lord Hoffmann was of the view that it would be wrong to impose a casual requirement which excluded liability. After considering *McGhee*[44] on the principle of authority, he erred on the side of caution and stated that the *Wilsher*[45] decision indicated the dangers of over-generalisation[46] although admitting that the principle was capable of development and could apply in new situations.[47]

XI LORD HUTTON'S VIEW

Lord Hutton analysed the authorities.[48] He confirmed the decision in *McGhee* and stated that it was in the interest of justice that trial judges follow the approach in *McGhee* where: (1) the facts were similar to the present one; (2) where the plaintiff could prove that the employer's breach of duty materially increased the risk

---

42 [2003] 1 AC 74, [61].
43 [2003] 1 AC 75, [63].
44 *Mc Ghee v National Coal Board* [1973] 1 WLR 1.
45 *Wilsher v Essex Area Health Authority* [1988] AC 1074.
46 [2003] 1 AC 77, [73].
47 [2003] 1 AC 77, [74].
48 [2003] 1 AC 78, [79]–[117].

of him contracting a particular disease; and (3) the disease occurred, but where, on the medical knowledge at the time, it was not possible to prove by medical evidence that the breach was a cause of the disease.[49] He disagreed with the view that the *McGhee* approach suggested that a new principle was being laid down. He stated:[50]

> 109 Whilst there is very little practical difference between the two views I prefer, with respect, to take the view that the *McGhee* approach is based on the drawing of a factual or legal inference leading to the conclusion that the breach of duty was a cause of the disease rather than that the decision in *McGhee* laid down a new principle that, in cases where medical evidence as to the precise nature of the causation cannot be adduced, the material increase in the risk is taken in law to be a cause of the disease without reliance on a factual or legal inference. As well as the passages in the speeches of Lord Simon of Glaisdale, Lord Kilbrandon and Lord Salmon to which I have referred in paras 96 and 97 of this opinion I incline to the view that Lord Reid's references to the legal concept of causation being based "on the practical way in which the ordinary man's mind works in the everyday affairs of life" and to a "broad and practical viewpoint" (see p 5B) point more to the drawing of an inference than to the laying down of a new principle of law. Moreover I think that in his speech in *McGhee*, at p 7, Lord Wilberforce recognised that there were two ways in which injustice to the pursuer could be avoided: one way was by drawing an inference (which he rejected in that case as a fiction), and the other way was, in effect, by reversing the burden of proof on causation. But as Lord Bridge observed in *Wilsher* [1988] AC 1074, 1087G, there was no support for the reversal of the burden of proof in the other speeches.

Justice will be achieved if the burden is placed on the employer, who has breached a duty imposed on him and who has materially increased the risk of the employee contracting the disease, to pay damages rather than concluding that the employee is not entitled to damages and is unable to receive any compensation.[51] Further he noted that liability should be joint and several, and each employer would be liable in full for the plaintiff's damage, although it was open to a defendant to seek contribution against other employers who were held liable for causing the disease.[52]

XII LORD RODGER'S VIEW

Lord Rodger agreed with the other lordships. He stated that the House of Lords should look at the state of medical knowledge at the present moment and that problems arising in future should be resolved when they occur at a later stage.[53] He went through the law of different jurisdictions[54] and stated as follows:

---

49 [2003] 1 AC 91, 108.
50 [2003] 1 AC 91, 109.
51 [2003] 1 AC 94, 114.
52 [2003] 1 AC 95, 117. However, Lord Hutton confined his opinion to the specific circumstances of the present case.
53 [2003] 1 AC 97, 125.
54 See [2003] 1 AC 118, 170.

First, the principle is designed to resolve the difficulty that arises where it is inherently impossible for the plaintiff to prove exactly how his injury was caused. It applies, therefore, where the plaintiff has proved all that he possibly can, but the causal link could only ever be established by scientific investigation and the current state of the relevant science leaves it uncertain exactly how the injury was caused and, so, who caused it. McGhee and the present cases are examples. Secondly, part of the underlying rationale of the principle is that the defendant's wrongdoing has materially increased the risk that the plaintiff will suffer injury. It is therefore essential not just that the defendant's conduct created a material risk of injury to a class of persons but that it actually created a material risk of injury to the plaintiff himself. Thirdly, it follows that the defendant's conduct must have been capable of causing the plaintiff's injury. Fourthly, the plaintiff must prove that his injury was caused by the eventuation of the kind of risk created by the defendant's wrongdoing. In McGhee, for instance, the risk created by the defenders' failure was that the pursuer would develop dermatitis due to brick dust on his skin and he proved that he had developed dermatitis due to brick dust on his skin. By contrast, the principle does not apply where the plaintiff has merely proved that his injury could have been caused by a number of different events, only one of which is the eventuation of the risk created by the defendant's wrongful act or omission. Wilsher is an example. Fifth, this will usually mean that the plaintiff must prove that his injury was caused, if not by exactly the same agency as was involved in the defendant's wrongdoing, at least by an agency that operated in substantially the same way. A possible example would be where a workman suffered injury from exposure to dusts coming from two sources, the dusts being particles of different substances each of which, however, could have caused his injury in the same way. Without having heard detailed argument on the point, I incline to the view that the principle was properly applied by the Court of Appeal in *Fitzgerald v Lane*.[55] Sixth, the principle applies where the other possible source of the plaintiff's injury is a similar wrongful act or omission of another person, but it can also apply where, as in McGhee, the other possible source of the injury is a similar, but lawful, act or omission of the same defendant.

However, he reserved his position as to whether these principles would apply where the other possible source of injury was similar but a lawful act or omission of someone else or a natural occurrence.[56]

8.3.2 Bolton Metropolitan BC v Municipal Mutual Insurance Ltd

8.3.2.1 The facts

In *Bolton Metropolitan BC v Municipal Mutual Insurance Ltd*,[57] the local authority, the employer, occupied a building site where an employee had accidentally inhaled asbestos fibres between 1960 and 1963. As a result, the employee started to develop chest symptoms in 1990 and was later diagnosed with mesothelioma in January 1991. He died the same year. A settlement was reached with the widower and, as a result, the plaintiff sought recovery through the public liability insurance policy against Municipal Mutual Insurance Ltd (MMI). The public liability policy had been in force since 1980 and provided for indemnity

---

55 [1987] 1 QB 781.
56 [2003] 1 AC 119, 170.
57 [2006] 1 WLR 1492.

by the company to the assured in respect of all sums which the assured shall become legally liable to pay as compensation which arose out of

> (a) accidental bodily injury or illness (fatal or otherwise) to any person other than any person employed under a contract of service . . . with the assured if such injury or illness arose out of the course of employment . . . occurs during the currency of the policy and arises out of the exercise of the functions of a local authority.

There was a further provision[58] which acted as an excess clause, and provided that if there was any occurrence which gave rise to a claim under the policy, and there was at the time another insurance policy in place, which applied to the claim, the company shall not be liable in respect of the claim, except in the amount of the excess beyond the amount which would be payable under such other insurance, had the present policy not been in force. Another requirement under the policy was that written notification had to be given, which had not been done in this case by the second defendant.

8.3.2.2 Trial judge's ruling
At trial, the judge ruled that the first defendant was liable to pay the plaintiff. Further, the second defendant was not liable because it was not on cover when the injury had occurred, since the second defendant had not given notification.

8.3.2.3 Appeal
On appeal, the first plaintiff's case was dismissed. The court rejected the argument that injury occurred at the point when there was inhalation of the fibres, that is when there was accidental injury. The contract between the parties was an agreement to indemnify against liability and there should not be liability when there is initial exposure or initial bodily reaction to this kind of exposure. Bolton should not be liable where indemnification could be required under any public liability insurance policy. Further it was well established that the words "injury" or "damage" in indemnity agreements would not include injury or damage which will happen in the future.[59] Longmore LJ went on to say that the proximity of the word "accidental" to "bodily injury" did not mean that both the accident and the injury had to be within the currency of the policy.[60] All that was required was that the injury occurs within the period of the policy and it was caused accidentally. He specifically stated that the triple trigger theory did not apply to employers' liability policy at present.

8.3.2.4 Analysis of Bolton's case
The decision[61] in *Bolton* provides that public liability policies give retrospective cover, which results in liability incurring when the negligent act occurs before

---

58 Condition 6 of the policy.
59 The case of *Promet Engineering (Singapore) Pte Ltd v Sturge (The Nukila)* [1997] 2 Lloyd's Rep 147, 157.
60 [2006] 1 WLR 1492, 1502 was referred to.
61 Merkin and Steel, *Insurance and The Law of Obligations* (2013), 12.3.2.

the inception of cover, but where injury results during the period of cover. However, this is contrary to the framework of the operation of public liability policies which are designed to give current or prospective cover, as retroactive cover only applies to claims made policies that respond to earlier negligent acts.[62] Therefore public liability policies now exclude liability for exposure in earlier years which give rise to injury during the currency of the policy.[63]

8.3.2.5 Application of principles to double insurance
There was discussion in *Bolton* as to whether the issue of double insurance and contribution arose – that is, whether CU could deny liability on the basis that Bolton had failed to give notice of the accident or claim under the policy, and as a result, MMI could argue that there was double insurance, and claim contribution from CU. The trial judge ruled that there was no contribution. Although the Court of Appeal did not want to decide whether the decision in *Legal and General Assurance Society Ltd v Drake Insurance Co Ltd*[64] or the decision of the Privy Council in *Eagle Star Insurance Co Ltd v Provincial Insurance plc*[65] were correct, Longmore LJ did however state that the Court of Appeal had the power to do so.

8.3.2.6 Doctrine of contribution
Longmore LJ preferred the reasoning of the Privy Council which held that the doctrine of contribution could be modified by contract and should be considered by reference to the parties' contractual liabilities. In his view, an insurer is entitled to rely on the fact that he has only agreed to insure on certain terms against the assured and against his co-assured. Double insurance does not arise where one of the insurers agrees to be liable without imposing any condition precedent to liability in relation to a notice requirement, and another insurer says that he will only be liable if due notice is given of an accident or claim.[66] It was different where the co-insurer, who was himself a party to an arrangement, was relieved from liability to an assured and a situation where you had a co-assured who tries to rely on a term of contract which existed at the time of loss.[67]

8.3.3 Barker v Corus: *revisiting Fairchild*

The next case in the string of decisions was *Barker v Corus*.[68] The decision in *Fairchild* was revisited in *Barker*, which has led to more uncertainty in the area of liability principles in mesothelioma claims. In *Barker*, the court dealt with three parties.

---

62 *Ibid.*
63 *Ibid.*
64 [1992] QB 887.
65 [1994] 1 AC 130.
66 [2006] 1 WLR 1492, 1508, [38].
67 [2006] 1 WLR 1492, 1508, [38].
68 [2006] 2 AC 572.

8.3.3.1 Barker: the plaintiff's husband
The first involved the plaintiff's husband who had been exposed to asbestos during his working life for a period of three years, while working for his first employer (the defendant) who had become insolvent, and finally while he was self-employed. The judge ruled that the defendant's liability was joint and severable with the insolvent company. The Court of Appeal agreed.

8.3.3.2 Barker: employees who had died
The two other cases involved a group of employers and where the employees had died as a result of exposure to asbestos. The problem which arose was that most of the employers had become insolvent and proceedings were then brought against the remaining ex-employers.

8.3.3.3 Trial judge's view
The trial judge held that liability of the defendants was joint and several.

8.3.3.4 The Court of Appeal
The Court of Appeal agreed with the trial judge's conclusion. The defendants appealed the ruling.

8.3.3.5 Lord Hoffmann's view
Lord Hoffmann, giving the judgment of the court,[69] reiterated the emphasis placed on the exceptional nature of such cases, in terms of the nature of liability.[70] He noted the importance of the court relying on fairness, and how the court had applied an exceptional and less demanding test for the necessary causal link between the defendant's conduct and the damage.[71]

8.3.3.6 Issues on appeal in Barker
Two important issues arose on appeal: (1) what were the limits to the exception of the decision in *Fairchild*; and (2) what is the extent of the liability?

The difference between the facts of *Fairchild* and the present case was that in the present case not all the exposures which could have caused the disease involved breaches of duty to the plaintiff or were within the control of the defendant.[72] The court had to decide whether the exception, as laid down in *Fairchild*, extended to such situations; if not, whether the defendant, Corus, was liable for all the damages suffered by the plaintiff, or only for its aliquot contribution to the materialised risk that he could have contracted mesothelioma.[73] Although it was not challenged in the other two appeals that their cases fell within the exception

---

69 With other Lords agreeing. Lord Rodger dissenting.
70 Lord Hoffmann was one of the judges in *Fairchild*.
71 [2006] 2 AC, 572, 580.
72 [2006] 2 AC 572, 580, [3].
73 [2006] 2 AC 572, 580, [3].

to *Fairchild*, the court still had to decide whether liability was joint and several or only several liability.[74]

8.3.3.7 The lordships' differing views

Lord Hoffmann noted the differing views and mechanisms[75] adopted by the lordships in their attempt to confine the approach as to the extent of the principle of liability.[76] For example, Lord Bingham's view required that all possible sources of asbestos should involve breaches of duty to the plaintiff. Lord Rodger went further to allow for non-tortious exposure by the defendant who was in some way responsible for a tortious exposure.[77] The other lords did not formulate the issues to exclude the possibility of liability in non-tortious exposures,[78] although agreeing that the formulations on the exceptions that were expounded in *Fairchild* could be adapted to different situations.[79]

8.3.3.8 The decision in *McGhee*

McGhee and its implications were considered. In particular, where there were other possible sources of the injury which were similar, but were a lawful act or omission of the same defendant. Lord Hoffmann stated that it did not matter whether the tortfeasor who committed the non-tortious act was the same tortfeasor who committed the tortious act.[80] The *Fairchild* exception would allow for situations where it would not matter whether the exposure to the defendant was tortious or non-tortious, caused by natural causes or human agency or if it was attributed to the defendant himself.[81] This would only be relevant to whether and to whom responsibility could be attributed to. However, where there was an argument of a causal link between the defendant's conduct and the plaintiff's injury, it did not matter.[82] Lord Hoffmann stated that it was difficult to prove an essential condition for the exception to apply as it could not be proved that it was the defendant who caused the damage due to the existence of other potential causative agents which operated in the same way.[83] It had to be shown that the mechanism which caused the damage must be the same.[84]

8.3.3.9 Apportionment

In relation to apportionment, the defendant argued that, as liability was approached in a novel way, the same should apply for apportionment. Lord

---

74 [2006] 2 AC 572, 581, [4].
75 [2006] 2 AC 572, 582, [8]–[10].
76 The lordships did not deal with the situation where the employee contributed to the significant exposure.
77 Although he did not deal with situations where there was the possibility of liability where there had been non-tortious liability.
78 [2006] 2 AC 572, 583, [11].
79 [2006] 2 AC 572, 583, [11].
80 [2006] 2 AC 572, 583, [11].
81 [2006] 2 AC 572, 585, [17].
82 [2006] 2 AC 572, 585, [17].
83 [2006] 2 AC 572, 587, [24].
84 [2006] 2 AC 572, 587, [24].

Hoffmann emphasised the importance of providing more protection to the plaintiff and the likely consequence of not following the "normal principles" where there was an indivisible injury. This applied even though, after time, the number of employers remaining solvent and traceable was diminishing.[85] Therefore, to prevent the plaintiff from being out of pocket, liability should be joint and severable, where there was a possibility that the tortfeasor was insolvent.

8.3.3.10 Whether liability was for the risk or the injury?
Another issue in *Barker* was whether liability was for the risk or for the injury. If the court characterised the damage by focusing liability on the wrongful creation of a risk or a chance of causing the disease, and where the damage caused by the defendant is the creation of such a risk or chance, it would not matter that the disease, namely mesothelioma, would be indivisible.[86] Chances were infinitely indivisible and different people could be separately responsible to a greater or lesser degree for the chances of the event happening.[87] These cases involved uncertainty as to the cause of a known outcome, which was mesothelioma. Lord Hoffmann considered that it was possible for the courts to quantify, as he put it, "the chances of X having been the cause of Y just as well as the chance of Y being the outcome of X". Again, the issue of fairness was considered in relation to the characterising of the damages as the risk of contracting mesothelioma. If a person may be liable, liability should be divided according to the possibility that one or the other may be liable.

8.3.3.11 Damages
Damages should be apportioned according to the defendants' contribution to the risk, according to the time of exposure for which the defendant was responsible, with allowance made for the intensity of exposure and the type of asbestos.[88] This issue was not discussed in detail, but the court commented that the parties, their insurers and advisers should devise a practical and economical criteria for dealing with damages.[89]

8.3.4 Durham v BAI (Run Off) Ltd – a review of the cases

8.3.4.1 The trial: trigger litigation
The next case in the line of authorities which reviewed *Fairchild*, *Barker* and *Bolton* in some detail was *Durham v BAI (Run Off) Ltd*[90] (referred to as "Trigger"). This case was subsequently referred to as the *Trigger* litigation.[91]

---

85 [2006] 2 AC 572, 588, [30].
86 [2006] 2 AC 572, 589, [35].
87 [2006] 2 AC 572, 589, [35].
88 [2006] 2 AC 572, 594, [48].
89 [2006] 2 AC 572, 594, [48].
90 [2012] 1 WLR 867.
91 *Merkin and Steel*, Chapter 12.

8.3.4.2 The facts

In *Trigger*, claims were brought against the employers' insurers who had policies under the employers' liability insurance. The policy covered situations where the employee had died from mesothelioma after inhaling asbestos fibres during their employment with the employer. There were policies in place which covered the period from 1940 to 1998. Although the specimen policies were worded differently, each policy would operate where there was disease which was "sustained" and/or when disease was "contracted during the policy period in question". Personal representatives of the deceased sued the employers who had paid out but wanted to obtain indemnity under their employers' liability insurance under the Third Parties (Rights against Insurers) Act 1930 from five employers' liability insurers – BAI (Run Off) ("BAI"), Excess Insurance Co Ltd, Independent Insurance Co Ltd, Municipal Mutual Insurance Ltd ("MMI") and Zurich Insurance Co.

8.3.4.3 The issue of employers' liability insurance

Under the Employers' Liability (Compulsory Insurance) Act 1969, all employers were required to maintain the approved policies under the Act. The insurers argued that under employers' liability insurance, the policy would only respond where the disease of mesothelioma developed, or manifested itself, during the relevant period of insurance, which could have occurred years ago. The employers and the personal representatives on the other hand argued that the insurance policy must respond to the disease of mesothelioma which develops and manifests itself at a much later stage and that, once the victim has been exposed during the insurance period, the tortfeasor should be liable as the law places such responsibility on the tortfeasor. These alternative bases of response (or "triggers" of liability) have been loosely described as an occurrence (or manifestation) basis and an exposure (or causation basis).[92]

8.3.4.4 The courts' view

Burton J, at first instance, held that the relevant insurances would only respond on an exposure basis. The majority[93] in the Court of Appeal agreed, especially where there was insurance which covered disease "contracted" during the relevant periods. The Court of Appeal however concluded that where there was a policy covering disease "sustained", then the policy would only respond on an occurrence or manifestation basis.

Further, Burton J held that all policies which were claims against the insurers, should respond where it was decided that the employer was liable on the basis that the inhalation by the employees occurred during the policy period. This was upheld by Rix, Smith and Stanley Burnton LJJ on appeal, who were of the view that this was the position where the policy provided for cover for diseases "contracted" during the period of insurance. However, they permitted the insurers'

---

92 [2012] 1 WLR 872, [3].
93 Rix, Smith and Stanley Burnton LJJ.

appeal, where the policy provided for cover for diseases "sustained" during the policy period.

8.3.4.5 Employers' Liability Act 1880

Burton J was of the view[94] that the single fibre theory as developed in *Fairchild* had been discredited and that the analysis of Lord Rodger, who provided an alternative explanation, should be accepted. He went on to state that it was common ground that the asbestos fibres in the body could not be causative of mesothelioma during the last ten years immediately prior to death, as the process started before that.[95] He noted that problems would arise for the purposes of the Employers' Liability Act 1880, which required that the employee show that the employer has caused the injury. Further, under s4 of the Employers' Liability Act 1880, the sustaining of the injury only referred to injury which had been so caused.

8.3.4.6 Workmen's Compensation Act

The Workmen's Compensation Act[96] was passed by Parliament due to the unfairness which resulted under the Employer's Liability Act 1880. Burton J noted the decision in *Fairchild* and *Barker v Corus*, and concluded that the majority view was as stated at para. [48][97] of the judgment. However, as a result of the decision in *Barker v Corus*, Parliament considered it necessary that legislation in the form of the Compensation Act 2006 be passed – in particular s3, which specifically deals with mesothelioma jurisprudence.

8.3.4.7 Section 3 Compensation Act 2006

Section 3[98] refers to "the responsible person" who has negligently or in breach of his statutory duty caused or permitted the victim to be exposed to asbestos

---

94 [2009] 2 All ER, 26, 42, [31].
95 [2009] 2 All ER, 26, 42, [31].
96 In 1897, 1900, 1906 and 1925.
97 Although the *Fairchild* exception treats the risk of contracting mesothelioma as the damage, it only applies when the claimant has contracted the disease against which he should have been protected. And, in cases outside the exception, as in *Gregg v Scott*, a risk of damage or loss of a chance is not damage upon which an action can be founded. But when the damage is apportioned among the persons responsible for the exposure to asbestos which created the risk, it is known that those exposures were together sufficient to cause the disease.
98 Mesothelioma: damages

> "(1) This section applies where – (a) a person ('the responsible person') has negligently or in breach of statutory duty caused or permitted another person ('the victim') to be exposed to asbestos, (b) the victim has contracted mesothelioma as a result of exposure to asbestos, (c) because of the nature of mesothelioma and the state of medical science, it is not possible to determine with certainty whether it was the exposure mentioned in paragraph (a) or another exposure which caused the victim to become ill, and (d) the responsible person is liable in tort, by virtue of the exposure mentioned in paragraph (a), in connection with damage caused to the victim by the disease (whether by reason of having materially increased a risk or for any other reason). 2. The responsible person shall be liable – (a) in respect of the whole of the damage caused to the victim by the disease (irrespective of whether the victim was also exposed to asbestos – (i) other than by the responsible person, whether or not in circumstances in which another person has liability in tort, or (ii) by the responsible person in circumstances in which he has no liability in tort), and (b) jointly and severally with any other responsible person."

and, as a result, the victim had contracted mesothelioma due to the exposure of asbestos. Further, due to the nature of mesothelioma which makes it difficult to identify with any certainty whether such exposure caused the victim to become ill, liability fell on the shoulders of the responsible person, in connection with damage caused to the victim by the disease, either by reason of having materially increased a risk or for any other reason. Under s3(2) the responsible person is liable in whole for the damage caused to the victim by disease. This would still apply regardless of whether the victim was exposed by persons other than the responsible person, as liability would be regarded as joint and several with any other responsible person. Therefore, a solvent employer will be facing liability where the employee was able to show that they had been tortuously exposed to asbestos while being exposed to it during their employment.

8.3.4.8 Insurer's liability: employers' liability insurance
The next issue which was discussed was an insurer's liability under the employers' liability insurance which is owed by the employer to the employee, until the establishment and ascertainment of which there is no right of indemnity by the employer against the insurance company.[99] Burton J stated that the wording of the insurance policies in place at the time when the employer is held liable to the employee is a decisive factor in determining what trigger or key unlocks a relevant period of cover.[100] Burton J identified that the court would consider the temporal limitation under an employers' liability policy which provided for indemnity against liability for compensation for bodily injury or disease which was suffered by a person to a contract of service which arose out of or in the course of the employee's employment with the employer. He then went to state that there were five kinds of liability insurance triggers which were relevant to employers' liability insurance, which included: (1) occurrence or event, which was at the date of breach; (2) causation/exposure; (3) occurrence of loss/damage, which was known as injury of fact; (4) manifestation/diagnosis/notice; and (5) claims made. It was stated that (1)–(4) are all known as "events occurring", which should be contrasted with (5).[101] Employers' liability[102] is causative, which required that liability of the employer had to be shown, and that the injury must have arisen out of the employment, which to that extent had to be caused by the employer.

8.3.4.9 "Sustained" and "contracted" and "caused" and "be caused"
Burton J concluded that the words "sustained" and "contracted" were to be construed in their context and within the factual matrix to be considered. The words "caused" or "be caused" are to be construed in the same way as causation. On

---

99 *Post Office v Norwich Union Fire Insurance Society Ltd* [1967] 2 QB 363.
100 [2009] 1 All ER 26, 52, [59].
101 [2009] 2 All ER 26, 53, [59].
102 Public liability insurance on the other hand does not have an employment relationship in existence.

the present case, such a reading is consistent with the commercial purpose of employers' liability. Burton J was of the view that this construction is consistent with (1) public policy, when considering the Workman's Compensation Act, (2) the courts' approach of giving protection to the employee who could make a claim against the employers, and (3) taking into consideration the likelihood that there would be a change of insurers during the period of the employees' employment. Further, by including the words "caused" or "sustained", which is construed as meaning "be caused", was the only way to achieve consistency with public policy and the Act, so protection would be provided "irrespective of what may happen thereafter".[103] He went on to say that on a construction of the words which apply on a causation or exposure basis, "contracted", "inflicted", was wide enough to mean "be caused". Looking at the wording of the policies, injury is "sustained" when it is "caused" and the disease is "contracted" when it is "caused".[104]

8.3.4.10 The Court of Appeal

In a split decision, Smith LJ in his analysis agreed with Burton J. The majority, comprising of Rix and Stanley Burnton LJJ, partially disagreed with the decision of Burton J. The majority in the Court of Appeal were of the view that "sustain" looked *prima facie* at the experience of the suffering employee rather than its cause. Therefore this would not cover situations where the mesothelioma was sustained long afterwards.

I RIX J'S ANALYSIS

Rix LJ stated that the concept of sustaining injury in its normal sense refers to the suffering of injury,[105] when dealing with the issue of the construction of the wording "sustain" injury, which he considered to be crucial when considering the terms of wording in all the policies. Injury he thought only occurred when it was suffered, or incurred, or occurs, or inflicted upon. The approach adopted by the trial judge was ambiguous, by substituting the word "caused" with the word "sustained". Therefore, the issue was whether one had to look at the injury or the cause of the injury. Rix LJ stated that *prima facie* one looked to the injury rather than its cause when considering the words "sustaining injury".[106] These were standard wordings included in contracts which would be renewed by the parties on a yearly basis and, in some cases, tariff wordings were used which tended to adopt the causative approach.[107] This approach starts off with the concept of sustaining injury but then goes on to suggest that what has to occur in the policy year is not the injury itself but the cause of that injury, because of the words "if any person under a contract of service . . . shall sustain bodily injury or

---

103 [2009] 2 All ER 26, 108, [240].
104 [2009] 2 All ER 26, 111, [243].
105 [2011] 1 All ER 605, 672, [230].
106 [2011] 1 All ER 605, 673, [233].
107 [2011] 1 All ER 605, 673, [234].

disease caused during the period of insurance".[108] Although he noted the conflict which may arise when looking at it in conjunction with the employers' liability insurance, such a definition would not be an absurd or meaningless or irrational interpretation.[109] He equated it with how the court defines "injury occurring" in public liability insurance. He stated that it was in "extraordinary circumstances" such as mesothelioma that such a test applied.[110] He went on to say that it would be possible that the test could also apply to other forms of cancers.

The phrase "disease contracted" could be considered in two ways. The first is if the phrase is considered together with the words "injury sustained". These words indicate that one would be dealing with the onset of the disease and not the origin of the disease. Such an approach would be consistent with the interpretation in *Bolton Metropolitan BC*. The second is to consider the phrase in a commercial context with regard to the purpose of employers' liability insurance contracts. Under such contracts it is the casual origins of the disease of the employee's exposure to noxious activities which he is subject to during his employment which has to be considered. Rix J preferred the latter view, and held that *prima facie* the phrase "disease contracted" referred to the time of the disease's causal origins.[111]

When considering injury, Rix LJ followed the decision in *Bolton Metropolitan BC*, which clearly stated that there was no injury until the injury's onset, even though he had serious doubts as to the correctness of the decision. He then went on to discuss *Fairchild, Barker* and *Rothwell* and concluded that, where mesothelioma develops, it is the exposure, and the risk of mesothelioma, which is the damage, and as a result the employer should be liable.[112] He relied on *Barker's* case where Lord Hoffmann stated that the underlying purpose of the *Fairchild* exception "is to provide a cause of action against a defendant who has materially increased the risk that the plaintiff will suffer damage", and where the risk has materialised.[113] This reflected a common sense approach. It was consistent with the medical literature at the time. Even though, following the decision in *Bolton's* case,[114] he still went on to state why he did not agree with the case.

If employers were liable for injuries which an employee received during his employment in any given policy year, and where the employee's exposure to the assured was caused as a result of the employers' activities in that year, this would prevent the "unknowable and serendipitous mystery"[115] of the problems of mesothelioma. This would occur where (1) an employee would not be able to identify whether there was liability, (2) if there was liability, which employer was

---

108 [2011] 1 All ER 605, 673, [234].
109 [2011] 1 All ER 605, 673, [235].
110 [2011] 1 All ER 605, 673, [235].
111 [2011] 1 All ER 605, 675, [245].
112 [2011] 1 All ER 605, 681, [281].
113 [2011] 1 All ER 605, 681, [281].
114 Where the court stated that there was no actionable injury at the time of exposure, and did so in a case where mesothelioma developed.
115 [2011] 1 All ER 605, 682, [285].

liable, or (3) whether or not the employee was covered at all.[116] Rix LJ ultimately concluded that the word "sustain" meant sustain, but that "disease contracted" looked towards the causative origins.

II SMITH J'S ANALYSIS

Smith J, although agreeing with the other judges, came to his conclusion based on the principal ground that the use of the word "sustained" should be interpreted by looking at the factual matrix of the policies and the user's understanding of the words in the policies, which had the same effect as causation.[117]

III BURTON LJ'S ANALYSIS

Burton LJ agreed with Rix J's decision but disagreed with his independent analysis[118] and conclusion that the 1969 Act required causation wording. Further, he was of the view that the issue of whether the definition of an employee included an ex-employee was a factor which also had to be considered.

8.3.4.11 The Supreme Court

The Supreme Court reviewed the principles as discussed by the court at first instance and by the Court of Appeal.[119] Reference was made to the policy wording. The insurers argued that the policies would not respond to many of the mesothelioma claims because the claims only emerged in the 1980s.

I LORD MANCE

A RESOLVING INCONSISTENCY IN INTERPRETATION

Lord Mance JSC was of the view that the correct way to resolve the inconsistent interpretation was to avoid looking at the meaning of single words or phrases, but to look at the wording of the insurance contracts more broadly. Five factors were considered which were indicative of a causative approach being preferred. First, the policy wording on its face required the course of employment to be contemporaneous with the sustaining of injury, although "sustain" equated with occurrence. Second, there was a close link between the actual employment undertaken during each insurance period and the premium payable for the risks that were undertaken by the insurer during that period. Third, there would be a potential gap in cover where there was an employers' breach of duty during a period which only led to injury or disease in another further period. This would occur where the insurance policies only address risks during the period of the policy. Fourth, insurers may not renew the employer's policy. Lord Mance JSJ was of the view that Rix LJ failed to take into account *Rainy Sky SA v Kookmin*

---

116 [2011] 1 All ER 605, 682, [285].
117 This was due to the acceptance of the development of the medical knowledge at different points of time.
118 [2011] 1 All ER 605, 696, [350].
119 [2012] 1 WLR 873, [6]–[10].

Bank[120] where it was held that where there was more than one interpretation, it would be appropriate to adopt an interpretation with business common sense. Further, even 1% of cases where there may be no cover was not insignificant.[121] Fifth, there was the issue of territorial scope, where there would be cover for the disease experienced during employment even though it was caused by pre-employment exposure, and a situation where disease caused by employment was not covered if only experienced while the employee was working abroad.

He went on to say that the wording of the BAI and MMI policies would still lead to uncertainty regarding disease and the difference between "injury sustained" and "accidents arising" could be read either as deliberate or as suggesting that no significance was attached to the difference or that the real concern was causation.[122]

B *DISCUSSION OF THE HISTORY OF THE WORKMEN'S COMPENSATION ACTS AND THE CASES*

Lord Mance JSC went on to deal with relevant parts of the history and the wording of the Workmen's Compensation Acts, and agreeing with the analysis by Rix LJ.[123] Lord Mance JSC agreed with Smith LJ's conclusion that public liability and employers' liability gave rise to different considerations, which, according to Smith LJ, was necessary due to the factual matrix of employers' liability rather than public liability policies.[124] The effect of the particular terms and consideration[125] had to be considered. He proceeded on the basis that *Bolton Metropolitan* was not binding on the court, without discussing the accuracy of the decision, but relied on the fact that it was unnecessary to decide the position regarding public liability insurance.

He agreed with the Court of Appeal's view that the word "contracted" considered together with disease looked to the initiating or causative factor of the disease. The word "sustained" may, at first glance, refer to the development or manifestation of such an injury or disease as it impacts employees. A more consistent approach would be to look to the initiation or causation of the accident or disease which injured the employee. This would occur when the disease was caused or initiated even though it would only develop and manifest at a much later stage. The case of *Fairchild*, which imposed liability for the mesothelioma on persons who have exposed the victim to asbestos and as a result created the risk of mesothelioma, is not a rule which, as he put it, even as between employers and employees, would deem that the employee has suffered injury or disease when there was exposure. Even if it is viewed that liability is retrospective on the employers, the insurance policies do not insure risk of physical injury or disease, but only actual injury or disease.[126]

---

120 [2011] 1 WLR 2900, 2911, [30].
121 [2012] 1 WLR 880, [26].
122 [2012] 1 WLR 880, 881.
123 [2011] 1 All ER 605.
124 [2011] 1 All ER 605, 692, 328.
125 [2012] 1 WLR 867, 877, [18]–[28], [42]–[47].
126 [2012] 1 WLR 867, 891, [52].

C THE DOUBLE INSURANCE PERSPECTIVE

This issue of double insurance and its application only became significant when it was raised by Lord Phillips PSC. He stated that exposure to the risk of mesothelioma was the correct application of the *Fairchild* rule. Further, exposure could not satisfy the concept of injury or the concept of causation for the purposes of the policies. If Lord Phillips' analysis and approach was adopted, all the present insurance claims that were settled by other insurers or by present insurers, would fail. The only exception would be situations where an employee was exposed to asbestos when employed by a single employer, who had assured with only one insurer throughout. The decisions of *Fairchild*, *Barker* and *Sienkiewicz* have developed a special rule which provides a deeming provision that once an employer had exposed an employee to asbestos and as a result that employee suffered mesothelioma, the insurance policies should pay out. The decision in *Fairchild* would create liability not for the disease but "for the creation of the risk of causing the disease". According to Lord Phillips' analysis, no assistance would be given to employers and employees where a person who suffers from mesothelioma was caused or initiated in any particular policy period. Therefore, even if the employers' policy responded, when there are injuries caused or initiated during their period, the employer and employee would fail for want of proof.[127]

Lord Mance JSC disagreed with this analysis. He relied on the decisions of *Fairchild* and *Barker*, and the House of Lord's decision which rejected this fictional approach, that each exposure would have caused or materially contributed to the disease.[128] Further, liability was not the causing of the disease but for materially increasing the risk of the mesothelioma.[129] One could conclude that the common law position after the decision in *Barker* was concerned with the issue of the "causal requirements" or "causal link" between the defendant's conduct and the disease. The precondition that the person actually develops mesothelioma was required.[130] The cause of action arises where the victim "has been" exposed to asbestos by the employer previously, "and because mesothelioma has been suffered by the victim". In relation to the exposure, "What materialised was at most a risk of the same kind to which someone, who may or may not have been the defendant, or something or some event had exposed the victim."[131] Therefore, the cause of action is "for" or "in respect of" the mesothelioma and the defendant who exposes a victim of mesothelioma to asbestos will be responsible "for" and "in respect of" both that exposure and the mesothelioma, which later develops.[132]

D MAIN ISSUE OF THE APPEAL

The main issue for the court to decide was on what basis the employers' liability insurance policies respond as a matter of construction, where it fell within the

---

127 [2012] 1 WLR 867, 893, [58].
128 [2003] 1 AC 32, [31], [61], [104].
129 [2003] 1 AC 32, [31], [36], [40], [53], [61] and [113].
130 As was stated in *Barker*.
131 [2012] 1 WLR 867, 895, [65].
132 [2012] 1 WLR 867, 896, [66].

framework of *Fairchild* and *Barker*. Lord Mance JSC was of the view that the employer must accept the possibility that the common law would develop where the employer's liability would be increased, if they were within the limits of the relevant insurance and insurance period.[133]

E ISSUE OF LIABILITY

Lord Mance JSC considered that liability only arose because of the incurring of the disease and is "for the disease"[134] when the employer had exposed the victim to the disease.[135] The same principle would apply in situations where there is vicarious liability. The insurance policies should be read on a causation basis which would effectively cover any liability which arose during the employers' activities during the period of coverage, and only if liability for mesothelioma flowed from the negligent exposure during an insurance period which is covered by the policies, otherwise the policy would not respond.[136] For the purposes of insurances, a more justified approach would be one where liability regarding mesothelioma, following the exposure to asbestos which was created when the policy of insurance, was in effect and during the insurance period, would provide a sufficient "weak" or "broad" causal link for the disease to be "caused" within the insurance period.[137] It would be unjust on the one hand for there to be a deeming provision of causation of the disease which could have created policy liability and, on the other, insist that the risk for such cases would be for the risk of causation. The risk, he went on to say, was no more than an element or condition necessary to establish liability for the mesothelioma. The 2006 Act was, in his view, there to impose liability on the employer for the mesothelioma.

For the purposes of the policy, the negligent exposure of the employee to the asbestos could have a sufficient causal link or be causally connected with mesothelioma subsequently arising, in which case the policy would respond to the claim. The fundamental focus of the policies was on the employment relationship, the activities during the insurance period and on liability arising out of and in the course of them, which would result in the liability attaching.

II LORD CLARKE

Lord Clarke preferred the view that the employers' liability insurers would be liable to indemnify the employers in respect of that liability. Further, on the present facts the employers were liable to the employees, and it would be remarkable if the insurers were not liable under the policies.[138]

---

133 [2012] 1 WLR 867, 898, [70].
134 [2012] 1 WLR 867, 899, [72].
135 This is a condition of such liability.
136 [2012] 1 WLR 867, 899, [72].
137 [2012] 1 WLR 867, 899, [73].
138 [2012] 1 WLR 867, 906, para. [88].

III LORD PHILLIPS PSC

Lord Phillips was of the view that the court should not redefine the special rule which permitted the claims to be brought under the employers' liability policy. The intention of the special approach, in the decision in *Fairchild* and *Barker*, was to ensure that an employer who had breached his duty, owed to the employee, did not escape liability because of the scientific uncertainty. It would be "judicial law-making" of a different dimension if the courts were able to create such a fiction as to the policy years in which mesothelioma cases were initiated in order to render liable insurers who could not otherwise be able to show that they were liable.[139] It would be a matter for Parliament and not for the courts, if it was necessary to establish a means which would result in the employers' liability insurers becoming liable. It would be wrong in principle for the Supreme Court to depart from the reasoning of the majority in *Barker* for the only reason and purpose of imposing liability on the employers' liability insurers.[140]

8.3.5 Zurich Insurance plc UK Branch v International Energy Group Ltd

8.3.5.1 IEG: time to run for cover?

Has the dust finally settled on asbestos litigation after the recent UK Supreme Court decision in *Zurich Insurance plc UK Branch v International Energy Group Ltd*?[141] Probably not. *IEG* has caused more confusion than certainty in the development of mesothelioma cases and insurance law. Whether the principles of equity, justice and fairness between the interest of victims, assureds and insurers have actually been achieved is questionable.

8.3.5.2 Tort liability: relationship between employer and employee

An individual who has been exposed to asbestos dust and fibres during his employment is open to the risk of developing mesothelioma, a malignant tumour. The condition can lay dormant for 30–40 years and may develop within a few years. An employee may not know that he has been exposed to asbestos. If the employee had to prove the employer's negligence, this would prove almost impossible, especially if he has worked for numerous employers or the employer has ceased business or become insolvent. The problem is less significant if he has

---

139 [2012] 1 WLR 867, 893, para. [135].
140 [2012] 1 WLR 893, 137. *Merkin and Steele*, p. 364:

> Our argument is that this would have been a vacuous goal for a special rule if it simultaneously negated the existing insurance cover, not least where (as in *Fairchild*) the defendants were plainly insurers. We therefore do not agree that the liability question and the compensation question are separable justifications for *Fairchild*. It follows that we also do not agree with Lord Phillips that defining the rules as set out in *Barker* to enable insurers to be liable would be to act for "reasons of policy", and should be a matter for "Parliament not the courts".

Lord Phillips PSC raised a few questions which he thought would lead to some difficulty if an employer was unable to prove that an employee's mesothelioma was caused in whole or in part by any particular period of exposure to asbestos dust.

141 [2015] 2 WLR 1471.

only worked for one particular employer who can easily be identified. The House of Lords in *Fairchild v Glenhaven Funeral Services Ltd*,[142] relaxed the principles of causation, to protect such victims (the "*Fairchild* enclave"). Therefore, all an employee needed to prove was some "weak" or "broad" causal link for the disease to be regarded as "caused" within the insurance period. The employer would be 100% liable. However, the House of Lords in *Barker v Corus*,[143] shifted from the principles in *Fairchild* and considered that liability should be apportioned according to the employer's contribution to the risk according to the time of exposure, the intensity of exposure and the type of asbestos. This formulation required an employee to sue each and every employer to recover. After the decision in *Barker*, and its unfair result, Parliament, within three months, felt it necessary to give protection to an employee by passing the Compensation Act 2006 to impose joint and several liability on all former employers.

8.3.5.3 Insurance liability: employers' liability insurance
Before the Supreme Court decision in *Durham*, an employer was held liable when the disease took hold. In *Bolton Metropolitan Borough Council v Municipal Mutual Insurance*,[144] the scene was set for the Court of Appeal to interpret liability for injury or illness in a policy which stated the disease "occurs during the currency of the policy", which, in a public liability context, meant when the disease took hold and not when the employee was exposed to the risk of asbestos. The tables were turned in *Durham v BAI (Run-Off) Ltd*[145] (also known as thne *Trigger* litigation), where the Supreme Court unanimously held that the words "injury sustained" or "disease contracted" by an employee in the insurance policies meant that liability would be triggered on any exposure by the employer and not the date when the onset of mesothelioma developed or manifested, although this was distinguished on the ground that the court here was dealing with employers' liability insurance.

8.3.5.4 Facts of IEG
Mr Carré was employed by GGLCL, later known as IEG, for 27 years from 13 November 1961 to 31 December 1988. Carré brought proceedings against IEG after contracting mesothelioma, as a result of his employment. GGLCL had liability insurance for only part of the 27 year with (1) Excess Insurance Co Ltd between 31 December 1978 and 30 December 1980 (two years) and (2) Midland Assurance Ltd, which Zurich had succeeded, from 31 December 1982 to 31 December 1988 (six years). Therefore, for a period of 19 years the employer was unassured or, if policies existed, they were untraceable. IEG settled Carré's claim. IEG then sued Zurich for the full amount of the settlement. Zurich claimed that it was only liable for a rateable proportion of the claim, i.e. 22.08% for its

---

142 [2002] 1 AC 32.
143 [2006] 2 AC 572.
144 [2006] 1 WLR 1492.
145 [2012] 1 WLR 867.

time on risk. The trial judge agreed, and awarded 100% defence costs. On appeal, the Court of Appeal ordered Zurich to pay 100% of both the claim and defence costs incurred by IEG. The Court of Appeal applied principles in the *Trigger* litigation, which placed the burden of the whole loss incurred on one employer. This was consistent with the effect of the Compensation Act 2006. The issues the Supreme Court had to decide was (1) whether the insurance policies respond to the full extent of an employer's liability to the employee or only a proportionate part of that liability fixed by reference to the periods of cover for which premiums have been assessed and paid, and (2) if the former, whether the insurer has a claim against insurers of the employer in respect of other periods of the employee's exposure and against the employer itself for periods in which it was unassured or in respect of which its insurer can no longer be identified or traced (see para. [99] of the judgment).

8.3.5.5 Implications of IEG

The Supreme Court unanimously agreed that *Barker* represented the common law position which applied in Guernsey. IEG was only liable for a proportionate part (ie, 22.08%) of the six-year period of Midland cover. The court was however split 4:3 on the extent of an insurer's liability when the insurance cover was only for part of the exposure to the employee. The majority view was that the employer's insurer was liable for the whole of the employer's liability to the employee. The insurer could then seek proportionate contributions from other insurers of other periods, and even claim from the employer himself. The minority view is that this loss should be limited to the proportion of the policy years to which there had been exposure.

The principles in *Barker* will apply in Hong Kong, and all the principles as laid down in *IEG* will be directly relevant to Hong Kong. It is important to look at the analysis adopted by the Supreme Court on the special issue and employers' liability insurance.

A common theme throughout the judgment was the importance of achieving "a fair balance of the interest of victims, assureds and insurers". The Supreme Court acknowledged the need to adapt "existing tools" of the law to meet the "unique situation" which arose in the *Fairchild* enclave. This can be seen in the solution to the anomalies identified regarding (1) liability, (2) contribution, and (3) recoupment/self-insurance, and how the courts have given new interpretation to existing cases or have been very selective when relying on cases to support propositions.

8.3.5.6 Liability

It is unclear whether the principles on liability only apply in situations like the present case, where cover is provided for a limited period or when dealing with unique situations or if it has a wider general application. At first blush it seems that if it is a situation that falls outside the parameters of the *Fairchild* enclave, the insurer will not be liable for a risk that falls outside the period of the policy. An assured will not be allowed to choose whichever order to sue to maximise allocation of his recovery. The application of *Barker* in Hong Kong will not afford full protection to the assured, who has paid premiums, and is at risk of receiving nothing. Insurers, on the other hand, will still have subrogation and contribution rights, after an employer who has taken out employers' liability insurance has been sued. It may be prudent for Hong Kong to implement similar legislation as the Compensation Act 2006, to avoid the narrow and unfair approach adopted by the courts under the common law.

8.3.5.7 Contribution
It is interesting to note that the majority in *IEG* was of the view that by imposing full liability upon Midland, Midland would then be able to seek insurance contribution from excess. The right of insurance contribution however only arises in cases of double insurance (i.e. where there are two or more policies taken out by one individual which covers the same interest, same subject matter covering the same risk). If the approach adopted is that there are separate losses in each year, this precludes double insurance, because the policies are not concurrent (as discussed in *Phillips v Syndicate 992 Gunner*[146]). The decision in *IEG* now suggests an extension of such principles to contribution across policy years. The majority view that the Civil Liability (Contribution) Act 1978 does not apply, even though s1(1) of the 1978 Act would be satisfied, is questionable. It could be said that the extension of such principles to ensure fairness and justice should be commended, but this is not a case of double insurance. The Supreme Court analysis has led to more uncertainty. Furthermore, the court did not state what the correct method for calculating contribution would be in such situations, but it seems that apportionment based on the independent actual liability calculation as in *National Employers Mutual General Insurance Association v Haydon*,[147] would lead to a fairer result.

8.3.5.8 Recoupment/Self-insurance
On the issue of self-insurance, the majority found that Midland could seek recovery from IEG, where IEG had no insurance. It extended the principles of restitution, which is normally applied between insurers, when dealing with the issue of contribution or subrogation rights, and not an assured. There is no authority that specifically deals with this principle. The only situation where there can be a distribution of such liability is under s81 of the Marine Insurance Act 1906, which deals with underinsurance, but this is not recoupment as such. This is yet another attempt by the Supreme Court to achieve a new result not supported by authorities. It is unclear on what basis the courts should allow for recoupment. The position should be that either the assured is completely covered under the insurance policy or, if there is no insurance, he will be unassured. If the majority view is correct, this means that the assured will now be treated as an insurer.

The implications in cases where there is reinsurance in mesothelioma cases is also unclear: can the reinsurers decide to base allocation on maximisation of

---

146 [2004] Lloyd's Rep IR 426.
147 [1980] 2 Lloyd's Rep 149.

recovery or should the reinsurer place the loss based on the year it occurs. However, the majority reasoning would suggest that the reinsurer will now only be liable to proportionate percentage of the loss, and not the whole of the loss.

It will have to be seen whether the extensions to the *Fairchild* enclave only applies to those cases which fall within the principle of *Fairchild* or will it extend outside these types of cases. Further guidance is needed before the dust finally settles.

8.3.6 Cape Distribution v Cape Intermediate Holdings plc

In *Cape Distribution v Cape Intermediate Holdings plc*,[148] Picken J had to consider consequential matters arising from the preliminary issues. One of them was whether Aviva, the insurer's successors, were precluded from pursuing indemnities not only in cases of employees who were exposed to asbestos after 25 November 1964 (the date of the endorsement) but also in cases of those employees who were exposed before and after (the Straddlers issue).

CDL, the plaintiff, produced asbestos-related products. On 1 January 1964, the business was sold to CIH and, under a sale agreement, CIH would indemnify CDL for claims made against CDL.CDL was assured with Aviva's predecessor against such liability. On 25 November 1964, CIH became a co-assured.

The insurer argued that each defendant was liable for the whole of the damage, and not proportionately under the Compensation Act 2006. Further, rights of subrogation applied for exposure caused before the parent company was joined as a co-assured. The parent company argued that the right to subrogation by the insurer was barred. The court referred to the legal context in light of the respective arguments of the parties:

> but for the particular position arrived at by the law in relation to mesothelioma claims specifically, there would likely have been agreement as to how "straddlers" should be dealt with in this case to the effect that they should be approached in the same way as divisible disease (diffuse pleural thickening) claims. The reason why there is no such agreement in relation to mesothelioma claims is that in relation to such claims, and only such claims, Parliament has enacted the Compensation Act 2006 (the "2006 Act"), thereby changing the position arrived at by the common law in relation to mesothelioma claims but not divisible disease (diffuse pleural thickening) claims.

He referred to *Zurich v IEG* to prevent the subsidiary limiting its claim under the clauses to liabilities incurred during the pre-25 November 1964 period, "with the result that there is then *"absolutely no question of CIH being made liable for any assured risk"* after 25 November 1964".[149] Further, CDL's attempt to limit its claim would constitute an unfair selection of the period to which a loss is to attach, and so would fall foul of the principle described in the *IEGL* case albeit in a different context:

---

148 [2016] Lloyd's Rep IR 499 (QB).
149 [2016] Lloyd's Rep IR 499 (QB), at para. [41].

> It is contrary to principle for insurance to operate on a basis which allows an assured to select the period and policy to which a loss attaches. This is elementary. If assureds could select against insurers in this way, the risks undertaken by insurers would be entirely unpredictable.[150]

At para. [51] of the judgment, he went on to distinguish the case of *Zurich v IEG*, as follows:

> In short, there is simply not the same call in the present case for a "Fairchild recoupment right" as there was in the IEGL case. Indeed, I am clear that, were I to take the view that Aviva should be afforded a "Fairchild recoupment right" on the facts of the present case, this would entail a significant and impermissible extension of the principle expounded in the IEGL case. Applying "a broad equitable approach," in my view, it would be neither fair nor equitable were Aviva to be allowed to recoup as against CIH simply so as to enable Aviva to avoid the financial consequences of having agreed, through the Endorsement, to provide CIH with cover under the Policy even though Aviva is liable to CDL under the Policy in relation to the entire period from 1965 to 1966. It was CDL which exposed its employees to asbestos, thereby attracting the liabilities which Aviva has had to bear under the Policy. In meeting these liabilities, Aviva has done nothing more than it agreed to do when it agreed to insure CDL. As a result of the Endorsement, CIH is also assured by Aviva for the same liability. Aviva does not find itself facing a claim by an assured such as IEGL under which it is contractually obliged to pay more than had always been envisaged and in relation to which it had not received an appropriate level of premium. I am satisfied that to afford Aviva a "Fairchild recoupment right" on the facts of the present case would not strike a "fair balance of the interests of victims, assureds and insurers" (the term used by Lord Mance in the IEGL case at [55]) but would merely permit Aviva to gain a commercial advantage to which it has no legitimate claim in circumstances where it had agreed to indemnify CDL throughout the life of the Policy and so was always obliged to meet liabilities stemming from CDL employee claims and in circumstances where it is accepted that, were CIH to have been confronted with such claims being made directly against it, Aviva would have been obliged similarly to meet those claims.

8.4 Reasoning of mesothelioma cases: what is the possible solution and does it apply to double insurance?

8.4.1 Approach of the courts

The courts have adopted different approaches to try and resolve the problems arising from mesothelioma cases. The courts have attempted to grant protection to such victims where it would be almost impossible for an employee to identify a particular employer, who is liable for the injury suffered by the employee, where numerous employers are involved. The same principles can be extended to double insurance cases when deciding which insurer to sue, where insurers argue that their policy does not cover the relevant period in question.

---

150 [2016] Lloyd's Rep IR 499 (QB), at para. [42].

8.4.2 The extension of the general rule of causation: double insurance cases

The courts have stretched the general rules of causation in mesothelioma cases. An employee can sue his employer to recover for the loss suffered under tort. The employer can then claim against the insurer in every year of exposure, and for every act of exposure which is on risk for any one year during which it is alleged that the exposure may have taken place. The courts will permit an assured to sue whichever insurer he wishes, by removing the requirement of the causative effect. The insurer will be liable to pay in full for the loss suffered. The employer will not need to respond to a request[151] by the insurer to identify a particular year, because a claim is present for every year.

8.4.3 Compensating mesothelioma victims

Under the law of tort, a person is entitled to compensation.[152] Payment of liabilities will only be considered in terms of mere practice, and is only of subsidiary concern,[153] because there is usually cover in place or legislative provisions in place, such as the Employers' Liability (Compulsory Insurance) Act 1969.[154] The Act specifically provides that an employer who carries on any type of business in Great Britain has to take out insurance, and is required to maintain insurance for liability regarding bodily injury or diseases which the employee may get.[155]

8.4.4 Does the Fairchild, Bolton and Durham line of cases provide a solution?

There has been suggestion that the decisions in *Fairchild*, *Bolton* and *Durham* have been far from satisfactory[156] and that it is unnecessary for the courts to analyse policies by distinguishing the policies based on the type of wording used as to whether there was cover or not. The problem is that the word "sustained" is genuinely unambiguous in its meaning.[157] It is the principles of contractual interpretation and the intentions of the parties which should be relevant when interpreting the contractual terms entered into between the parties. If such an approach were adopted, such an ambiguity would not arise.[158] Therefore, whether the employer is covered or not would depend on the wording of the policy. If the policy contained the words "injury sustained", the assured would be unassured against exposure. However, if the wording used was "injury sustained or disease contracted", this suggests that there was cover and a claim could be made under

---

151 This request may only be relevant for dealing with any reinsurance claims.
152 Merkin and Steele, "Compensating Mesothelioma Victims" (2011) 127 LQR 329.
153 *Ibid*.
154 *Ibid*, p. 330.
155 Section 1(1).
156 Merkin and Steele, "Compensating Mesothelioma Victims" (2011) 127 LQR 329, 331.
157 *Ibid*.
158 *Ibid*.

the policy.[159] A reading of the policies in this way, may not reflect the intention of the parties.

8.4.5 Investors Compensation Scheme Ltd v West Bromwich Building Society

The House of Lords in the case of *Investors Compensation Scheme Ltd v West Bromwich Building Society*[160] provided guidance on how the wording in the contracts should be construed. The interpretation of the policy wording should be looked at from the perspective of a reasonable person having all the background knowledge that would reasonably have been available to the parties at the time when they entered into the contract.[161] Background would be anything that would have affected the way in which the language of the document would have been understood by a reasonable man.[162] The present law is unclear[163] as to the kind of "injuries" needed, due to the changing nature of the mesothelioma cases, where more medical literature on the issue is needed.[164] Some commentators have said that the commercial purpose of the parties should take significance over the actual wording of the policy.[165]

8.4.6 Further criticism

It has been argued that the Court of Appeal decision[166] is wrong in the following four respects (1) that the distinction raised by the courts regarding "injury sustained" and "disease contracted" is artificial; (2) the ruling seriously undermines the legislative provision in the form of the 1969 Act; (3) the wider policy context;[167] and (4) the failure to distinguish[168] the decision in *Bolton*.

For point (1), it is unclear why the courts should read into the words in such a way that is contrary to the intention of the parties. These are standard wordings in policies and should also be adopted in employers' liability policies.

For point (2), the whole point for the implementation of the Employers' Liability (Compulsory Insurance) Act 1969 was to give protection to an employee by ensuring that the employer takes out such insurance for the employee. The ambiguity in the terms of the contract[169] is not required for contextual issues for it to be considered relevant, but the ambiguity in the wording "disease contracted"

---

159 *Ibid.*
160 [1998] 1 WLR. 896.
161 [1998] 1 WLR 896, 912.
162 [1998] 1 WLR 896, 913.
163 By the time it reached the Court of Appeal.
164 *Ibid.*
165 R Merkin and J Steele, "Compensating Mesothelioma Victims" (2011) 127 LQR 329, 333. Also see *Rainy Sky SA v Kookim Bank* [2011] 1 WLR 2900 (which considered the correct approach where the meaning of a contractual provision is ambiguous); *BMA Special Opportunity Hub Fund Ltd v African Minerals Finance Ltd* [2013] EWCA Civ 416 (where the Court of Appeal considered the principles of interpreting commercial documents).
166 Merkin and Steele, "Compensating Mesothelioma Victims" (2011) 127 LQR 333, 334.
167 When one looks at the *Fairchild* decision and the Compensation Act 2006.
168 As the Court of Appeal could not do so.
169 See *Oceanbulk Shipping & Trading SA v TMT Asia Ltd* [2010] 3 WLR 1424.

could have been considered as interchangeable when considering or using the phrase "injury sustained".[170]

For point (3), it is questionable how the process of trying to determine how words used by the parties, which the parties had drafted years ago, and which applied to unforeseen circumstances, is considered as an artificial exercise.[171] It seems unlikely that after the legislature decided to implement the Compensation Act, as a result of the decision in *Barker* to protect the victim, that it would now remove such protection.[172]

For point (4), the law of tort, does not focus on the physical harm that has been caused, but the earlier cause.[173] This was consistent with *Rothwell v Chemical & Insulating Co Ltd*[174] that one had to focus on the injury that has been caused, and not the damage in an insurance policy.[175] The markets have criticised the decision in *Bolton* where emphasis was placed on the effects of the obligation placed on a public liability insurer to provide cover for torts which have occurred some four decades ago.[176] Therefore injury cover is now almost changed to claims made cover, which creates retroactivity for public liability policies, which does not seem to be the intended effect.[177] However this does not apply in situations where you have employers' liability policy due to the effect of the decision in *Durham*, which provided that once you have clear wording in an occurrence-based policy, the employee has to be working for the employer at the time of the exposure, and at the time of the injury.[178] The problem with the suggested approach is that occurrence-based policy will not cover the employers' liability to pay compensation to the former employee, as public liability and employers' liability policy will only achieve their purpose when one is operating on an exposure-based structure.[179] Further, if the Supreme Court overturns the decision in *Durham*, another important issue is the allocation of responsibility as between the consecutive annual insurers if there is only one employer, as the courts have now stated that it is unnecessary for an employee to identify any single year of exposure, because of the protection given to the employee, due to the unique situation arising from such cases, for him to bring his claim.[180]

8.4.7 The implications of the Employers' Liability (Compulsory Insurance) Act 1969

The 1969 Act itself, does not provide specific provision or wording as to the type of policy required to be taken out to comply with the wording of the Act.[181] One

---

170 Merkin and Steele, "Compensating Mesothelioma Victims" (2011) 127 LQR 329, 333.
171 *Ibid*.
172 *Ibid*.
173 *Ibid*, 334.
174 [2008] 1 AC 281.
175 *Ibid*.
176 R Merkin and J Steele, "Compensating Mesothelioma Victims" (2011) 127 LQR 329, 334.
177 *Ibid*.
178 *Ibid*.
179 *Ibid*.
180 *Ibid*.
181 This was the view of the Stanley Burnton and Smith LJJ.

view[182] is that the approach adopted by Rix LJ was correct. His approach was that an exposure-based cover was the only type of policy which could satisfy the wording of the 1969 Act. This was subject to the insurer having a right of recourse to the employer if the policy was otherwise written on an injury basis. The reason why Rix LJ's view is considered logical is that the policy, if it is an occurrence-based policy, will only apply to current employees. Therefore, all ex-employees who had contracted mesothelioma would not have any protection or be able to recover under the policy, as they must remain employed at the date of the onset of the injury.[183] If the analysis of Stanley, Burnton and Smith LJJ[184] is followed, employees who have left the employment of their employer would not be covered. Further, the legislation does not make express provision for ex-employees to be covered, and to do so would lead to the prohibition of contractual exclusions for liability which arose from previous acts.[185] The correct approach is that adopted by Lord Mance, where he held that the insurance contracts must be looked at in broad terms, when one tries to interpret the construction of the contracts.

8.4.8 Is there sufficient protection under the law of tort?

An employee has protection under the law of tort. Lord Clarke correctly pointed out that it would be remarkable if the insurers were not liable under the policies. If that is the case, the deemed causation approach would be most beneficial to the insurer. However, there are differences in application of the deemed causation approach and the new tort approach in mesothelioma cases.

The *Fairchild* decision adopted the causative approach and, as a result, an employee can choose to sue either or both of his employers. The employer can then submit the claim to his insurer to recover the whole loss for any year. If the new liability of materially increasing the risk of mesothelioma is adopted, the employer will have to identify a particular exposure which had caused the injury. This may prove difficult and would result in the employer being unable to submit his claim.[186] Further, liabilities could be unassured, even though there is a legislative requirement to do so.[187] There may also be re-insurance problems, where the re-insurer will refuse to pay out if a particular insurer could not be identified.

8.4.9 Does the type of liability insurance matter?

The issue becomes more complicated depending on the type of liability insurance.[188] It could be possible that, one year, the insurance taken out is under a causation policy, which would make the employer liable and, another year, the

---

182 Merkin and Steele, "Compensating Mesothelioma Victims" (2011) 127 LQR 329, 335.
183 *Ibid*.
184 Who agreed with Burnton LJ's decision.
185 *Ibid*.
186 Merkin and Steele, *Insurance and The Law of Obligations* (2013), 12.3.4, p. 374.
187 *Ibid*, p. 375.
188 Liability insurance can be divided into a causation basis, injury basis and claims made basis.

policy may be that of an injury policy. An employer may choose different insurers during different years, and each insurance policy may be different. The implications of this become significant depending on the year of exposure and the year in which the injury is suffered by the employee. The date of the trigger is important, and the status of the employee has to be considered.[189]

8.4.10 Implications for insurers?

The case of *Durham* is of broad significance.[190] The approach adopted by the courts is a "transparent illustration of holistic law making, identifying an injustice in the application of the rule in causation and then allowing the matching of insurance with the modified approach".[191] Adopting this approach results in a more balanced and fair result being achieved.

8.5 Should liability be divided proportionately?

In cases which involve the inhalation of asbestos, it may be impossible to know whether any particular inhalation of the asbestos, which occurred years ago, played a part in contributing to the death of the employee. This is what happened in *Phillips v Syndicate 992 Gunner*,[192] *Fairchild v Glenhaven Funeral Services Ltd*[193] and *Barker v Corus (UK) Ltd*.[194] There have been differences of opinion, such as whether each employer was liable to the employee or was each employer liable only for a proportionate share.

8.5.1 Fairchild v Glenhaven Funeral Services Ltd

It is likely that the courts will follow the approach as laid down in *Fairchild* where, although not directly dealing with rateable proportion clauses, it was held that the employers were liable for the loss suffered to the employee. Situations like those in *Fairchild* would arise when (1) two separate potential causes expose the plaintiff to the same risk, one involving the act of the defendant, (2) either one gives rise to the risk and (3) one does, but (4) neither of which can, as a matter of probability, be shown to have done so. This has now been extended, as a result of *Barker* and *Sienkiewicz v Grief (UK) Ltd*,[195] to cases where there is an act or

---

189 *Merkin and Steel*, 12.3.1.
190 *Ibid*, 12.3.4, p. 375.
191 *Ibid*.
192 [2004] Lloyd's Rep IR 418. Also see *Durham v BAI (Run Off) Ltd* [2012] 1 WLR 867 and *International Energy Group Ltd v Zurich Insurance plc UK* [2012] EWHC 69 (Comm).
193 [2002] 3 WLR 89.
194 [2006] 2 WLR 1027.
195 [2011] 2 AC 229. In *Sienkiewicz*, there were two mesothelimoa claims. The court stated that with the present state of medical knowledge victims were unable to prove on a balance of probabilities the source of exposure to asbestos which initiated the process which caused the illness, where only one defendant could be proved to have tortuously exposed the victim and where the victim could have been exposed to asbestos due to environmental circumstances, this would be no different if the

omission exposing a person to asbestos, which may have caused mesothelioma, but where it was not possible to prove it as a matter of probability.

8.5.2 Barker v Corus (UK) Ltd

In *Barker*, the court concluded that a person's liability should be proportionate to the extent that he had exposed another to the risk of mesothelioma. However, this was reversed due to the enactment by Parliament of the Compensation Act 2006,[196] which made each person liable in respect of the whole of the damage[197] caused by the mesothelioma. The Financial Services Authority has the power to make rules for compensation to victims where employers' liability insurers have become insolvent for claims made before 1 December 2001. This Act will assume liability and only alters the measure of recovery[198] as seen in *Sienkiewicz*.

8.5.3 Phillips v Syndicate 992 Gunner

In *Phillips v Syndicate 992 Gunner*, the deceased employee who had been exposed to asbestos dust for a period of time had contracted malignant mesothelioma. The defendant relied on express terms of the employer's liability policy which stated that, if there was other insurance covering the same liability when a claim arose, the underwriters would not be liable to pay or contribute more than their due proportion of any such claim. The defendant further argued that the rateable proportion clause should be implied into the contract to give business efficacy. Eady J concluded that the wording relied on by the insurers would not be sufficient to cover situations where there are successive policies of insurance, which covered different periods and different risks. It was unnecessary to imply into the contract a rateable proportion clause to give it business efficacy. Subsequent cases[199] have held that liability for mesothelioma, following exposure to asbestos created during an insurance period, involved a sufficient "weak" or "broad" casual link for the disease to be regarded as "caused" within the insurance period.

8.5.4 Conclusion

There has only been a recent peak in such cases due to the condition developing decades later. The fact that these events took place a long time ago should not

---

victim was in fact able to point to multiple defendants. The court should apply the special rule devised under common law and s3 of the Compensation Act 2006 for multiple defendants, where what would have to be established by the victim was that the defendant had breached his duty by exposing the victim to asbestos fibres and this materially increased the risk that he would develop mesothelioma – material meaning more than minimal. This was for the judge to decide. The test for causation had no place in such cases.

196 Whether by reason of having materially increased a risk or for any other reason: s3(1)(d).
197 Section 3(2)(a).
198 Lord Phillips PSC, Lord Rodger and Lord Brown of Eaton-under-Heywood JJSC [70], [131] and [183].
199 See for example, *Durham v BAI (Run off) Ltd* (SC(E)) [2012] 1 WLR 867, 899.

matter. It is clear that there was a need to provide protection to such employees, as indicated in the *Fairchild* decision and the implementation of legislative provisions in the form of the Compensation Act 2006. The nature of such cases makes it almost impossible to identify one particular employer especially where the employee has been employed by numerous employers over a period of time. In some cases, the employer may have become insolvent or the employers' insurers no longer exist when the condition of the employee develops. In such situations, the employee will not be protected by any cover. The position would be different where the employee has worked for only one employer, who is still in business, and the employer's insurers still exists. It is important that the law develops to ensure that an assured is protected. Therefore, it can be argued that the courts should not adopt Lord Phillips' approach, and it is unnecessary to implement legislation if the court applies principles which favour an assured.

8.6 Can these principles be extended to double insurance?

Double insurance will arise where there is one employer, who takes out insurance cover for a particular employee, with numerous insurers, and the period of cover overlaps. In *Phillips v Syndicate 992 Gunner*, Eady J held that successive periods of insurance cover would not be treated as covering the same liability. Therefore, it can be argued that double insurance does not arise in mesothelioma cases as there is no overlap between the policies, as the policies are consecutive.

When an employee seeks full compensation from his employer, the employer then has to look to his insurers. An insurer is on risk when there was exposure to the employee, and is generally under an obligation to pay out under the policy. However, there may have been different insurers during a number of years or the amount recoverable has varied due to the exhaustion through other claims or policy terms.[200] If the insurers are still in operation, the employer can seek to recover full indemnity from them.[201] Should an insurer on risk be liable in full or should an apportionment basis be applied? The preferred view[202] is that the increase of an employer's liability is a risk which the insurers must accept.

Liability should be 100%,[203] since the law has developed to entitle an employee to recover 100% from the employer. It would then be for the employer to receive 100% indemnity from whichever insurer he chooses.[204] However, contribution does not arise because each insurer is only liable for the risk of a particular period of time or year and there are no concurrent policies in place. This argument is incorrect. As the Supreme Court in *Durham* has confirmed, there is only one claim which the employee can make. There is a single indivisible loss. Double insurance should apply in such cases. The insurer can seek contribution from

---

200 Merkin and Steele, *Insurance and The Law of Obligations* (2013), 12.4, p. 376.
201 An employer has to consider carefully which insurer he seeks to recover from.
202 As stated per Lord Mance JSC.
203 This was confirmed in *International Energy Group Ltd v Zurich Insurance plc UK* [2015] 2 WLR 1471.
204 This would be consistent with the approach in *Fairchild* and the Compensation Act 2006.

other insurers. It does not have to be shown that the loss arose in one particular year, as s3 of the Civil Liability (Contribution) Act 1978 applies. Under the 1978 Act one responsible person can then claim contribution from another, for his proportion of liability. It has been suggested that the common law should not redefine liabilities.[205]

---

205 *Merkin and Steel*, 12.1.1.

CHAPTER 9

Contribution under common law and its equitable position

9.1 Contribution under common law and equity

The term "common law" has been described as the law that has developed through case law, and differs from statutes. It has been described as the body of rules originally developed by Chancery courts, before the Supreme Court of Judicature Acts 1873 and 1875 came into effect.[1] Lord Mansfield approved the development of parties bringing contribution claims under unjust enrichment,[2] and principles of co-sureties into principles of contribution[3] from Scottish law.[4]

9.2 Joint liability and contribution: its implication for insurance

Generally, liability arises where a plaintiff suffers loss or damage due to the torts committed by a tortfeasor. In some situations, there may be joint liability by tortfeasors, which impacts on how liability should be distributed. The liability of tortfeasors can be ascertained by identifying (1) whether the cause of action against each tortfeasor is the same, (2) whether they are both responsible and (3) if the same evidence can be used to bring the action.[5] This would not be the

---

1 Charles Mitchell, *The Law of Contribution and Reimbursement* (2003), 4.03, p. 66.
2 *Deker v Pope* (1757) Selw NP (1812 edn), Vol. 1, 71–2.
3 For example, in the case of *Mahoney v McManus* 36 ALR 545, 549–550, at para. [17] as follows:

> A surety is entitled to contribution from his co-sureties so that the common burden is born equally and so that no surety is required, as between himself and his co-sureties are bound jointly, jointly and severally, or severally, and whether by the same or different instruments, and whether or not the sureties knew of each other's existence, provided that they are liable in respect of the same debt. The right to contribution arises when a surety has paid or provided more than his proper share of the principal debt . . . The amount of contribution recoverable depends on the number of sureties who are solvent at the time when contribution is sought and on the proportion for which each is liable . . . The doctrine of contribution is based on the principle of natural justice that if several persons have a common obligation they should as between themselves contribute proportionately in satisfaction of that obligation. The operation of such a principle should not be defeated by too technical an approach.

4 JH Baker, "The History of Quasi-Contract in English Law", in WR Cornish et al. (eds), *Restitution: Past, Present and Future* (1998), 37, 46.
5 *The Koursk* [1924] P 140 (shipping case); *Brook v Bool* [1928] 2 KB 578 (landlord and lodger); but contrast principles as enunciated in *Mutua v Foreign and Commonwealth Office* [2012] EWHC 2678 (QB); *Fish & Fish Ltd v Sea Shepard UK* [2015] AC 1229.

case where each is independently responsible for a separate tort and the two torts cause the same damage.[6] If so, they are joint tortfeasors.[7]

9.2.1 Does the same damage mean the same tort?

Scrutton LJ in *The Koursk*[8] stated that the same damage did not mean the same tort, and therefore did not mean same cause of action.[9] Where there are numerous tortfeasors, and there is a distinct cause of action against each tortfeasor, each tortfeasor will only be liable for the part of the damage for which he is responsible.[10] Where the amount which the tortfeasor will be liable for is not stipulated, the amount will be distributed equally between the tortfeasors.[11] This situation arose in *Barker v Corus (UK) plc*,[12] and is relevant in cases of industrial diseases where there were several former employers who owed a duty of care to the plaintiff and who had breached that duty of care.[13]

9.2.2 Same damage: joint tortfeasors and several tortfeasors

Where joint tortfeaors are liable for a separate tort, successive actions can be brought against them even though the damage is one and indivisible.[14]

9.2.2.1 Civil Liability (Contribution) Act 1978

Section 3 of the Civil Liability (Contribution) Act 1978, governs proceedings against persons who are jointly liable for the same debt or damage. It states that judgment recovered against any person liable in respect of any debt or damage shall not be a bar to an action, or to the continuance of an action, against any other person who is (apart from any such bar) jointly liable with him in respect of the same debt or damage. The courts have been reluctant to permit a plaintiff from bringing an action against numerous defendants for the same damage suffered. In *Talbot v Bekshire County Council*[15] the court relied on the principles of res judicata, stating that as the plaintiff's claim against the council arose out of substantially the same facts as the cause of action[16] as

---

6 *Clerk and Lindsell on Torts* (20th edn 2010), p. 273, para. 4–03.
7 *Ibid.*
8 [1924] P 140.
9 [1924] P 140, 156. In *Re The Alexandros T* [2013] UKSC 70, the UK Supreme Court looked to see whether there was a same cause of action. The court was of the view that there should be "*le meme objet et la meme cause*" (although not specifically dealing with double insurance but with claims which mirror each other in England and Greece).
10 *Performance Cars Ltd v Abraham* [1962] 1 QB 281, where the court was dealing with successive independent tortfeasors.
11 *Bank View Mill v Nelson Corp* [1942] 2 All ER 477 at 483.
12 [2006] 1 AC 572.
13 *Clerk and Lindsell on Torts*, p. 273, para. 4–06.
14 *Ibid*, para. 4–07.
15 [1994] QB 290.
16 [1994] QB 290, 298.

the passenger's claim, which had been made out, the plaintiff's appeal should be dismissed. In such situations, the courts have stayed or struck out litigation for abuse of process.[17] Therefore a plaintiff in such a case should sue all likely defendants.[18] Wigram V-C in *Henderson v Henderson*[19] stated that parties to the litigation should bring forward their whole case and the courts will not permit the same parties to open the same subject matter of litigation on issues which might have been brought forward as part of the litigation in previous litigation.[20]

9.2.3 Where there is a release of one tortfeasor

In *Gardiner v Moore*,[21] Thesiger J was of the view[22] that a release by one joint tortfeasor, either by way of deed or by accord and satisfaction, would release all other joint tortfeasors.

9.2.4 Possibility of double recovery

There could be the possibility of double recovery in some situations under the Civil Liability (Contribution) Act 1978. It has been suggested that, prior to accepting settlement, a party should expressly leave open the option to bring proceedings against the other concurrent tortfeasors.[23]

9.3 Contribution or reimbursement: restitutionary in nature

Remedies provided under contribution or reimbursement are restitutionary in nature. The main purpose is to prevent the likelihood of unjust enrichment by a defendant who has been conferred a benefit by the plaintiff's payment.[24]

9.4 Distinction between common law and equity

The courts have drawn a distinction between common law and equitable principles of liability. In *Bonner v Tottenham and Edmonton Permanent Investment Building Society*,[25] a landlord sued for breach of a covenant to pay rent, where

---

17 *Brisbane City Council v Attorney General for Queensland* [1979] AC 411, 411G.
18 *Clerk and Lindsell on Torts*, p. 273, para. 4–08.
19 (1843) 3 Hare 100.
20 (1843) 3Hare 100, 114–115.
21 [1969] 1 QB 55 at 92F.
22 Although not a point which he relied on to decide the case.
23 *Clerk and Lindsell on Torts*, p. 273, para. 4–11, where the case of *Jameson v Central Electricity Generating Board* [2000] 1 AC 455 was discussed.
24 *Grupos Torras SA v Al-Sabah (No 5)* [2001] Lloyd's Rep Bank 36 at 64.
25 [1899] 1 QB 161. This has been followed in the decisions of *FBI Foods Ltd – Aliments FBI Ltée v Glassner* 86 BCLR (3d) 136; *Friend v Brooker* [2009] HCA 21 at [44]; *Whitham v Bullock* [1939] 2 KB 81 at [87].

the tenant assigned his lease out, which had then been mortgaged to the defendant. The tenant paid the landlord, then pursued a claim for recovery against the defendant. The claim for recovery did not succeed as the liability of the defendant had not been discharged, as the defendant was only a sub-lessee.[26] Vaughan Williams LJ stated:

> There is a common law principle of liability, and also a principle of liability in equity, and these two principles differ. The common law principle requires a common liability to be sued for that which the plaintiff had to pay, and an interest of the defendant in the payment in the sense that he gets the benefit of the payment, either entirely, as in the case of the assignee of a lease, or pro tanto, as in the case of a surety who has paid, and has his action for contribution against his co-surety. The principle in equity seems wide enough to include cases in which there is community of interest in the subject-matter to which the burden is attached, which has been enforced against the plaintiff alone, coupled with benefit to the defendant, even though there is no common liability to be sued.

Further, equitable principles require that the burden will be borne equally between the parties even if there are requirements of the law or the parties themselves agree that the burden will be attached by one of the parties for the benefit of others who are associated with him for that interest.[27] In *Whitham v Bullock*,[28] the Court of Appeal, applied these principles when dealing with the lessee of land who had assigned the lease partly to X and partly to Y. It held that as the plaintiffs paid the whole amount which was claimed by the landlord under the threat of the distraint,[29] the Court of Appeal was of the view that they could seek reimbursement from the defendant.

9.5 Co-sureties

The doctrine of contribution is not confined to double insurance but to co-sureties as well. Co-sureties must be liable in respect of the same debt. The amount which is recoverable depends on the number of sureties.[30]

---

26 Contrast *Moule v Garrett* (1872) LR 7 Exch 101, where the defendant was an assignee. See *Brook's Wharf and Bull Wharf Ltd v Goodman Bros* [1937] 1 KB 534, 544, per Lord Wright MR, where he stated: "The case is analogous to that of a payment by a surety which has the effect of discharging the principal's debt and which, therefore, gives a right of indemnity against the principal."
27 *Whitham v Bullock* [1983] 2 KB 81.
28 At para. [89] per Clauson LJ.
29 Friedmann, "Double Insurance and Payment of Another's Debt" (1993) 103 LQR 51, 53, discussed the public interest factor in trying to settle claims, but also the problem of where payment is made where the plaintiff pays out when they are not liable to make such payment. The problem he identified was that the payor was not the debtor as such, and the rules of contribution would not apply. England does not look favourably on those who would come under the category of "volunteers".
30 *Mahoney v McManus* (1981) 36 ALR 545, 549–550. This was confirmed in *Stratti v Stratti* [2000] NSWCA 358.

9.6 Law Commission: Law Reform (Married Woman and Tortfeasors) Act 1935

The Law Commission reviewed s6(1)[31] of the Law Reform (Married Women and Tortfeasors) Act 1935,[32] which was later suspended.

Section 6(1)(c) permitted a tortfeasor to claim contribution from any other tortfeasor who was or, if sued, would be liable in respect of the same damage suffered. The legislation was considered unsatisfactory when dealing with a contractor situation,[33] and the Law Commission[34] looked into the issue. The Law Commission concluded that the 1935 Act should apply to all wrongdoers, and successive actions should be allowed for the same damage.[35] These changes were implemented in the Civil Liability (Contribution) Act 1978.[36]

9.7 Implementation of the Civil Liability (Contribution) Act 1978

The Civil Liability (Contribution) Act 1978 developed in relation to the liabilities that arose where there was damage that was the same and applied to tortfeasors who had liabilities that were joint and several.[37] It was thought that the law

---

[31] "(1)Where damage is suffered by any person as a result of a tort (whether a crime or not) – (a) judgment recovered against any tort-feasor liable in respect of that damage shall not be a bar to an action against any other person who would, if sued, have been liable as a joint tort-feasor in respect of the same damage; (b) if more than one action is brought in respect of that damage by or on behalf of the person by whom it was suffered, or for the benefit of the estate, or of the wife, husband, parent or child, of that person, against tort-feasors liable in respect of the damage (whether as joint tort-feasors or otherwise) the sums recoverable under the judgments given in those actions by way of damages shall not in the aggregate exceed the amount of the damages awarded by the judgment first given; and in any of those actions, other than that in which judgment is first given, the plaintiff shall not be entitled to costs unless the court is of opinion that there was reasonable ground for bringing the action; (c) any tort-feasor liable in respect of that damage may recover contribution from any other tortfeasor who is, or would if sued have been, liable in respect of the same damage, whether as a joint tort-feasor or otherwise, so, however, that no person shall be entitled to recover contribution under this section from any person entitled to be indemnified by him in respect of the liability in respect of which the contribution is sought. (2) In any proceedings for contribution under this section the amount of the contribution recoverable from any person shall be such as may be found by the court to be just and equitable having regard to the extent of that person's responsibility for the damage; and the court shall have power to exempt any person from liability to make contribution, or to direct that the contribution to be recovered from any person shall amount to a complete indemnity."

[32] Ireland, Ontario and Tasmania do not follow the Law Reform (Married and Tortfeasors) Act 1935.

[33] *McConnell v Lynch Robinson* [1957] NI 70 where there were different contractual obligations, and where the architect was sued but was unable to claim contribution from a builder, for defective construction of a building.

[34] Report on Contribution 1977 (Law Com. No 79). See also the Apportionment of Civil Liability [1992] NZLCPP 19.

[35] "The Civil Liability (Contribution) Act 1978" (1979) 42(2) MLR 182.

[36] The legislation came into effect on 1 January 1979.

[37] For some examples of this can be seen in the cases of *Weld-Blundell v Stephens* [1920] AC 956, *Horwell v London General Omnibus Co Ltd* (1877) 2 Ex D 365, 379 and *Royal Brompton NHS Trust v Hammond* [2002] 1 WLR 1397.

should cater for contribution between tortfeasors.[38] In cases of double insurance the Civil Liability (Contribution) Act 1978 does not apply.

9.8 Application to double insurance

As a result of the recommendation in the Law Commission's Report, the Civil Liability (Contribution) Act 1978 was enacted by Parliament. There have been comments[39] that the Act is not without its problems.

The general principle as stated in *Merryweather v Nixon*[40] was that where the damage is the same, regardless of whether it was caused by a joint tortfeasor or several tortfeasors, there could not be contribution or indemnity between them unless there was an express or implied agreement. The Civil Liability (Contribution) Act 1978 however now permits contribution to persons who are liable for the same damage.[41] The long title to the Civil Liability (Contribution) Act 1978 Act provides for contribution between persons who are jointly and severally liable for the same damage, and in some cases where two or more persons have paid or may be required to pay compensation for the same damage.

Under s1(1) of the Act any person who is liable in respect of any damage suffered by another person may recover contribution from any other person liable in respect of the same damage, whether jointly with him or otherwise. This is subject to the other provisions in the Act itself which lists certain situations where liability may cease in respect to the damage in question. Section 6(1) of the Act provides that a person is liable in respect of any damage, for the purposes of the Act, if the person who suffered it is entitled to recover compensation from him in respect of the damage, regardless of the legal basis of his liability.

9.8.1 Interpretation of ss1(1) and 6(1) Civil Liability (Contribution) Act 1978

The Court of Appeal in *Royal Brompton Hospital NHS Trust v Hammond*[42] interpreted ss1(1) and 6(1) of the Civil Liability (Contribution) Act 1978. In *Royal Brompton Hospital NHS Trust* the architect granted an extension of time provided under a building contract. The contractor sued for the loss and expenses incurred due to delay. The contractor commenced arbitration against RBH for the balance unpaid by the hospital, which was subsequently settled. RBH then sued the architect and the professional team for negligence to recover the sums paid to the contractor. Lord Steyn considered that s1(1) and s6(1) should be read together, and that the 1978 Act should be given a broad interpretation. The main question before the court was in relation to the words "liable in respect of the

---

38 This can be seen in the Law Revision Committee's *Third Interim Report* of 1934. Legislation such as the Law Reform (Married Women and Tortfeasors) Act 1935, s6(1) was implemented but was inadequate to meet the needs of recovering contribution.
39 Charles Mitchell, *The Law of Contribution and Reimbursement* (2003), 4.27 p. 82.
40 (1799) 8 TR 186.
41 Section 1(1).
42 [2002] 1 WLR 1397.

same damage". The court stated that the words of the legislation would not justify an expansive interpretation of the words "the same damage" to mean substantially or materially similar damage, due to the unfairness that would arise, and the uncertainty of the application of the law. It was held that the correct approach was to interpret and apply a correct evaluation and comparison of claims alleged to quantify contribution under s1(1).[43] The natural and ordinary meaning of the words of "the same damage" was sufficient[44] and "no glosses, extensive or restrictive, were warranted".[45]

9.8.2 Does the Civil Liability (Contribution) Act 1978 apply to claims between indemnity insurers?

9.8.2.1 Bovis Lend Lease Ltd v Saillard Fuller & Partners

Whether contribution claims between indemnity insurers fall within the confines of the Civil Liability (Contribution) Act 1978 depends on the exact wording of the relevant policies.[46] The preferred view was found in the case of *Bovis Lend Lease Ltd v Saillard Fuller & Partners*,[47] where liability for "damage" under the 1978 Act was made out where the insurer had to pay damages for a breach of the contract stated under s6(1), on the basis that the insurer had committed a wrong by not preventing the assured from suffering a risk.[48]

9.8.2.2 Bovis Construction Ltd v Commercial Union Assurance Co plc

The case of *Bovis Construction Ltd v Commercial Union Assurance Co plc*[49] clearly settled the issue of whether an insurer could rely on the Civil Liability (Contribution) Act 1978, and discussed the issue of subrogation. In *Bovis*, two claims were made. First, by the first plaintiff, Bovis Construction Ltd (Bovis) relying on their policy of insurance, and the second was that of the insurers, Eagle Star Insurance Co Ltd (Eagle Star), relying on their right to contribution. Eagle Star had at the time assured Bovis under a public liability policy. Commercial Union Assurance Ltd (CU) assured Rosehaugh Estates Ltd (Rosehaugh), with which Bovis was also assured at the time. There was then a claim made by CU seeking indemnity or contribution for the amount of damages and costs which were paid by Bovis to General Accident Life and Assurance Ltd (GA), who were the assignees of Rosehaugh. A contract was entered into between Bovis and Rosehaugh for the management of the construction, which Bovis was in charge of. Rosehaugh was required to obtain and maintain an insurance policy, which

---

43 [2002] 1 WLR 1410, para. 27. Section 1(4) of the 1978 Act deals with situations where the claim has been settled. Also see *Dubai Aluminium Co Ltd v Salaam* [2001] QB 113.
44 [2002] 1 WLR 1410, para. 27.
45 [2002] 1 WLR 1410, para. 27.
46 *Mitchell*, 4.43, p. 88.
47 [2001] 77 Con LR134, 184–5.
48 *Mitchell*, 4.44, p. 89.
49 [2001] Lloyd's Rep IP 321. The principles were followed by the Supreme Court of Appeal of South Africa in *Samancor Ltd v Mutual &Federal Insurance Co Ltd* (Case Number 565/03).

covered their liabilities for injury and damage to the property, which resulted during the contract period. The cover had to be taken out in the joint names of Rosehaugh and Bovis. Further, joint name insurance had to be taken out for all executed works, goods and materials, which were to be incorporated into the works, construction works and other materials. This policy was taken out with CU, which included an "all risks" in s1 and another part for "public liability" under the policy. It was argued that the Civil Liability (Contribution) Act 1978 applied and, as a result, the plaintiff should be entitled to claim indemnity or contribution under s3. Bovis, on receiving GA's claim, referred it to CU, which repudiated the claim on the basis that the claim was not one which was covered under the policy. Therefore, Bovis had to turn to its own liability insurer, Eagle Star, which had provided the indemnity for the amount that GA was given. The repudiation by CU was not accepted. CU argued that the claim was not covered by either s1 or s3, and that, since indemnity was already provided for by Eagle Star before the proceedings had started, Bovis should not be entitled to obtain contribution.

The court then considered the issue of double insurance. Steel J started by looking at the position of Bovis's claim. The first "hurdle" for Bovis was that Eagle Star had already made payment to Bovis and, as a result, Bovis should not be allowed to make a claim under another policy.[50] Steel J stated that the right to contribution between insurers existed where there is more than one policy which covered the risk which gave rise to the claim. He relied on the case of *Albion Insurance Co Ltd v Government Insurance Office of New South Wales*[51] and confirmed *Caledonia North Sea Ltd v London Bridge Engineering*.[52] On the facts of the present case, Bovis was unable to satisfy the elements required and, for that reason alone, their claim failed.

It was further argued that, based on a breach of the Civil Liability (Contribution) Act 1978, both Bovis (through the management contract) and CU (under the policy) were liable to Rosehaugh. Steel J held[53] that there was no liability against CU under the heading of "in respect of the same damage". Therefore, Rosehaugh could not claim against CU for compensation as CU had no "responsibility for the damage" which Rosehaugh had received. No apportionment of liability could be received. To hold otherwise would be to override principles relating to contribution between the insurers. Bovis's liability for flood damage and CU's liability under the policy of insurance did not fall within the meaning of "in respect of the same damage". The case of *Royal Brompton Hospital National Health Service Trust v Hammond*[54] was relied on to emphasise the point that it was not the same damage.

---

50 Reliance was placed on the cases of *Sickness & Accident Assurance Association v General Accident Assurance Corporation Ltd* (1892) 19 R 977.
51 [1969] CLR 342.
52 [2000] 1 Lloyd's Rep IP 249.
53 [2001] Lloyd's Rep IP 321, 326 at para. 27.
54 [2000] Lloyd's Rep PN 643.

9.8.2.3 *Co-operative Retail Services Ltd v Taylor Young Partnership Ltd*

I THE TRIAL

Where there are terms in the contract excluding liability or there are limitation clauses, and where the damage is covered by a joint names insurance policy, there is no contribution. This was the position in the case of *Co-operative Retail Services Ltd v Taylor Young Partnership Ltd*,[55] where there was a standard form contract entered into with the main contractor, W Ltd. The defendants were architects and engineers. The electrical sub-contractors were H Ltd, who were hired by W Ltd under a standard form subcontract. In addition to this, H Ltd entered into a warranty agreement with the building owner and W Ltd. Liability was excluded for damage caused before practical completion of the works which were due to the contractors' negligence or breach of statutory duty, under the main contract. The contractors were required to take out policies in their joint names for all risks insurance which provided cover against loss or damage to the works in respect of specified perils, which included fire. A fire broke out prior to practical completion. The defendants issued proceedings[56] under ss1 and 6 of the Civil Liability (Contribution) Act 1978 against W Ltd and H Ltd, for liability for the fire damage from whom the owners of the building were entitled to seek compensation. The judge stated that such a claim could not be brought by the defendant.

II THE COURT OF APPEAL

This decision was appealed and the Court of Appeal looked at the structure of the contractual scheme. It concluded that it provided for the restoration and completion of the damaged works which was funded under the joint names policy, and that the building owner and the contractors would each bear other losses themselves. There was no requirement for the contractors to compensate the building owner for the damage caused by the fire and, as a result, the defendant could not seek contribution under the 1978 Act.

III THE HOUSE OF LORDS

The House of Lords stated that the usual rules which applied to compensation for negligence and breach of contract did not apply here. The building contractor could only require reinstatement works to be carried out. They were entitled only to insurance moneys which were used for payment of those works. Further, according to s6(1), H Ltd were not within the category of persons who could claim compensation from the building owners.

---

55 [2002] 1 WLR 1419. Although different considerations apply where there is one co-defendant liable for the deceit, where the party then cannot rely on the exclusion or limitation clauses, as was seen in the case of *Nationwide Building Society v Dunlop Haywards (DHL) Ltd and Cobbetts (A Firm)* [2010] 1 WLR 258.

56 This was a Part 20 action.

9.8.2.4 Application of s1(4) Civil Liability (Contribution) Act 1978?

The Civil Liability (Contribution) Act 1978 does not apply to double insurance. An insurer cannot rely on s1(4) of the 1978 Act, which provides that contribution may be obtained where

> a person has made or agreed to make any payment in bona fide settlement or compromise of any claim made against him in respect of any damage (including a payment into court which has been accepted) he shall be entitled to recover contribution in accordance with this section without regard to whether or not he himself is or ever was liable in respect of the damage provided, however, that he would have been liable assuming that the factual basis of the claim against him could be established.

Damage is to be given its natural and ordinary meaning as stated in the case of *Royal Brompton Hospital NHS Trust v Hammond (No 3)*.[57]

9.8.2.5 Apportionment: s2(1) Civil Liability (Contribution) Act 1978

Under s2(1) of the 1978 Act, the amount of the contribution recoverable from any person shall be an amount found by the court to be just and equitable having regard to the extent of that person's responsibility for the damage in question. Further, s2(2) of the 1978 Act provides that the court shall have power in any such proceedings to exempt any person from liability to make contribution, or to direct that the contribution recovered from any person shall amount to a complete indemnity. The courts will take into account (1) the faults of the respective parties and (2) causative relevance.[58]

9.8.2.6 Liability in tort: s7(3) Civil Liability (Contribution) Act 1978

When dealing with liability in tort, it is very common for the parties who have committed the tort to seek contribution or indemnity from a third party, for example their insurers. In most cases this would be done by way of an agreement[59] or required by statue.[60] Section 7(3) specifically provides that:

> the right to recover contribution in accordance with s1 above supersedes any right, other than an express contractual right, to recover contribution (as distinct from indemnity) otherwise than under the Act in corresponding circumstances; but nothing in this Act shall affect – (a) any express or implied contractual or other right to indemnity; or (b) any express contractual provision regulating or excluding

---

57 [2002] 1 WLR 1397, 1410.
58 *Downs v Chappell* [1997] 1 WLR 426, 445.
59 *Spalding v Tarmac Civil Engineering Ltd* [1967] 1 WLR 1508. For example, in the decision on *Spalding v Tarmac Civil Engineering Ltd* [1967] 1 WLR 1508, both the first and second defendant were liable for the loss. The first defendant was liable under the Factories Act 1961 and the second defendant was liable under the tort of vicarious liability. The wording of the clause which was stated in the liability would fall solely on the second defendant for claims which arose from operating the excavator by the driver. In this case, indemnity from the first defendant could be obtained from the second defendant. However, where the claimant failed to take precautions himself, then no contractual indemnity in respect of the damages which would be payable to third party could happen, unless it had been expressly or impliedly provided for.
60 *Sims v Foster Wheeler Ltd* [1966] 1 WLR 1508.

contribution; which would be enforceable apart from this Act (or render enforceable any agreement for indemnity or contribution which would not be enforceable apart from this Act).

Therefore, this section provides that statue will supersede the common law position.[61] The 1978 Act does not render valid an agreement for indemnity that was originally void.[62] The problem with the apportionment of damages, the 1978 Act and common law is the likelihood of uncertainty, due to the different results that could occur. It has also been stated that where there is a contractual indemnity, which is provided for against liability for an unintentional tort, it will be considered valid.[63] In an employer and employee situation, the same principles of joint tortfeasor apply. The employer can claim contribution from the employee, where the employee is negligent.

9.9 Subrogation and indemnity

The Court of Appeal dealt with the issue of subrogation and indemnity in *Morris v Ford Motors Co Ltd*,[64] although the point regarding the right of subrogation was not pleaded or argued. Lord Denning held that where the risk of a servant's negligence was covered by insurance, his employer should not seek to make the servant liable for it, and just and equitable principles applied. In *Morris v Ford Motors Co Ltd*, Ford had employed a firm of cleaners to clean the factory under a contract which contained general clauses. One of the clauses provided that the cleaners were bound to indemnify Ford against their liability to Morris, who was an employee at the firm of cleaners. The plaintiff was injured due to the negligence of Ford's servant, R. Third party proceedings were brought against the cleaners who claimed an indemnity as provided for in the contract. R was then brought in as a fourth party under the doctrine of subrogation, to enjoy the rights which Ford had against R. Lord Denning commented that the decision in *Lister v Romford Ice and Cold Storage Co Ltd*[65] was an unfortunate decision, and its effects have only been avoided by agreement between insurers not to enforce it, and should not be followed. It was not just and equitable for Ford to allow their name to be lent to the cleaner to sue their servant R. Neither was there an implied term that the cleaners were entitled to.[66]

---

61 *Clerk and Lindsell on Torts*, p. 273, para. 4–33. See The Law Report Commission of Hong Kong, *Report on The Law Relating to Contribution Between Wrongdoers* (Topic 5) at p. 1, para. 1.4 where it was stated, "This Act broke down more of the barriers imposed by common law."
62 *Clerk and Lindsell on Torts*, p. 273, para. 4–33.
63 *Ibid*, paras 4–34.
64 [1973] QB 792.
65 [1957] AC 555. The effects of the decision on employers and workers was examined in the *Report of the Inter-Departmental Committee appointed in 1957 by the Mister of Labour and National Service*.
66 [1973] QB792, 801, 802.

In *Drayton v Martin*[67] Sackville J stated that an insurer, under an indemnity policy, who sought contribution from a co-insurer must establish (1) it is liable to indemnify the assured under its own policy; (2) it has paid out sums in respect of that liability; (3) the co-insurer is also liable under its policy to indemnify the assured; and (4) the co-insurer had not paid out moneys to meet its liability to the assured.

9.9.1 The difference between contribution and subrogation

It has been stated that the doctrine of contribution and subrogation are complimentary in nature.[68] The difference between contribution and subrogation is that, for contribution, there is usually (1) the existence of more than one insurance contract and (2) the insurer can seek contribution from other insurers, if one of the insurers has paid out to the assured.[69]

Subrogation, on the other hand, involves the presence or the requirement that the assured who has taken out insurance obtains the amount of indemnity to which he is entitled.[70] The insurer then steps into the shoes of the assured and exercises its rights against third parties. It is well-established[71] that where a person is entitled to two or more indemnities, he is not permitted to enforce more than one of them.

9.9.2 Austin v Zurich Insurance

In *Austin v Zurich Insurance*,[72] MacKinnon LJ and Uthwatt J, when dealing with the issue of subrogation and contribution, and deciding on who is the correct party to bring the proceedings, held that this issue was very much a technical matter. MacKinnon LJ expressed the view that, if the case was one of subrogation, the claim should be brought in the name of Austin himself. However, he went on to explain that Bell's claim was one of contribution and not subrogation, as they were looking to recover from Zurich Insurance, through double insurance. The underwriters were the correct party to bring proceedings against the defendants. MacKinnon LJ was of the view that the correct claim should be a contribution claim and not a subrogation claim. Uthwatt J agreed that, as the plaintiff had already obtained indemnity from one insurer, he could not seek indemnity for something for which he has already been indemnified. In a situation where you have two insurers, the correct approach would be one of contribution.[73]

---

67 (1996) 137 ALR 145. This was followed in the *Lumley General Insurance Ltd v QBE Insurance (Australia) Ltd* [2008] VSC 216.
68 *Stratti v Stratti* [2000] NSWCA 358.
69 *Colinvaux's Law of Insurance in Hong Kong* (2nd edn 2012).
70 *Ibid.*
71 *The Sydney Turf Club v Crowley* [1972] 126 CLR 420, 423–424. In this case, the court was dealing with a partnership situation.
72 [1945] 1 KB 250.
73 [1945] 1 KB 250, 258.

9.9.3 Caledonia North Sea Ltd v London Bridge Engineering

The case of *Caledonia North Sea Ltd v London Bridge Engineering*[74] was an appeal from the Inner House of the Court of Session[75] to the House of Lords. This case is referred to as the *Piper Alpha* case. In 1988, there was an explosion which destroyed the Piper Alpha oil platform, injuring and killing numerous people. The employees were employed by the contractors to build and maintain the platform. Settlement had been reached regarding the victims' claims. The amount of the settlement which was accepted by the operator, other participants and their respective insurers were at levels far greater than the amount that would have been awarded by the Scottish courts, but less than what would have been awarded in Texas. It was after settlement figures were agreed and paid out that the contractors were asked to indemnify the operator and other participants. The contractors refused. Due to the numerous insurance policies in place at the time, the insurers of the operator and other participants decided to pay most of the settlement figures. The terms of the agreements[76] required the contractors to indemnify the operators where, as a result of the contractor's default, the operators may incur liability. The insurers paid out, as a result of the agreement. The insurers then brought proceedings claiming subrogation rights against the contractors.

The issues to be decided were (1) whether on a proper construction of the contract between the parties, the operator was entitled to indemnity in respect of claims arising from death or injury of the contractor's employees in circumstances where the contractor was not liable at common law or for breach of statutory duty in respect of the death or injury in question; (2) whether in so far as the action was a subrogated claim, the contractor's liability to the operator had been discharged by the payments made by the underwriters; and (3) whether, on a proper construction of the contract between the parties, recovery of the excess above the Scots law value of the claims was excluded by clause 21, which provided that they should not be liable for indirect or consequential losses suffered.[77]

When dealing with the issue of subrogation, Lord Bingham agreed with the conclusions expressed by Lord MacKay, where he stated that it was a well-established principle that an insurer who has fully indemnified an assured against a loss which has been covered by a contract of insurance between them may ordinarily enforce, in the insurer's own name, any right of recourse available to the assured.[78]

The trial judge's reasoning was overruled on appeal. It was argued that Caledonia's rights were not extinguished as a result of the insurers paying out. They would be entitled to proceed on the basis of a subrogated action in Caledonia's

---

74 [2002] Lloyd's Rep IP 261.
75 2000 SLT 1123, Ct of Sess (Inner House).
76 The indemnity provision was found in clause 15(1) under contractor's indemnities, in particular clause 15(1)(c).
77 As stated in the headnote [2002] 1 Lloyd's Rep 553, 554.
78 He relied on the cases of *Randal v Cockran* (1748) 1 Ves Sen 98; *Mason v Sainsbury* (1782) 3 Dougl 61, which was cited by Lord Mackay; *London Assurance Co v Sainsbury* (1783) 3 Dougl 246; *Yates v Whyte* (1838) 4 Bing NC 272; *Dickenson v Jardine* (1868) LR 3 CP 639.

name. The insurers would be able to bring the proceedings. However, the contractors argued that Caledonia's rights and contractual obligation to indemnify no longer existed once the insurers satisfied Caledonia's loss under their contractual responsibility. The correct party to the proceedings should have been the insurers.

On appeal, the court looked at who would be liable for the sum that was to be paid out under the contract, and concluded that the contractor's rights and obligations were not extinguished or discharged. Lord Hoffmann[79] stated that the general principle is that a person cannot claim more than he is entitled to; he can only be indemnified once. There were numerous ways one could give effect to such principle, for example (1) a person should be entitled to subrogation against those who are liable, where the liability is of a secondary party; and (2) one payment would discharge the liability, where the liability of the party who has made payment was primary or equal and co-ordinate.

It has been suggested that this analysis is wrong[80] for the following reasons: (1) it goes against the authorities in countries such as Australia and Canada[81] which laid down the principle that a discharge of a third party's contractual liability to indemnify was permitted where payment was made by an insurer liable to indemnify the assured; (2) it did not conform to the decision in England where 100% contribution could be ordered by the court against tortfeasors; and (3) where a surety pays the principal debtor's liability.

---

79 [2002] 1 Lloyd's Rep 553, 571.
80 *Mitchell*, 9.14, p. 181.
81 For example, *Trenton Works Lavalin Inc v Panalpina Inc* (1994) 126 Nova Scotia Reports (2d) 287 (Nova Scotia High Court) and *Sydney Turf Club v Crowley* (1971) 1 NSWLR 324; *Mitchell*, 9.14 p. 181.

CHAPTER 10

Conclusion

This book has tried to illustrate the problems which arise in double insurance when insurance policies are taken out with numerous insurers in the following ways: (1) by mistake; (2) where the assured is not aware of the existence of other policies; and (3) where an assured over insures his property.

The main issue of double insurance is whether an assured who has taken out policies with more than one insurer should be permitted to claim from any one of the insurers where a policy has been taken out. The requirements for double insurance are that the insurance policies cover: (1) the same subject matter; (2) the same assured; (3) the same interest; (4) the same risk; and (5) the same policy period.

The types of clauses that can be found in insurance policies are: escape clauses, excess clauses, rateable proportion clauses and other insurance clauses. The main reason for insurers imposing these clauses is to prevent possible fraud, i.e. where the assured is indemnified for more than the loss he has suffered. In some cases, there can be a combination of such clauses, which adds to the complexity. An escape clause completely excludes the liability of an insurer if an event occurs which is specifically provided for under the policy. An excess clause applies to cover the excess where there is another policy in existence. A rateable proportion clause limits the insurer's liability to the proportional rate for the loss suffered by the assured.

The assured pays a high premium in the hopes that when a loss is incurred the assured can look to the insurer to ensure that payment will be made. An insurer however can refuse to pay out for the loss incurred by the assured by relying on exclusion clauses or limiting the amount that can be recovered.

When balancing the interests between the parties, the interest of the assured is paramount. The insurer can impose terms of notification in the policy to ensure that, if an assured knows that there is another policy in existence, this should be disclosed. The insurer can then decide how this will affect the terms of the policy. This can then be done by way of limiting or excluding liability completely.

In cases where the assured is not aware of other policies in existence, the insurer should not be allowed to rely on such limiting or exclusion provisions. In some jurisdictions, for example Australia, this has been given legislative effect.

A comparative study of the courts in the United Kingdom, the United States, Canada, Australia, South Africa, China, Singapore and India reveals the courts struggling to avoid dealing with double insurance situations by concluding in many cases that, on the facts, double insurance does not arise. There is copious case law on double insurance in the United States, but the UK courts have stated clearly that these authorities provide no guidance in the United Kingdom. The Canadian courts have preferred to follow the UK authorities.

The practical problem with double insurance can be seen in the way the cases have developed. For example, the lower courts may rule that there is no double insurance but, on appeal, it is held that double insurance exists, and vice versa. If double insurance arises, the cases suggest that the courts are more likely to find the insurers liable, and so payment should be made to the assured. This usually results in the similar clauses (e.g. excess/excess or ratable proportion/ratable proportion) "cancelling out" each other and both insurers paying out up to the total of the loss with the insurers fighting it out between themselves when dealing with contribution.

A better solution to the problem, which could lead to more certainty, is in the form of legislative provisions similar to that in Australia under s45 of the Insurance Contracts Act 1984, with some modifications. The United Kingdom has not followed Australia by imposing a similar statutory framework.

Therefore, from a common law perspective, a workable possible solution to double insurance would be as follows:

> If there is double insurance, regardless of the type of clause present and its wording, an assured should be able to choose whichever insurer from which he wishes to recover for the loss he has suffered, and the insurers will then have to seek contribution amongst themselves.

This would give greater protection to the assured, particularly consumer assureds.

It must be noted that contribution only arises when there is double insurance. There are three methods for calculating contribution (1) independent actual liability; (2) the common liability test; and (3) maximum potential liability. The judge has absolute discretion as to which method of calculation is appropriate, depending on the facts of the case.

The approach which should be adopted by the courts in the United Kingdom are that excess clauses, ratable proportion clauses and escape clauses in the policies should be treated as void. Only the application of such clauses are void, and not all the terms of the contract. This is the position adopted by the courts in Australia. The assured can then claim from whichever insurer he wishes for the loss suffered. This should be the general position, but exceptions should be provided which are similar to Australian legislative provisions. There is express provision that such clauses will not be void where there is a true excess liability in a policy or where there is a requirement under statute that such clauses are not void.

If English law does not implement such legislative provisions, the courts should strive to change the common law position. The cases at present in this area have not provided much assistance. The courts in such circumstances should rule that the combination of the clauses is irrelevant and that, in such situations, the clauses cancel out each other and each insurer will be equally liable under the policies. The assured can seek indemnity from any of his insurers. The insurer who has paid out can then seek contribution from the other insurers, through common law principles of contribution.

This may seem drastic, but the courts in England have devised a similar result when dealing with mesothelioma cases, where an employee is now entitled to recover damages of 100% from whichever employer he chooses. The same principles should also apply in cases of double insurance. However, it is questionable whether there is double insurance in such cases, as there are numerous policies over many years and it is difficult to identify whether there is an overlap of policies and the period of overlap.

The above suggestions could provide a possible solution to the problems arising in double insurance. However, there are a lot of unresolved questions, mainly because of the wordings in policies which have been developed by using eighteenth-century principles. There is also a lack of consistency in approach adopted by the courts. In conclusion, whichever method or principles are adopted by the courts, in a consumer market it is suggested that the ultimate beneficiary who should be protected is the assured. This is because an assured pays premiums and expects to be covered under the insurance policy when an incident arises.

INDEX

absolute escape clauses *see* exclusion clauses
Albion Insurance Co Ltd v Government Insurance Office of New South Wales 142, 143
America: double recovery, prohibition on 13n32; "other insurance" clause 104–107; stacking cases 13n32
apportionment method for contribution 148
asbestos litigation: apportionment 182, 183; approach of the courts to resolve problems 198–203; *Barker v Corus* revisiting Fairchild 180–183, 204; *Bolton Metropolitan BC v Municipal Mutual Insurance Ltd* 178–180, 199; *Cape Distribution v Cape Intermediate Holdings plc* 197, 198; case law development 169, 170; causation principle 173, 186, 187, 199; contribution, doctrine of 180; damages, apportionment of 183; development of mesothelioma 169; damages 183; double insurance, application 191, 198–203, 205, 206; *Durham v BAI (Run Off) Ltd* 183–193, 199, 203; Employers Liability (Compulsory Insurance) Act 1969, point of and implications of 200–202; employers' liability insurance 184, 186, 194; *Fairchild v Glenhaven Funeral Services Ltd* decision 170–178, 199, 203, 204; history and medical aspect of mesothelioma 170, 171; *Investors Compensation Scheme Ltd v West Bromwich Building Society* 200; liability for risk or injury 183; *Phillips v Syndicate 992 Gunner* 203–205; law of tort 202; proportionate division of liability 203–205; "sustained" and "contracted" 186–189; tort liability 193, 194, 202; type of liability insurance 202, 203; Workmen's Compensation Acts 185, 190; *Zurich Insurance plc UK Branch v International Energy Group Ltd* 193–197
assured: distinction between "an assured" and "the assured" 56, 57
Austin v Zurich General Accident and Liability Insurance Co Ltd 43, 44, 218
Australia: adoption and application of Marine Insurance Act 1906 13; "an assured" and "the assured", distinction between 56, 57; approach to double insurance 6, 7; case law 11, 11n13, 12; combination of clauses 53, 54; comparison of insurance market with that of the UK 32; contractual and legislative exclusions 20, 21; contribution, right of recovery 163; control of policy terms, legislative provisions 111, 112; cover note 54; "entered into", meaning 57–63; exclusion clauses, legislation barring 51; Explanatory Memorandum (Insurance Contracts Bill 1984 *see* Explanatory Memorandum (Insurance Contracts Bill 1984; fairness, test of 112–114; Financial Ombudsman Service 111; General Code of Insurance Practice 111; Insurance Contracts Act 1984 (Australia) s45 *see* Insurance Contracts Act 1984 (Australia) s45 "other insurance" provisions; Marine Insurance Act 1909 11; meaning of "the assured" 56, 57; other legislative provisions 111, 112; severance 55, 56; specified terms in contracts 88–99; unfair terms 112–114

225

INDEX

Australian Corporations Act 2001
Australian Eagle Insurance Co Ltd v Mutual Acceptance (Insurance) Pty Ltd 147, 148
Australian Insurance Law 143
Australian Law Reform Commission, Report on Insurance Contracts, Report No 20 (1982): calculating contribution 157, 158; combination of clauses 53, 54; consideration of English law 6, 7; cover note 54; draft legislation 53; existing problems 53; fairness, test of 112–114; guiding principles 52; "other insurance" provisions 53–56; recommendations 52, 75, 76; severance of void parts in clauses 86–88; specifying terms in contracts 88–99; terms of reference 51; true excess liability in a policy 76–85
Australian Prudential Regulatory Authority 111
Australian Securities and Investment Commission Act 2001 111

balancing the interest between parties 128, 129, 221
Bankers & Traders Insurance Co Ltd v National Insurance Co Ltd 33–35
Barker v Corus revisiting Fairchild 180–183, 204
Battle of Lagos 4
Bolton Metropolitan BC v Municipal Mutual Insurance Ltd 178–180
Bovis Construction Ltd v Commercial Union Assurance Co plc 213, 214
Bovis Lend Lease Ltd v Saillard Fuller and Partners 213
Bubble Act 1720 4, 12, 110, 111

calculation methods for contribution: common liability test 6, 154, 222; criticisms and possible solutions 157, 158; independent actual liability 6, 151–154, 222; maximum potential policy 6, 148–151, 222
Caledonian North Sea v London Bridge Engineering 129, 219, 220
Canada: adoption of Marine Insurance Act 1906 13; notification requirement 70–72; position on double insurance 107–110
Cape Distribution v Cape Intermediate Holdings plc 197, 198
case law (asbestos litigation): *Barker v Corus revisiting Fairchild* 180–183; *Bolton Metropolitan BC v Municipal Mutual Insurance Ltd* 178–180; *Cape Distribution v Cape Intermediate Holdings plc* 197, 198; case law development 169, 170; development of mesothelioma 169; *Durham v BAI (Run Off) Ltd* 183–193; *Fairchild v Glenhaven Funeral Services Ltd* decision 170–178; *Zurich Insurance plc UK Branch v International Energy Group Ltd* 193–197
case law (Civil Liability (Contribution) Act 1978) 212–217
case law (contribution): Australia 142–145; calculation of insurer's liability 148–153; co-insurers 126; common law contribution 117, 118; co-sureties 121–123; covering the same risk 134–141; entitlement to 147; equitable contribution 119, 120, 147; guarantor's right 123–126; independent actual liability 151–154; maximum potential policy 148–151; principle behind 129; same assured, same subject matter and same interest 131–134; wide range of events covered by policy 154, 155
case law (double insurance): absolute escape clauses 33–36; combination of clauses 46–50; excess clauses 43, 44; escape clause against excess clause 42, 43; identifying whether double insurance arises 14–18; illustrating complexities of double insurance 30–32; interpreting clauses 20–22; marine insurance 13–16; rateable proportion clauses 45; recovery from insurers 18–20; return of premiums 25–27; self-cancelling clauses held ineffective 36–39; *Weddell* principle in other jurisdictions 39–41
case law (double insurance America), "other insurance" clause 104–107
case law (double insurance Australia): analysis of cases 102–104; "an assured" and "the assured", distinction between 56, 57; conclusion on facts of the case 62, 63; "entered into", meaning 57–63; marine insurance 11, 11n13, 12; notification clause, validity of s45(1) 68–72; "other insurance" 59–62; specifically, meaning under s45(2) 65–68; specifying terms in contract 88–99; tests adopted by the courts 102; true excess clause 77–86, 102

INDEX

case law (double insurance Canada) 107–110
case law (subrogation and indemnity 217–220
categories of insurance 5n17
causation principle, mesothelioma cases 173, 186, 187, 199
Chamber of Assurance, establishment 4, 9
Civil Liability (Contribution) Act 1978: application to double insurance 6, 212–217; apportionment 216; claims between indemnity insurers 213–217; implementation 211, 212; joint liability 208, 209; liability in tort 216
claims: choice of policy 22; limitation period 130
clauses: combination in policies 30; escape clauses *see* exclusion clauses, excess clauses *see* excess clauses; exclusion clauses *see* exclusion clauses; in combination 46–50; interpretation of policy wording 20–22; limiting or excluding liability 20–22; "other insurance" 29, 30; policy considerations 32; rateable proportion clauses *see* rateable proportion clauses; restriction of assureds' rights 29; self-cancelling clauses held ineffective 36–39; suggested solutions 110–114; types of 6, 29, 32, 33, 221; uncertainty of 33
co-insurer's right to contributions 126
combination of clauses 46–50; 53, 54
common law principle: Australia, right of recovery 95; contribution and 6, 117, 118, 129, 130, 207–220; co-sureties 121, 126; distinction between equity and 209, 210; exclusion/limitation clauses 29; indemnity up to extent of loss 75; premiums 27
common liability test 6, 154, 222
Compensation Act 2006 185, 186
compensation, entitlement of mesothelioma victims 199, 183, 185, 186, 190, 199
concept of double insurance 5, 13, 14
consideration 3
contract of insurance, definition 3
contribution: apportionment, policy providing method of 148; balancing interest of insurer and the assured 128, 129; calculation of insurer's liability 6, 148–154; case law *see* case law (contribution); Civil Liability (Contribution) Act 1978 *see* Civil Liability (Contribution) Act 1978; common law 6, 117, 118, 129, 130, 207–220; co-sureties 120–123, 207, 210; doctrine modified by contract 180; double recovery, possibility of 209; elements of double insurance 126–128; entitlement to 147, 148; equitable principle 23, 147, 209, 210; event after loss and insurer denying liability 163; factors to be satisfied 127, 128; general concept 22–24; history 117–126; joint liability 207–209; limitation period for claims 130; marine insurance 156; origins of 23; overlaps allowing for contribution 164–167; property insurance 155, 156; reimbursement or 209; requirements to be satisfied 24; restitution in nature 109; right of contribution arising *see* right of contribution arising; same damage not same tort 208; subrogation and indemnity 217–220; tortfeasors, joint and several 207–209, 211; unjust enrichment 207, 209; voluntary payment 159–163; wide range of events covered by policy 154, 155
Co-operative Retail Services Ltd v Taylor Young Partnership Ltd 215
co-sureties, contribution and 120–123, 207, 210
cover note 54

Deering v Earl of Winchelsea 119, 120, 121
definition of double insurance 5, 9n3
double insurance: America 104–107; apportionment of loss 24; asbestos litigation 191, 198–203, 205, 206; Australia *see* Australia; Canada 107–110; case law *see* case law (double insurance); complexities of 30–32; concept of 5, 13, 14; definition 5, 9n3; effect on claims 29–50; excess clauses *see* excess clauses; exclusion clauses *see* exclusion clauses; history of 9–11; identifying, case law 14–18; legislative reform, Australia *see* Australia; overview 3–7; premiums 25–27; rateable proportion clauses *see* rateable proportion clauses; recovery from insurers 18–20; requirements for 5, 221; unclear legislation 6
double recovery, possibility of 209

Drake Insurance Co v Provident Insurance Co 161–163
Durham v BAI (Run Off) Ltd 183–193

Eagle Star Ltd v Provincial Insurance plc 161
employers, asbestos litigation *see* asbestos litigation
Employers' Liability Act 1880 185
Employers Liability (Compulsory Insurance) Act 1969, point of and implications of 200–202
employers' liability insurance, asbestos litigation 184, 186, 194
"entered into": beneficial third parties 61, 62; meaning 57–63; question of construction 94–96
Equitable Fire & Accident Office 30–32
equitable principle, contribution and 6, 119, 120, 129, 147, 149, 158, 209, 210
escape clauses *see* exclusion clauses
excess clauses: America 104–107; Australia *see* Australia; combination of clauses 46–50; concurrent 43, 44; escape clause against 41–43; inclusion of 6, 29, 32; self-cancelling 43; true excess clause 77–85; *Weddell* principle 37–39
excess coverage 64, 65, 167
exclusion clauses: absolute escape clauses 33–35; all policies containing absolute clauses 35, 36; America 104–107; Australia *see* Australia; combination of clauses 46–50; concurrent 33–39; excess clause, against 41–43; inclusion of 6, 29, 32; self-cancelling clauses held ineffective 36–39; uncertainty of such clauses 33; *Weddell* principle 36–39
ex gratia payments 148
Explanatory Memorandum (Insurance Contracts Bill 1984): categories of clauses 87; effect of type of policy provision 87; mechanisms used for protection by insurers 88; severance of void clause 87, 88; situations where double insurance could arise 86, 87; types of policy provisions 86, 87

Fairchild v Glenhaven Funeral Services Ltd decision 170–178, 199, 203, 204
Financial Services and Markets Act 2000 111
fire insurance, history 4

Fire Life Insurance Duty Act 1782 4
"floater" policy 59n35
fraud, risk of 3, 9, 20, 52
fraudulent trading 4

Gale v Motor Union Insurance Co 35, 36
Godin v London Assurance Co 16, 138, 147
Great Fire of London 4
guarantor's right to contribution 123–126

HIH Casualty and General Insurance Co v Pluim Construction Pty Ltd 65–67, 89–91, 93
history of contribution: common law contribution 117, 118; co-insurers 126; co-sureties 120–123; equitable contribution 119, 120; guarantor's right 123–126
history of double insurance: Bubble Act 1720 12; Chamber of Assurance 9; Marine Insurance Act 1906 9–11
Home Insurance Co of New York v Gavel 70, 71
Hong Kong: adoption of Marine Insurance Act 1906 13

identifying double insurance, case law 14–18
indemnity, requirement 13, 18
independent actual liability test 6, 151–154, 222
insolvent insurers 5, 45
Insurance Conduct of Business Sourcebook the Insurance Ombudsman Bureau 111
Insurance Contracts Act 1984 (Australia) s45 "other insurance" provisions: application 54; effects of s76 74, 75; "entered into" 59–63, 94–96; exceptions under 63–65; excess clause, impact on 75, 76; excess layers of cover 64, 65; exclusion clause, impact on 75, 76; Explanatory Memorandum *see* Explanatory Memorandum (Insurance Contracts Bill 1984); implementation 6, 7; not being a contract of insurance required to be effected by or under law (exception 1) 63, 64; notification clause, validity of s45(1) 68–73; proposed legislative provision 73, 74; provision, meaning of 97, 98; public liability insurance 63, 64; rateable

proportion clauses, impact on 75, 76; rationale for 53; recovery of loss suffered under contract 95; review of the Act 100, 101; severance 55, 56; some or all of loss not covered by a contract of insurance that is specified in first-mentioned contract (exception 2) 64, 65; "specifically", meaning under s45(2) 65–68; specifying terms in contracts 88–99; text of s45 53; time "other insurance" entered into 54, 55
Insurance Contracts Bill 1982 Clause 77 158
Insurance Contracts Bill 1984 Explanatory Memorandum *see* Explanatory Memorandum (Insurance Contracts Bill 1984)
insurance industry: development and regulation of 4
insurance premiums *see* premiums
Investors Compensation Scheme Ltd v West Bromwich Building Society 200

joint liability: Civil Liability (Contribution) Act 1978 211–217; contribution and 207–209

landlords and tenants, overlapping insurance 165, 166
Law Commission recommended reforms 1980 111
Law Council of Australia, clarification of Insurance Contracts Act 1984 101
Law of Contribution and Reimbursement 118
Law of Restitution 120
Law Reform Committee's Report 1957 111
Law Reform (Married Woman and Tortfeasors) Act 1935 211
Legal & General v Drake Insurance 159–162
Limitation Act 1980 130
limitation of liability *see* exclusion clauses
limitation period for contribution claims 130
Lloyd's Coffee House 12
Lloyd's underwriters 5, 12
London Assurance 4, 12

marine insurance: history 4; registration 4; right to contribution 156; source of 12
Marine Insurance Act 1906: definition of double insurance 9n3; other jurisdictions 11, 13; overview 9–11;

situations covered 10; valued policy 10; United Kingdom 10; unvalued policy 10
Marshall on Insurance 26
Mathie v The Argonaut Marine Insurance Co Ltd 14, 15
maximum potential liability test 6, 148–151, 222
Merchant Insurers Bill 1693 4
Merryweather v Nixon 212
mesothelioma *see* asbestos litigation
Morris v Ford Motors Co Ltd 217
mortgagor and mortgagee, overlapping insurance 164, 165
mutual societies 5

National Employers Mutual General Insurance Association Ltd v Haydon 37–39; 77–79
National Farmers Union Mutual Insurance Society Ltd v HSBC Insurance (UK) Ltd 46–50
New Zealand: adoption of Marine Insurance Act 1906 13; escape clause against excess clause, self-cancelling 42, 43; Marine Insurance Act 1908
Nicholas v Wesfarmers Currangh Pty Ltd 59–62
1986 Statement of Practice, Insurance Conduct of Business Rulebook 111
North British and Mercantile Insurance Co v London, Liverpool and Global Insurance Co 131, 132, 164
North British Insurance v London, Liverpool & Globe Insurance 14
notification requirements: Australian case law 68–72; Canadian position 72; correct approach 72, 73; effect of s76 Insurance Contracts Act 1984 74, 75; notification clause, validity of s45(1) of Insurance Contracts Act 1984 68; suggested legislative provision 73, 74

"open cover policy" 59n35
"other insurance" clauses: America 104–107; Australia *see* Insurance Contracts Act 1984 (Australia) s45 "other insurance" provisions; Canada 108; effect of 29, 30
overlapping insurance, allowing for contribution 164–167

parent and subsidiary companies, "top and drop" policies 68, 103
Phillips v Syndicate 992 Gunner 203–205

229

policy considerations 32
premiums: outline 3; return of 25–27
primary policies 167
property insurance: history 4; right to contribution 155, 156
public liability insurance 63, 64

rateable proportion clauses: combination of clauses 46–50; contribution, both policies containing rateable proportion clause 161, 162; effect of 44, 45; inclusion of 6, 29, 32, 33; policies not concurrent 45
Rathbone Brothers plc v Novae Corporate Underwriting Ltd 17, 18
recovery from insurers: assureds' rights 18–20; 147
regulation of the insurance industry in the UK 4, 5, 110, 111
reimbursement 39, 40, 117, 118, 207, 209
return of premiums: insurer refusing to pay 25; legislative framework 25, 26; principle in *Tyrie* 25, 26; prior to legislation 26, 27; risk attached 27
review of Insurance Contracts Act 1984 100, 101
right of contribution arising (Australian position): case law 142–145; requirement for policies to be in force and valid 144, 145
right of contribution arising (UK position): case law 131–141; covering the same risk, essential requirement 134–141; factors required 131; same assured, same subject matter and same interest covered 131–134
rights of assured persons: recovery from insurers 18–20; restriction by insurers 29
rights of parties regarding clauses 110
risk, covering 18; 134–141
Royal Brompton Hospital NHS Trust v Hammond 212, 213, 216
Royal Exchange Assurance 4, 12

self-insurance, asbestos litigation 196, 197
severance of underlying clause 55, 56, 98, 99
Sickness & Accident Assurance Association Ltd v The General Accident Assurance Corporation 144, 145

Singapore: adoption of Marine Insurance Act 1906 13; contribution, right of recovery 162, 163; interpreting clauses 21, 22; *Weddell* principle 39–41
South Sea Company 4
specifically, meaning under s45(2) 65–68
specifying terms in contracts: actual effect of provision 91–93; definition of specified 89–91; legislative effect of s45 Insurance contracts Act 1984 88–99; meaning of provision 97, 98; parties specifying terms 88, 89; potential effect of provision 92, 93; range of ways 88, 89; severance of underlying clause 98, 99
speculative trading 4
stacking, definition of 13
Steadfast Insurance Co Ltd v F&B Trading Co Pty 68–70
subrogation and indemnity 217–220
sureties: common law contribution 117, 118; co-sureties 120–123, 210; equitable contribution 119, 120
Sutton on Insurance Law 62n53, 68n82

"top and drop" policies 68, 103
tort, principles of 6
tortfeasors, joint and several 207–209, 211–217
Trade Practices Amendment (Australian Consumer Law) Act 2010 112, 114
true excess liability: exemptions, true excess clause 77–85, 102; limits on recommendations 76, 77
types of clauses 6, 29, 32, 33

umbrella policies 167
Unfair Contract Terms Act 1977 111
Unfair Terms in Consumer Contracts Regulations 1999 111
unfair terms, test of 112–114
unjust enrichment 120, 207, 209
Union Marine Insurance Co Ltd v Martin 15, 16, 17
unvalued policy 10, 11

validity of policy 18
valued policy 10, 11
vendors and purchasers, overlapping insurance 166
Vero Insurance Ltd v QBE Insurance (Australia) Ltd 58, 59

void clauses: severance 86–88
voluntary payment by insurer 159–163

Weddell v Road Traffic and General Insurance Co Ltd 36–41
Workmen's Compensation Act 185, 190

Zurich Australian Insurance Ltd v Metals & Minerals Insurance Pte Ltd 57–59, 67, 79–85, 88–99
Zurich Insurance plc UK Branch v International Energy Group Ltd 193–197